WA 1382982 3

A Community Guide to Environmental Health

by Jeff Conant and Pam Fadem

hesperian

Berkeley, California, USA

D1341466

Copyright © 2008 by Hesperian Foundation. All rights reserved.
First edition: May 2008
Printed in Canada on recycled paper
ISBN: 978-0-942364-56-9

Library of Congress Cataloging-in-Publication Data

Conant, Jeff.

A community guide to environmental health / by Jeff Conant and Pam
Fadem.

p. cm.

Includes bibliographical references and index.

Summary: "Covers topics: community mobilization; water source
protection, purification and borne diseases; sanitation; mosquito-borne
diseases; deforestation and reforestation; farming; pesticides and toxics;
solid waste and health care waste; harm from mining and oil extraction.
Includes group activities and appropriate technology instructions."

ISBN 978-0-942364-56-9 (alk. paper)

1. Environmental health--Popular works. 2. Community leadership. I.
Fadem, Pam. II. Title.

RA566.C666 2008

362.196'98--dc22

2008015042

Hesperian Foundation encourages others to copy, reproduce, or adapt
to meet local needs any or all parts of this book, including the illustrations,
provided that the parts reproduced are distributed free or at cost—not for
profit. Any organization or person who wishes to copy, reproduce, or adapt
any or all parts of this book for commercial purposes must obtain permission
from Hesperian Foundation.

Before beginning any translation or adaptation of this book or its contents,
please contact Hesperian Foundation for suggestions, for updates on the
information it contains, and to avoid duplication of efforts. Please send
Hesperian a copy of any materials in which text or illustrations from this book
have been used.

Learning Resources
Centre

13829823

hesperian

1919 Addison Street, #304
Berkeley, California 94704, USA

CREDITS

Editorial Oversight: Sarah Shannon

Editing and editorial management:
Pam Fadem, Todd Jailer

Copy editing: Todd Jailer, Jane Maxwell,
Susan McCallister

Additional writing and research:
Pratap Chatterjee, Ann Hawkins, Todd
Jailer, Elaine Knobbs, Cynthia Knowles,
Susan McCallister, Tracy Perkins,
Sarah Shannon, Elizabeth Shapiro

Art Coordination:
Mary Israel, Elaine Knobbs, Tracy
Perkins, Susan Quass, Leana Rosetti

Community review coordination:
Jeff Conant, Pam Fadem, Mary Israel,
Elaine Knobbs, Tracy Perkins, Susan
Quass

Project support:
Mary Israel, Elaine Knobbs, Elena
Metcalf, Tracy Perkins, Susan Quass,
Leana Rosetti, Maya Shaw

Additional project support:
Kay Alton, John Balquist, Shipra Bansal,
Amy Cantor, Kris Carter, Frances
Chung, Erin Donnely, Deanne Emmons,
Leslie Fesenmyer, Rachel Freifelder,
Scott Friedman, Yuri Futamura, Rachel
Golden, Kate Hahner, Sonja Herbert,
Sarah Hill, Casey Jackson, Lea Joans,
Liz Johnson, Aparna Kollipara, Leona
Kwon, Sherin Larijani, Sara Mahdavi,
Sandy McGunegill, Sumi Mehta,
Patricia Navarro, Liv Nevin, Victor M.
Polanco, Gregory Rowe, Devon Shannon,
Frederick Shaw, Sarah Shulman, Sara
Sloan, Jeremy Weed, Agnes Wierzbicki,
Tse-Sung Wu, Kirby Zelgowski, and
Kytja Weir, at the end of the list but our
first volunteer

Proofreading: Sunah Cherwin

Indexing: Victoria Baker

Production management: Todd Jailer

Design and production:
Iñaki Fernández de Retana, Jacob
Goolkasian, Shu Ping Guan, Leana
Rosetti, C. Sienkiewicz

Cover design: Jacob Goolkasian

Artists:
Roberto "Galo" Arroyo, Sara Boore,
Heidi Broner, Barbara Carter, Rossina
Cazali de Barrios, Gil Corral, Raza Do,
Regina Faul-Doyle, Victoria Francis,
Sandy Frank, Jesse Hamm, Haris
Ichwan, Mary Israel, Anna Kallis,
Delphine Kenze, Susan Klein, Elizabeth
López, June Mehra, Mabel Negrete, Jane
Norling, Gabriela Núñez, Leana Rosetti,
Petra Röhr-Rouendaal, C. Sienkiewicz,
Chengyu Song, Yoly Stroeve, Oran
Suta, Sally Sutton, Ryan Sweere,
Yakira Teitel, Arunadha Thakur, Kjell
Torstensson, Bambi Tran, Yors de
Waard, Sarah Wallis, David Werner,
Christine Wong, Leah Wong, Mary Ann
Zapalac

Cover photos:
brown: © Don Mason/Brand X/Corbis;
green: © Datacraft/Getty Images; blue:
© Bloomimage/Corbis; Left: GEF Small
Grants Programme, Vietnam; Center:
People's Grocery, Oakland, CA USA;
Right: GEF Small Grants Programme,
Montañoso de Guamuhaya, Cuba

Artwork permissions:
For permission to use illustrations, we
thank: Aquamor, IRC International
Water and Sanitation Centre, CODEL/
VITA, EAWAG/ SANDEC, PAN Asia/
Pacific, People's Workbook Collective,
Proyecto Zopilote, Solidarity Center/
AFL-CIO, *Training for Transformation*,
Urban Resource Systems, Inc., World
Neighbors, Zimbabwe Natural Farming
Network, Unicef Nepal

After leading a needs assessment with Hesperian partners in 1996-97, Todd Jailer
developed the original vision and outline for this project, and shepherded it through
early stages of development. From 2000, Jeff Conant's commitment to environmental
and social justice and full-time writing propelled the project forward. Upon joining in
2004, Pam Fadem's energy, engagement, and organizational skill pulled the project into
book form. Todd Jailer stepped in again to help finish the book in 2007-08. The organized
review input of Hesperian's talented staff (book packers, designers, promotional and
editorial workers, fundraisers and administrators) also shaped the book at every step.

Community Reviewers and Grassroots Collaborators

This book was developed in collaboration with grassroots organizations and community groups around the world. We gratefully acknowledge the contribution of those who gave of their time, their experience, and their devotion to community health by reviewing early drafts and sharing their perspectives. Their efforts ensure this book will be useful to people living in widely varying conditions and in countries throughout the world.

Argentina:
El Alamo Cooperative

Bangladesh:
Center for Environmental Protection and Arsenic Free Water
Gonoshashtaya Kendra (People's Health Centre)

Cameroon:
Mbingo Baptist Hospital
Mutengene Tiko Health District

China:
Greenpeace
Pesticida Eco-Alternatives Center

Ecuador:
Acción Ecológica
Community of Amazanga
Frente por la Defensa de la Amazonia
Guacamayo Bahiatours
Intag Solidarity Network
Salud Para El Pueblo

El Salvador:
Peace Corps El Salvador, Agroforestry and Environmental Education Program and Rural Health and Sanitation Program

Ethiopia:
Bale Region Dalo Health Center

Ghana:
Community Partnerships for Health and Development
Ghana Coalition Against Water Privatization
Sunkwa Clinic

Guatemala:
Association of Community Health Services
Remedios

Guinea:
Rural Women Health Care Project

Honduras:
Community of Guadelupe Carney
Movimiento Campesino del Aguan
Pastoral Social de la Diócesis de Trujillo

India:
Centre for Resource Education
CHESS
Christian Medical Association
Community Health Cell
Community of Plachimada
Comprehensive Rural Health Project
Forum for Corporate Accountability and Environmental Health
Foundation for Ecological Security
India Centre for Human Rights and Law
Gravis Centre for People's Science for Rural Development
HEDCON
K.E.M. Hospital Community Project
Manavi
Mumbai MedWaste Action Group
Occupational Health and Safety Center
Orissa Mines Area People's Action Network
SAMATA
Santulan
Sarvodaya Youth Organization
Shri J.G. Co-operative Hospital and Research Institute LTD
Shrishti
Solutions in Action
St. Xavier's Hospital
Thanal
Tibetan Community-in-Exile
Vipra Clinic
Zero Waste Kovalam

Indonesia:
Community IPM Program, Southeast Asia
Jatam Mining Advocacy Network
The Institute for Coastal and Hinterland Community Development
Tropical Forest Trust, Sulawesi Program
World Neighbors

Karakalpakstan:
Karakalpak Center for Reproductive Health and Environment
Perzent

Kyrgyzstan:
Tree of Life Human Development Center

Kenya:
Akyona Women's Group
Green Towns
Ilima
Jasho Village Health Center
Kiambiu informal settlement, Nairobi
World Agroforestry Center

Malawi:
Kaluluma Rural Hospital
Kasungu District Hospital

Mali:
Association pour le développement des activités de production et de formation (ADAF Galle)

Mexico:
Centro de Innovación en Tecnología Alternativa, A.C.
Centro de Investigación y Capacitación Rural, A.C.
Community of Vicente Guerrero
Desarollo Economico y Social de los Mexicanos Indígenas
Huicholes Contra Plaguicidas
Proyecto Zopilote
Sarar Transformacion, SC

Mozambique:
ESTAMOS
United Nations Food and Agriculture Organization, Junior Farmer Field Schools

Nepal:
Asha/Nepal
Centre for Public Heath and Environment Development
NGO Forum for Urban Water and Sanitation

Nigeria:
Environmental Rights Action
Atiem Coalition for Environment

Pakistan:
Shirkat Gah Women's Resource Centre

Philippines:
Barangay Health Workers, Mindanao
Cabubuhan Rural Water and Sanitation Association
CHESTCORE

Davao Doctors Hospital
EcoWaste Coalition
GAIA, Philippines
Mother Earth Foundation
The Philippine Center for Water and Sanitation – International Training Network Foundation (PCWS-ITNF)
Save the Abra River Movement
Streams of Knowledge Foundation

Somalia:
Horn of Africa Relief and Development Organisation

South Africa:
Capetown Department of Public Health
Groundwork
University of Capetown

Tanzania:
Safina Group
Tanzania Compassion Society

Thailand:
Green Empowerment
Images Asia
Mea Tao Clinic

Togo:
COGESTEN

Uganda:
Centre for Environment, Technology, and Rural Development
Climate and Development Initiatives
Gwalimutala Women's Development Group
Nakonte Community Development Organization
Pro-biodiversity Conservationists

USA and other North America:
California Rural Legal Assistance
CHAMACOS
Clear Lake Pomo Tribe
International Indian Treaty Council
Migrant farmworkers, Arvin, California
Migrant Health Promotion
People's Grocery
Pit River Tribe
University of New Mexico
Wintu Tribe
Yukon River Intertribal Watershed Council

Vietnam:
National Institute of Occupational and Environmental Health

Zimbabwe:
Aquamor

THANKS!

An enormous number of people contributed time, ideas, suggestions, and critical information, hosted and guided us as we visited projects around the world, and offered vision, inspiration, and support. For making this book possible, we thank:

Hilary Abell
Al-Hassan Adam
Ferrial Adam
Anu Agarwal
Ravi Agarwal
Brahm Ahmadi
Azuibuke Akaba
Cecilia Allen
Laura Allen
Marceline Almojera
Miguel Altieri
Anton Alvarez
Ingvar Andersson
Annu
Cesar Añorve
Patrick Apoya
Shobha Arole
Francisco Arroyo
Oral Atanyazova
Shailendra Awale
S.A. Azad
Christine Bachman
Sarita Bahl
Catherine Baldi
Davis Baltz
Rolando Barillas
Robin Barr
Andrew Kang Bartlett
Nnimmo Bassey
Shenyu Belsky
Peter Berg
Wen Bo
Asa Bradman
Daniel Breneman
Lindsey Breslin
Ned Breslin
Kenny Bruno
Jacinto Buenfil
Robert Tumwesigye Baganda
Roland Bunch

Beth Burrows
Timothy Byakola
Jayakumar C.
Alejandra Caballero
Francisco Caballero
Sandy Cairncross
Manny Calonzo
Chris Canaday
Lyn Capistrano
Joy Carlson
Andrea Carmen
Ryan Case
Robert Chambers
N.M. Chandrashekar
Prabir Chatterjee
Eric Chaurette
Zafrullah Chowdhury
Enrique Cifuentes
Tony Clarke
Mary Coalter
Gary Cohen
Carol Colfer
Joana N. Cooper
Gilles Corcos
Ramon Coyle
Mr. Daromar
Darlena David
Gopal Dayaneni
Dick de Jong
David de Leeuw
V. Ramana Dhara
Russ Dilts
Carol Djeddah
Catherine Doe
Brock Dolman
Amity Doolittle
Brendan Doyle
Valentine Doyle

Deepika D'Souza
Madhumita Dutta
Jorge Emmanuel
Robert Engleman
Jeroen Ensink
Rico Euripidou
Ianto Evans
Yael Falicov
Karl Flecker
Shirley Fronda
Ndong Joseph Fuoh
Gene Gallegos
Linthoin Gambi
Karen Garfinkle
Anna Garwood
Carmelo Gendrano
Ginger Gibson
Mickey Gimmel
Tracy Glynn
Lisa Goldman
Chris Graecen
Nelly Gram
Liza Grandia
Reuben Granich
Kristen Graser
Abebe Gulma
Cheryl Hackworth
Ross Hagan
Robert Hamm
Eva Harris
Alden Henderson
Jennifer Hinton
Wilbur Hoff
Philan Horo
Robert Hrubes
O. O. Imediegwu
Aviva Imhof
Regina P. Ingente
Gloria Iñiguez
Balu Iyer
Sarah Janssen
Selene Jaramillo

Ravi Jayakaran
Nityanand Jayaraman
Harry Jeene
Manas Jena
Matt Jeschke
Apolonio Jiménez
Tunkaminyire John
Paul Joicey
David Kaimowitz
Bhanumathi Kallurim
Dennis Kalson
Rachel Kamande
Laila Iskandar Kamel
Vijay Kanhere
Assetou Kanoute
Nalini Kant
Godfrey Kasozi
Susan Kegley
Christie Keith
Kate Kelly
Mamta Khanna
Sayokl'a Kindness
Misa Kishi
Eckhard Kleinau
Jamie Kneen
Ram Babu Koirala
Timothy Krupnik
Rongping Kuang
Dennis Kuklok
Satomi Lander
Shanna Langdon
Denny Larson
Allen Lassey
Anne Leonard
Stephen Lester
Ana Leung
John Limo
Elizabeth Linder

Chun Long
Jesús Lopez
Simone Lovera
Art Ludwig
Wanjira Maathai
James MacNeil
Firuzeh Mahmoudi
Siti Maimunah
Paul Maina
Hugh Mainzer
Irma Makalinao
Kelly Malahy
Adolfo Maldonado
Deepak Malik
Gnana Surabhi
   Mani
Shyamala Mani
M.A. Mansur
Esperanza Martinez
Jacqueline Mason
Jakesh May
Kathy McAfee
John McCracken
Patrick McCully
Chris McGahey
Toby McGrath
Sandy McGunegill
Anne McKinnon
James McNeil
Glenn McRae
Nicola Meares
Regula Meierhofer
Hanna Melnitsky
Atutambire Melone
Sonia Mendoza
Gustavo Merten
Leslie Minot
Zini Mokhine
Kalia Moldogazieva
Robert Mollel
Rita Monroy
Julio Monsalvo
Alicia Montoya
Roger Moody
Monica Moore
Robert Moran
Peter Morgan
Marion Moses

Cynthia Muang
Santos Nelida
   Murga-Gutierrez
Catherine Murphy
Innosanto Nagara
Anil Naidoo
Shibu Nair
Pratep Nayak
Joseph Ndong
Ashley Nelsen
Kara Nelson
Margaret Nelson
Dan Nepstad
Gila Neta
Nguyen Ngoc Nga
Lisa Nichols
Sherri Norris
Ms. Meher
   Noshirwani
Mrs. Nyirenda
Mae Ocampo
Odigha Odigha
Elly Ongola Ogweno
C. Obichukwu
   Onwudiwe
George Odindo
   Opiyo
Peter Orris
Rikki Ott
Erlinda Palaganas
Cindy Parker
Prashant Pastore
Bobby Peek
Rebecca Perlmutter
Valentin Post
Dario Proano-
   Leroux
L. D. Puranik
Rob Quick
Romeo Quijano
Cresenciano G.
   Quintos
Ausaf Rahman
Narendra Rana
Y.E.C. Ratsma
Ravi Rebbapragada
D. Narasimha
   Reddy

Margaret Reeves
Diana Reiss-Koncar
Bastu Rege
Pallavi Rege
Sarojeni Rengam
Maggie Robbins
Kim Rodrigues
Mario Rodríguez
Marni Rosen
Rob Rosenfeld
Fred Rosensweig
Andrea Rother
Rosario Rubio
Ram Charitra Sah
Alberto
   Saldamando
Payal Sampat
Flavio Santi
Rafael Santi
Jorge Santiago
   Santiago
Feliciano dos Santos
Satinath Sarangi
Atanu Sarkar
Alicia Sawyer
Ron Sawyer
Anne Scheinberg
Alexa Schirtzinger
Steve Scholl-
   Buckwald
Cassandra Scott
Briony Seoane
Shalini Shah
Sarah Shamos
Devinder Sharma
Lonny Shavelson
Ang Rita Sherpa
Bob Shimeck
Mira Shiva
Marco Simons
Ratna Singh
Subrat Kumar
   Singh
Jo Smet
Kirk Smith
David Sohail
Gina Solomon
Kevin Starr

Dean Still
Ginés Suarez
Sally Sutton
Brent Swallow
Susan Sykes
Rhoda Bafowna
   Takyi
Fe Tan-Cebrian
Anelle Taylor
Michael Terry
Abou Thiam
Kalindi Thomas
Felix Thomson
Beverly Thorpe
Hope Traficante
Bambi Tran
Circe Trevant
Mrs. Shashi Tyagi
John Urness
Nora Urrutia
Aditi Vaidya
Angel Valencia
Arnold van de
   Klundert
Isaac Vanderburg
Marcello Veiga
Kathleen Vickery
Rory Villaluna
Yerome Wambura
Tom Watson
Martin Wegelin
Merri Weinger
Emily West
Andy Whitmore
Dave Williamson
Monica Wilson
Scott Wittet
Hannah Wittman
Agung Wiyono
Cleo Woelfle-
   Erskine
Kevin Woods
Stephanie Wright
Maglo Yao
Angelina Zamboni
Jeffrey Zayach

These organizations have been invaluable in supporting the development of this book in many ways:

APROVECHO Research Institute, CARE International, Center for Health, Environment, and Justice, Cob Cottage Company, DESMI, Global Alliance for Incinerator Alternatives (GAIA), HealthCare Without Harm, Indigenous Environmental Network, International Campaign for Justice in Bhopal, International Development Exchange (IDEX), London School of Hygiene and Tropical Medicine, Pesticide Action Network, People's Health Movement, Population Action International, Program for Appropriate Technology in Health (PATH), Project Underground, Public Health International, Sambhavna Trust SANDEC, Solar Cookers International, Tearfund, WASTE-Netherlands, Water Aid UK, WELL, World Neighbors

We thank the following foundations and individuals for their generosity in financially supporting this project:

Arntz Family Foundation, Christensen Fund, Conservation, Food and Health Foundation, Edward S. Moore Foundation, Ersa S. and Alfred C. Arbogast Foundation, Ford Foundation, Goldman Environmental Prize, Grousbeck Family Foundation, Harris and Eliza Kempner Fund, Homeland Foundation, International Foundation, Jenifer Altman Foundation, Laura Jane Musser Fund, Lawson Valentine Foundation, Marisla Foundation, Mitchell Kapor Fund, Moriah Fund, Mulago Foundation, Overbrook Foundation, Panta Rhea Foundation, Public Welfare Foundation, Rockefeller Brothers Fund, Solidago Foundation, Summit Foundation, Swedish International Development Agency, The Flora Family Foundation, The Summit Foundation, United Nations Development Program, Unitarian Universalist Service, Water Aid, West Foundation

CONTENTS

Stories

Activities

How-to...

1 Promoting Community Environmental Health

In this chapter: page

Promoting Community Environmental Health

It is clear what it means to improve the health of a child or of a family. But how do you improve the health of the environment?

When we talk about environmental health, we mean the way our health is affected by the world around us, and also how our activities affect the health of the world around us. If our food, water, and air are contaminated, they can make us sick. If we are not careful about how we use the air, water, and land, we can make ourselves and the world around us sick. By protecting our environment, we protect our health.

Improving environmental health often begins when people notice that a health problem is affecting not just one person or group, but is a problem for the whole community. When a problem is shared, people are more likely to work together to bring about change.

In this chapter we tell the story of a health center in the town of Manglaralto, Ecuador, where health workers stopped a cholera epidemic. Afterward, people in the community found ways to work together to overcome other health problems as well.

Health Promoters Stop Cholera

On the coast of Ecuador, for 6 months it is very dry and for 6 months it is very wet. This makes it hard to grow food. There are few markets, and the government does little to provide schools, health clinics, and other basic services like clean water and sewers. When cholera struck the area in 1991, most people were not prepared for it, and many became very sick.

Day after day, people brought family members to the local health center in the town of Manglaralto. They were weak, trembling, feverish, and suffering from terrible, watery diarrhea and **dehydration** (loss of too much water in the body). The health promoters realized this was a cholera epidemic and many people would die if they did not act quickly to stop it.

Because cholera contaminates drinking water and passes easily from one person to the next, the health promoters knew that treating the sick people was not enough. To prevent cholera from spreading, they would have to find a way for everyone in Manglaralto and the nearby villages to have clean water and safe toilets.

The health promoters began to organize the villagers who were still healthy, and they asked local groups for help. They persuaded an organization that had partners in other countries to give money to start an emergency program to provide clean water and toilets.

Calling their project *Salud para el Pueblo* ("Health for the People" in Spanish), the health promoters organized public health committees in every village. Committee members selected "village health educators" who were trained to teach people about water and **sanitation** (building and maintaining toilets and washing hands to prevent the spread of germs). In this way, the health promoters enabled the villagers themselves to take responsibility for important parts of the fight against cholera and for environmental health in their communities.

Having money to do something was good, but it was not enough. We needed people to take action to do the work it takes to prevent cholera from spreading.

Working together for change

The first thing the village health educators did was teach people how cholera and other diseases that cause diarrhea can spread (see pages 47 to 51). Then they helped each household and each village make sure its water supply was clean (see pages 92 to 99). They also taught people how to stop dehydration, the main cause of death from diarrhea, by making a **rehydration drink** of sugar and salt in boiled water and giving it to children and anyone else who had diarrhea (see page 53). They taught people in schools, churches, community centers, and public gathering places to prevent cholera by washing their hands and by building and using safe toilets. After a few weeks, the cholera had nearly disappeared.

But the health promoters knew they had more work to do to make sure cholera would not strike again.

With help from local engineers, people came together to build piped water systems, to improve pit toilets in every village, and to make sure every household had enough water for bathing. The villagers themselves did the work, and learned how to clean and maintain the water systems and toilets. They also made sure animals were fenced in (to keep animal wastes out of the water supply) and that water containers were covered to prevent disease-carrying mosquitoes from breeding.

As this work went on, people from other villages joined in. Starting with 22 villages, Salud para el Pueblo reached 100 villages not long after it began. Soon there was no cholera in the entire region, and other illnesses had been reduced as well.

What made this health organizing successful?

Salud para el Pueblo was very successful at stopping cholera and moving on to solve other problems. This happened because the health promoters:

- **worked with people in their homes.** Salud para el Pueblo workers trained people house by house to keep their water supply clean. This helped the health teams learn about other problems and gain trust in the community.

- **brought many groups together.** Local organizations, local government, national and international non-governmental organizations (NGOs), and the Ministry of Health all worked together. This made sure all of their resources and experiences were available to help stop the epidemic. Because they worked together, they avoided the problem of one organization doing the same job as another organization, or working against one another.

- **valued people as the most important resource.** They did not blame the villagers for the health problems, and they did not depend only on help from outside the communities. Instead, they used the peoples' own experience to work toward a common goal. They used games, puppets, songs, discussions, and popular education activities to bring people together to share their knowledge and abilities. These activities built self-confidence and motivation as the villagers saw how their own knowledge and participation solved serious health problems.

Community Health depends on clean water

How the vision of environmental health began to grow

Over time, the health promoters also realized disease-carrying insects were breeding in trash and trash dumps. They held community meetings about the need to clean up the streets and to improve the dumps. Each village formed a group of "environmental health promoters" who organized work days for everyone to pick up trash. With help from an engineer, the environmental health promoters turned waste dumps into safe pits called **sanitary landfills** (see page 412). Over the next few years, the promoters talked about starting a recycling program (see page 404) to reduce the amount of trash in the landfills. When an international agency donated a big truck to haul trash to the city, they were able to do just that. The money earned from recycling helped pay for gasoline and the costs of maintaining the truck.

By 1996, Salud para el Pueblo had built hundreds of toilets, installed many piped water systems, dug 2 sanitary landfills, started a recycling program, and began to help people plant community gardens.

Then in 1997 disaster struck. The rainstorms known as El Niño hit the coast of Ecuador. For 6 months there were strong winds and rain nearly every day. The winds tore up the trees, rain turned the hills to muddy landslides, and the valleys filled with raging brown rivers. The rivers overflowed and changed course, destroying whole villages. Toilets, water pipes, and years of hard work were washed away.

As the hills collapsed, the work of Salud para el Pueblo nearly collapsed with them. To better understand why this happened, we must look at the history of the region.

A hill with no trees is like a house with no roof

The hills and mountains on the coast of Ecuador were once covered in thick tropical forests. Mangrove trees grew where fresh water from the rivers mixed with salt water from the sea. The mangroves protected the coast from storms and were home to many kinds of fish and shellfish. Bamboo trees grew along the streams, keeping their banks from being worn down or washed away (**erosion**). Forests were filled with giant ceibo trees that gave shade. Their deep roots held water and soil. Carob trees grew on the steep mountain slopes, holding the soil in place and keeping the hillsides from falling down. Leaves from the trees enriched the soil when they fell to the ground.

The forests were home to people, and also to deer, birds, insects, lizards, and countless other animals. People built their houses out of bamboo and palm tree leaves. There were animals to hunt, wild berries to eat, and water and rich soil for gardens and small farms.

But over the last 100 years, many of the trees were cut down to make a railroad and to build houses. Then a company from Japan came and cut down most of the remaining trees, using the railroad to carry the wood to a port on the coast, and shipped it to Japan. Because tropical forest trees are very strong, they sold for a good price. When the trees were gone, the company left. The railroad fell into disrepair. Over time, it was abandoned.

before

Now, the mountains on the coast of Ecuador look like a desert. The hills are brown and there is no shade. In the dry season, the soil blows away and the air is full of dust. In the rainy season, the soil turns to mud and the hillsides tumble down. When the El Niño storms came in 1997, there were no trees to protect the villagers from their destructive force.

after

Finding the root cause of the problem

When they saw how the rains washed away whole villages — taking the new piped water systems and toilets with them — the health workers of Salud para el Pueblo realized they needed to do different kinds of work to prevent disasters like this in the future. Building water systems and promoting safe sanitation only solved one part of the problem.

There is a saying in the villages: a hill with no trees is like a house with no roof. This means trees protect the hills and prevent them from being eroded in the wind and rain, just as a roof protects the people in a house. The health workers began to see promoting tree planting and protecting natural resources was as important as promoting health — because they are one and the same!

With this in mind, the health promoters started a tree-planting project. But some villagers did not want to plant trees. One man named Eduardo refused to join the tree-planting project.

"Too much work," Eduardo said. "They just want us to work for nothing." He convinced some other villagers to go against the health promoters.

A health worker named Gloria in Eduardo's village gathered people together and organized an activity called "But why...?" to help everyone look more deeply at why they lost their toilets and piped water.

By asking "But why?" questions, Gloria helped the villagers look at all the ways their health problems were related to their environment. At the end of the discussion, most of the villagers agreed it was important to plant trees to prevent erosion and protect the soil. But Eduardo was still not convinced.

Planting trees is too much work when we have no crops and no money. We need something that will feed us now, not in 10 years!

Learning to be an effective environmental health promoter

Gloria returned to the health center discouraged. "Even though they understand the importance of trees, they still will not do the work to plant them," she thought. "How can I convince them?" Just then, a bee flew into the room and startled her. Gloria shooed it away, and then saw it fly out the window and land on the red flower of a carob tree. This gave her a new idea.

The next day, Gloria gathered the villagers together again. She asked another question, and Eduardo was the first to answer.

You need to earn more money to improve your lives now, not just in 10 years. You also believe it is important to plant trees. Is there any way to earn money from trees?

Ha! Of course — we can cut them down and sell the wood. But it will take 10 years, because trees take that long to grow.

The other villagers thought hard, and this is the conversation they had:

We can make pillows from the cotton of the silk-cotton tree and sell them.

We can raise livestock that eat the pods of the carob tree.

We can carve handicrafts from the nuts of the tagua palm.

These are all great ideas! And they give us even more reasons to plant trees. I had an idea myself that I wanted to share. Does anybody here like honey?

Gloria said, "If we grow trees with flowers that bees like, we can start a bee-keeping project and sell the honey. It will take only 1 year for the flowers to blossom." The villagers liked this idea. Even Eduardo agreed to try planting trees if he could learn how to produce honey.

Eduardo stopped Gloria as she was leaving. He told her, "When my grandson was sick with diarrhea we made him a drink from the pods of the carob tree. It cured him better than any medicine from the doctor. I think it would be a good idea to plant carob trees. Then we can make the curing drink and use the honey we produce to make it sweet."

Gloria returned to the health center excited about these new projects. After thinking about how the meetings had gone, she realized it would never work for her to tell the villagers what to do. She had to learn to see things with their eyes, hear their ideas, and understand their needs if she was to be an effective environmental health promoter.

2 Understanding and Mobilizing for Community Health

In this chapter:

Understanding and Mobilizing for Community Health

When Gloria and other health promoters realized many people in Manglaralto and the surrounding region were getting sick, they quickly knew the problem was cholera, a community health problem with an environmental cause: contaminated water. The health promoters and village health educators went from house to house to educate everyone about the problem and what to do. Once the success of the basic treatments had earned people's trust, the community began to work on the root causes of the cholera and other health problems.

Working on the root causes through community participation and education, the community was able to begin making many environmental health improvements. With each improvement, the villagers gained greater confidence in their ability to change their own lives.

It is necessary to ask many questions and collect information in various ways to find the cause of a health problem. Often there are strong conflicts in a community that require long processes of discussion and struggle to resolve. While each community will find its own way toward making changes and use different activities as it organizes, the experiences of Salud para el Pueblo give some examples of how communities can learn about the root causes of environmental health problems and work to change them.

Mobilizing for Environmental Health

After many years of poverty and isolation, the people living on those muddy hills on the coast of Ecuador were discouraged. They did not know how to improve their lives. Everyday life was so hard, it was difficult to believe in or plan for a better future.

By working to solve the immediate health problem – cholera – Gloria and the health workers of Salud para el Pueblo saved many lives. The success of the health promoters, local organizations, and the villagers in working together to stop the epidemic motivated and prepared them to overcome other problems as well. When the big storm destroyed much of their work, they were able to organize and recover from the storm's damage. Then they were able to move on to solve other problems. Their work to make communities healthier continues, as they improve present-day conditions and build for the future.

Work to understand root causes

Health problems may be caused by many things: germs, toxic chemicals, accidents, hunger, exposure to extreme cold or heat, and so on. These are examples of immediate causes of illness. Illnesses have many immediate causes, but they also have root causes.

Identifying root causes can help us to identify what we may need to do to solve the problem in the long term. You can see how using the "But why...?" activity, as Gloria did (see page 7), can help people understand how a single problem may have several different root causes.

Why did so many people get sick with cholera?

Because there were germs in the water.

This is a physical cause of illness.

But why were there germs in the water?

Because we do not have toilets that keep germs out.

This is an environmental cause of illness.

But why don't we have good toilets?

Because we have no money to build them.

This is an economic cause of illness.

Change takes time

Improving environmental health does not happen quickly. In Manglaralto, the health workers first treated cholera by giving rehydration drink and also worked to prevent it by making the water clean. Then they organized the community to build new water systems and pit toilets to prevent cholera in the future. But it was only after the big storm came and washed away all of these improvements that they understood the problems of **erosion** and flooding caused by **deforestation** (the loss of trees). They needed this understanding of root causes to be able to make lasting changes.

Improvements in environmental health happen step by step. Have patience. Sometimes change that happens quickly wears away just as quickly.

Sometimes, we must struggle and fail several times before we succeed. Often, it is only by seeing what does not work that we learn what does — and why. Improving environmental health takes time because it often requires 4 different kinds of changes:

- changes to improve water systems, housing, or other things we build for ourselves (**infrastructure**).

- changes in what we buy, such as refusing to buy junk food, toxic cleaning products, or products wrapped in plastic (**consumption**).

- changes in our habits, such as regular hand washing, separating trash so more can be recycled, or growing crops in new ways (**behavior**).

- changes in how much power local people, corporations, central governments, and others have in making decisions that affect the environment (**political**).

All of these changes take time and affect each other.

We must be the change we wish to see in the world.

Work with young people

One way to make sure change lasts is to work with young people, because they will take what they learn into the future. Each of us, no matter what age we are, can adopt the attitude of a young person — to always be willing to learn and try new things.

Activities for Learning and Mobilizing

Group activities can help people understand root causes of health problems and make plans for change. Which activities you use will depend on what you need to know, what you hope to do, and what resources are available. Activities can:

- Bring people together to identify common problems.

- Find out what people feel they need most.

- Gather information about what is causing a health problem.

- Analyze problems to discover their immediate causes and their root causes.

- Gather all points of view in the community. A project will not be successful if some groups or opinions are left out. People will not want to help if their opinions are ignored!

Environmental health is always a community issue, and requires people working together to make improvements. Whether the goal is to reduce the risk of an epidemic, to plant a community garden, to improve the health and safety of people living near a factory or working in a mine, or to address some other environmental health issue, the more people have a shared understanding of the problem and a shared commitment to solving it, the more successful they will be.

Women need a voice

In some communities, women and girls are more likely to participate in organized activities if they are in a group separate from men. The women's group then presents their ideas to the larger group. This way, women and girls have a chance to speak in a strong united voice before the whole community. By strengthening the voice of women and girls, and building their leadership skills, the whole community is made stronger.

If you want to solve a problem, work with the people affected by the problem.

Guided discussion

To have a shared understanding of health problems, people need to talk to each other. A guided discussion is a way for a group of people to talk to each other and to ask and answer specific questions. The "But why...?" activity (see pages 7, 12, 38, 48, and 422) is one kind of guided discussion. Drawings for Discussion (see pages 59 and 260) and Body mapping (see page 266) are also kinds of guided discussions.

The person who guides the discussion is sometimes called a facilitator or animator. Most of the activities in this book require a facilitator to make sure each person participates to the best of his or her ability, and to help make sure the discussion or activity leads to action.

Community mapping

Community mapping is an activity in which people make a map together based on what they see and know about their community. By making a community health map, you can learn:

- **where** health problems are.

- **who** these problems affect.

- **how** these health problems may happen because of conditions in the environment.

Make maps with pens or paint on paper, or on the ground with rocks, sticks, and anything else available.

Making a map can help people see patterns in health problems, begin to identify root causes of these problems, and see how conditions in the community have changed over time. A map can also help people identify important community resources and strengths they may not have been aware of. And mapping can be used as a step in protecting important traditional or sacred places. (For examples of mapping, see pages 68, 164, and 443.)

Finding out what a community needs

People often have different opinions about what the problems are in their community and how best to fix them. Making everyone aware of the range of problems that exists and the various causes of the problems, and helping people decide which ones to work on in the short and long term is sometimes called a "needs assessment." (For examples of needs assessment activities, see pages 72, 110, and 221.) A good needs assessment process can help make sure everyone's needs and abilities are considered in planning.

Health walks

During a health walk, people take a closer look at their community. They try to find things that may be causing health problems, such as an unsafe water source, a polluting business, or a lack of firewood. When a health walk is done as a group, people share with each other the different things they know about problems. Then they can work together on possible solutions. The more people involved, the better. (For examples of health walks, see pages 391 and 443.)

Change over time

Another way to understand problems and needs in a community is to compare conditions now to how it was in the past. Then think about how you would like it to be in the future. One way to do this is to gather stories from elders in your community.

Encouraging young people in the community to lead these activities helps build respect and understanding between the generations. It also helps preserve those community traditions that everyone wants to keep.

A community timeline can help people understand how changes have occurred from generation to generation, and take into account significant events such as a road being paved, a factory opening, a dam being built, and so on. Mapping environmental changes is another way to share knowlege of community history through pictures or maps of changes over time in fields, farms, forests, settlements, rivers and lakes. (For an example, see page 164.)

Drawing activities

Making and looking at drawings can help us see solutions to problems that we might not see otherwise. Drawings can be used to start guided discussions, and drawing can be a way for people who cannot read or write well to express themselves and to participate in group leadership. (For examples of drawing activities, see pages 50, 54, and 275.)

Some communities work together to paint pictures on the walls of buildings (murals) that express their problems and hopes for a better, healthier future. (For ideas on making and using drawings in community education, see Hesperian's book, *Helping Health Workers Learn.*)

Community surveys

Community surveys are an organized way to gather information. They can be used to find out what health issues people have, to consider similarities and differences in what people think or believe, or to measure the support for different plans or actions in the community.

In a survey, the same questions are asked in the same way to all of the people participating. Surveys can be done in homes, workplaces, schools, places of worship, other gathering places, or even over the telephone or by post.

Surveys allow people to share their thoughts privately, without having to come to meetings or other public events. They can be a way for people who might be afraid, or who are not allowed to participate in the community decision making process, to have their concerns and ideas considered. (For an example of a community health survey, see pages 500 to 505, "Communities affected by oil organize a health study.")

Theater

Theater is a way to explore problems and propose solutions while entertaining and having fun. People can act out their own experiences and imagine the experiences of others. Some issues and conflicts may be easier to consider if they are portrayed in another time and place. (See the next page for ways to use theater.)

Sociodrama

A sociodrama allows people to act out a problem and demonstrate some of its causes and effects. An example of how sociodrama is used to talk about a forest resource conflict is on pages 186 to 188.

Sociodramas can bring up lots of emotions. Some community organizers like to end by having people sing a song together or do some other 'cooperation' activity.

Interactive theater is a kind of sociodrama in which everyone both watches and participates. Any person in the audience can tell the actors to stop, and then can take the place of an actor and act out a different solution to the problem. This is especially helpful in situations where people take turns playing the role of the person who has little or no power.

Any story can be turned into a sociodrama as long as it has characters and a problem to be worked out.

Role play

A role play does not require as much preparation as a sociodrama, and can help explain different points of view or resolve conflicts. People act out different roles in real-life situations to show what they would do. You can discuss and repeat a role play to understand why people behave a certain way.

Changing the way people in power act is easy on the stage, but very difficult in real life. Using a drama to practice how we interact with people who have power over us helps people prepare different ways to respond to power in real life.

Puppet show

A puppet show uses puppets instead of people to act out the story of a community conflict. They make people laugh, and can help them see things in ways they are not used to. Some people find it easier to talk through puppets than to act on a stage.

A Guide to Which Activity to Use When

The activities in this book are good for exploring the particular environmental health issues of the chapters in which they are described. And they can also help you move forward while organizing in your community. They can:

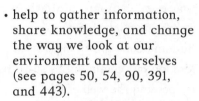

- help identify problems or start a conversation about a particular subject (see pages 59, 69, 72, 260, and 468).

- help a group make decisions or choose between different needs and options (see pages 138 and 191).

- help to gather information, share knowledge, and change the way we look at our environment and ourselves (see pages 50, 54, 90, 391, and 443).

- help to learn new ideas, to relearn ideas we already knew or to learn old ideas in a new way (see pages 158, 284, 289, 336, and 514).

- help to begin organizing to solve a particular problem (see pages 110, 164, 221, and 275).

- help to teach difficult ideas or understand and resolve conflicts (see pages 110 and 186).

Some activities can be used together, such as making community maps during or after a health walk, or using a role play as part of a needs assessment activity. What is most important is that activities help people to gather information, share knowledge, and deepen understanding. This will support their organizing, empowerment, and work to solve the root causes of community health problems.

3 Protecting Natural Resources for All

In this chapter: **page**

Protecting Natural Resources for All

How we use natural resources affects our health and the health of our communities. Because everyone uses natural resources, we all have some part to play in protecting, preserving, and sharing these resources.

Unfortunately, natural resources are not shared equally among everyone. The poor use the least, and the rich use the most. Powerful corporations, governments, and militaries often take a large share of natural resources. Even within a single community, wealthier people use more natural resources than poor people. Often the poor are forced to fight among themselves for what is left. This unfair distribution of resources leads to serious health problems for the poor.

We can talk about conserving natural resources all day long, but so long as inequality continues, environmental health will be a right only for the few who have wealth and power and not the many who need these resources for daily survival. As the Indian leader Mahatma Ghandi said, "There is enough for everyone's need, but not for everyone's greed."

Causes of Environmental Health Problems

One way to think about causes of environmental health problems is:

- **scarcity** (not enough) of essential things we need for a healthy life, such as clean air and water, healthy soil and forests, safe and comfortable shelter, and safe working conditions.

- **excess** (too much) of harmful things we do not need, such as trash, toxic chemicals, **pollution,** and **junk food**.

In the story from Ecuador (see Chapter 1), health problems were caused by the scarcity of basic necessities such as clean water, toilets, and trees. In a story from Bhopal, India (see Chapter 4), health problems were caused by an excess of toxic chemicals.

In each story, improving environmental health depended on people preventing the conditions that caused both a scarcity of essential resources for life and an excess of pollution. By protecting our communities and our natural resources, we are protecting the future for our children, and our children's children.

Too many people, too few resources?

The amount of water, trees, minerals, and other natural resources on Earth is limited, while the number of people using these resources is growing rapidly. But the number of people is not the real problem. The problem is how these natural resources are distributed and used. Any time one person or a group of people uses more than their fair share of resources, or causes an excess of pollution, this imbalance can lead to environmental health problems for others.

The rich man's explanation of poverty and environmental destruction: Too many people, too little land and resources.

The poor people's explanation of poverty and environmental destruction: Unfair distribution of land and resources, too much in the hands of too few.

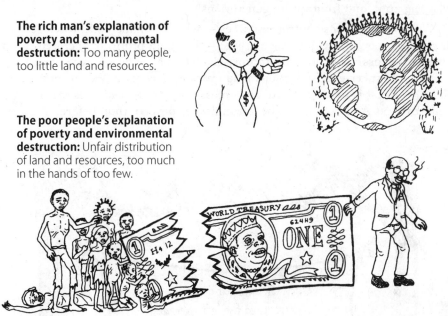

Some people believe the best way to prevent harm to our environment is to reduce the number of people. This way of thinking leads to 'population control' programs. These programs have failed to improve the lives of people anywhere because they do not address the root causes of environmental destruction, poverty, and poor health. When families have the resources they need to live with health and dignity, many choose to have fewer children. Only when communities, governments, and development programs plan for the survival of children, and the improvement of the social, political, and economic status of women, will the so-called "population problem" be solved.

But reducing the number of people in the world will not address the problem of the unequal use of resources. The best way to reduce the harmful effect people have on the environment is for the rich to use fewer resources, and to use them in a way that conserves resources for the future and does not create an excess of pollution. By first changing the behavior of those who use the most, we can begin to make sure there will be enough for a healthy life for everyone.

Corporate control is bad for our health

The health crisis on the coast of Ecuador (see Chapter 1) was caused by a big corporation that paid local people to clear the forest. Not only did people lose the trees that kept the soil healthy and protected them from storms, they also lost important resources for daily survival such as food, fuel wood, medicines, fiber, and other basic needs. When a resource like a large forest cannot be put back, it is the same as if it had been stolen – from nature, from communities who rely on it, and from future generations.

When corporations control resources — whether timber, oil, water, seeds, or the labor power of people themselves — they gain profit for themselves, and have little reason to protect or improve the lives of the people who need those resources to survive. Corporations may provide short-term jobs or income, but if their interest is to export local resources, when those resources are gone they will leave too. And people will be left in deeper poverty than before.

Building community institutions

Fair and equal control of natural resources means that all people have a voice in decisions about how natural resources are used and shared. Fair and equal control can take many forms, but all are based in education and organization of people to work together for change.

Environmental health is always a community issue. People must work together, as a community, to protect the resources they share in common. To work together over the long term, people usually form some sort of community group or institution.

When the cholera epidemic began to spread in Ecuador, Salud para el Pueblo organized public health committees to raise awareness and get people to act. To better respond to the cholera epidemic, the public health committees offered knowledge (how to make rehydration drink) and services (building new toilets and water systems). They also helped to restore and strengthen their communities by maintaining a health clinic, and providing health education and training at schools, parks, and in people's homes. And they inspired other people to form groups and institutions, such as the environmental health promoters and the recycling program.

Salud para el Pueblo also worked with organizations from outside their communities to provide money, engineering skills, medicines, and other resources. They made sure these resources were used and managed by the villagers themselves. The communities were also involved in the planning and decision making about expanding the program.

When each village formed a committee of health promoters, they were able to decide which health problems were most important to resolve.

When governments do not provide for the basic needs of their people, the people must build institutions for themselves, as Salud para el Pueblo did, to make sure the future is healthy. Often, when communities organize, the government then responds by fulfilling its responsibilities to the people.

The different resource needs of men and women; of workers, farmers, foresters, and ranchers; and of industries, land developers, and others, can bring conflict into your community and your organization. Sometimes problems can be particularly difficult, such as balancing short-term needs for income and long-term health needs. Building strong community institutions often takes so much time because recognizing these differences and trying to settle these conflicts is difficult. Making long-term health a goal, and finding ways for everyone to work toward meeting this goal together, can help resolve difficult conflicts and build strong institutions that protect the common good.

Making Our Communities Sustainable

Sustainability means the ability to keep something going for a long time. Whether we are talking about a community institution such as a health clinic or recycling program, or a natural resource such as a forest, field, or spring, if it is not developed and used in sustainable ways, serious environmental health problems may result.

Sustainability also means being able to meet the daily needs of people now while planning for the needs of future generations. One of the greatest challenges facing people today is trying to meet all of our needs without harming the environment that feeds, houses, and clothes us, that gives us water, energy, and medicine, and is the very source of our survival.

All around us we see the signs of development that is not sustainable. There is an increasing scarcity of healthy food, clean air and water, and safe livelihoods. And there is an excess of pollution, deforestation, and illness. When communities grow in ways that are not sustainable, they create big problems for themselves and for future generations.

Throughout this book, especially in the stories we have collected, we give examples of some basic principles of sustainability. Some of the most important principles are described in the following pages.

Respecting the web of life

The natural world is made up of a great variety of living things. The scientific word for the great number of different kinds of people, plants, animals, and insects that live on Earth is **biodiversity.** Long before scientists gave this name to the variety of living things, many people taught their children about the web of life. Just as a spider's web is made strong by the many threads connecting it, biodiversity depends on the web of life connecting all living things.

For example, people gather fruits to eat, which have nutrients that keep them healthy. These fruits grow on trees and bushes **pollinated** by insects. Without pollination, the fruit will not grow. Birds eat the insects, and the birds are hunted by foxes. A balance in the web of life means that there are just enough flowers, insects, birds, and foxes for all to live in the area. If you kill too many foxes, maybe because they are killing your chickens, then perhaps the number of birds will grow and they will eat too many of the insects. In this way, killing too many foxes can mean you have less fruit as well.

An important part of protecting human health, now and in the future, is protecting the web of life.

Unfortunately, the world is facing a great loss of biodiversity, with many plants and animals disappearing every year. Biodiversity is valuable in itself, but it is also valuable in the many ways this web of life protects human health.

Damage to the web of life leads to new illnesses

Loss of biodiversity means there are fewer kinds of plants and animals, and the natural balance among plants, animals, and people is disturbed. This can cause new illnesses. Here are 2 examples of how a loss of biodiversity from **deforestation** caused new illnesses:

- Where people cut down tropical forests for farms and towns in Africa, there have been outbreaks of leishmaniasis, yellow fever, and sleeping sickness. These are diseases spread by insects that thrived when water pooled instead of being absorbed by the soil, and the animals that eat the insects lost their forest homes.

- When large numbers of trees were cut down in North America, the number of white-footed mice grew because their food supply increased and the number of animals that hunted them got smaller. These mice carried an illness called Lyme disease, which then spread to people.

Plant medicines depend on biodiversity

Most medicines are made from plants. When forests are cut down, and rivers and wetlands dry up, we lose many of these plants. We also lose traditional knowledge of how to use these plants for healing.

Protecting biodiversity and the web of life protects our cultures and our healing traditions.

People who use medicinal plants often cultivate and care for them, protecting both biodiversity and traditions.

A healthy diet depends on biodiversity

Good health depends on eating a variety of foods, such as fruits, vegetables, grains, and wild foods such as berries, fish, and game. When we lose biodiversity, we lose many of the foods we rely on for a healthy diet. Then entire communities are faced with the health problems that come from poor nutrition.

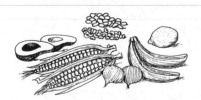

Planting a variety of crops promotes both biodiversity and a healthy diet.

Gloria, the health worker with Salud para el Pueblo, understood the web of life. Because honey bees need flowers to make honey, and flowering trees need bees to help them bear fruit, planting trees and raising bees helped the community produce food and restore the web of life at the same time.

Biodiversity improves crop yields

All food crops, including rice, maize, and wheat, were cultivated over thousands of years from wild plants. These crops still depend on insects and other animal life to grow well.

Industrial farming, with its use of big farm machines and toxic chemicals, promises bigger crop yields. But these chemicals kill helpful plants and insects, and damage the soil. If production increases, usually it is for one crop only, and only for a short time. After several years, there is less food and fewer varieties of the foods necessary for good health.

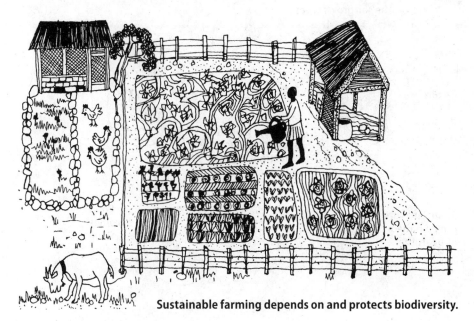

Sustainable farming depends on and protects biodiversity.

Farms can produce more crops and suffer fewer pest problems with sustainable methods. These methods promote healthy insect and animal life, enrich soil with natural fertilizers, and protect land with trees and plants (see Chapter 15). A diverse crop yield provides improved nutrition and better health for all.

Biodiversity protects water resources

Both deforestation and industrial farming lead to a loss of soil moisture and streams drying up in the dry season. Chemical fertilizers and pesticides run off industrial farms and pollute rivers and lakes.

Biodiversity protects communities

Many different livelihoods depend on access to natural resources. When those resources disappear, poverty grows. In farming areas, industrial farming increases debt for some and landlessness for many others.

Restoring the web of life

In the web of life, when a living thing dies, it affects many others, including people. In the story in Chapter 1, when the people of Manglaralto lost their forest, they also lost food sources and income. When the storms struck, they lost their homes as well. When they started replanting trees, the villagers found they were doing more than preventing erosion or producing honey. Their work to restore the land to a state of health brought back many plants and animals important to the health of their communities.

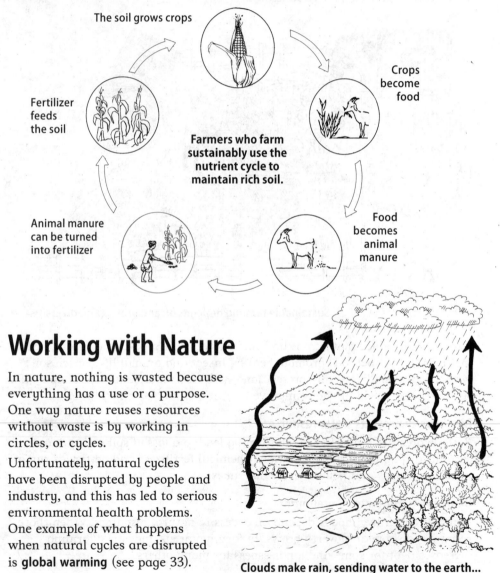

The soil grows crops

Crops become food

Food becomes animal manure

Animal manure can be turned into fertilizer

Fertilizer feeds the soil

Farmers who farm sustainably use the nutrient cycle to maintain rich soil.

Working with Nature

In nature, nothing is wasted because everything has a use or a purpose. One way nature reuses resources without waste is by working in circles, or cycles.

Unfortunately, natural cycles have been disrupted by people and industry, and this has led to serious environmental health problems. One example of what happens when natural cycles are disrupted is **global warming** (see page 33).

**Clouds make rain, sending water to the earth...
Water evaporates to form clouds....**

How we can copy natural cycles

Environmental health promoters in the Philippines have a saying:

> *What comes from the earth must return to the earth.*

By understanding the importance of returning to the earth what comes from the earth, we can copy nature and protect our natural resources and health. The cycles we create in our homes, communities, and factories are small steps we can take toward improving environmental health. For example, composting, and reusing or recycling glass bottles and tin cans, are ways to follow nature's example by creating a cycle instead of a waste dump.

How industry can copy natural cycles

Environmental health promoters in the Philippines also have another saying:

> *What comes from the factory must return to the factory.*

Industry causes the most toxic pollution. But even industry can learn from natural cycles to reuse energy and materials in a process called **clean production.**
The first step would be for industry to take back all the waste it creates. If wastes, such as toxic chemicals, cannot be recycled, industry must safely dispose of them, and reduce and eventually eliminate their use. If industry is to have a place in a sustainable future, it must be based on prevention, precaution, and the right to health for all, not on the right to profit from danger, dumping, and disease.

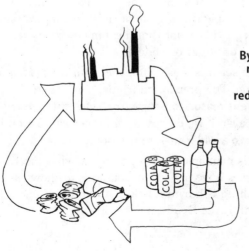

By using fewer resources, and recycling and reusing what they do use, industry can reduce the harm it causes to our environmental health.

Preventing harm from pollution

Pollution is the harm to people and the environment caused by an excess of poisonous or toxic substances from peoples' activities, especially wastes from industry, transportation, and agriculture. Toxic pollution travels through the environment in our air, water, and soil.

Most pollution comes from things we use and are exposed to in our daily lives. The most common ways people are exposed to toxic pollution include:

- **smoke from fires,** especially when plastic is burned. We breathe in toxic smoke, and toxic ash pollutes our drinking water and our crop land.

- **smoke from factories** that pollutes air, water, and soil.

- **chemicals** used in factories, mining, and oil drilling and production that are dumped into water sources, and also pollute the air and land.

- **pesticides** used and handled near food, water sources, and at home. When sprayed, they travel far through the air, causing great harm.

- **chemicals** in batteries, paints, dyes, and from making electronics that harm the people who work with them.

- **motor exhaust** from automobiles that pollutes air, water, and soil.

Toxic pollution causes serious harm to people, plants, and animals not only where it is released but also far from the source. Protecting ourselves from the harm caused by pollution and toxic substances is an important part of sustainability (see pages 42, 368, 410, 440, and Chapters 14, 16 and 20 to 23).

The precautionary principle

In their search for new products and more profit, corporations have developed thousands of chemicals that never existed in nature. Most of these chemicals have not been tested to prove they are safe. Still, they are used in products sold to us every day. Even when people think some of these chemicals might be harmful, if they cannot prove beyond a doubt that a chemical is dangerous, it cannot be kept off the market — or out of our bodies.

Some community leaders and scientists use what they call the **precautionary principle** to guide decision making. The precautionary principle says:

An ounce of prevention is worth a pound of cure.

If there is reason to believe that something may cause harm, even if we do not know for certain, then it is better to avoid it than to risk doing harm.

This principle is the opposite of what most countries have now. Now you have to show that something is harmful before it can be stopped. We call it the Dead Bodies Principle.

Global warming

All over the world, the web of life is being torn apart. Deforestation, increased pollution of our water and air, and loss of wildlife are all visible examples. Less visible is the increase in temperature caused by pollution.

This problem, called **global warming,** is changing the **climate** (what the weather is like in a place over a long period of time) in most parts of the world. What seem like small increases in temperature are leading to big changes. Some places are having more floods and severe storms, and other places are having less rain and more droughts. Climate change caused by global warming is causing disasters all around the world, year after year, creating serious problems for people's health.

- Flooding, severe storms, and drought cause crop loss, famine, destruction of homes, mass migration, injury, and death.

- Diseases worsen or spread because changing weather brings more insects and disease-carrying animals, and lets them move to new places.

- Hotter temperatures sometimes lead to increased illness and death.

Root causes of global warming

The environment has a natural ability to absorb pollution. But if too much pollution is put into the environment, the earth cannot absorb it. Over the last 100 years, when people started to remove and burn large amounts of **fossil fuels** such as oil and coal, the amount of pollution released into the environment increased faster than ever before. This is one of the root causes of global warming. Also, some chemicals invented for manufacturing pollute the air and cannot be absorbed. They too contribute to global warming.

Another root cause of global warming is the unfair, unequal, and unsustainable use of resources. Wealthy countries such as the United States of America started global warming by using too many resources and causing too much pollution in pursuit of higher profits and a higher standard of living. When poorer countries start following the same unsustainable paths toward development, the pollution becomes even more impossible for the earth to bear. To prevent disasters caused by global warming, like the ones listed above and worse ones still to come, both developed and "underdeveloped" countries must change to a sustainable use of resources. We especially need to stop depending on fossil fuels and start using more clean energy (see Chapter 23).

4 Environmental Rights and Justice

In this chapter: page

Environmental Rights and Justice

Every person in every community has the right to health, and to a safe and healthy environment. Unfortunately, these rights are often not respected. Many people suffer from serious health problems caused by a scarcity of basic necessities and an excess of harmful substances. The most vulnerable people are those who have low status because of race, ethnicity, religion, gender, class, caste, poverty, or for other reasons. They usually suffer first, and worst.

The struggle to live in a healthy, safe, productive, and enjoyable environment by communities whose rights are not well respected by people in power is sometimes called the struggle for environmental justice.

There are many stories from around the world of communities suffering unjustly from environmental health disasters, just as many stories can be told of people organizing to protect and defend their right to health and environmental justice in the wake of these disasters. This chapter tells such a story.

The Bhopal Toxic Gas Disaster

On the night of December 3, 1984, in the city of Bhopal, India, a terrible disaster happened. A pesticide factory in a crowded and poor neighborhood of Bhopal leaked many tons of poison gas into the air. The warning system in the factory was turned off, so the community heard no alarms of any kind.

One survivor, Aziza Sultan, remembers:

I woke in the night to the sound of my baby coughing badly. The room was filled with a white cloud. I heard people shouting 'Run! Run!' Then I started coughing with each breath as if I was breathing in fire.

Another survivor, Champa Devi Shukla, remembers:

People just got up and ran in whatever they were wearing, even if they were wearing nothing at all. They were only concerned with saving their lives and the lives of their loved ones, so they just ran.

It felt like somebody had filled my body with red chilies, my eyes had tears coming out, my nose was watering, I had froth in my mouth.

The poison gas killed many people that night. After 3 days 8,000 people had died. But this was not the end of the disaster. In fact, it was only the beginning.

Over the next 20 years, more than 20,000 people died from the poison that remained in their bodies. Many more developed terrible illnesses, including pain and difficulty breathing, constant cough, fever, loss of feeling in their arms and legs, weakness, fear, depression, and **cancer.** Children and grandchildren of the survivors suffer from severe **birth defects,** including withered limbs, slow growth, and many different reproductive and nervous system problems. More than 150,000 people have been harmed by the poison gas released that night in Bhopal.

The Struggle for Rights and Justice

To this day, the site of the toxic gas leak has never been cleaned up and the abandoned factory remains as a deadly reminder of the disaster. Piles of toxic chemicals still lie in the open air, and the groundwater beneath the city is poisoned. Many people never received the medical treatment they needed for their health problems. For these reasons, the people of Bhopal do not think of the disaster as something that happened in the past only. They see it as an ongoing disaster they must face every day.

The pesticide factory was owned by a **multinational corporation** (a big company that works in many countries) called Union Carbide. Survivors of the disaster knew it was not right that their lives had been so damaged by the disaster. The people affected did not have money to treat their illnesses or to care for their family members who could no longer work. They wanted the company to take responsibility. But Union Carbide said the disaster was caused by a worker in the factory, and refused to take any responsibility.

Like other people struggling for rights and justice, the people affected by the Bhopal disaster knew that their poverty not only made their problems worse — it was a large part of why the disaster happened in the first place.

Why did the disaster happen?

The Bhopal disaster was, and is, a horrible event that should never have happened. But, as horrible as it was, it is not surprising. The "But why...?" activity can help understand the root causes of the Bhopal disaster.

All over the world, corporations build their polluting factories, toxic dumps, and other dangerous industrial projects among people who are most oppressed by poverty and low status. In this way, poor countries and communities become dumping grounds for toxic industries, products, and pollution. This is why protecting environmental health is not just a matter of each of us changing the products we use and how we dispose of them, but of all of us challenging how the powerful abuse their power and how the most vulnerable among us are made to suffer damage to their health.

The international campaign for justice in Bhopal

Survivors of the Bhopal gas leak worked together to bring attention to their suffering and to make the company take responsibility. They organized hunger strikes, and refused to eat until they were heard. They marched with no food or water for 750 kilometers (466 miles) to the state capital. They also marched to the national capital to demand justice. Women set up a tent in front of the office of the state's chief minister. They camped out there for 3 months. Every day from dawn to dusk they chanted their demands.

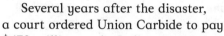

Never again!

Several years after the disaster, a court ordered Union Carbide to pay $470 million to the Indian government. This was an important victory, but it was not enough. Most of that money never reached the survivors.

Soon after, Union Carbide was sold to another multinational corporation called Dow Chemical. Dow Chemical also refused to take responsibility or to help the affected people get treatment. Neither the government of India, where the disaster happened, nor the government of the United States, where both corporations are based, is willing to bring to justice the top corporate officials responsible for the disaster.

The survivors organized an international campaign to continue their struggle for justice. They built support among students, environmental groups, and human rights organizations. With support from people all over the world, the Bhopal survivors delivered their demands for justice to the headquarters of Union Carbide and Dow Chemical Company. The survivors inspired others to go on hunger strikes and to take actions to bring attention to their suffering. And through it all, they have supported their families, organized their own health care (see page 345), supported victims of other toxic disasters, and survived.

The rallying cry of the campaign for justice in Bhopal is "Bhopal, never again!" Their goal is to prevent similar environmental disasters in the future. By making their struggle international, they have taught people around the world important lessons about the long-term effects of toxic exposure. The Bhopal survivors have shown industrial accidents can happen at any time, and that the poor are always more affected by them than anyone else. Their struggle for rights and justice has become a model for community organizers everywhere.

How Toxic Substances Get into our Bodies

Eating and drinking   **Breathing**   **and**   **Through the skin**
(ingestion)   **(inhalation)**   **(absorption)**

The longer someone is exposed to (in direct contact with) a toxic chemical, the more harm it can cause. In Bhopal, thousands of people were exposed all at once by breathing the gas and getting it on their skin. This was the immediate disaster. Because the chemical disaster was not cleaned up and the chemicals spread widely throughout the areas around the factory, the poison got into the soil and the groundwater beneath the city. Now, many years later, people are drinking water with the poison in it. This is part of the ongoing disaster.

Whether in a large-scale toxic exposure such as the one in Bhopal or a simple exposure to toxics in paints, solvents, or other ordinary products, the first thing to do is to get away from the chemicals, or get them away from you, so that the exposure does not last. After that, work to prevent future exposures. (For more about health problems from toxic chemicals, see Chapter 16.)

A health clinic designed to protect the environment

People in Bhopal are fighting for environmental justice. At the same time, they are working to heal from the disaster. Survivors and other volunteers started the Sambhavna Clinic to provide health care to the whole community, regardless of ability to pay, or religious or caste differences. *Sambhavna* means "possibility" in the Sanskrit and Hindi languages.

The Sambhavna Clinic is a model of environmental health. It was built and operates as safely and sustainably as possible. For example:

- Only hot water and soap are used to clean the clinic, to make sure that no one is harmed by toxic cleaning products.

- Clinic workers started a garden to grow plant medicines. No chemicals are used in the garden. People treated at the clinic work in the garden and collect their own herbs for treatment.

- When new clinic buildings are needed, only nontoxic building materials are used. The buildings use local materials, and are designed to allow natural light and air to pass through.

- Rainwater is collected from tiled roofs during the wet season and stored in underground tanks, providing water for the dry season.

- After water is used for washing, it is piped into a pond and then irrigates the grounds and the herb garden.

- Electricity is made by **solar panels,** which cause very little pollution.

The Sambhavna Clinic shows how achieving health for all means not only treating the sick, but preventing illness in the first place. Their example of reducing harm from toxics can be followed in schools, businesses, government offices, and our homes. But even if we change our homes and institutions to make them healthier and more sustainable, all of us, especially the most vulnerable, are still at risk, as long as industries continue to produce and use toxic substances. (To learn more about the Sambhavna Clinic, see page 345.)

Working for change

By organizing their community to struggle for long-term health and well-being, the survivors of Bhopal have inspired people around the world to act for environmental rights and justice. These principles of organizing to reduce harm from toxic chemicals have proven useful:

- **Avoid toxics in daily life.** Use nontoxic chemicals for cleaning at home, in community institutions, or at the workplace (see pages 372 to 374). Do not use chemical pesticides or fertilizers in the garden, eat food grown without chemicals, and wash fruits and vegetables carefully before eating (see Chapter 14). Because we are likely to be exposed to toxics in our communities, we must pressure governments to stop allowing corporations to expose people, especially the most vulnerable.

- **Organize to prevent pollution.** Use different actions to prevent toxic disasters, including hunger strikes, sit-ins, and marches, as well as popular theater, the media, the internet, and other communication methods to educate people. If a factory is polluting, look for other ways that workers can earn their livelihood, because all people need jobs and income.

- **Force companies to clean up.** Although this is very hard to achieve, demanding that a corporation clean up its toxic mess is an important part of every struggle for environmental rights. People agree, even if corporations do not, that corporations must take responsibility to prevent harm and to repair any damage they cause.

If our governments protected us and our environment the way I protect my family, we would all be healthier.

- **Pressure governments for better safety standards.** Unfortunately, most governments protect corporate profits more than they protect people. This promotes environmental injustice and leads to disasters when the companies see safety as an avoidable cost, not a responsibility. Governments must change their priorities to protect all people, especially the most vulnerable.

- **Change the way industry makes things.** The Union Carbide factory in Bhopal made pesticides to control crop pests. But there are better ways to control pests than using these chemicals. In fact, there are less harmful and more sustainable ways to do just about everything. Why is it that we are allowed to be poisoned by industry, but not allowed to decide how things should be made?

Acceptable risk? For whom?

Industries and governments often justify the risk of environmental damage, even disasters such as the one at Bhopal, by saying that a certain amount of risk is acceptable as "the cost of development." This usually means that the most vulnerable of us are sacrificed in order for business to continue making profits as usual. For most of us, that is not acceptable. The pursuit of profit is no justification for causing so much harm and violating people's human rights to health and a healthy environment.

If the Union Carbide company or the Indian government had been guided by the precautionary principle (see page 32), perhaps the Bhopal toxic gas disaster would not have happened.

Demanding precaution

Safety measures can reduce harm. But even when safety measures are taken, there is always some risk in industrial factories. If risks cannot be avoided, then at least they should be shared equally and not affect only the poorest people and communities.

In the long term, to be as safe as possible, industries must be organized in a way that values safety and sustainability more than high profits. To achieve this, we should demand that corporations develop safer and more just ways of doing things, and that governments hold them accountable by making and enforcing laws that protect health and the environment. One way to promote environmental justice for all is to demand that our leaders and those in power make decisions guided by the precautionary principle.

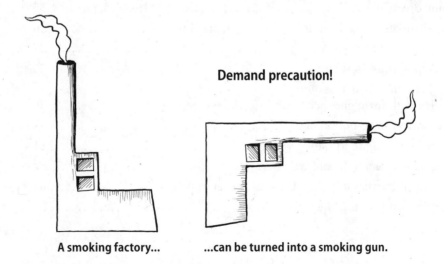

Demand precaution!

A smoking factory...   ...can be turned into a smoking gun.

5 Health Problems from Unsafe Water

In this chapter: page

Health Problems from Unsafe Water

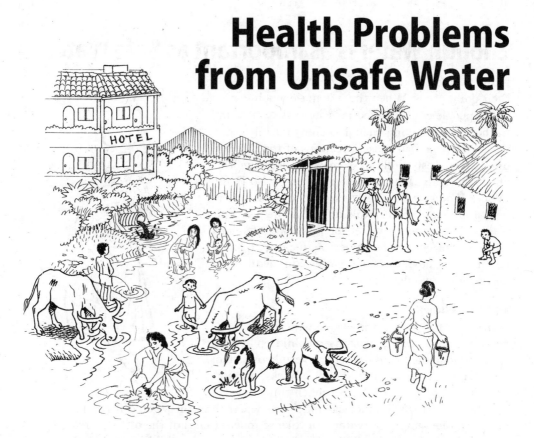

No one can live without water. To be healthy, people need enough water and they need the water to be safe. Water is not safe when germs and worms from human and animal wastes (urine and feces) get into it. The germs and worms can be passed through the water or from one person to another, causing many serious health problems and affecting a whole community.

Chemicals from agriculture, industry, and mining, and trash dumping can also make our water unsafe and cause illnesses such as skin rashes, cancers, and other serious health problems.

Not having enough water for drinking, cooking, and washing can lead to sickness. Especially when there is no way to wash hands after using the toilet, diarrhea diseases spread quickly from person to person. A shortage of water for personal cleanliness can also lead to infections of the eyes and skin. Lack of water can cause **dehydration** (losing too much water in the body) and death.

Not having enough water may be due to **drought** (dry weather for a long time), the high cost of water, or because water has not been well **conserved.**

Contamination of water can make the effects of water scarcity worse, and likewise, water scarcity can make contamination more serious. (For information on protecting water sources and making water clean and safe, see Chapter 6. For safe sanitation, see Chapter 7.)

Enough Water is as Important as Safe Water

Many people do not have enough water to meet
their daily needs. When there is not enough water to
wash, people can get infections such as **scabies** and
trachoma. Not having enough water to drink and
wash with can also cause infections of the bladder
and kidneys, especially in women. (To learn more
about these illnesses, see *Where There is No Doctor,
Where Women Have No Doctor,* or another general
health manual.) In hospitals and other health centers,
if there is not enough water for washing, infections
can spread from person to person. Especially for
children, not having enough water can mean
dehydration and death.

Women's burden

When water is scarce, the people who collect and
carry water — usually women and children — have
to travel long distances and carry very heavy loads.
This leads to injuries to their necks, backs, and hips.
Collecting water often takes so much time and strength
that they and their families use much less water than they would if it was
plentiful. The search for water can take so much time that the other work
women do to support family health, including caring for children and tending
crops, does not get done.

Water can prevent and treat many illnesses

Water is used to reduce fevers and to clean wounds and skin infections.
Drinking a lot of water helps to prevent and treat diarrhea, urinary infections,
coughs, and constipation. Washing hands with soap and water after using the
toilet and before eating or handling food also helps prevent many illnesses.

Cleaning wounds with
soap and water helps
prevent infections.

Treat minor burns
by holding them
in cold water.

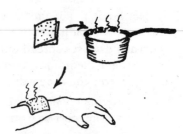

Hot soaks and compresses
treat abscesses, boils, sore
muscles and stiff joints.

What Makes Water Unsafe?

Water is unsafe when it contains germs, worms, or toxic chemicals (for more about toxics, see Chapters 16 and 20). Germs (tiny living things, too small to see, that cause many kinds of illness) and worms, such as whipworm, hookworm, and roundworm, cause many serious illnesses.

Germs and worms live in human and animal waste (urine and feces) and can cause serious and long-lasting illnesses when:

- there is not a good way to get rid of human and animal wastes.
- water supplies are not protected and kept clean.
- there is not enough water to wash.

Some of the illnesses they cause, such as cholera, spread quickly and can cause many deaths. Other illnesses from germs and worms can cause years of sickness and lead to other health problems such as dehydration, infections, **anemia** (weak blood), and malnutrition. Because the most common sign of illnesses from germs and worms is diarrhea, these illnesses are sometimes called diarrhea diseases.

Timothy's story

Njoki lived in a village with her one-year-old son Timothy. Like the other villagers, she collected water from a tube well built many years before by a development group. Back then, when the pump would break, the development workers brought new parts to repair it. But after the development workers left, no one in the village knew how to repair the pump or where to get parts. And they had no money to buy parts anyway.

So when the pump broke, the women had to go collect water from a water hole outside the village. The water hole was also used by animals, and was contaminated with worms and germs. After drinking water from this hole, Timothy became sick with severe watery diarrhea. He grew weaker and weaker. Njoki had no money to take him to the health center many hours away. Within a few days, Timothy died.

Dehydration from diarrhea diseases is the most common cause of death for children in the world. The discussion of how people get diarrhea diseases continues on the next page.

Understanding why Timothy died

The "But why...?" activity (see pages 7 and 12) can help to understand the different causes of Timothy's illness and death.

What caused Timothy's death? Diarrhea and dehydration.

But why did he have diarrhea? There were germs in the water.

But why were there germs in the water? It was an unprotected water hole contaminated with germs and worms.

But why did Timothy drink from an unprotected water hole? The village pump was broken.

But why couldn't it be repaired?

Continue the "chain" until you run out of questions. You can also return to an earlier link and ask for more underlying causes. For example:

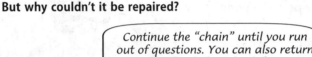

But why didn't Njoki make the water safe to drink? There was little firewood to boil the water and no money to disinfect it with chlorine.

The "But why...?" questions continue as people come up with reasons for Timothy's death. A chain of causes drawn on paper or on a chalkboard, or made of cardboard or flannel, can show how each cause is connected to the other causes. For each reason given, a link is added to the chain. In this way, people can understand the different causes of illness, and how these causes can be prevented.

Pump broken

Animal waste in water

No wood to boil water — Timothy gets diarrhea — No rehydration drink — No money for doctor

Timothy dies

A simple story about how germs travel

1. A man has diarrhea outside.

2. A dog eats the man's feces.

3. A child plays with the dog and gets feces on his hands.

4. The child starts to cry and his mother comforts him. He wipes his hands on her skirt.

How germs and worms spread disease

Sometimes it is easy to know where germs and worms are, especially on unclean things such as feces, rotting foods, dirty toilets, and so on. But sometimes they are in places that look clean, like clear water, or on our hands.

Germs and worms can pass from person to person through touch, and through the air with dust or when people cough or sneeze. They can spread through food and drinking water, or be carried by flies, other insects, and animals. They may also live on uncooked or poorly cooked food. Some worms can be passed by drinking, stepping into, or washing with contaminated water, or eating uncooked shellfish or plants from contaminated water. Germs and worms that cause diarrhea travel on these paths:

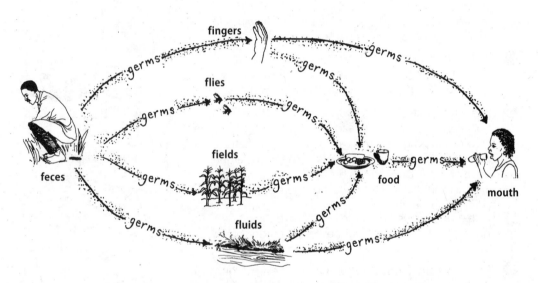

One way to remember the paths germs travel is they are all words beginning with the letter F: fingers, flies, feces, fields, foods, and fluids (water).

5. The mother cooks. The germs on her skirt get on her hands. She serves the food with her hands.

6. The family eats the food.

7. Later, the whole family has diarrhea.

How Diarrhea Diseases Spread

This activity helps to show how germs that cause diarrhea pass from person to person. People make drawings and put them together to form a story.

Time: 1 to 1½ hours

Materials: Small drawing paper, large drawing paper, colored pens or markers, sticky tape, sample drawings

❶ Form groups of 5 to 8 people. Each person draws a picture that shows something about how she thinks people get diarrhea. Each drawing should show just one part of the story of how diarrhea spreads. If a person has difficulty drawing, she can write a word instead or get help from someone else. It may help to have sample drawings to stimulate group discussion.

❷ Each person shows her drawing in her small group. The other people in the group tell what they see. This is so every person understands the drawings.

❸ Each group puts their drawings in an order that makes a story about how germs spread. If the group sees there are drawings missing, they make new drawings to fit the story. When the drawings are in order, tape them to a larger piece of paper. Draw arrows between the drawings to make a chart that tells a story of how germs spread.

❹ Each group shows its chart to the other groups. The group showing the drawings tells the story of how diarrhea passes from one person to another.

❺ The whole group discusses the activity. Is every group's story the same? How are the stories different? Why? Talk about the ways diarrhea spreads. How do economic and social conditions put people at risk? What behaviors and beliefs put people at risk? What other ways do diseases spread that were not illustrated in the activity?

Diarrhea diseases

Most diarrhea diseases are caused by a lack of water for personal cleanliness, toilets that are not clean and safe, and contaminated water and food.

Signs

The most common sign of diarrhea disease is frequent, runny or liquid feces. Other signs include fever, headache, trembling, chills, weakness, stomach and intestinal cramps, vomiting, and swollen belly. What treatment to give depends on the kind of diarrhea a person has.

These signs can help you know which diarrhea disease a person has:

- **Cholera:** diarrhea like rice water, intestinal pain and cramping, vomiting.

- **Typhoid:** fever, severe intestinal pain and cramping, headache, constipation or thick diarrhea (like pea soup).

- **Giardia:** diarrhea that looks greasy, floats, and smells bad, intestinal pain, low fever, vomiting, gas, burps sometimes smell like rotten eggs.

- **Bacterial dysentery (Shigella):** bloody diarrhea 10 to 20 times a day, fever, severe intestinal pain and cramping.

- **Amebic dysentery:** diarrhea 4 to 10 times a day, often with white mucus, fever, intestinal pain and cramping, and diarrhea right after eating.

- **Roundworm:** swollen belly, weakness, large pink or white worms that may come out in feces or through the mouth and nose.

- **Hookworm:** diarrhea, weakness, anemia, pale skin. Children with hookworm may eat dirt.

- **Whipworm:** diarrhea, thin pink or grey worms in feces.

To learn more about treating diarrhea diseases and worm infections, see Chapters 12 and 13 in *Where There Is No Doctor.*

Treatment for diarrhea diseases

Diarrhea is best treated by giving plenty of liquids and food. In most cases, but not all, no medicine is needed. (For more information, see a health worker or a general health book such as *Where There Is No Doctor.*)

- **Amebic dysentery** is best treated with medicines.

- **Typhoid** is best treated by antibiotics because it can last for weeks and lead to death.

- **Cholera** is best treated with rehydration drink, lots of fluids, and easy-to-digest foods to replace nutrients lost through diarrhea and vomiting. Medicines may be used to prevent cholera from spreading.

If a person has bloody diarrhea, fever, or is very sick, he or she needs to go to a health center right away.

Diarrhea and dehydration

Many people die from diarrhea diseases, especially children. Most often, they die because they become dehydrated.

People of any age can become dehydrated, but serious dehydration can happen very quickly to small children and is most dangerous for them.

Any child with watery diarrhea is in danger of dehydration. Give lots of liquids and take young children with signs of dehydration to a health center right away.

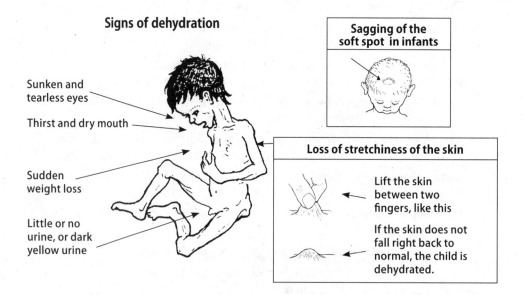

Signs of dehydration

Sunken and tearless eyes

Thirst and dry mouth

Sudden weight loss

Little or no urine, or dark yellow urine

Sagging of the soft spot in infants

Loss of stretchiness of the skin

Lift the skin between two fingers, like this

If the skin does not fall right back to normal, the child is dehydrated.

To prevent or treat dehydration

When a child has watery diarrhea or diarrhea and vomiting, **do not wait for signs of dehydration. Act quickly.**

- **Give lots of liquids to drink,** such as a thin cereal porridge or gruel, soup, water, or rehydration drink (see next page).

- **Keep giving food.** As soon as the sick child (or adult) can eat food, give frequent feedings of foods he likes. To babies, keep giving breast milk often — and before any other foods or drinks.

- **Rehydration drink** helps prevent or treat dehydration. It does not cure diarrhea, but may support the sick person until the diarrhea stops.

How to make rehydration drink

Here are 2 ways of making rehydration drink. If you can, add half a cup of fruit juice, coconut water, or mashed ripe banana to either drink. These contain potassium, a mineral that helps a sick person accept more food and drink.

Give a child sips of this drink every 5 minutes, day and night, until he begins to urinate normally. A large person needs 3 or more liters a day. A small child usually needs at least 1 liter a day, or 1 glass for each watery stool. Keep giving the drink often, and in small sips. Even if the person vomits, not all of the drink will be vomited. After one day, discard the drink and make a new mixture if necessary.

Made with powdered cereal and salt.
(Powdered rice is best. But you can use finely ground maize, wheat flour, sorghum, or cooked and mashed potatoes.)

In 1 liter of clean WATER put half of a level teaspoon of SALT,

and 8 heaping teaspoons of powdered CEREAL.

Boil for 5 to 7 minutes to form a liquid gruel or watery porridge. Cool the drink quickly and begin to give it to the sick person.

CAUTION: Taste the drink each time before you give it to make sure that it has not spoiled. Cereal drinks can spoil within a few hours in hot weather.

Made with sugar and salt.
(You can use raw, brown or white sugar, or molasses.)

In 1 liter of clean WATER put half of a level teaspoon of SALT,

and 8 level teaspoons of SUGAR. Mix well.

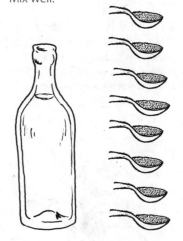

CAUTION: Before adding the sugar, taste the drink and be sure it is less salty than tears.

IMPORTANT: If dehydration gets worse or other danger signs appear, get medical help.

Stop the spread of diarrhea

This activity uses the stories from the activity "How diarrhea diseases spread" (page 50) to show how to prevent diarrhea from being spread.

Time: 30 minutes to 1 hour

Materials: large sheet of drawing paper, colored pens or markers, sticky tape, pictures from the activity "How Diarrhea Diseases Spread" (page 50)

❶ Work in the same small groups as in the previous activity, How Diarrhea Diseases Spread. Each group looks at the pictures from How Diarrhea Diseases Spread. They then talk about how to stop the spread of disease by washing hands, using toilets, protecting food and water, and so on. Each of these actions is a barrier that blocks the spread of diarrhea.

❷ When the group has agreed on what barriers will stop the spread of germs, have the group draw pictures that show the different ways to stop the spread of diarrhea diseases.

❸ The group then talks about how to change the story from How Diarrhea Diseases Spread to Stop the Spread of Diarrhea. Where do the new drawings fit in the story so that they will stop the spread of illness? The new drawings are taped in place in the old story to show how the story can change.

❹ Each group shows its new stories. The whole group talks about which disease barriers they use and which ones they do not use. Do all the disease barriers work all the time? Why, or why not? Why is it hard to use some of these barriers? How can the community work together to make sure that diarrhea diseases do not spread?

Guinea worm

Guinea worm is a long, thin worm that lives under the skin and makes a painful sore on the body. The worm, which looks like a white thread, can grow to be more than 1 meter long. Guinea worm is found in parts of Africa, India, and the Middle East.

Signs

A painful swelling usually on the ankle or leg, but can develop elsewhere on the body. A few days to a week later, a blister forms which then quickly bursts open and forms a sore. This often happens when standing in water or bathing. The end of a white thread-like guinea worm can be seen poking out of the sore. The worm works its way out of the body over the next week. If the sore gets dirty and infected, or if the worm is broken by trying to pull it out, the pain and swelling spread and walking can become very difficult.

Guinea worm is spread from person to person like this:

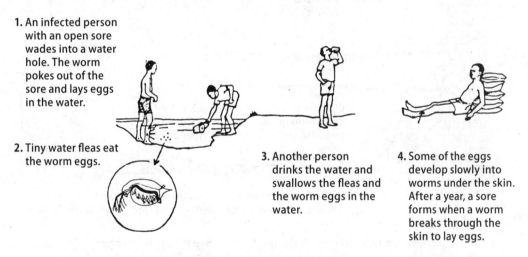

1. An infected person with an open sore wades into a water hole. The worm pokes out of the sore and lays eggs in the water.

2. Tiny water fleas eat the worm eggs.

3. Another person drinks the water and swallows the fleas and the worm eggs in the water.

4. Some of the eggs develop slowly into worms under the skin. After a year, a sore forms when a worm breaks through the skin to lay eggs.

To treat guinea worms, see a health worker or a general health book such as *Where There Is No Doctor*. Also, take steps to prevent new contact with worms.

To prevent guinea worms, protect water sources (see pages 75 to 85) and filter water (see pages 94 to 97). If nobody wades or bathes in water used for drinking, the infection cannot be passed on and will eventually disappear from the area.

Blood flukes (schistosomiasis, bilharzia, snail fever)

This infection is caused by a kind of worm that gets into the blood through the skin after wading, washing, or swimming in contaminated water. The illness can cause serious harm to the liver and kidneys, and may lead to death after months or years. Women have a greater risk of infection from blood flukes because they spend a lot of time in and around water — collecting it, washing clothes, and bathing children.

Sometimes there are no early signs. A common sign in some areas is blood in the urine or in the feces. It can also cause genital sores in women. In areas where this illness is very common, even people with only mild signs or belly pain should be tested.

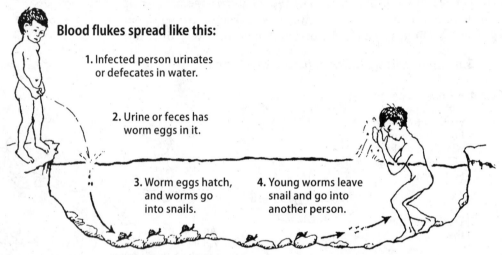

Blood flukes spread like this:

1. Infected person urinates or defecates in water.

2. Urine or feces has worm eggs in it.

3. Worm eggs hatch, and worms go into snails.

4. Young worms leave snail and go into another person.

5. In this way, someone who washes or swims in water where an infected person has urinated or defecated also becomes infected.

Treatment

Blood flukes are best treated with medicines. See a health worker about which medicines to use, or a general health book such as *Where There Is No Doctor.* Genital sores and blood in the urine are also signs of sexually transmitted infections (STIs). Some women will not seek treatment because they are afraid they will be blamed for having an STI. Lack of treatment can cause other serious infections and can make women infertile (unable to become pregnant).

Prevention

Blood flukes are not passed directly from one person to another. For part of their life, the blood flukes must live inside a certain kind of small water snail. Community programs can be organized to kill these snails and prevent blood flukes. These programs work only if people follow the most basic preventive step: never urinate or defecate in or near water.

Preventing the Spread of Germs and Worms

While germs and worms are found everywhere, there are simple steps that every person can take to help prevent illness. To stop the spread of germs and worms:

- **Protect water sources and use clean water** for drinking and washing. Unless you know water is safe, it is best to treat it (see pages 92 to 99).

- **Always wash hands after using the toilet, and before handling food.** Use clean water and soap if available. If not, use clean sand or ash. **Cut fingernails short.** This will also help keep hands clean.

- **Use a toilet.** This puts germs and worms out of contact with people. If there is no toilet it is best to defecate far from water sources, in a place where feces will not be touched by people or animals. Cover feces with dirt to keep flies away.

- **Use clean and safe methods of preparing and storing food.** Wash fruits and vegetables, or cook them well before eating them. Feed left-over food scraps to animals, or put them in a **compost** pile or toilet. Get rid of spoiled food, keep meat and seafood separate from other foods, and make sure meat, eggs, and fish are cooked well before eating. Wash dishes, cutting surfaces, and utensils with hot water and soap after using them, and allow them to dry well in the sun if possible.

- **Keep animals away** from household food and community water sources.

- **Wear shoes** to prevent worms from entering through the feet.

- **Make fly traps and cover food** to prevent flies from spreading germs. Toilets that control flies or stop them from breeding can also help (see Chapter 7).

How to make a fly trap from a plastic bottle

❶ Cut the top part off a plastic bottle.

❷ Attach wire or string to the bottle for hanging.

❸ Put some sweet bait, like sugar or fruit, in the bottle.

❹ Put the top back in the bottle upside-down.

❺ Flies will fly in but will not be able to fly out.

❻ When the bottle is full, empty it into a toilet or compost pile. Make sure all the flies are dead before the trap is emptied.

To reduce flies, hang this trap near toilets and places where food is prepared.

Washing hands

One of the best ways to prevent health problems from
germs and worms is to wash hands with soap and water
after defecating or cleaning a baby's bottom, and **before**
preparing food, feeding children, or eating.

Keep a source of clean water near your home to make hand washing easier.
But washing with water alone is not effective enough. Use soap to remove dirt
and germs. If no soap is available, use sand, soil, or ashes.

Rub hands together with soap and flowing water from a pump, tap (faucet),
or tippy tap. If there is no flowing water, use a washbasin or bowl.

Lather soap (or rub sand or ashes) all over your hands and count to 30 as
you rub them. Then rub your hands together under the water to rinse off.
Dry with a clean cloth or let your hands dry in the air.

The tippy tap: A simple hand-washing device

The tippy tap allows you to wash your hands using very little water.
It also allows the user to rub both hands together while water runs
over them. The tippy tap is made of materials that are freely available and
can be put wherever people need to wash their hands, for example, near the
cooking stove, at the toilet, or in a market.

How to make a plastic tippy tap

To make this tippy tap you need 1) a plastic bottle with a screw-on cap (the sort
soda drinks come in), and 2) a drinking straw, or the tube from a ballpoint pen, or
some other small, stiff, hollow tube.

❶ Clean the bottle.

❷ Using a heated piece of wire, make a small hole in the lower part of the bottle.

❸ If you do not have a drinking straw, clean the inside tube from a ballpoint pen.
Cut it off at an angle, and push it through the hole in the bottle.
The tube should fit tightly.

❹ Fill the bottle with water and replace
the cap. When the cap is tight, no
water should flow through the tube.
When the cap is loose, water should
flow out in a steady stream. When
you are sure that it works, hang it or
place it on a shelf where people can
use it for hand washing. Keep soap
nearby, or thread a bar of soap with
string and tie it to the bottle.

❺ To use the tippy tap:
Loosen the cap just
enough to let water
flow. Wet your hands,
add soap, and rub
your hands together
under the water
until they are
clean.

Toxic Pollution in Water

Agriculture, mining, oil drilling, and many other industries dump chemical wastes into water sources. This makes the water unsafe to drink or to use for preparing food, for bathing, or irrigation.

In some places, water may be contaminated by toxics that naturally exist in the earth, such as arsenic (see page 61) and fluoride (a natural substance that causes brown spots on teeth and severe bone weakness). As the **groundwater** is used up, the risk of natural toxics grows because they are concentrated in the water that is left.

Whether they are from industry or from the earth itself, toxic chemicals are usually invisible and difficult to detect. Testing water in a laboratory can help detect both natural toxics and chemicals from industry.

Drawing for discussion: **How do toxic chemicals get in the water?**

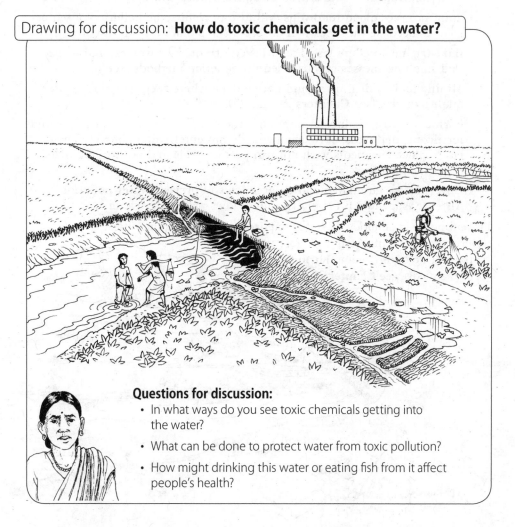

Questions for discussion:
- In what ways do you see toxic chemicals getting into the water?
- What can be done to protect water from toxic pollution?
- How might drinking this water or eating fish from it affect people's health?

Preventing toxic pollution

The only way to make sure water is free of toxic chemicals is to prevent pollution at the source. If you think your water is contaminated, you can organize your community to map water sources and find problems with your water supply (see pages 68 to 70), and then to take steps to stop the pollution. But the only way to know for certain what chemicals are in water is to test it at a laboratory (see page 70).

IMPORTANT: Remember: making water safe from worms and germs will NOT make it safe from chemicals. And protecting water from chemicals will NOT make it safe from germs and worms.

To prevent contamination from toxic chemicals:

- Roads and bridges can be planned with drainage channels to carry pollution from cars and trucks away from waterways.

- Planting trees along roadways will also prevent some pollution of water sources because the trees will absorb some pollution from the air.

- Industry must pollute less. Factories can treat their wastes, and large and small businesses can use clean production methods (see page 458).

- Mining and oil drilling should not be done where they will place water quality at risk (see Chapters 21 and 22).

- Farmers need to reduce or eliminate their use of chemical pesticides and fertilizers, and make sure chemicals do not enter water sources. They can replace chemicals with natural pest controls and natural fertilizers (see Chapter 15).

- Governments can make and enforce laws to prevent water pollution. Also see Appendix B for international laws protecting water.

Preventing toxic pollution of water requires action by communities, governments, and industry. For more information on preventing and reducing harm from toxic chemicals, see Chapter 20.

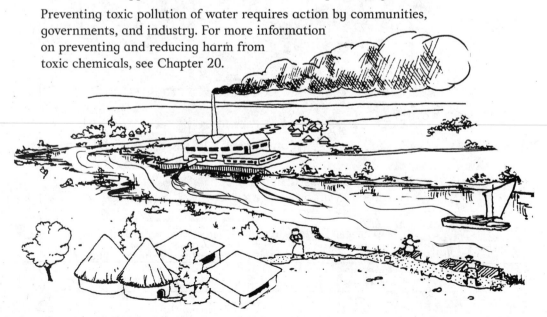

Arsenic in "safe" water

For centuries, most people in Bangladesh drank surface water from carefully protected ponds. But to bathe and wash dishes and clothes, they used rivers, ditches, and other unprotected water sources. This water was often contaminated with germs, causing diarrhea, cholera, hepatitis, and other health problems. So the government worked with international agencies to build shallow tube wells all over the country. Public health campaigns encouraged people to use the "safe" groundwater from tube wells instead of surface water.

But a large number of toxic poisonings were reported, starting around 1983. Many people got very sick with skin sores (lesions), cancer, nerve damage, heart disease, and diabetes. Many people died. No one knew what was causing these illnesses. By 1993, scientists agreed the illnesses were caused by arsenic in the groundwater. Nobody had tested the groundwater for arsenic. However, about half the tube wells draw water with too much arsenic in it.

How did the arsenic get into the water? While arsenic naturally existed in the groundwater before, the amount people were consuming must have increased to make them so sick.

The same technology that brought "safe" water out of the ground in villages also made it possible to irrigate vast pieces of land, leading to the development of big commercial farms. Drawing too much groundwater for irrigation made the arsenic concentrate (get stronger) in the groundwater that was left for drinking. Also, the use of chemical fertilizers (which often include arsenic) increased, and a variety of toxic pesticides were sprayed on fields. The poisoning of Bangladesh got worse as toxic waste from leather tanneries and other factories was dumped into waterways too.

About 40,000 people in Bangladesh are now sick from arsenic poisoning, mostly women, poor people, and domestic workers. Arsenic-related health problems take years to develop, so many more people will become sick. Better water is the only way to treat the health problems from too much arsenic.

This disaster got worse for so long, and remained without much study or remedy, because the people suffering are among the world's poorest. If water in the capitol city of Dhaka was contaminated (it is not) or the sickness was happening in a wealthy country, action would have happened more quickly.

The poisoning in Bangladesh shows the dangers of polluting surface and groundwater. It also shows the importance of testing water sources and acting quickly if there is any doubt about water safety.

To remove arsenic from drinking water

A simple filter has been developed in Bangladesh that uses iron nails to take arsenic out of the water (see page 97 and Resources). This reduces the number of poisonings, but it does not solve the problem of contaminated water.

The Right to Enough Safe Water

Around the world people are working to protect their right to health, including the right to a good supply of safe water. Private companies say they can provide better service than governments and still make a profit. But when private companies take control of water services (called water privatization), prices often go up, forcing people to use less water than they need for good health. Many people then have no choice but to collect water wherever they can for free, even if the water is contaminated with germs, worms, or toxic chemicals. This leads to serious health problems.

Governments and communities must work together to improve and extend water systems so they provide a safe and sufficient supply of water, especially for those most in need.

Partnership improves the water supply

In Ghana, West Africa, community groups have taken control of their water supply. In the town of Savelugu, the government-owned Ghana Water Company supplies piped water, and community members are responsible for pricing, distribution, and repair of the water system. They call this a "government-community partnership."

Because the community is responsible for managing the water, safe and sufficient water is guaranteed by popular decision making. If some people cannot afford to pay for water, the community pays for their water until they can afford to pay. People's needs are met not because they have money to pay, but because they are part of the community. The Ghana Water Company benefits because the community always pays them for supplying the water.

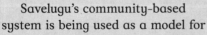

Savelugu's community-based system is being used as a model for towns throughout Ghana. By managing their own water system, the people of Savelugu have shown that privatization is not the only way to provide water. Since their government-community partnership began, there is less illness, and everyone has enough water. Their success shows that community decision making and responsibility is one way to improve water security for all.

Bottling and selling the right to water

When people do not trust that water from their taps is clean, those who can afford to, buy bottled water. If there are germs in tap water, drinking safe bottled water is a way to avoid illness. But just because water is sold in a bottle does not mean it is safe. In many cases, bottled water is just tap water in a bottle, but sold at a much higher price. The best way to support the health of both people and the environment is to improve water quality and reliability by improving the public water supply.

When you consider the health problems caused by making the plastic bottles water is sold in, as well as filling, transporting, and disposing of them, the cost of bottled water is higher than providing safe water for everyone.

Companies sell bottled water because it is very profitable. They often advertise their water products in ways to make people think that publicly supplied water is not healthy or "good enough." Multinational companies that sell water, like Coca Cola, often harm the local economy by driving local soft drink companies out of business. Sometimes they use so much water they harm people by creating a shortage of water for household needs, irrigation of crops, and other local activities (see story on page 67).

MUNICIPAL TAP WATER

MOUNTAIN SPRINGS superior water

Safe, healthy piped water systems are one of the most important ways to improve health for everyone. In Europe and North America, safe water systems are the very foundation of public health. There is no reason why people in less wealthy countries should suffer from a lack of safe water and be forced to buy expensive bottled water.

Having enough clean water to live a healthy life is a human right. Protecting and fulfilling people's right to water is best achieved by publicly managed or community controlled water systems. To make sure government provides good service, community members are increasingly involved in overseeing water utilities. This helps make sure they are managed with people's health as the top priority.

6 Protecting Community Water

In this chapter: page

Protecting Community Water

Water is essential for life. People, animals, and plants all need water to live and to grow. But in many places people do not have enough water to stay healthy. Many people have to travel long distances to collect water. And often, the water that is available is not safe to drink.

When a community has a water supply that is safe and easy to get to, everyone has a better chance of having good health. If women and girls are freed from the daily labor of carrying water and making sure it is clean, they have more time to go to school and be part of community life. This improves the well-being of everyone. With enough safe water, children grow healthier and have less diarrhea disease caused by contaminated water.

Water and Community Health

Water is nature's gift. And **water security** (regular access to enough safe water) is a necessary part of community health. When people make decisions together about how to collect, store, and use their common water resources, they can ensure community water security.

To have enough safe water, most people are willing to do the work required or to pay a reasonable price. But in many places, water people need for drinking is contaminated by germs, worms, or toxic chemicals, is taken instead by industry or industrial farming, or is sold at a price people cannot afford. People's needs for water for survival and health must have more importance than other uses when decisions are made about how much it costs and how it is protected, conserved, distributed, and used.

Everyone needs water

Industry takes a community's water

Plachimada is a small village in the south of India where farmers grow rice and coconuts. Farmers used to make a good living there because there was plenty of rain and good soil. But a few years ago this began to change after the Coca-Cola company built a bottling factory on the edge of the village.

The company drilled deep wells to get to the groundwater they needed to bottle the sugary drink. Every day the factory used 1½ million liters of water. 2 years after the factory opened, the villagers' crops were dying and their household wells were drying up. When they cooked rice, it turned brown and tasted bad. When they drank or bathed in the water, they suffered skin rashes, hair loss, pain in the joints, weak bones, and nerve problems. They learned that the company had polluted their groundwater with toxic chemicals. To protect their health, the villagers started collecting water far from their homes.

One year, the rains didn't come at all. But the Coca-Cola company continued to take water during the drought. Villagers watched as trucks left the factory day after day, carrying away the precious liquid that once gave life to them and their crops. Even sources away from the village dried up. As more and more people began to get sick, they gathered together to talk about how they could get the Coca-Cola company to stop taking their water.

After the meeting, more than 2,000 peaceful protestors marched to the Coca-Cola factory and demanded the company leave and pay the villagers for the loss of their water. The company responded by sending a truckload of water to the village every day. But this was not enough water to meet the villagers' needs. After 50 days of protests, police arrested 130 women and men. Months later, 1,000 people marched to the factory and again the police arrested many of them.

The struggle caused hardships for the people of Plachimada, but it also brought them together to demand respect of their right to safe water. After several years, the local government began to support the people and ordered the company to stop using groundwater in times of drought. But the state government said the company should be allowed to continue using groundwater. The conflict went to court where finally the people of Plachimada won the case and the Coca-Cola factory was closed.

When the people of Plachimada fought for their right to water, their campaign received attention throughout India and the world. Their struggle has inspired many others. In a world where people do not have enough safe drinking water, it makes no sense to use this limited resource to produce sweet luxury drinks, especially if a factory's use of the water makes people sick.

Raise Community Awareness

A woman who carries water long distances every day does not need to be told it is hard work. But she may not feel she has the power to change that.

When people see the need for a reliable and safe water supply as a problem shared by all, they can begin to work together to make changes. Raising community awareness is often the first stage in making changes, and usually involves a group of people taking several steps together.

Talk to the people in charge of the water

Is there a person, group, or business responsible for wells, pipes, or other water supply systems? Is there a person or group responsible for sanitation? Which people or groups most often collect, carry, treat, and store the water?

Together with the people responsible for the water, list all the water sources in the area. What do people say about drinking water quality and quantity? How much water is used every day? Are different sources used for drinking, cooking, bathing, watering livestock, farming, and other needs? Is there enough water for all these needs? Is there a water source or water storage for emergencies?

Visit the places where people collect water

Different kinds of water sources can have different problems and different solutions. Visit springs, wells, sources of surface water (rivers, streams, lakes, and ponds), and rainwater catchment sites. At each water source, start a discussion about how this water is used and whether anyone suspects it is contaminated (not safe).

Make a map of local water sources and sources of contamination

Your map can show where the water sources are in relation to people's homes and to sources of contamination. Use different colors to show safe water sources and contaminated sources.

Is your water safe?

It is difficult to know if water is safe or not. Some things that cause health problems are easily noticed by looking at, smelling, or tasting the water. Others can be found only by testing the water. Understanding what makes water unsafe and taking steps to protect water from contamination prevents many health problems (see Chapter 5.)

Clear water might not be clean water

This activity shows how there may be something harmful in the water even if it cannot be seen, smelled, or tasted.

Time: 15 to 30 minutes

Materials: 4 clear bottles, mud, salt, sugar, treated water

1 Before the activity, fill 4 clear bottles with water that has been boiled, treated with chlorine, or had some other treatment to make it safe. To one bottle, add a spoonful of mud. To another, add a spoonful of sugar. To a 3rd, add a spoonful of salt. Shake the bottles well. Add nothing to the last bottle. Bring these bottles to the group.

2 Ask people in the group to smell the water in all the bottles. Then invite them to drink water from any of the bottles. Most likely no one will drink the muddy water, but many will drink from the other bottles.

3 After several people have drunk the water, ask them why they did not drink from the muddy water bottle. Then ask what their water tasted like, and what did they think was in it. Did anyone drink the water with nothing added to it? Ask them how they knew it was just water, and did not contain something they could not see, smell, or taste.

4 Begin a discussion about things that may be in your water that make it unsafe to drink. This could include germs that cause diarrhea, blood flukes that cause schistosomiasis, and pesticides or other chemicals. Are there reasons to believe these things may be in your water? Are there other ways besides looking and smelling to know if water is safe or unsafe?

Testing for water safety

Water quality testing is often done by examining samples of water in a laboratory. These tests show the type and amount of contamination and are usually necessary to find chemical contamination.

But they can be costly. While useful, water quality testing is usually less important than raising community awareness of water issues and careful protection of water sources (see page 75).

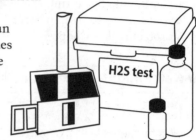

Some water testing kits can be used locally to test water for germs. For example, the "H2S test" is low cost (5 tests cost about 1 dollar) and gives quick results. But this test sometimes mistakes harmless living things for germs, and it does not show if chemicals or parasite eggs are in the water.

Water quality tests show only if the water was contaminated at the time and place the water sample was taken.

Improve Your Water Supply

Before trying to develop a new water supply, it will probably be easier to make your current water sources produce more and cleaner water. When making a plan to improve the water supply, start by making a list of local resources. Resources include water sources, building materials, and most important, people. Include the people with skills to build wells or tanks or install pipes, people who can facilitate group activities and organize work parties, and older people who remember how water was collected years ago.

Identify solutions

What your community does to improve the water supply may depend on which problems are most urgent or which problems are easiest to solve first. It is important to make a plan that addresses the root causes of the problems and satisfies the needs of everyone in the community.

Decide what each water source should be used for, especially if there is little water or it is difficult to get to. Building rainwater catchment tanks, storage tanks, or a piped water system may help bring water closer to the community (see pages 86 to 91). If this is not possible, the community can still try to make sure there is enough safe water for everyone:

- share the work of collecting water
- show everyone how to keep water safe from germs (see pages 92 to 99).

If there already is a water system, the community can:

- improve the ways water is collected
- fix broken pipes and pumps
- protect water sources upstream
- find new ways to protect and save water

If there is a possibility the water may be contaminated by toxic chemicals, use a different water source until a water quality test can be done. If a test shows the water is contaminated, keep using a different water source and work toward getting rid of what caused the contamination. Try to prevent the pollution of your water by demanding that industries dispose of their waste safely and use cleaner production methods, and by asking farmers to use fewer pesticides and chemical fertilizers.

Health workers and water safety promoters can help the community improve water security.

Women are important in planning

Women may have different needs for water than men. It is usually women who collect and treat water for family use. But it is often men who are in charge of building and maintaining water systems. Because of these differences in men's and women's work, it is helpful to use planning activities that involve women.

2 circles

This activity helps women think about their water needs and the barriers they face in meeting these needs.

Time: 45 minutes to 1 hour
Materials: Large drawing paper, drawing pens

❶ Divide into groups of no more than 10 women each. Give each group drawing pens and paper.

❷ Each group draws 2 circles on their paper, a large circle with a smaller circle inside.

❸ Inside the larger circle each person draws or lists the water, sanitation, and health-related problems that affect the whole community. Inside the smaller circle they draw or list the problems that affect women in particular.

❹ Bring the groups back together and discuss: How do the problems in the 2 circles differ? How are the problems similar? What solutions can be found for both? How can we make sure the women's problems receive enough attention?

This activity can also be done with women and men together. If men participate, have one of the groups be only men, and have each group draw 2 small circles inside the large circle rather than only one. Let one of the smaller circles include problems that affect women and the other include problems that affect men.

When the groups come back together, ask the men to think about how they can help improve conditions that affect women. This may include building toilets closer to homes, having men collect and carry water, spend more time with children, and so on. It may be more comfortable to have the women discuss their issues in private before the men discuss theirs, especially in communities where men and women may have strong differences of opinion.

Barriers to improving your water supply

There may be many reasons why a community does not have safe water. Problems might include lack of money, not knowing how to build water systems, no government support, or lack of participation by people in the community. To have a constant and safe water supply, the barriers must be identified and removed, one by one. People are more likely to improve and maintain their water system when it results in:

- immediate improvements, such as more water, easier access, or less disease.

- low cost.

- only small changes in daily activities.

- improvements in the local environment, such as less mud, fewer mosquitoes, or more water for home gardens.

A sustainable water project should remove physical and social barriers, and help everyone in the community equally.

Look for solutions within the community

Throughout history, every community has developed ways to find, transport, and protect water. People have used sticks (called divining rods) to find water, invented devices for lifting and moving water, built many kinds of structures to capture the rain, and planted trees to protect water sources and watersheds. They have also made agreements to help neighboring communities share water. Protecting water and preventing conflicts over water can help to preserve water resources for future generations, even as we learn new ways to collect and treat water to make sure it is safe and abundant.

Villagers teach development workers

A group of development workers came to a mountain village in Colombia to help the villagers fight diarrhea by protecting their water sources. When they visited the village spring, they saw that cattle and soil erosion were damaging the spring. The development workers suggested 2 simple solutions: Put up a barbed wire fence to protect the spring, or graze the cattle elsewhere.

The villagers did not like these ideas. They predicted that the barbed wire would be stolen before long, and they did not have enough land and money to make proper cattle pastures. But seeing the problem, they came up with a solution that would work. They organized a work day when everyone from the village came out to plant prickly plants upstream from the spring. This forced the cattle to drink water at lower places along the river, and solved the problem for the village.

Protect Water Sources

Water is either surface water (from rivers, streams, lakes, and ponds) or groundwater (water that collects underground and comes up from springs or wells). Because surface water is often contaminated, it should not be used for drinking unless it is treated first (see pages 92 to 99). Groundwater is usually free of germs because it is filtered when it seeps through sand and soil. However, groundwater can be contaminated by natural minerals such as arsenic or fluoride (see page 61), by leaking sewer lines, septic tanks, or toilets, by waste dumps, or by toxic chemicals from industry and agriculture.

When land and waterways are not well cared for, the amount of groundwater can also become dangerously low. Where land has been cleared of trees and vegetation, rain that once soaked into the ground and was stored as groundwater can run off to rivers and the ocean.

The best ways to protect both groundwater and surface water are to:

- practice sustainable farming (see Chapter 15).
- build and use safe toilets (see Chapter 7).
- protect the area where water collects, called the **watershed** or **catchment area** (see Chapter 9).

As more people settle around and use a water source, it becomes harder to protect. In places with industrial activity, water may be overused and polluted and the people who need it most may not be able to prevent the problem. These problems can be solved only when a community organizes for water security, puts pressure on governments, and enforces rules on industry.

Protected Wells

There are many kinds of wells for drawing up groundwater. The simplest is a hand-dug water hole, sometimes called a **scoophole.** The most costly kind of well, called a **tube well,** is a narrow pipe going deep into the ground with a pump at the top to draw water out.

A well is useful only if people can get water out of it. The best well for any community depends on the depth of the groundwater and the resources available for digging, drilling, and building a well. In many cases, simple shallow wells where people draw water in buckets may be better than costly deep wells that require pumps. Several shallow wells are often better then one deep well, because if one well goes dry, the others can still provide water.

When people stand on the lip of the well or use unclean buckets, the water in the well can be made unsafe.

Steps to safer wells and water holes

Before digging a well, make sure it is the best kind of well for everyone's needs. Well water becomes unsafe if wells are dug:

- too close to pit toilets, sewer pipes, garbage dumping pits, or livestock. Keep at least 30 meters away.
- near industrial activity such as mining or oil drilling, fields where chemical pesticides or fertilizers are used, or waste dumps.
- where waste water or surface runoff can flow into the well.

Shallow hand-dug wells can provide good, safe water. But the water can dry up or be easily contaminated. During rainy seasons, surface runoff may drain into a water hole, carrying germs and other contamination. People or animals who use the water may carry germs on their feet to the water hole. Buckets and ropes around the rim of the well may also collect germs, and can easily contaminate the water when they are lowered into the well.

Simple improvements can prevent contamination. For example, make sure only clean buckets and ropes are lowered into the water. Build up earth around the hole or line the top with bricks or a concrete ring to keep water safer. Lining the hole also makes it less likely to dry up or collapse, and allows for a deeper well that can store more water. (For some ways to improve wells, see the drawings on the next page.)

Before drilling new wells or making costly improvements to water systems, consider making small improvements like these to make your water sources safer.

Improvements to open water holes

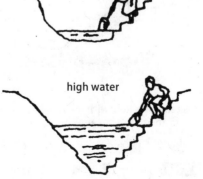

low water

high water

Build stone steps into the water hole so a person can draw water up from a step, without getting wet. Always use the last dry step. Never walk into the water.

Improvements to basic wells and scoopholes

1. Unimproved scoophole

2. Mouth of hole built up to keep out runoff

3. Mouth closed off
   with barrel and lid

4. Top strengthened with bricks
   and small drainage platform

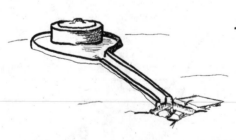

5. Protected water hole with drainage
   platform and runoff channel

6. Protected water hole with drainage
   platform, runoff channel, and garden

IMPORTANT: Never drink directly from a water hole. Filtering the water through a cloth and letting it settle before drinking will remove some germs. Other water treatment methods are described on pages 92 to 99.

Protect the family well

Many communities have tube wells or boreholes with pumps built by governments, or local or international agencies. These deep, closed wells protect water from contamination by people and animals. But years after they are drilled, many of these wells can no longer be used because the pumps have broken, or spare parts are no longer available, or the people who knew how to fix them are gone. This leads to no regular supply of clean water. People must walk long distances or collect contaminated surface water to fill their needs. In some parts of Africa, protected family wells are replacing tube wells.

A protected well is a hole dug by hand with a lining, a concrete cover, a windlass to raise water, and a drainage platform. Each of these things adds protection to the well. With all of them in place, and with careful handling of the water, a family well can be very safe.

Where to dig a well

When digging a well, the best sign there will be water is when you see other wells nearby. But if the other wells are deep boreholes, the groundwater may be too deep to get to by hand digging. Another good sign is the year-round presence of plants that need a lot of water to survive. Low areas are more likely to have water than higher ground. But if a well is dug in a low area, it will need to be protected from rainwater runoff.

The well lining

In very firm soils, lining the well may seem unnecessary. But it is wise to line at least the top 1 to 2 meters below ground to prevent the side walls from collapsing. If the entire well is lined it will make the water source more dependable, but it will be more difficult to dig the well deeper at a later time. A well can be lined with stones or rocks, with fired bricks, or with concrete.

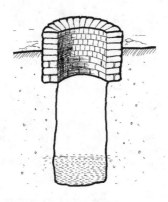

Top 1 to 2 meters lined

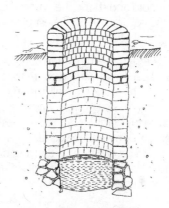

Fully lined well

How to make a cover slab for a well

Once a well has been lined, the next step is fitting a concrete cover slab. The cover helps prevent polluted wastewater or objects from falling into the well. It also makes the well safer for children and provides a clean place to put buckets as people collect water.

Make a mold for the slab.

1 The cover should fit neatly over the upper well lining. Clear a flat place to pour a concrete slab and mark out a circle the size of the cover slab to fit the well. Place a ring of bricks around the marked circle. This ring is the slab mold.

2 Leave a hole in the slab to pass a bucket through or to fit a pump. The size of the hole depends on the kind of bucket or pump used, but generally the hole should be large enough for a 10 liter bucket. A tin drum big enough for a bucket to pass through can be used to form the hole.

Place reinforcing wire and a mold for the hole.

3 Place reinforcing wire (3 mm) within the slab mold to form a grid, with spaces 10 cm apart.

4 Remove the reinforcing wire grid and make a concrete mix of 3 parts gravel, 2 parts washed river sand, and 1 part cement. If gravel is not available, use 4 parts washed river sand and 1 part cement. Pour concrete in the mold, halfway to the top. Place the wire grid on top of the wet concrete. Add the remaining concrete and level it with a piece of wood.

Pour the concrete slab and form the protective collar.

5 Let the slab cure for 1 hour. Remove the tin drum mold, and fill the central hole with wet sand. Replace the mold on top of the sand and place a ring of bricks around it, leaving 75 mm of space between the bricks and the mold. Fill the space between the bricks and the mold with concrete and let it cure for an hour. After an hour, remove the bricks and the tin mold and shape the protective collar. For the collar to give the best protection, a tin cover should fit snugly over it.

Shape the protective collar.

6 Let the slab harden overnight and cure for at least 5 days, keeping it wet the entire time. Before putting the slab on a well, test its strength. After it has cured for 7 days or so, place 4 blocks of wood 1 or 2 inches high under the 4 sides of the slab to raise it off the ground. Then dance on it! A well-made slab will not break even with several people dancing on it. Place a bed of cement mortar on the top of the well lining and carefully set the well cover in place.

Set the well cover in place.

The windlass, bucket and chain

A windlass is a shaft fitted with a handle that makes raising the bucket easier and provides a place to wrap the bucket chain or rope. If a pump is fitted to the well later, the windlass can easily be removed. Attach a bucket to the end of the chain or rope. Chain is best because fewer germs will grow on it, but it is costly. Rope is less costly and can be replaced easily if it breaks.

Set windlass supports in concrete on each side of the well.

Cut slots in the poles and place the windlass.

Drive bolts through the posts above the windlass to keep it in place as it turns.

This design shows wooden windlass supports set in the ground. Windlass supports may also be made of bricks.

The drainage platform

The drainage platform carries runoff away from the well to a drainage area. This prevents the area around the well from getting muddy, and breeding germs and insects. Germs can grow in cracks, so it is important that the platform is well made.

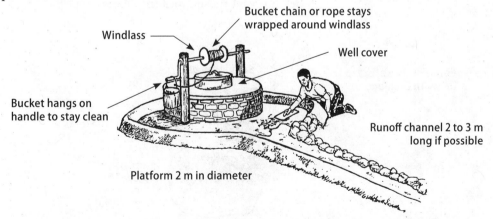

Windlass

Bucket chain or rope stays wrapped around windlass

Well cover

Bucket hangs on handle to stay clean

Runoff channel 2 to 3 m long if possible

Platform 2 m in diameter

Pour concrete to a depth of 75 mm, with a raised outer rim 150 mm high. The entire platform and rim should be reinforced with 3 mm wire to prevent it from cracking.

Maintain your well

Well water is easily contaminated when dirty buckets and dirty ropes or chains are lowered into it. To keep well water clean, keep one bucket attached to the well and use it to fill other containers. Washing hands before collecting water and building a fence to keep animals out will also prevent contamination.

You can also protect your well water when you:

- keep the well cover in place.
- keep the platform and runoff channel clean.
- grease the handle bearing often to make it easier to use.
- do not let children play with the well or pump.
- fence the area to keep livestock out.
- have a person be caretaker of the well.

Drain runoff from wells and taps

Wherever people collect water, water spills. When water collects in puddles, it becomes a breeding ground for mosquitoes that carry malaria and other illnesses. Wells, taps, outlets from storage tanks, and other water collection areas need good drainage to allow spilled water to flow away or to drain into the ground.

To take advantage of water that runs off, plant a tree or a vegetable garden where the water drains. If you cannot plant a tree or garden, make a hollow in the ground filled with rocks, gravel, and sand for the water to seep into. This is called a "soakaway pit." It will help prevent mosquitoes from breeding.

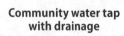

Community water tap with drainage

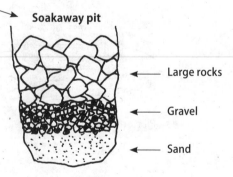

Soakaway pit

Large rocks

Gravel

Sand

Pumping water from wells

To move water up from a well, a pump is needed. Pumps use various kinds of energy, including electricity, gas, solar energy, or human power. If a pump is difficult to use or if it is often out of service, people will start to collect water from unsafe sources.

How to choose a pump

All pumps have one thing in common: if they break, there is no water. For most people, the best pump is one they can build, operate, and repair by themselves, or that can be repaired by trusted local mechanics. Consider the following when choosing a pump:

- Will it be usable by and meet the needs of both men and women? Were women involved in selecting the community pump?

- What kind of energy source is available? If a pump uses costly fuel, or electricity that is not available, it will not be useful.

- Is the pump easy to repair with available spare parts? Would it be better to have a pump that breaks easily but is very easy to repair locally, or a pump that will break after many years but cannot be easily repaired by local people?

The rope pump: a low cost, easy way to lift water

The rope pump is based on an ancient design from China. It is used to pump water from wells up to 15 m deep with little effort. As a person turns the wheel, water is lifted and pours out of a spout at the top of the well.

This pump costs little to make and is easy to fix. The rope is the part most likely to break, but even if it is fixed rather than replaced, the pump still works. People in many countries have adapted rope pumps to fit their needs and the materials they have. (See Resources.)

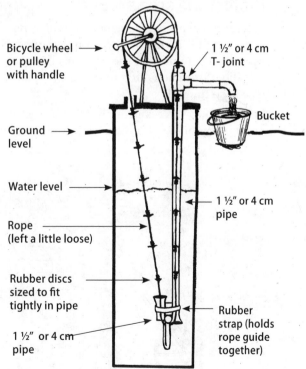

Bicycle wheel or pulley with handle →

1 ½" or 4 cm T- joint

Bucket

Ground level →

Water level →

1 ½" or 4 cm pipe

Rope (left a little loose)

Rubber discs sized to fit tightly in pipe

1 ½" or 4 cm pipe

Rubber strap (holds rope guide together)

The rope pump is made from low cost, durable parts.

Protect your Spring

Springs are where groundwater naturally comes to the surface. Because spring water is filtered through rock and soil and moves quickly, it can be considered safe unless it is contaminated at the surface. To know if a spring is safe, find its source (where it comes out of the ground) and ask these questions:

- Is it the true source, or is there a stream or other surface water that goes underground above the spring? If so, what appears to be a spring may in fact be surface water that flows a short distance underground. In this case it will likely be contaminated, or may flow only during the rainy season.

- Are there large openings in the rock above the spring? If so, check the water in the spring after a heavy rain. If it appears very cloudy or muddy, contamination from surface runoff is likely.

- Is there a possibility of contamination near or just above the source of the spring? This could include pastures for livestock, pit toilets, septic tanks, use of pesticides and fertilizers, or other human activity.

- Is the soil very loose or sandy within 15 m of the spring? This could allow contaminated surface runoff to enter the groundwater.

Protect the area around the spring

Protecting a spring is cheaper than digging a well or borehole. Once a spring is protected it is relatively easy to run pipes from the spring closer to the community. To protect the area around a spring, fence the area all around it and dig a drainage ditch to carry away surface runoff and waste. This will also keep animals out.

Plant native trees near the spring to protect it even more. Trees will prevent erosion, and make it a more pleasant place to collect water.

Build a spring box to capture the water

A spring box is a covered container made of masonry, brick, or concrete that helps protect spring water from contamination. A spring box also makes it easier to collect water at the spring or direct water into pipes to community taps or storage tanks. The kind of spring box that is best depends on the lay of the land and the materials that are available.

Parts of a spring box

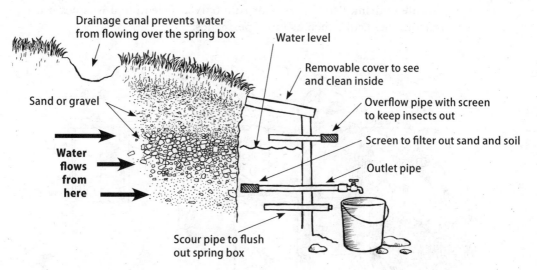

This shows one kind of spring box with the hillside cut away to show what is inside.

Pipes and spring boxes need cleaning often

Spring boxes need to be checked to make sure the spring continues to provide safe water. Silt, leaves, dead animals, and other things can collect in the pipes and spring box and block the pipes or contaminate the water. Put a wire screen on the pipe leading into the spring box to prevent unsafe things from entering pipes. Cleaning the screen every now and again will make sure there is a steady flow of water.

Collect Rainwater

Collecting rainwater is one of the easiest and most effective ways to have a safe supply of water. Rainwater is safe to drink except in areas with a lot of air pollution. Rainwater collection is a good solution to both water scarcity and water safety.

Above ground tanks can be placed next to the house. The roof will catch rainwater and divert it into the tank. Roofs made of tin or corrugated metal are best. Roofs made of thatch may collect too much dirt to be safe. Roofs made of lead, asbestos, or tar have toxic chemicals in them that will make the water unsafe to drink. Make sure your rain barrel is clean and was never used to store toxic chemicals, such as oil or pesticides.

Using a tin roof to collect rainwater

Ground **catchments** can collect surface runoff and rainwater. To make a simple catchment, dig a depression into the ground and press down the earth or line it with clay, tile, concrete, or plastic sheeting. These reservoirs can be used to give water to animals or to collect water for bathing. If a ground catchment is used for drinking water, it should be fenced to keep animals out. Water from ground catchments should be cleaned (see pages 92 to 99) before drinking.

Water collected on roofs or in ground level catchments can also be diverted into underground tanks for storage. This is a good way to keep water cool and covered. It may also be less costly than building or buying above-ground tanks.

Make rainwater safe to drink

Rainwater must be kept free of contamination to be safe to drink. To make sure the water you collect will be safe:

- Clean the tank, entrance pipe, roof, and roof gutters before the rainy season.
- Never collect water in containers that have been used for oil, pesticides, or other toxic chemicals.
- Allow the first rains of each year to run through the tank to clean it.
- Cover the tank and place a filter or screen over the inlets to keep out insects, leaves, and dirt. This will also help prevent mosquitoes from breeding.
- Take out water through taps, if possible. If water is removed with buckets or other containers, make sure they are clean.
- For added safety, add chlorine to the tank (see page 99) or connect a water filter to the tank (see page 96).
- Do not stir or move the water. That way, any dirt or germs in the tank will settle and stay at the bottom.
- Sweeping the roof from time to time will also help keep collected rainwater clean.

Collecting rainwater in the desert

One way rainwater is collected in the Thar Desert of Rajasthan, India, is in village ponds, called naadi. Everyone in the village, and even people passing by, may use naadi water.

Everyone in the village works together to maintain the naadi. Ancient laws prohibit any trees from being cut near the edges of the naadi, or in the area where rainwater collects and runs into the naadi. Animals are kept away from the naadi, and people are not allowed to urinate or defecate near the naadi. Once a month, on the day of no moon, the entire village works to dig out any sand and silt that has collected in the naadi. Digging out the naadi makes it deeper and also removes germs that may have settled on the bottom. After digging it out, the villagers allow the water to settle so it becomes clear again. In these ways the community comes together to protect their water.

Safe Water Transport

Care must be taken to keep water safe and clean while it is being moved from its source to where people need it. Carrying water is some of the hardest daily work done in any community, and it is often done by women and girls. Carrying heavy loads of water on the head, on the back, or with a head strap can lead to frequent headaches, backache, harm to the spine, and can cause a pregnant woman to lose her baby due to strain.

Water improvement projects can reduce this burden. Sometimes simple changes can make it easier to carry water. Water systems can be built so there will be no need to carry water long distances. And homes can be built closer to the water source. Community health will improve if men understand the importance of this work in family life and share the tasks of collecting and carrying water.

Piped water

There are many advantages to a piped water system. Piped water reduces the risk of contamination and there are fewer places for snails and mosquitoes to live. However, a piped water system that is poorly built and used unsafely may make water contamination worse than no system at all. A piped water system must be planned carefully, with an understanding of how much water is needed and available now, and how much water may be needed in the future as your community grows.

Water can be piped from almost any water source, but springs and reservoirs are the most common. The least costly source is one that is uphill from the community, so that gravity will carry the water downhill. Most piped water systems bring the water to a large storage tank. The tank may be treated with chlorine or have a filter attached to treat the water. Water is then piped from the storage tank to taps in people's homes or to public water taps around the community.

A piped water system needs regular maintenance. Keeping records of where pipes are laid can prevent accidents and make it easier to find and repair broken pipes. Leaking pipes can waste a lot of water, draw in sewage and other contamination from the soil, and make breeding grounds for mosquitoes and snails. If pipes have been fixed with jute, hemp, cotton, or leather, germs may grow on these things and contaminate the water inside the pipes.

An important part of any piped water system is making sure that someone is responsible for fixing damage to the pipes.

Women and men talk about water

When the water committee in a small Mexican village planned to pipe water to the village from a large spring, they decided they had enough money to install a shared tap for every 2 houses. At the village assembly the men from the water committee announced that the taps would be used to provide water for drinking and cooking. This was good for the village, they said, because now the women would not spend all day carrying water from the river and boiling it to make it safe to drink.

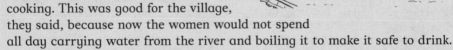

A woman at the assembly stood up and asked, "What about washing clothes?" One of the men from the water committee said, "You can continue to wash clothes in the river as you always have done." A second woman stood up and asked, "What about bathing our children?" The man said, "You can continue to bathe the children in the river as you always have done." A third woman stood up and asked, "What about our home gardens? We need water to grow vegetables."

The women felt their voices had not been heard. They said there was not a single woman on the water committee and so women's needs would not be met. The women demanded that they be allowed to join the water committee and help make a new plan. The rest of the assembly agreed.

The new water committee made a different plan. Rather than a tap for every 2 houses, they would install a tap and a wash basin for every 6 houses. Though the women would still walk to collect water, they would also be able to wash clothes, bathe children, and clean maize right in the village. The tap would be used for drinking water and the washbasin for everything else. This would help make sure that the drinking water stayed clean. And they would use the wastewater from the washbasin to water their home gardens.

The plan was popular among the men as well because it would give them a place to wash their tools when they returned from the cornfields each day. In this way, the villagers met many of their needs at once.

Store Water Safely

If water is not handled carefully while it is being collected, carried, and stored in containers, it can be easily contaminated. Water stored in tanks with cracked walls, or containers with loose, poorly made, or missing covers can be contaminated by animal waste and germs.

Detective story: **How did the drinking water get contaminated?**

This activity helps explore how water drawn from a well, spring, or tap can become contaminated before it is consumed. It can be done with 4 people or more.

Time: ½ hour

❶ The facilitator explains to the group they are health detectives, then gives the detectives their briefing. Here's an example: 10 families collect clean drinking water from a well. During the next few days, children from one family become sick from drinking contaminated water at home. The other families are fine. The task for the detectives is to find out how the water became contaminated after it was drawn from the well.

❷ The facilitator asks for 1 to 3 volunteers. Away from where the rest of the group can hear, the facilitator explains that their role is to give "clues" as the group asks questions to try to discover how the water became contaminated. Then the facilitator can either tell the volunteers, or ask them to quickly decide, how the water got contaminated before they rejoin the rest of the group.

❸ The group then takes turns asking the volunteers questions, who respond with "clues" until someone is able to guess correctly how the water became contaminated.

❹ If the group is large, it can be divided into several teams. Limit the number of questions, for example, allow each team or person up to 4 questions. The first person or team to guess the right answer wins.

Repeat the activity several times with different ways the water became contaminated. Afterwards, the facilitator can lead a discussion to explore the different ways that drinking water becomes contaminated. Talk about what can be done to keep drinking water clean and how to do that at home and throughout the community.

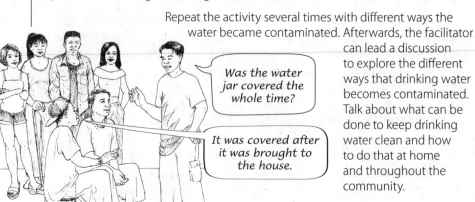

Was the water jar covered the whole time?

It was covered after it was brought to the house.

Keeping water containers clean

Stored water can become unsafe when it is touched by people with dirty hands, when it is poured into a dirty container, when dirt or dust gets in the water, and when dirty cups are put into it. To prevent water from becoming unsafe at home:

- Wash hands before collecting and carrying water.
- Clean and cover the container that is used to carry water.
- Regularly clean the container where water is stored in the house.
- Keep water containers off the floor and away from animals.
- Pour water out without touching the mouth of the container, or use a clean, long-handled dipper to take water out of the container.
- Clean all cups that are used for drinking.
- Never store water in containers that have been used for pesticides or toxic chemicals.
- If possible, do not treat more water than you need for short-term use. For drinking and cooking, that is usually less than 5 liters for each person each day.

Narrow mouthed containers are safest for storing water.

Cover tanks and cisterns

Covered tanks and cisterns are safer for storing water than open ponds because mosquitoes and snails cannot live in closed tanks. Covering storage tanks also reduces water loss from evaporation. If water is stored in ponds or ditches, digging them deeper will expose less water to the air and so will reduce the amount lost to evaporation.

Cisterns should be placed as close as possible to where the water will be used.

Fix leaks

A lot of water can be lost through leaks, evaporation, and seepage. To save water, make sure taps are closed when they are not in use. Fix or replace broken or leaky pipes and cracked tanks as soon as leaks are found. Leaks are also a sign of possible contamination, because germs and dirt enter the cracks in tanks and pipes.

Make Water Safe to Drink

It is better to protect and use a source of safe water, such as a spring or protected well, than to treat and use water from a contaminated source, such as a river or waterhole. But water from any source will need to be treated if it has been contaminated, if people refuse to drink it due to color or taste, or if it is carried and stored in the home. (Water from pipes, tanks, and wells will also need treatment before drinking if it has been contaminated.)

The methods you choose to treat water will depend on how much water you need, what it is contaminated with, how you will store it, and what resources are available. No matter how it is treated, it is best to either let the water settle and pour it into another container, or to filter the water before disinfecting it (see page 94). This removes the sediment (particles of dirt). Removing sediment makes disinfection easier and more effective.

The methods shown here do not make water safe from toxic chemicals. Water that contains toxic chemicals is never safe for drinking, bathing, or washing clothes. It may lead to cancer, skin rashes, miscarriages, or other health problems.

To make water safe from germs, follow these 2 steps, filter and disinfect:

❶ Let the water settle for a few hours and pour it into a clean container, or filter it:

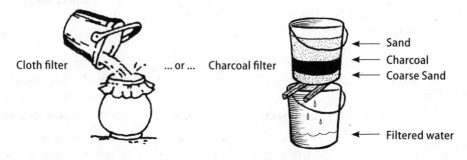

Cloth filter   ... or ...   Charcoal filter

Sand
Charcoal
Coarse Sand

Filtered water

See pages 93 to 97 for other ways to settle and filter water.

❷ Disinfect the water using 1 of these methods:

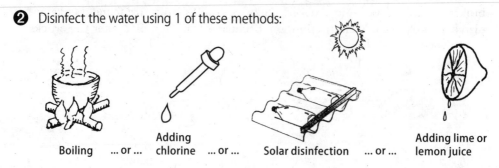

Boiling   ... or ...   Adding chlorine   ... or ...   Solar disinfection   ... or ...   Adding lime or lemon juice

Settling water

Settling water allows dirt, solids, germs, and worms that cause some illnesses to fall to the bottom of the container. Storing water for 5 to 6 days will reduce the number of germs in the water. But some germs, such as **giardia,** will not be killed by any length of storage. For this reason, use another method after letting water settle to make it safe, such as filtering, chlorinating, or solar disinfection.

3-pot method

The 3-pot method settles water so germs and solid matter fall to the bottom. This method is safer than settling water in 1 pot, but it does not make the water completely free of germs. The 3-pot method should always be followed by disinfection (see page 97).

Morning, Day 1: Fill pot 1 with water. Cover the top and let it settle for 2 days.

Morning, Day 2: Fill pot 2 with water. Cover it and leave for 2 days. The dirt in pot 1 is beginning to settle.

Morning, Day 3: Pour the clear water from pot 1 into empty pot 3, making sure not to pour out the sediment at the bottom of pot 1. The water in pot 3 is now ready for disinfecting. The dirty water and sediment left in the bottom of pot 1 can be poured out. Wash pot 1 and refill it with water. Cover it and let it settle for 2 days. (It will be poured out and ready for disinfecting on Day 5.)

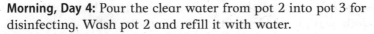

Morning, Day 4: Pour the clear water from pot 2 into pot 3 for disinfecting. Wash pot 2 and refill it with water.

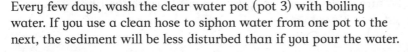

Every few days, wash the clear water pot (pot 3) with boiling water. If you use a clean hose to siphon water from one pot to the next, the sediment will be less disturbed than if you pour the water.

Using plants

In many places, people use plants to make water safer to drink. Moringa seeds are used in East Africa. Moringa is called malunggay in the Philippines, horseradish tree or drumstick tree in India, and benzolive tree in Haiti and the Dominican Republic. To use moringa seeds:

1. Dry the seeds for 3 days.

2. Grind the seeds to powder. It takes 15 ground moringa seeds to clear 20 liters of water.

3. Mix the powder with a little water to make a paste, and add it to the water.

4. To dissolve the paste, stir for 5 to 10 minutes. The faster it is stirred the less time is needed.

5. Cover the container and set it aside to let it settle. After 1 to 2 hours, pour the water into a clean container. Be careful to leave the solids in the first container.

Filtering water

There are many ways to filter water to make it safer from germs. Some filters, like the ceramic filter below, require special equipment. Others need no special equipment and can easily filter small or large amounts of water before disinfecting.

Cloth filters

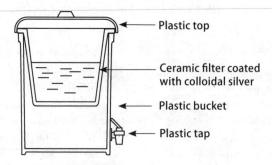

In Bangladesh and India, a filter made of finely woven cloth is used to remove cholera germs from drinking water. Because the cholera germ often attaches to a tiny animal that lives in water, filtering out these animals also filters out most cholera germs. This method also filters out guinea worms.

You can make a cloth filter out of handkerchiefs, linen, or other fabric such as the cloth used to make saris. Old cloth works better than new cloth because worn fibers make the spaces in the weave smaller and better for filtering.

1. Let water settle in a container so that solids sink to the bottom.
2. Fold the cloth 4 times and stretch or tie it over the mouth of another container or water jar.
3. Pour water slowly from the first container through the cloth into the second container or jar.

Always use the same side of the cloth, or germs may get into the water. After using the cloth, wash it and leave it in the sun to dry. This kills any germs that may be left in the cloth. In the rainy season, disinfect the cloth with bleach. Be sure to clean the container you use to store the filtered water in, at least every 2 to 3 weeks.

Ceramic filters

A small water filter can be made from fired clay coated with colloidal silver (a substance that kills germs). With basic training, any potter can easily make these filters. (For more information, see Resources.)

Plastic top

Ceramic filter coated
with colloidal silver

Plastic bucket

Plastic tap

Ceramic filter used inside a plastic bucket

How to make a charcoal filter

This filter is easy to make and removes most germs from small amounts of water.

Materials: 2 metal or plastic buckets, a hammer and 1 or 2 large nails, a bucket of coarse sand (not sea sand), a quarter bucket of wood charcoal

1 Make holes in the bottom of 1 of the buckets. Wash the bucket. This is now the filter bucket.

2 Clean the sand by rinsing it in water and draining until the water that drains off is clear.

3 Crush charcoal into small pieces. Activated charcoal works best, but ordinary wood charcoal will also work. Never use charcoal briquettes! They are poison!

4 Put a layer of washed sand 5 cm deep into the filter bucket and pour water over it. Water should run out through the holes. If no water runs out, make the holes bigger. If sand runs out, the holes are too large. If this happens, remove the sand, place a thin cloth over the holes, and replace the sand.

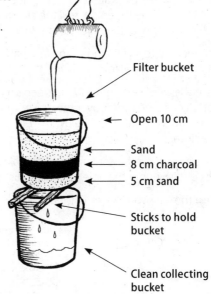

Filter bucket

Open 10 cm

Sand
8 cm charcoal
5 cm sand

Sticks to hold bucket

Clean collecting bucket

5 Place a layer of crushed charcoal about 8 cm deep on top of the sand. Now fill the bucket with more sand, until the sand is 10 cm below the top of the bucket.

6 Place 2 sticks on top of the second bucket and set the filter bucket on these sticks. Pour clean water through the filter bucket several times until the water comes out clear into the collecting bucket. Now the filter is ready for use.

7 To use the filter, allow the water you collect to settle before pouring it through the filter. Drinking water collects in the clean, bottom bucket. To be safest, after filtering, disinfect the water (see page 97 to 99.)

Because the germs that are filtered out will grow on the charcoal, it is important to remove and clean the charcoal every few weeks if the filter is used daily, or any time the filter has been unused for a few days.

How to make a household slow sand filter

This is one of the safest, most effective, and cheapest ways to filter water for a household. This filter can treat enough water for a small family (at least 50 liters per day).

❶ Clean a watertight 200 liter container and disinfect it with bleaching powder. Make sure the container did not contain toxic materials.

❷ Drill a hole ⅓ of the way down from the top of the container for the valve or tap. The hole should be sized for the fitting on the tap. (For example, if the tap has a 12 mm fitting, the hole should be 12 mm wide.)

❸ Fit the tap to the hole and fix it in place with hard-setting putty. If a brick container is used, the valve can be cemented within the wall.

❹ Prepare the flexible water collecting pipe. Drill or punch many small holes in the first 35 cm of the hosepipe, seal the end, and form it into a ring on the bottom of the container with the holes facing downward.

❺ Connect the top of the hosepipe (the end with no holes) to the tap. Seal the pipe fittings with hose clamps or wire.

❻ Place a layer of clean gravel 7 cm deep on the bottom of the barrel to cover the water-collecting pipe. Cover the gravel with fine cloth and fill the barrel with clean river sand to about 10 cm below the tap. Then cover the sand with a second fine cloth.

❼ Make a cover for the container, with a hole in it to pour water through. Place a flat rock or dish under the hole to prevent disturbing the sand when water is poured in.

❽ Flush the filter with water. Once the filter is cleaned, it is ready to use.

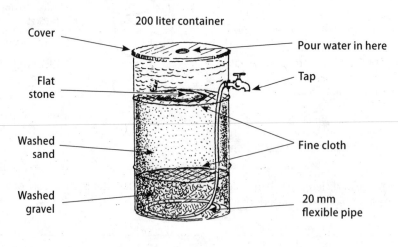

200 liter container

Cover

Pour water in here

Flat stone

Tap

Washed sand

Fine cloth

Washed gravel

20 mm flexible pipe

To use and maintain a slow sand filter

After a few days of use, a layer of green scum (bacteria and algae) will grow on top of the sand. This helps to treat the water, so do not remove it. For this scum to work, the sand must always be covered with water. (This is why the tap is placed above the sand layer.) Fill the filter daily and remove water only in small amounts. If the filter is drained completely it will not work well, and will need to be cleaned and refilled.

Allow solids to settle out of the water before pouring it into the filter. This will reduce the need to clean the filter because the water will be cleaner when it enters. Letting water flow like a waterfall as you pour it will add air into the water and make it taste better.

When the water flow from the tap slows down, clean the filter. Drain all the water and remove the green layer and about 1 cm of sand from the top. After many cleanings, when more than half of the sand has been removed, replace all the sand and gravel with new cleaned sand and gravel and start over. This may be necessary 1 or 2 times a year.

Arsenic filter

To filter out arsenic from water, add a container filled with iron nails to the top of a slow sand filter. Use 3 to 5 kg of the smallest sized iron nails. Do not use "galvanized" nails because the nails must be able to rust for the filter to work. Arsenic binds to the rust on the iron nails and is removed from the drinking water. (For more information, see Resources.)

Disinfecting water

Disinfecting water kills germs and worms, making water safe to drink. The best methods are boiling, solar disinfection, or using chlorine.

IMPORTANT: These methods will NOT make water safe from toxic chemicals.

Boiling water

Bring water to a rapid, rolling boil. Once it starts boiling, let it boil for 1 full minute before taking the pot off to cool. In high mountain areas, water needs to boil for 3 minutes to kill germs because water boils at a lower temperature high in the mountains.

Boiling changes the taste of the water. After boiled water cools, pour it into a bottle and shake it strongly. The shaking will add air to the water and improve the taste.

Where firewood is scarce, boiling water can be difficult. Planning to boil water after food is prepared but before the fire dies is one way to reduce your use of wood.

Boiling water for 1 minute makes it safe from germs.

How to disinfect water with sunlight

Solar disinfection is an effective way to disinfect water with only sunlight and a bottle. Filtering or settling the water first will make it clearer so it will disinfect more quickly. Solar disinfection works best in countries close to the equator, because the sun is strongest there. The farther north or south you are, the more time is needed for disinfection to work. (For more information about solar disinfection, see Resources.)

1 Clean a clear plastic or glass bottle, or a plastic bag. Bottles made of PET plastic work best.

2 Fill the bottle half full, then shake it for 20 seconds. This will add air bubbles to the water. Then fill the bottle or bag to the top. The air bubbles will help to disinfect the water faster.

3 Place the bottle where there is no shade and where people and animals will not disturb it, such as the roof of a house. Leave the bottle for at least 6 hours in full sun, or for 2 days if the weather is cloudy.

4 Drink directly from the bottle. This will prevent contamination from hands or other vessels.

Solar disinfection can be done faster and more completely by putting the bottle in a solar cooker (see page 364).

Use 1 lime or lemon for every liter of water.

1 LITER

Lime or lemon juice

Add the juice of a lime or lemon to 1 liter of drinking water and let it sit for 30 minutes. This will kill most cholera and some other germs as well. This does not make water completely safe, but is better than no treatment in areas where cholera is a threat. Adding lime or lemon juice to water before using solar disinfection or the 3-pot method will make the water safer.

Chlorine

Chlorine is cheap and easy to use to kill most germs in drinking water. But if too little chlorine is used, it will not kill germs. If too much is used, the water will taste bad. Chlorine is best used in community water systems, because it can be difficult for a single household to do it well all the time. To use chlorine to disinfect household water, follow the instructions on the next page.

Large amounts of chlorine are harmful to people and the environment, but the amounts used to disinfect home and community water are generally safe. It is safer to disinfect water with chlorine than to risk the health problems caused by germs.

How much chlorine to use?

The amount of chlorine needed to disinfect water depends on how contaminated the water is (how many and what kinds of germs it contains). The more germs there are in the water, the more chlorine you need to get rid of them. It is important to add enough chlorine so that some is left in the water after the germs are killed. The chlorine that is left is called free chlorine. This will kill any new germs that get into the water. If the water has free chlorine in it, it will smell and taste just slightly of chlorine. This tells you it is safe to drink. If it has too much, the smell and taste will be strong and unpleasant.

To use the right amount of chlorine, you need to know how strong your chlorine solution is. Chlorine comes in different forms — gas, bleaching powder, high-test hypochlorite (HTH), and household liquid bleach. Because household bleach is the most common form of chlorine, this book shows how to disinfect water with household bleach.

Household bleach may have different amounts of chlorine. Most common are 3.5% and 5%. The easiest way to measure the amount of bleach needed is to first make a 'mother solution' (about 1% chlorine) and then add this solution to the water you want to disinfect. To prepare the mother solution:

1. Add 1 cup of bleach to a clean, empty 1 liter bottle.
2. Fill the bottle with clean water.
3. Shake the bottle for 30 seconds.
4. Let it sit for 30 minutes. Your mother solution is ready.

If there is a lot of solid matter in the water, the chlorine will not work as well, so filter the water (see page 94), or let the water settle. Pour the clear water off into a clean container and then add chlorine.

Water		Bleach 'Mother Solution'
For 1 liter or 1 quart		3 drops
For 1 gallon or 4 liters		12 drops
For 5 gallons or 20 liter		1 teaspoon
For a 200 liter barrel		10 teaspoons

Add these amounts of the mother solution to clear water and wait at least 30 minutes before drinking. If the water is cloudy, you need twice as much of the bleach mother solution.

Wastewater: A Problem or a Resource?

Because the amount of water in the world stays the same, all water is used over and over again. But runoff water and water that has been used for washing, farming, sanitation, or industry often contains germs and chemicals that make it unsafe for drinking, bathing, or washing.

Water that is not contaminated with toxic chemicals or human waste can be reused after simple treatment. The method best suited for your household or community depends on the amount of wastewater to treat, what it is contaminated with, what it is to be used for, and how much time, space, and labor you have to treat the water.

Greywater solutions

Greywater is wastewater that has been used for washing and other household chores, but does not contain human wastes. As long as you do not use toxic soaps or cleaners (see page 373 for how to make safer cleaning products), greywater needs only simple treatment before being reused in the garden, or no treatment at all before being disposed of into the ground.

IMPORTANT: Greywater is never safe for drinking.

There are many different types of greywater systems (see Resources). Any greywater system works best when:

- it is easy to build and maintain.
- grease, concentrated bleach, solvents, and other chemicals are kept out of the water.

Constructed wetlands (reed beds) filter greywater

One way to treat greywater is to copy nature's way of cleaning water by making a wetland. Constructed wetlands (also called reed beds) treat greywater by filtering water through layers of plants, soil, and rocks. Nutrients in the wastewater feed the plants, and the plants add oxygen to the water, which helps clean it. Reed beds also:

- provide irrigation water for food crops.
- grow plants you can harvest for other uses, such as bamboo or reeds.
- replace stagnant water with beautiful gardens.

IMPORTANT: Constructed wetlands cannot treat solid human wastes (feces).

To make a constructed wetland

In planning a constructed wetland, consider these issues:

- How much area do you need and how deep does it need to be? The more water that flows through the system, the bigger and deeper it needs to be to safely filter greywater. If water flows too quickly, the reed bed cannot clean it well.

- Is the water source higher than the wetland? Water must flow through the wetland, so it needs to come from a source above, or be pumped.

- Where will cleaned water flow to? Can it be collected in a storage tank or directed to a garden?

Wetlands can be built anywhere there is enough space. If there is little space, they can be built above ground in basins, such as a 200 liter drum. In areas with well-drained soil or high groundwater, dig a pit and line it with thick plastic or cement. In areas with clay soil, no lining is needed.

To maintain a constructed wetland

A constructed wetland dug into the ground can treat large amounts of greywater.

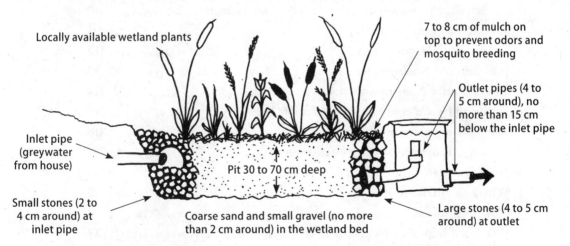

Locally available wetland plants

7 to 8 cm of mulch on top to prevent odors and mosquito breeding

Outlet pipes (4 to 5 cm around), no more than 15 cm below the inlet pipe

Inlet pipe (greywater from house)

Pit 30 to 70 cm deep

Small stones (2 to 4 cm around) at inlet pipe

Coarse sand and small gravel (no more than 2 cm around) in the wetland bed

Large stones (4 to 5 cm around) at outlet

Every constructed wetland has different needs depending on the amount of water, the type of soil and plants, and other conditions. Experiment to find the best way to make your constructed wetland work.

- **If plants dry out or die,** not enough water is running through. More water sources can be added to the system, the pit can be made smaller or less deep, or new plants can be added.

- **If water does not flow through,** try bigger stones and less sand, or lower the outlet pipe.

7 Building Toilets

In this chapter: page

Building Toilets

Human waste (feces and urine) can pollute water, food, and soil with germs and worms, leading to serious health problems (see pages 51 to 58). The safe disposal of human waste (sanitation) by building and maintaining toilets and washing hands prevents the spread of germs and is necessary for good health.

Whether your community uses pit toilets, toilets that turn human waste into fertilizer **(ecological sanitation),** toilets that flush human wastes and water **(sewage),** or another type of toilet, the main goal is to prevent human waste from contaminating drinking water, food, and our hands. Just as important as a safe and comfortable toilet is a way to wash hands after using it. Safe toilets and hand washing together can prevent most of the illnesses that come from germs in human waste.

Poorly built toilets and sewage systems are a major cause of illness and groundwater contamination. As clean water becomes more scarce, disposing of human waste in ways that do not cause more water contamination becomes increasingly important.

Promoting Sanitation

Some health workers believe health problems and death from poor sanitation can be prevented only if people change their personal habits, or "change their behaviors," for staying clean. But promoting behavior change often fails because the conditions people face in their daily lives, such as poverty, or a lack of clean water or decent toilets, do not change. And when their behavior does not change, the people themselves are blamed for their own poor health.

Experts may offer technical solutions, such as modern toilets that use no water, or costly sewage treatment systems. But just because these technical solutions may work elsewhere does not mean they will respond to the traditions or conditions of the community. Some of the toilets in this book may not be right for some communities. Offering technical solutions without understanding people's cultures, living conditions, and real needs can create more problems than it solves.

Diseases caused by poor sanitation will continue if people are blamed for their own poor health or if technical solutions that ignore local conditions are promoted. To improve health in a lasting way, health promoters must listen carefully and work with people in the community to develop solutions based on their needs, abilities, and desire for change.

What People Want from Toilets

Health is not always the main reason why people want improved sanitation. People also want:

- **privacy:** A toilet can be as simple as a deep hole in the ground. But the need for privacy makes it important for a toilet to have a good shelter with a door. The best shelters are simple and are built from local materials.

- **safety:** For a toilet to be safe it must be built well and in a safe place. If a toilet is badly built it can be dangerous to use. And if the toilet is far from the home, or in an isolated place, women may be in danger of sexual violence when they use it.

- **comfort:** People will more likely use a toilet with a comfortable place to sit or squat, and a shelter large enough to stand up in. They will also be more likely to use a toilet that is close to the house and is sheltered from wind, rain, or snow.

- **cleanliness:** If a toilet is dirty and smelly, no one will want to use it. Traditionally the job of low status people in the community, sharing the task of cleaning will help make sure that toilets are properly used and cared for.

- **respect:** A well-kept toilet brings status and respect to its owner. This can be an important reason people spend the money and effort to build one.

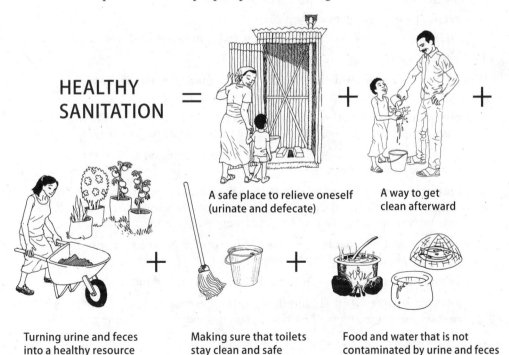

HEALTHY SANITATION =

A safe place to relieve oneself (urinate and defecate)

\+ A way to get clean afterward

\+

Turning urine and feces into a healthy resource

\+ Making sure that toilets stay clean and safe

\+ Food and water that is not contaminated by urine and feces

Planning for Toilets

Every person and every community has a way of managing human waste, even if it just means that people go into the bush or forest to urinate and defecate. Not all people in a village use the same method, and not every person disposes of their waste the same way all the time. Some people may want to change, while others may not. Whether it means building a new kind of toilet, improving access to safe toilets, or some other kind of change, almost every sanitation method can be improved.

A plan that leaves women or anyone else without toilets will not prevent illness in the community.

Small, step by step changes are easier than big changes all at once. Examples of small changes that can have a big impact on health, safety, and comfort are:

- keeping wash water and soap near the toilet.
- adding a screened vent to a pit toilet to let air flow and also trap flies.
- adding a durable platform to an open pit.

When planning or making changes in the way human waste is disposed of in your community, keep in mind that every method should:

- **prevent disease** — it should keep disease carrying waste and insects away from people and food, both at the site of the toilet and in nearby homes.

- **protect water supplies** — it should not pollute drinking water, surface water, or groundwater.

- **protect the environment** — toilets that turn human waste into fertilizer (ecological sanitation) can conserve and protect water, prevent pollution, and return nutrients to the soil. (See pages 124 to 135.)

- **be simple and affordable** — it should be easy for people to clean and maintain, and to build for themselves with local materials.

- **be culturally acceptable** — it should fit local customs, beliefs, and needs.

- **work for everyone** — it should address the health needs of children, women, and men, as well as those who are elderly or disabled.

Sanitation decisions are community decisions

When decisions about toilets are made by the people who will use them, it is more likely that people's different sanitation needs will be met. And because household, neighborhood, and village sanitation decisions can affect people downstream, when neighboring communities work together, health can improve for everyone.

Community participation can make the difference between success and failure when a government or outside agency tries to improve sanitation.

The wrong toilets?

In 1992, the government of El Salvador spent over US $10 million to build thousands of toilets. These toilets were meant to turn waste into fertilizer, but they needed more care and cleaning than the old toilets people were used to. The government did not involve anyone in the communities to help build them, and there was no training in how to use them. So people did not learn how they worked.

After the project was finished, the government studied how the toilets were being used. They learned that many of the toilets were not being used well, and others were not used at all.

When people participate in planning, the result is more likely to fit their needs.

Someone must clean the toilet

No one likes to clean the toilet. But someone has to do it.

Often, the job of planning, building, and fixing toilets is considered men's work or work for specialists. The less pleasant and more constant task of cleaning toilets often falls to women or people of lower social classes. It is unfair if tasks that are unpleasant always fall to women and poor people who usually do not make the decisions in the first place.

Sharing unpleasant tasks is a way to make sure the work gets done, though it often creates social conflicts.

Women and Men Have Different Needs

Women and men have different needs and customs when it comes to using the toilet. Men may be more comfortable than women relieving themselves in public or in open spaces. Women have a greater share of family work such as caring for children, collecting water and firewood, cooking, and cleaning. This affects their access to toilets that are safe, clean, comfortable, and private.

It is generally easier for men to relieve themselves than it is for women.

Planning toilets with women's needs in mind

Leaving women out of sanitation planning puts them at a greater risk for health problems because it is less likely that their needs will be met. Men must also keep women's needs in mind when changes are made in community sanitation if they are to improve health for everyone.

To make it easier for women to participate in community sanitation planning in a way that does not simply give them more work to do:

- Organize meetings at times when women can participate.
- Make sure that women are invited and feel comfortable speaking out.
- Have separate meetings for women if they make it easier for women to speak up.
- Share decision making power.

Women usually teach and care for children. When women's needs are not met, the needs of children may be unmet as well. When women are not included in planning household and community sanitation, the whole community suffers.

If you teach a man, you teach one person. If you teach a woman, you teach a whole nation.
—African proverb

Removing barriers to toilets for women

This activity helps people talk about issues that may prevent women from having access to safe and healthy toilets. The goal is to decide what changes might be necessary to improve health for everyone. After the activity has been done with just women, a session can be organized with men and women.

Time: 1 to 1½ hours

Materials: Large drawing paper, pens, sticky tape

❶ Write statements about toilets on a large piece of paper. Then read each statement to the group, and ask each person to decide whether she agrees or disagrees. (Ask people to raise a hand if they agree, or to leave their hand down if they do not.) For every 'yes' answer, make a mark next to the phrase.

Here are some statements that might be used.

❷ Count the marks beside each statement. Choose the problems that were mentioned most often and begin a discussion about them. What is the cause of the problem? What illnesses may result from this problem? What can be done to improve the situation? What are the barriers to improving the situation?

❸ End with the group deciding on some actions that can be taken by both men and women to make sure everyone's needs are met.

Making toilets easier to use

There are many ways to make toilets easier for children and adults with disabilities to use. People need different adaptations depending on their abilities, so it is best to involve disabled people in the planning. Be creative in finding solutions that fit everyone's needs.

Removable front bar can be added if needed

If a person has **difficulty squatting,** make a simple hand support or a raised seat. Or, if the toilet is set in the ground, make a hole in the seat of a chair or stool and place it over the toilet.

If a person has **difficulty controlling her body,** make supports for her back, sides, and legs, and a seat belt or bar.

Use a rope or fence to guide **blind** people from the house to the toilet.

If a person has **difficulty adjusting clothing,** adapt the clothing to make it loose or elastic. Make a clean, dry place to lie down and dress.

If a person has **difficulty sitting** you can make moveable handrails and steps.

Toilet adapted for wheelchairs

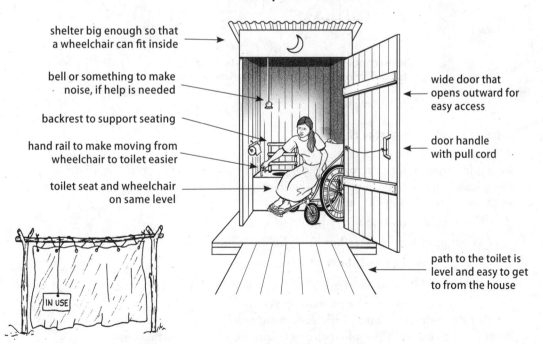

shelter big enough so that a wheelchair can fit inside

bell or something to make noise, if help is needed

backrest to support seating

hand rail to make moving from wheelchair to toilet easier

toilet seat and wheelchair on same level

wide door that opens outward for easy access

door handle with pull cord

path to the toilet is level and easy to get to from the house

IN USE

Remember, a person with a disability feels the same need for privacy as anyone else and should get the privacy he or she needs.

Toilets for Children

Children have a high risk of illness from poor sanitation. And while adults may live with diarrhea diseases and worms, children can die from these illnesses (see page 51).

When children have toilets they feel safe using and have an easy way to stay clean, they get sick less. Pit toilets can be dangerous and frightening for small children because of the darkness and the large hole. Many children, especially girls, leave school because schools lack safe toilets.

Allowing children to help build toilets and teaching them about illnesses caused by poor sanitation helps them develop healthy behaviors.

Every school should have safe toilets and a way for children to wash hands after using them.

Helping small children stay clean

All feces carry harmful germs, and handling them can cause serious illness in children and adults. In rural areas, parents can help children too small to use a toilet by making a hole near the house and adding a handful of soil after each use. It is also important to:

- Wash babies and young children after they defecate.
- Wash your hands after handling babies' feces.
- Bury the feces or put them in a safe toilet.
- Wash soiled clothes away from drinking water sources.

Teach boys and girls to wipe or wash carefully, and to wash their hands after using the toilet. Girls especially should be taught to wipe from front to back. Wiping forward can spread germs into the urinary opening and the vagina, causing bladder infections and other health problems.

Sanitation for Emergencies

More and more, large numbers of people are forced to live in emergency situations due to wars, natural disasters, and other reasons for displacement. In emergency settlements such as refugee camps, sanitation is a first priority.

Simple trench latrine

Simple trenches can be made quickly using local materials. One enclosed trench for each family, or for a small group of families, will allow for the most comfort.

Trench latrines should be built downhill and away from water sources, but close enough to family settlements so people do not have to walk long distances to use them.

A trench latrine has shelves for the feet to make it easier to use than a simple trench. The trench latrine should be as deep as possible (up to 2 meters), but can be shallow if little labor is available for digging. Each user covers his or her feces with a small amount of soil. When the trench is close to full, fill it completely with soil. Plants and trees will benefit from the rich soil.

A portable shelter can be built over the trench to give privacy and to protect users from rain. Screens can be made from cloth, reeds, or whatever materials are available. Special care should be taken to make sure latrines are private and safe for women and children.

A partially built trench latrine shelter

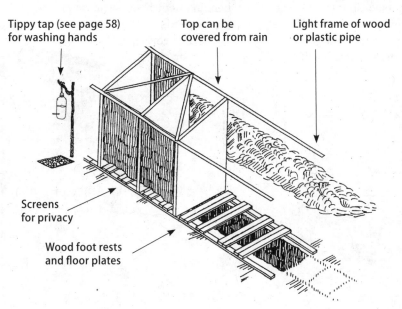

Tippy tap (see page 58) for washing hands

Top can be covered from rain

Light frame of wood or plastic pipe

Screens for privacy

Wood foot rests and floor plates

Sanitation for Cities and Towns

In cities and towns, health problems can spread very quickly. It is difficult to improve sanitation services in crowded cities and towns without a lot of help from governments, NGOs, and other partners. This book can offer only some guidelines to help think about possible solutions.

The main barriers to good sanitation services in cities are:

- **physical.** Often, sanitation is considered only after neighborhoods and settlements have roads, electricity, and water. Yet once a city is built, it is much harder to plan for and build toilets and sewage systems.

- **economic.** Sewage systems and public toilets are costly to build and maintain. If there is little government support, it is difficult to afford sanitation.

- **political.** Local governments may not want to deliver services to informal settlements and poorer neighborhoods. And there may be laws that prevent people from planning and building their own toilets and sewage systems.

- **cultural.** People and officials in cities often want flush toilets and costly sewer systems, making it difficult to agree on more sustainable and affordable alternatives.

Creative solutions for healthier cities

Any kind of toilet, including the ones in this guide, can be built and used in cities. And if sanitation services are combined with parks, urban farming (see page 310), resource recovery and recycling (see Chapter 18), and clean energy (see Chapter 23), cities can become healthier and more pleasant places to live. When city governments work with neighborhood groups to come up with creative solutions, the result will be cleaner, healthier cities.

Urban community sanitation

Not long ago, Yoff was a typical West African fishing village outside of Dakar, the capital city of Senegal. Families lived in compounds connected by walking paths and open spaces. But as Dakar grew and swallowed Yoff, it became part of a large urban area with an international airport and a lot of automobiles.

As the town grew, many houses installed flush toilets connected to open pits where the sewage sat and bred disease. Other people, too poor to afford toilets, used open sandy areas. But with many people living close together, this quickly became a health problem.

A town development committee came together to solve the sanitation problem. They began by looking at the resources they had: strong community networks, skilled builders, and people committed to keeping village life. They also had some new ideas about **ecological sanitation.**

In the village, houses were grouped around open common areas where people could gather and talk. After talking to many villagers, the committee made a plan to use this open area for a sanitation system that would make the area more attractive, rather than uglier. Instead of promoting household toilets and underground sewage tanks, they would promote community ecological sanitation.

The committee worked with residents to build urine-diverting dry toilets. Each set of toilets would be shared by the whole compound. The urine would run through pipes into beds of reeds. The feces, after being dried out, would be used to fertilize trees. All of this would help to keep the village green. Local masons and builders were hired to construct the toilets and to maintain the common areas.

This urban sanitation project not only prevented health problems, it helped to preserve the way the people of Yoff wanted to live.

The Problem of Sewage

Sewage systems use water to carry waste away in pipes. They can improve community health, especially in crowded urban areas. But to prevent health problems, sewage must be treated to make the water safe to return into waterways and for reuse.

Sewage treatment is costly, and more often than not, sewage is dumped without being treated. This spreads waste and all the germs, worms, and toxic chemicals it may contain, causing health problems such as hepatitis, cholera, and typhoid in places where sewage is dumped.

Even with costly sewage treatment, using water to carry away waste is often not sustainable and can lead to problems such as:

- contamination of drinking water sources downstream.
- contamination of land where people live and farm.
- loss of nutrient resources (fertilizer) for farming.
- contamination of water sources used for drinking, bathing, and farming.
- bad smells.

Sewage systems also cause health problems when different kinds of waste are mixed together, such as when factories dump toxic chemicals into sewers. This contamination makes the treatment and safe reuse of wastewater very difficult.

The safest low cost way to manage sewage is to treat it close to where it is produced, and then to allow the water to absorb into the soil and nourish plants. The most common way to do this is to use a **septic tank** (a large container underground where solids collect and decompose) and a **leach field** (where liquid flows out and into the soil). This method, however, requires technical planning beyond the scope of this guide. (For more information, see Resources.)

Sewage systems use a lot of water to do a job that can often be done with very little or no water. Communities with little water, or that cannot afford a sewage system, will benefit from other types of toilets.

The people most affected by untreated sewage are those who live where it is dumped.

People build their own sewers

Orangi Township is a settlement of 900,000 people in Karachi, Pakistan. For many years, Orangi had no safe water or sanitation services. Sewage and wastewater ran in open ditches, breeding flies and mosquitoes, and causing illness. In 1980, Dr. Akhtar Hameed Khan began the Orangi Pilot Project, or OPP, to help people identify their health problems and come up with solutions.

Orangi residents decided an underground sewage system would most improve their lives. At first they expected the government to build it, but Dr. Khan knew that the Karachi government would not give them money to build a sewage system. After much discussion, the people of Orangi decided that even though they had no money, they could build the sewers themselves.

The first step was to develop community organizations. Each lane consisting of 20 to 30 houses was organized to build a sewer and applied to the OPP for assistance. The OPP surveyed the lane and prepared plans. The lane organization then collected money from the people to build their sewer.

At first, many people did not know how to mix concrete or to dig sewer pits that were flat and level, so some of the work was not done well. After 2 years, many faulty sewers had been built and others were still not built. The OPP organizers realized they had not trained people well enough, so more training sessions were held. This time, women and children were included. The work improved, and design changes were made to better serve the community, reduce costs, and finish the system more quickly.

After a few years, every lane had sewers to take waste away from people's homes. Health conditions improved and Orangi became a more pleasant place to live. But there was still a problem. The people of Orangi could build sewers, but they needed government support and money to build a sewage treatment plant. The government would not give the money. Many years later, the government found and funded a lower cost solution. They connected the sewers to a filter system that cleaned the sewage as it moved downstream. By working together to build their own sewers, the community took an important first step. The OPP helped the government and many experts to see that community health could be greatly improved by building a local sewage system to fit both the needs and the abilities of the community.

Toilet Choices

No kind of toilet is right for every community or household, so it is important to understand the benefits of each toilet. Toilets connected to sewer systems are complicated to build, so this book describes only toilets that use little or no water. (The activity on page 138 can help decide which toilet may be best for your community's needs.)

Toilets that use little or no water

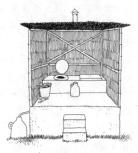

Simple compost toilet for tree planting
Best in places where people wish to plant trees and can manage a movable toilet (see page 126).

Urine diverting dry toilet
Best in places where people will use treated human waste as fertilizer, and where the groundwater is high or there is risk of flooding (see page 129).

2 pit compost toilet
Best in places where people will use treated human waste as fertilizer (see page 128).

Pour flush toilet
Best in places with deep groundwater and where people use water for anal washing (see page 136).

Ventilated improved pit (VIP) toilet
Best in places with deep groundwater and no risk of flooding (see page 123).

Closed pit toilet
Best in places with deep groundwater and no risk of flooding (see page 120).

Note: These drawings show toilets with no doors and no covers over the toilet hole, so you can see what they look like inside. All toilets should have doors, and toilet holes should be covered when not in use. Also, toilets should be made so that everyone in the community can use them (see page 111).

Where to build a toilet

When deciding where to build a toilet, make sure you will not pollute wells or groundwater. The risk of groundwater pollution depends on local conditions such as the type of soil, the amount of moisture in the area, and the depth of the groundwater. But some general rules can make sure conditions are safe.

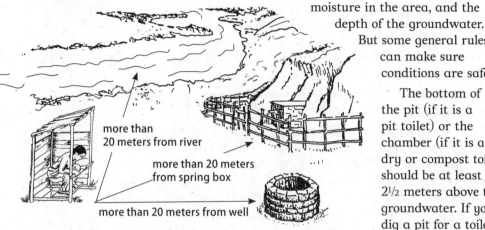

more than
20 meters from river

more than 20 meters
from spring box

more than 20 meters from well

A toilet should be at least 20 meters from water sources.

The bottom of the pit (if it is a pit toilet) or the chamber (if it is a dry or compost toilet) should be at least 2½ meters above the groundwater. If you dig a pit for a toilet and the soil is very wet, or if the pit fills with water, this is a bad place to put a toilet. Keep in mind that water levels are much higher in the wet season than in the dry season. Do not build pit toilets on ground that gets flooded.

When there is a risk of groundwater pollution from pit toilets, consider building an above ground toilet (such as the dry toilet on page 129).

Groundwater flows downhill. So, if there is no choice but to build a toilet in a place where there is a risk of groundwater pollution, place the toilet downhill from nearby wells.

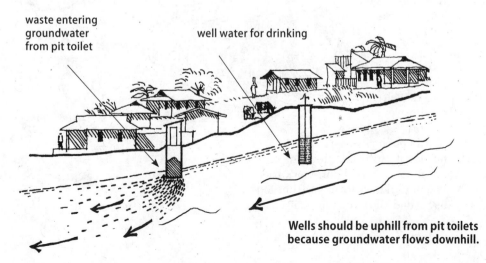

waste entering
groundwater
from pit toilet

well water for drinking

**Wells should be uphill from pit toilets
because groundwater flows downhill.**

Closed pit toilets

A closed pit toilet has a platform with a hole in it and a lid to cover the hole when it is not in use. The platform can be made of wood, concrete, or logs covered with earth. Concrete platforms keep water out and last many years. A closed pit toilet should also have a lining or concrete ring beam to prevent the platform or the pit itself from collapsing. (To make a concrete platform and ring beam, see pages 121 and 122.)

The ventilated improved pit (VIP) toilet shown on page 123 uses a vent pipe to reduce smells and flies.

A problem with pit toilets is that once the pit is full, the toilet can no longer be used. To take advantage of the waste in full pits, plant a tree on the site. To do this, remove the platform, ring beam, and shelter, and cover the waste with 30 centimeters (2 handwidths) of soil mixed with dry plant matter. Allow several months for the waste to settle, fill it with more soil, and plant a tree.

Another option is to add soil frequently while the toilet is in use and let it sit for 2 years to allow the waste to decompose. Then dig it out, use the waste as fertilizer, and use the pit again. Always wash hands after handling and digging the soil around toilets.

To make a closed pit toilet

1. Dig a hole less than 1 meter across and at least 2 meters deep.

2. Line the top of the pit with stones, brick, concrete or other material that will support a platform and prevent the pit from collapsing. A concrete ring beam works well (see page 122).

3. Make a platform and a shelter to put over the pit. A concrete platform works best, but local materials like logs or bamboo and mud can work too. If you make a platform from logs, use wood that does not rot easily.

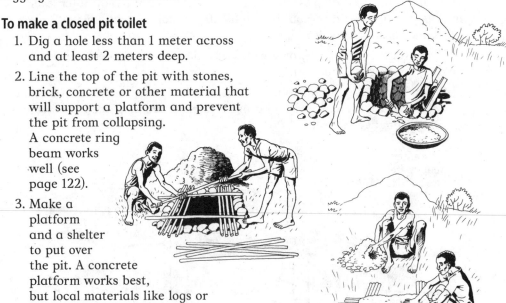

How to make a concrete toilet platform

A well made concrete platform will last many years. One 50 kilo bag of cement will make 4 platforms, or 2 platforms and 2 ring beams (see next page). You will also need reinforcing wires, bricks, and boards to form the mold, and wood cut to the shape of a keyhole to mold the hole. Platforms can be square or round.

1 Lay down a plastic sheet or used cement bags on flat ground. On top of this, make a mold of bricks or boards about 120 cm long, 90 cm wide and 6 cm deep.

2 Place a wooden keyhole mold in the center, to shape the toilet hole. You can also use bricks to block out the hole, and shape the hole after you pour the concrete.

3 Make a concrete mix of 1 part cement, 2 parts gravel, 3 parts sand, and enough water so that it is wet but holds together well. Pour the concrete into the mold until it is halfway to the top.

4 Place reinforcing wires 3 mm thick on top of the wet concrete. Use 4 to 6 wires going in each direction. Make handles of wire 8 to 10 mm thick, and set them in the concrete near the corners.

5 Pour the rest of the concrete, and level it with a block of wood.

6 Remove the keyhole mold when the concrete begins to harden (after 3 hours). If you used a brick mold, remove the bricks and form the hole into a keyhole shape. Cover the slab with wet sacks, damp cloth or a plastic sheet overnight. Wet it several times a day to keep it damp for 7 days. Keeping it wet lets the concrete harden slowly and become strong.

7 When the concrete has hardened, place the platform over the pit. To make the pit more secure, also use a ring beam.

8 Make a cover for the hole out of concrete or wood. It can have a handle, or make it to be moved by foot to keep germs off the hands.

Platform improvements

Because germs and worms can collect near the hole, foot rests will reduce the risk of health problems. If people prefer to sit, make a round hole and a concrete seat (see next page).

To make a mold for a seat, use 2 buckets of different sizes, one inside the other. There must be several inches between the sides of the inner bucket and the outer bucket. Weight the inner bucket with rocks so it stays on the bottom. Pour concrete into the space between buckets.

How to make a concrete ring beam

A ring beam is a square or round piece of cast concrete with an open center that supports the toilet platform and shelter, and keeps the pit walls from collapsing. The ring beam described here can be used along with the platform on page 121 for all pit toilets. The size of the ring beam you make depends on the width of the pit.

1 Lay down a plastic sheet or cement bags on level ground.

2 Make a mold of bricks, wooden boards, or both. For a platform that is 120 cm by 90 cm, the ring beam will be 130 cm by 1 m on the outside, and 1 m by 70 cm on the inside.

A mold for the ring beam

3 Make a concrete mix of 1 part cement, 2 parts gravel, 3 parts sand, and enough water so that it is wet but holds together well. Pour the concrete into the mold until it is halfway to the top.

4 Place 2 pieces of reinforcing wire 3 mm thick on top of the wet concrete on each side of the ring beam. If you want, you can make handles of wire 8 to 10 mm thick, and set them in the concrete near the corners.

Pouring the concrete

5 Pour the rest of the concrete, and smooth it with a block of wood.

6 Cover the concrete with wet cement sacks, wet cloth, or a plastic sheet, and leave it overnight. Wet it several times a day to keep it damp for 7 days.

7 When the ring beam is solid, carry it to the site of the toilet. Level the ground, place the ring beam, and dig a pit inside of it. Pack soil around the outside of the ring beam to set it in place.

Reinforcing wire

8 Place the toilet platform on top, then build a shelter.

Ventilated improved pit toilets (VIP)

The VIP toilet is an enclosed pit toilet that reduces smells and flies.

How the VIP works

Wind blows across the top of the vent pipe and carries away
smells. The shelter keeps the toilet dark so the flies in the pit will
go toward the light at the top of the pipe, get trapped by a wire
screen, and die.

To make the VIP toilet

1. Dig the pit 2 m deep and 1½ m wide. Line the top with bricks or a
   concrete ring beam sized to fit the pit (see page 122). If the shelter will be
   very heavy (brick, concrete, or heavy wood), line the whole pit, except the
   bottom. Leave gaps in the brickwork to let liquids out.

2. Make a platform (see page 121) 1½ m by 1 m, with
   2 holes in it. The second hole,
   near an edge of the platform,
   is for the vent pipe. Make
   the vent pipe hole no less
   than 11 cm wide.

3. Build a shelter over the pit
   and platform.

4. Fit a vent pipe at least 11 cm
   wide tightly into the smaller hole.
   Paint the vent pipe black to absorb heat and improve
   ventilation. Cover the top of the vent pipe with a mosquito
   screen (aluminum or stainless steel will last longest). Make the vent pipe
   rise at least 50 cm above the roof so the wind can pull out bad smells.

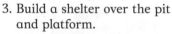

Make the vent
pipe hole the
same size around
as the vent pipe.

To use and maintain a VIP toilet

- Keep the hole covered when not in use.

- Keep the shelter dark inside.

- Keep the toilet clean and wash the platform often.

If the vent pipe gets blocked by spiderwebs, pour water down it.

If the wire screen breaks
or comes off the pipe,
replace it at once.

VIP toilets can have these problems :

If the shelter is not dark enough, or if the hole is left
uncovered, flies will not fly up into the pipe. And
if the shelter has no roof, or if the screen breaks or
comes off the vent pipe, there is little fly control.

Ecological Toilets

Ecological toilets turn feces and urine into soil conditioner and fertilizer. This improves people's health and the environment by preventing the spread of germs and turning harmful waste into a valuable resource.

Ecological toilets also protect and conserve water because no water is needed for their use, except for washing. They are safer for groundwater than other toilets because they sit above ground or use shallow pits.

Ecological toilets can be built and used in cities, towns, or villages. They need more maintenance than pit toilets (but not as much as pour-flush toilets), so it is important for people to understand how they work.

Turning waste into fertilizer

Rich, healthy soil needs **organic matter** (what is left when plants and other living things die and decompose). This natural process of organic matter breaking down into soil is called **composting** (see page 287).

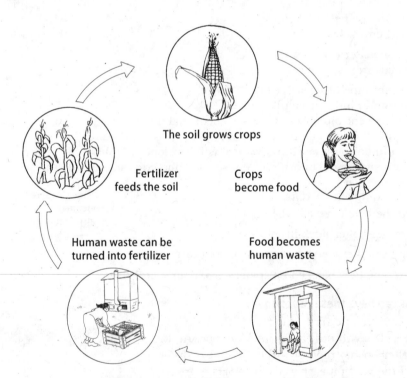

The soil grows crops

Fertilizer feeds the soil

Crops become food

Human waste can be turned into fertilizer

Food becomes human waste

Ecological sanitation turns waste into a resource.

Farmers make compost from food scraps and animal manure and add it to the soil. This keeps the soil full of **nutrients** for growing crops. Just as people need nutrients from food to grow strong and healthy, plants need nutrients in soil to grow strong and bear fruit.

Fertilizer can also be made from human waste. Human waste contains nutrients that can be used to improve soil. But it also carries germs that cause disease. For this reason, making fertilizer from human waste takes more care than composting animal manure and food scraps.

Feces should never be used fresh. But once made into fertilizer, feces safely help grow food, trees, and other crops without chemical fertilizers.

Urine carries fewer germs than feces and has more nutrients than feces. This makes it safer to handle and very valuable as fertilizer. But urine is too strong to use directly on plants, and also needs special treatment first (see page 134).

Compost toilets and urine diverting dry toilets

There are 2 main types of ecological toilets: 'compost toilets' and 'urine-diverting' or 'dry' toilets. Both of these can create safe fertilizer. Many people call both of these toilets 'compost toilets.' But there are some important differences.

In compost toilets:

- Feces and urine go into a container, like a shallow pit or a large concrete box that will not leak into the groundwater.

- The user adds a mix of dry matter such as straw, leaves, sawdust, soil and ash after each use. This reduces smells and helps the waste break down and become compost.

- Time will kill most germs, including roundworm eggs (the hardest to kill).

- After the mix has had a long time to kill germs in the feces (usually 1 year), the dry matter is removed for use as fertilizer.

In dry toilets:

- Urine is kept separate from feces (see page 129). It is collected, processed, and used as fertilizer.

- Feces go into a container, like a large concrete box or a hard plastic movable container that will not leak into groundwater.

- The user adds soil mixed with dry plant matter and ash to the feces after each use. This reduces smells and helps the waste dry out.

- The feces never get mixed with water. A dry mix will kill most germs, including roundworm eggs.

- The feces are stored for up to 1 year, until it has the texture of dry soil.

For both of these toilets, the aged feces mixture is ready after a year to be mixed into a compost pile, emptied into a shallow pit for planting a tree, or added directly into the soil for planting.

Dry toilets help local economy

In several towns in Morelos, Mexico, many people use ecological dry toilets. One neighborhood called La Cienega, has a special need for dry toilets because it is in a wet, lowland area where pit toilets get flooded. To solve the problem, members of the community bought a special kind of toilet bowl that separates urine from feces. These toilet bowls are built locally in small workshops with several local workers. The workers train community groups how to use these new toilet bowls.

Many people in La Cienega make a living by growing and selling fruit trees and other plants. The first people in the neighborhood to use dry toilets discovered they could use the urine and compost from their toilets as fertilizer for the trees. When their neighbors saw the trees grow big and healthy, they too wanted to try these new toilets that give free fertilizer.

Now, almost every family in La Cienega uses these toilets. The local workshop is busy making them, and the community has grown both healthier and wealthier.

Simple compost toilet for tree planting

This toilet makes fertilizer for planting trees. It is simple to build, and is made so the shelter can be moved when the pit is full.

This toilet is best where there is space and a desire to plant trees. It is also good for places with high groundwater, because the pit is shallow. Covering the toilet pit with soil and planting a tree there helps to decompose the waste.

This is a great way to start an orchard of fruit trees or other useful trees. If you do not plan to plant trees, use a different type of toilet.

Build a simple toilet for tree planting

Level the ground and place a concrete ring beam (see page 122) where you want the toilet. Inside the ring beam, dig a pit 1 meter deep. Secure the ring beam in place. Make a platform to put over the pit and ring beam. Build a light shelter for privacy that will be easy to move.

To use and maintain this toilet

- Before using, put dry leaves or straw in the pit. This will help feces decompose.
- Add a handful of soil mixed with ashes or dry leaves after every use.
- When the pile gets too high, stir it down with a stick.
- Sweep and wash the platform often. Be careful not to get much water in the pit.
- When the hole is nearly full, remove the shelter, platform, and ring beam.
- Fill the hole with 15 cm of soil mixed with plant matter. After several weeks, the waste will settle. Add more soil and plant matter, water, and plant a tree. Fruit trees grow well and bear safe and abundant fruit.
- Move the shelter, platform, and ring beam to another place, dig another hole, and do it again.

2 pit compost toilet

The 2 pit compost toilet is like the simple compost toilet for tree planting, but instead of planting a tree in the pit, the compost is dug out and used in the garden or fields. This toilet tends to be safer for groundwater than traditional pit toilets because the waste is mixed with soil in a shallow pit, allowed to dry out and kill germs, and then removed.

To build a 2 pit compost toilet

Dig 2 pits 1 to 1 ½ m deep, 1 m wide, and 30 cm apart. Add a lining or ring beam to both pits (see page 122). Place a platform and a simple shelter over one pit, and a concrete or wood cover over the second pit. Use the first pit until it is nearly full. A family of 6 will fill the pit in about 1 year.

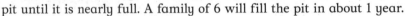

1. When the first pit is almost full, fill it with 30 cm of soil and cover it with a board or concrete slab. Move the platform and shelter to the second pit. Use it until it is nearly full.

2. Leave the first pit alone. Or, after it has settled for 2 months, add more soil and plant a seasonal vegetable like tomatoes right in the pit. Because the waste in the pit is still being processed, it is best to avoid crops that grow under the ground, such as carrots and potatoes.

3. When the second pit is full, empty the first pit with a shovel. Wear gloves, and wash hands after handling the fresh fertilizer.

4. Store the dry matter from the pit in open bags or buckets for later use, or add it to a compost pile or garden. (To know when the contents are ready, see page 133.) Move the platform and shelter back to the first pit, while the contents of the second pit settle. And so on...

To maintain a 2 pit compost toilet

- Keep a bucket of soil mixed with dry plant matter in the shelter. After each use, throw a handful in the pit.

- When the contents of the pit get too high, stir it down with a stick.

- Sweep and wash the platform often. Be careful not to get much water in the pit.

After 1 year, the contents of the 2 pit compost toilet should be safe to mix into garden soil as fertilizer. But it is still best to wear gloves and shoes when handling it.

Urine diverting dry toilets

Dry toilets do not use pits. They are built above ground so it is easier to remove the contents. They also have a toilet bowl with separate compartments that keep urine and feces separate. This helps the contents of the toilet stay dry, which kills germs and reduces smells. This also allows the urine to be used as fertilizer. Because they are built above ground and lined on the bottom, well built dry toilets do not contaminate groundwater.

Dry toilets are more costly to build than pit toilets. Their safe use requires training, because they are used differently than pit toilets and flush toilets. And it takes some work to keep them well maintained. But they are very good for people who want to produce fertilizer from their wastes. They are also a good choice in places where:

- The groundwater is too high for pit toilets.
- Flooding is common.
- The ground is too hard to dig.
- People want a permanent toilet in or near their house.

2 chamber dry toilets

This dry toilet has 2 chambers where feces break down into safe fertilizer. One side is used as the toilet while the feces on the other side dry and break down. A special toilet bowl that works for both men and women separates urine from feces. The urine drains through a tube into a container outside of the toilet. After about a year, the dried feces are removed and added to a compost pile or used on fields or gardens. The collected urine can be mixed with water and used as fertilizer (see page 134).

Parts of the 2 chamber dry toilet

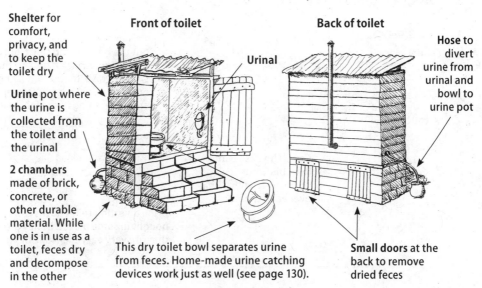

Shelter for comfort, privacy, and to keep the toilet dry

Front of toilet

Urinal

Back of toilet

Hose to divert urine from urinal and bowl to urine pot

Urine pot where the urine is collected from the toilet and the urinal

2 chambers made of brick, concrete, or other durable material. While one is in use as a toilet, feces dry and decompose in the other

This dry toilet bowl separates urine from feces. Home-made urine catching devices work just as well (see page 130).

Small doors at the back to remove dried feces

3 ways to build a dry toilet

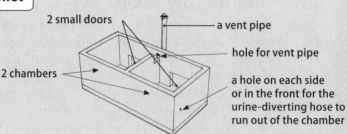

All 3 have a base made of concrete, brick, or any other waterproof material with these parts:

2 small doors

a vent pipe

hole for vent pipe

2 chambers

a hole on each side or in the front for the urine-diverting hose to run out of the chamber

BUILDING THE BASE

DIVERTING THE URINE

TYPES OF TOILETS

❶ For squatting

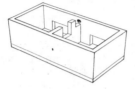

Leave a space in the dividing wall for a urine separating container to serve both chambers.

Cut the bottom off a 20 liter water bottle. Attach it, upside-down, to the space in the wall dividing both chambers. Attach a tube to the spout to divert urine, making sure there are no leaks between the jug and the tube. Put a fine mesh screen in the jug to keep feces and other things from falling in.

❷ For sitting, with a bench...

Cut the bottom and side from a plastic jug. Attach a tube to the spout to divert urine. Put a fine mesh screen in the jug to keep feces and other things from falling in.

❸ ...or with a toilet bowl

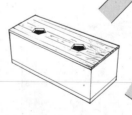

Cover the base with a level platform of wood or concrete with a hole over each chamber.

Urine diverting toilet bowls can be built or bought in some places. If they are available, they are very easy to install and use.

For all 3, build a shelter and steps. Attach doors in the back (concrete slabs held in place by lime mortar work well). Run the urine diverting tube out the hole in the toilet base to a container, a drainage pit, or into the garden to fertilize the soil.

FINISHING THE BASE

BUILDING A SHELTER

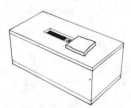

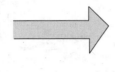

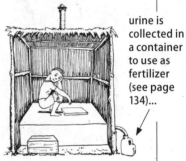

urine is collected in a container to use as fertilizer (see page 134)...

Cut a long squatting hole in a platform, with the upside-down bottle in the center. Urine goes into the bottle and feces into the chambers below either end of the hole. Put a cover on half of the hole, over the chamber that is not in use.

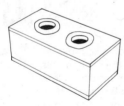

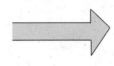

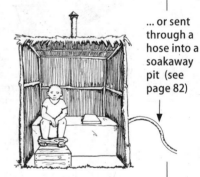

... or sent through a hose into a soakaway pit (see page 82)

Attach a urine diverter to the front of each hole. Put toilet seats over the holes.

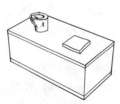

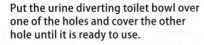

Put the urine diverting toilet bowl over one of the holes and cover the other hole until it is ready to use.

To use and maintain a 2 chamber dry toilet

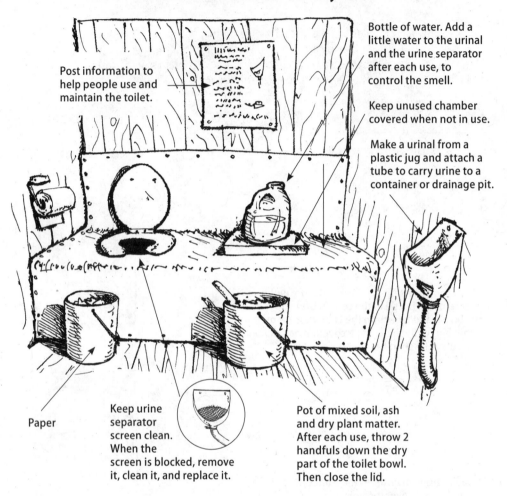

Post information to help people use and maintain the toilet.

Bottle of water. Add a little water to the urinal and the urine separator after each use, to control the smell.

Keep unused chamber covered when not in use.

Make a urinal from a plastic jug and attach a tube to carry urine to a container or drainage pit.

Paper

Keep urine separator screen clean. When the screen is blocked, remove it, clean it, and replace it.

Pot of mixed soil, ash and dry plant matter. After each use, throw 2 handfuls down the dry part of the toilet bowl. Then close the lid.

- Make sure no water gets in the feces holding part of the toilet chamber.
- If the contents of the toilet get wet, add more dry matter.
- If the toilet smells bad, add more dry matter, and make sure the vent pipe is clear.
- If the pile of feces builds up too high, use a stick to push it down.
- When the urine pot is full, empty it and make fertilizer (see page 134).
- When one chamber is full, use the other chamber. Be sure to cover the chamber that is not being used.
- It is best to let the feces sit for a full year before emptying the chamber. After a year, or when the second chamber is full, empty the first chamber and repeat the process.

Do not put garbage in the toilet

For ecological toilets to work, they must be used only for human waste. Women having monthly bleeding may safely use ecological toilets. But sanitary pads and other products should not be put in the toilet.

Do not put garbage in the toilet.

Ecological toilets cannot be used to dispose of things that will not break down, such as cans, bottles, plastic, tampons, or large amounts of paper. It is OK to use small amounts of paper, leaves, sawdust, and other plant matter because these things break down into soil.

When solid fertilizer is safe to use

The contents of a dry toilet are ready to remove when they are dry and have little or no smell. For this to happen, they should be kept dry inside the toilet chamber for 1 year.

When you think the contents are ready to remove, open the chamber. If the pile is wet, add dry plant matter or soil mixed with ash and let it sit for several more weeks. If the pile is dry and does not have a strong smell, it is ready. Remove it with a shovel.

After drying out for 1 year, most germs will be dead and the material should be safe to add directly to garden soil. But if there is any doubt, the waste can be stored in open bags or buckets in a dry, sunny area or added it to a compost pile.

Remove dry material for use as fertilizer.

It is important to wear gloves and shoes when handling human waste, and to wash well after emptying the toilet.

Urine fertilizer

Some farmers use urine mixed with water as a fertilizer because urine carries valuable nutrients such as nitrogen and phosphorous that can help plants grow. Urine is much safer to handle than feces. However, the same nutrients that make it a good fertilizer can pollute water sources. Also, urine can carry blood flukes (see page 56). Because of this, it is important not to put urine into water sources, or near where people drink or bathe.

To make simple urine fertilizer

Store urine for a few days in a closed container. This will kill any germs the urine contains, and will also prevent nutrients from escaping into the air.

To make fertilizer, mix 3 containers of water for every 1 of urine. You can fertilize plants with watered down urine as often as 3 times a week.

Plants fertilized with urine can grow as well as plants grown with chemical fertilizers, and need less water. Plants that have leaves you can eat, like spinach or other dark green leafy vegetables, grow best. Always wash your hands after handling urine.

3 jugs of water plus 1 jug of urine = safe fertilizer

To make fermented urine fertilizer

Adding compost to urine, and letting this mixture rot and turn sour (ferment), can create new soil for planting.

1. Collect urine from dry toilets. For each liter of urine, add 1 tablespoon of rich soil or compost.

2. Let the mix sit uncovered for 4 weeks. This will smell bad, so do it in a place away from people. The urine mixture will ferment and turn brown.

3. Fill a large container with dry leaves, straw, or other dry plant matter. Line the container with thick plastic to prevent water leakage through the hole in the bottom.

4. Add fermented urine. The best mix is 7 parts plant matter to 1 part urine (about 3 liters of urine for every 30 cubic centimeters of plant matter.)

5. Cover with a thin layer of soil (no more than 10 cm). Plant seeds or seedlings.

6. Water every 2 days with a mix of 1 part urine to 10 parts water. (This is a weaker mix than we suggest above, because it will be used in closed containers rather than in open gardens or fields.) The dry plant matter will turn to rich soil in 10 to 12 months.

The new soil can be used for planting.

Improved and adapted dry toilets

The toilets in this book are only some of the choices for ecological sanitation. They can be improved and adapted to meet the needs of different communities. Some things that will make a dry toilet work better are:

- **Heat from the sun** will help the waste decompose. Build the toilet so the chamber doors face the sun, and paint the door panels black. This will make the chambers heat up, improve air flow, and kill germs faster.

- **More air flow** will also help the waste decompose. Laying bamboo, corn stalks, branches, or other dry plant matter inside on the bottom of the chamber before use will help air flow through the feces for faster drying.

A wash toilet with plant bed

People in India have adapted the dry toilet to let both urine and wash water drain into a plant bed.

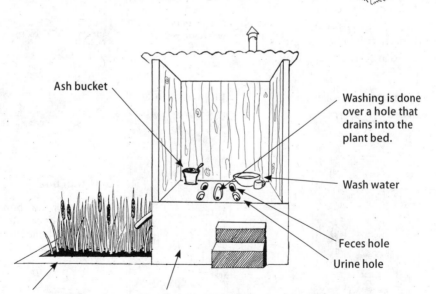

Ash bucket

Washing is done over a hole that drains into the plant bed.

Wash water

Feces hole

Urine hole

The plant bed where the wash water and urine go is filled with sand and gravel and planted with reeds or other local, non-edible plants. When the plants grow too big, they are cut back and thrown into the toilet.

The chambers under the toilet are lined with straw before use, to absorb moisture and make a good bed for the compost. Every time it is used, 1 or 2 handfuls of soil or ash are thrown in. Every now and then, some dry plant matter is added to help the material dry and decompose. After one year of use, the first chamber is opened and the material is put in a compost pile or into the soil for planting.

Pour Flush Pit Toilets

water seal trap

Pour flush toilets use water to flush waste into a pit. These toilets are common in both urban and rural areas where water is used to clean the anus after defecating. They are not much more costly than pit toilets. Because well built pour flush toilets prevent smells, they can be built in or near the home.

water seal trap set in concrete platform

Pour flush toilets use a plastic, fiberglass, or cement bowl or squatting pan set into a concrete platform. The bowl or pan often has a 'water seal trap' that prevents smells and insect breeding in the wet pits. The concrete platform is placed directly over a pit. Or it can be connected by pipe to 1 or 2 pits.

How to use a pour flush toilet

When there is 1 pit, the toilet is used until full, and then it must be emptied before it can continue to be used. When there are 2 pits, there is a junction box that directs waste towards the pit in use. The first pit is used until near full. Then waste is diverted into the second pit.

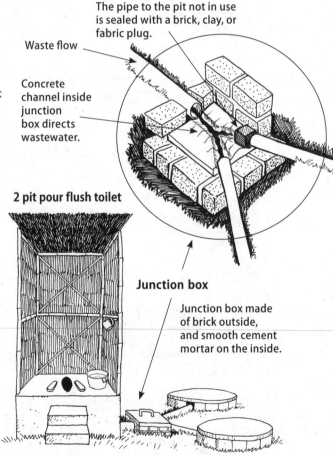

The pipe to the pit not in use is sealed with a brick, clay, or fabric plug.

Waste flow

Concrete channel inside junction box directs wastewater.

Junction box

Junction box made of brick outside, and smooth cement mortar on the inside.

1 pit pour-flush toilet

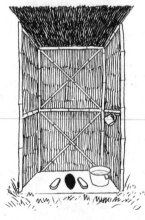

One lined pit underground, 2 meters deep. A family of 5 will fill this pit in about 5 years time.

2 pit pour flush toilet

Above ground chamber allows wastewater to flow down to pits. With regular care, this toilet will last many, many years.

When building a 2 pit pour flush toilet

Depending on soil conditions and groundwater level, pour flush toilets should never be built less than 3 meters from wells. In wet soil conditions the toilets should be at least 20 meters from wells.

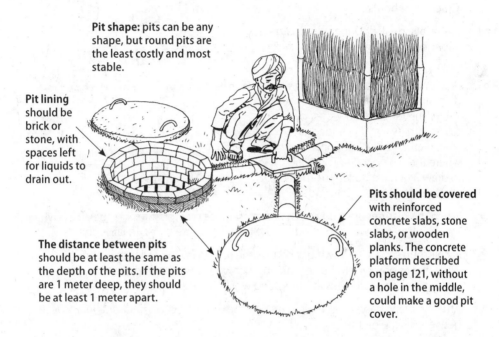

Pit shape: pits can be any shape, but round pits are the least costly and most stable.

Pit lining should be brick or stone, with spaces left for liquids to drain out.

Pits should be covered with reinforced concrete slabs, stone slabs, or wooden planks. The concrete platform described on page 121, without a hole in the middle, could make a good pit cover.

The distance between pits should be at least the same as the depth of the pits. If the pits are 1 meter deep, they should be at least 1 meter apart.

To maintain a pour flush toilet

Water must be poured in after every use. Pouring a little water in before using will also help keep the pan clean. Clean the toilet daily. To clean the squatting pan, use detergent powder and a long handled brush. The pits can overflow if:

- The water seal gets blocked. If this happens, the toilet will not work.
- The groundwater is less than 3 meters deep. When this is true, there is also a risk of groundwater contamination.

Emptying the pit

If the pits are built well and soil conditions and moisture are favorable, the waste will slowly and safely absorb into the surrounding soil, and the pits should not need emptying.

If waste does not decompose and absorb into the soil, the pit will need emptying. Remove the pit cover, add a layer of soil about 30 cm (2 handwidths) deep, and replace the cover. After 2 years, the contents can be removed with a shovel and used as fertilizer.

Choosing the right toilet

No toilet is right for all situations, and each sanitation method has room for improvement. This activity helps people think about what toilets are available and decide which one is best for them.

Time: 1 to 2 hours

Materials: small drawing paper, large drawing paper, colored pens or markers, sticky tape

❶ Make groups of 5 or 6 people. Each person draws a picture of every toilet or way of disposing of human waste that they know. They should draw their own toilets, others they have seen, and even pictures of what people do where there is no toilet. The goal is to draw a range of toilets, from the most simple to the most modern.

❷ When the pictures are ready, each group arranges their pictures in order, from what they think are the worst methods to the best. These are taped to large sheets of paper.

❸ Each group shows its drawings and tells the reason for the order they chose. What makes one system better and another worse? Each group member also tells which toilet he or she uses at home, and which he or she would like to have.

❹ After everyone has shown their drawings, the group talks about the differences between all the methods.

Ask questions such as:

- Does everyone agree about which toilet is the worst and which is the best?

- Is there one toilet that seems best to everyone? Is this because of health reasons, cost, or for some other reason?

- Are there some toilets that no one in the group uses? Why?

This can lead to a discussion of the reasons for people's choices.

- What health benefits are most important?

- What environmental benefits are most important?

- Would any of the improvements people want require changes in local conditions or how people think about sanitation? Are there simple things that can be done to improve what already exists?

- If the group includes both men and women, are their answers different?

❺ Introduce other toilets that people may not know about. This may include small changes to their current toilets such as vent pipes, or a new type of toilet. (It may include all the methods in this book, and others you may know of.) The group discusses these new ideas.

> To know what changes are **needed**, decide what health benefits and environmental benefits matter most.

> To know what changes are **possible**, decide which sanitation systems people want and can afford.

❻ Lead a discussion about the different methods, asking the group to think about the questions in the chart below. Each person shares his or her opinion about the benefits and risks of each toilet, using numbers to show how strongly he or she feels. For example, 5 may mean the best and 0 may mean the worst. Mark each person's opinion on the chart and count to see which method is judged best.

	Health benefits?	Environmental benefits?	Cost?	Work to clean and maintain
No toilet				
Closed pit toilet				
VIP toilet				
Compost toilet				
Dry toilet				
Pour flush toilet				

❼ The group makes new drawings based on the discussion of benefits and the new methods they have learned about. They tape the new and old drawings to large sheets of paper in order from worst to best. Finally, they compare the new order of the methods to the earlier order they had chosen.

- What differences are there?

- What ideas or information caused people to change their minds about what toilets are worst and best?

Based on this discussion, the group can decide what toilet or improvement is best for them.

Communication between men and women is an important part of choosing safe and healthy toilets.

8 Health Problems from Mosquitoes

Health Problems from Mosquitoes

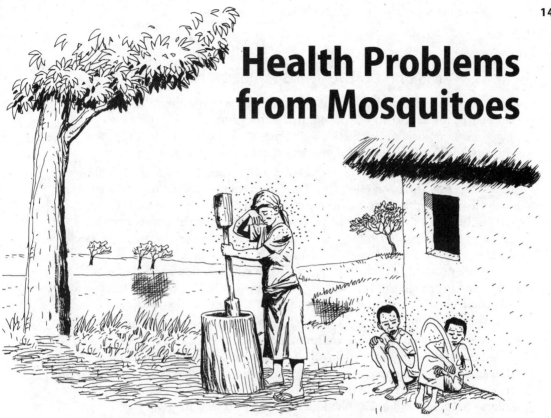

Mosquitoes carry serious diseases such as malaria, dengue, and yellow fever. These diseases spread quickly from one person to the next. Mosquitoes breed in water that does not move **(stagnant water)**, sometimes called "standing water."

To prevent diseases spread by mosquitoes:

- **Reduce the risk of being bitten.** Use window screens, safe insect repellents, mosquito coils, clothes that cover as much of the body as possible, and insecticide-treated bednets.

- **Control the spread of disease with treatment.** Make sure that people get quick and effective treatment, regardless of their ability to pay.

- **Get rid of mosquito breeding sites.** Cover household and community water supplies such as water barrels and cisterns. Create good drainage for taps, wells, and water run-off channels.

- **Prevent new breeding sites** through careful land and water management.

Rapid changes in land use, such as cutting down too many trees, building dams and diverting rivers, or removing vegetation from large areas of land, all create conditions that allow mosquitoes to breed.

Illnesses carried by mosquitoes spread even more quickly during emergencies such as wars, large movements of people, and natural disasters, when people find it difficult to take ordinary preventive measures.

Malaria on the Trans-Amazon Highway

For many years, the government of Brazil worked with communities throughout the country to prevent and treat malaria. After years of work, there was no longer much malaria in Brazil. But over time, with changes in land use, and with less health care and health promotion, malaria began to come back.

In 1970, the government began to build a new road through the rainforest called the Trans-Amazon Highway. The government built houses and farms along the new highway and moved people from the poorest and most crowded parts of Brazil to live there. Cutting a road through the rainforest destroyed millions of trees and left a large area with no groundcover. Rainwater collected in ditches and pools, making places for mosquitoes to breed. Animals and birds that would normally eat the mosquitoes were killed or fled from the area the road passed through. And there were few clinics or health workers to care for the people building the road and moving into the new settlements.

Wherever the highway went, malaria followed. Many of the people who built the road caught malaria, and many died from it, as did the people who settled along the completed highway. The new settlers suffered greatly because the soil was not rich enough for farming and rains damaged the road, making travel difficult. Poverty and isolation made health problems worse. Once again, malaria became the number one killer in the entire country.

How Mosquitoes Cause Illness

Three serious illnesses carried by mosquitoes are malaria, dengue fever, and yellow fever. Each of these illnesses has different signs and is carried by a different kind of mosquito with different breeding habits. (For malaria see page 144, for dengue, see page 147, and for yellow fever see page 148.) But these diseases can be prevented in the same ways because they are all passed from mosquitoes to people.

Prevent mosquito bites

All mosquito-borne illnesses can be prevented by preventing mosquito bites. To prevent mosquitoes from breeding, see page 149. To reduce the danger of being bitten:

- Wear clothes that completely cover the arms, legs, head, and neck (long sleeves, pants and skirts, and a head covering).

- Use mosquito coils and repellents like citronella, neem oil, or basil leaf. Repellents are especially important for children because they can prevent mosquito bites even when other preventive steps are not taken.

- Use screens on windows and doors.

- Use mosquito netting and bednets treated with insecticide to prevent bites while you or your children sleep. Tuck the edges of the nets under the bed or sleeping mat so there are no openings. In many places, pregnancy care programs offer bednets at low cost or no cost to women and young children. To be effective, bednets must be re-treated every 6 to 12 months. Also use a net when sleeping outdoors.

Note: Bednets are most effective for malaria, and less effective for dengue and yellow fever. See page 146.

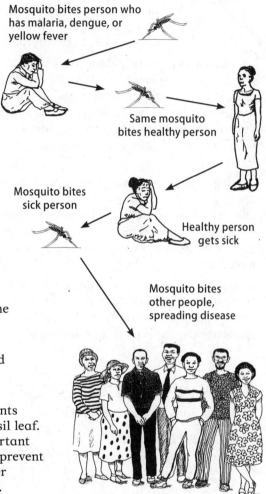

How mosquito-borne diseases spread

Mosquito bites person who has malaria, dengue, or yellow fever

Same mosquito bites healthy person

Mosquito bites sick person

Healthy person gets sick

Mosquito bites other people, spreading disease

Malaria

Malaria is an infection of the blood that causes high fever and chills. It is caused by a parasite (called plasmodium) that is passed to people by a certain kind of mosquito that bites mostly at night. Millions of people die from malaria every year, and many millions more live with the disease.

Malaria is especially dangerous to children under 5 years old, pregnant women, and people with HIV/AIDS. Pregnancy lowers a woman's ability to fight illness and infection. If she becomes ill with malaria, she may also get severe anemia (weak blood) which increases the chance of death during or after giving birth. Malaria in pregnancy can also cause her to lose the baby (miscarriage) or cause the baby to be born too soon, too small, or dead (stillbirth).

There are many kinds of malaria. People can live for many years with some kinds of malaria, and most kinds of malaria can be cured. But cerebral malaria (Plasmodium falciparum or P. falciparum) can cause death within 1 or 2 days of being infected. In areas where cerebral malaria exists, it is especially important to seek testing and treatment right away if you suspect you have malaria.

Usually malaria causes fevers every 2 or 3 days, but in the beginning it may cause fever every day. Anyone who suffers from unexplained fevers should have a blood test for malaria. This can be done at most health centers. **If the blood test is positive for malaria, or if testing is not available, get treatment right away.**

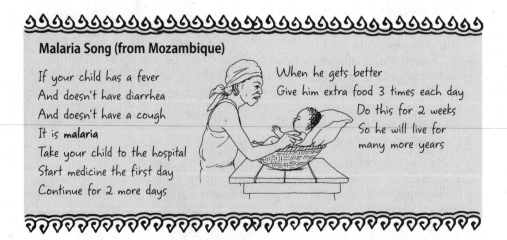

Malaria Song (from Mozambique)

If your child has a fever
And doesn't have diarrhea
And doesn't have a cough
It is **malaria**
Take your child to the hospital
Start medicine the first day
Continue for 2 more days

When he gets better
Give him extra food 3 times each day
Do this for 2 weeks
So he will live for
many more years

Signs

A malaria attack has 3 stages:

1. The first signs are chills and often headache. The person shivers for 15 minutes to 1 hour.

2. Chills are followed by high fever. The person is weak and at times not in his right mind (**delirious**). The fever may last hours or days.

3. Finally the person begins to sweat and the fever goes down. After the fever drops, the person feels weak.

Treatment

If possible, get a blood test. Start treatment as soon as the first signs show. Because malaria is passed from person to person by mosquitoes, treating a sick person also protects others from getting infected. After you have been treated, mosquitoes that bite you will not pass malaria on to others.

Find out what medicines for malaria your local health authorities recommend. In many regions, the malaria parasite has developed **drug resistance.** This means that medicines that once worked to prevent or treat malaria are no longer effective. Medicines that cure malaria in one region may not cure the malaria found in a different place.

There are new medicines or combinations of medicines now being given to treat malaria in different regions. One of these, artemisinin (used for many years in China), is often taken with another antimalaria medicine or with an antibiotic. In some areas, chloroquine (the most common medicine for many years) still works. The only way to know what medicine will work in your area is to check with your local health authorities.

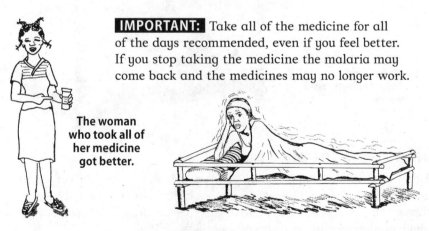

IMPORTANT: Take all of the medicine for all of the days recommended, even if you feel better. If you stop taking the medicine the malaria may come back and the medicines may no longer work.

The woman who took all of her medicine got better.

The woman who did not finish all her medicine is still sick in bed.

Prevention

Malaria occurs most often during hot, rainy seasons because the mosquitoes that carry it breed in warm, stagnant water. But in some areas of the world, malaria is also found in the dry season, when mosquitoes find breeding sites in small standing pools of water. As with dengue and yellow fever, the best way to prevent malaria is to avoid mosquito bites (see page 143) and to use community mosquito control (see pages 149 to 153).

Sleeping under an insecticide-treated bednet is a good way to prevent and control malaria. These bednets are treated with an insecticide called "pyrethrins," which is relatively safe, especially compared to getting malaria. The greatest dangers from insecticide-treated bednets are when they are dipped in the insecticide (leading to exposure through the skin), when children suck or chew on them (leading to exposure through swallowing), and when they are washed (because the insecticide can poison water sources and harm fish, insects, animals, and people downstream).

Bednets only protect if any holes or tears are quickly repaired. Also, the insecticide on the bednet wears off after 6 to 12 months, or sooner if it is often washed. If the bednet is still in good condition, new pesticide can be mixed and applied, but if the bednet has many rips or tears it may be safer to replace it. When reapplying pesticide, wear gloves and pay careful attention to the directions.

Malaria mosquitoes bite at night. To prevent malaria, sleep under an insecticide-treated bednet.

Treatment for all

Malaria is most common among poor people, and the number of deaths is growing each year. When people cannot afford blood tests and medicines, they are forced to live and die with this disease. And as long as one person has malaria, the infection can spread to others.

Malaria occurs most often in communities suffering from poverty and social injustice. For prevention campaigns to be successful, they must address the root causes of poverty and injustice as well as making treatment available for all.

Dengue Fever (Breakbone Fever)

Dengue fever is caused by a virus spread by a black mosquito with bands of white dots that look like white stripes from a distance. Their legs are also striped. This mosquito is sometimes called the "yellow fever mosquito" because it can also carry yellow fever (see page 148). Dengue usually occurs during the hot, rainy season. It is most common in cities, in places where water collects, and where there is poor drainage.

The first time a person gets dengue, she can usually recover with rest and lots of liquids. But when a person gets it a second time, it can be much more dangerous and may even cause death.

Signs

When first sick, a person gets a sudden high fever with chills, severe body aches (dengue is sometimes called "bone-break" or "breakbone" fever), a headache, and sore throat. The person feels very ill and weak. After 3 to 4 days, the person usually feels better for a few hours to 2 days. Then illness returns for 1 or 2 more days, often with a rash that begins on the hands and feet. The rash spreads to the arms, legs, and body (but usually not the face).

Babies, young children, and older people, or people with weak immune systems (such as people with HIV/AIDS), are especially at risk for a more severe form of dengue called hemorrhagic dengue. If not treated right away, this form of dengue causes bleeding from the skin and can lead to death.

Treatment

There is no medicine to treat dengue, and no vaccine to prevent it. It most cases, dengue can be treated at home with bed rest, drinking plenty of fluids, and taking **ibuprofen** or **paracetamol** (not aspirin) to reduce pain and fever.

IMPORTANT: Hemorrhagic dengue can only be treated by quickly replacing body fluids and blood. Go to a hospital immediately if the person starts to bleed from the skin, is unable to eat or drink, or acts confused (a result of fever, weakness, and the inability to stay awake). It is also important to get help right away if the sick person is a baby, young child, an elder, or has some other serious health problem, such as diabetes, heart disease, or HIV/AIDS.

Prevention

The mosquito that spreads dengue breeds in clean standing water. Unlike the malaria mosquito, the dengue mosquito bites mostly during the day. For this reason, bed nets have little effect except for small children or older people who sleep during the day. Dengue mosquitoes usually stay in shady, dark places, such as under tables or beds, or in dark corners.

To prevent dengue, avoid mosquito bites (see page 143) and practice community mosquito control (see pages 149 to 153).

Yellow Fever

Yellow fever is carried by mosquitoes in Africa and some parts of South America. There are two kinds of yellow fever and they spread in different ways:

Jungle yellow fever is spread from infected mosquitoes to monkeys, and back again from monkeys to mosquitoes. People get infected when they are bitten by mosquitoes that have been infected by monkeys. Jungle yellow fever is rare and mostly affects people who work in tropical rain forests.

Urban yellow fever is the cause of most yellow fever outbreaks and epidemics. Like malaria and dengue, urban yellow fever spreads when a mosquito bites and sucks the blood of an infected person, and then passes the infection to the next person it bites.

Urban yellow fever is spread by the same black mosquito that spreads dengue. It has white dots along its back and legs. These mosquitoes live and breed in standing water in cities, towns, and villages.

Signs

Yellow fever causes fever, chills, muscle pain (especially backache), headache, loss of appetite, nausea and vomiting, high fever and slow pulse. For most people, the illness goes away after 3 or 4 days.

But for some people, about 1 out of every 7, the fever returns 24 hours after the first signs go away. **Jaundice,** abdominal pain, and vomiting may be followed by bleeding from the mouth, nose, eyes, and stomach. Death may occur within 10 to 14 days, but half of the people sick with this second round of yellow fever survive with no serious damage to their health.

To help prevent yellow fever, get rid of places where mosquitoes can breed and keep water containers covered.

Treatment

The best treatment for yellow fever is bed rest and drinking plenty of fluids. Most people recover completely over time and develop a resistance to it. A small number of people do get the disease again, before they have recovered from getting it the first time. But they too usually recover.

Prevention

Like malaria and dengue, the best way to prevent yellow fever is to avoid mosquito bites (see page 143) and control mosquitoes (see pages 149 to 153). Vaccination is the only sure prevention for yellow fever, but may not be available or may be expensive.

Community Mosquito Control

Mosquitoes lay eggs in standing water. It takes about 7 days for mosquito eggs to hatch. By getting rid of standing water once a week, or by making water move and flow, mosquito breeding is interrupted and they do not live to spread diseases. To prevent mosquitoes from breeding:

- Get rid of places where water collects (standing water) such as old car tires, flower pots, oil drums, ditches, uncovered water storage containers, and any standing water inside the house.
- Manage land in ways that prevent water from collecting so the water will instead soak into the ground.
- Make sure watersheds are protected so that water will keep flowing (see Chapter 9).

Remove mosquito breeding sites around the house and community:

Clear drainage ditches so water can flow through.

Use screens on windows and doors.

Keep water containers covered.

Make sure there is proper drainage around community wells and water taps.

Clear away old cans, tires, or broken pots that collect water, and fill any pits.

Biological controls, such as a bacteria called BTi, are used in some places to kill young mosquitoes without harming the environment. (For more information about BTi, see Resources.)

Other methods used in community mosquito control programs include:

- **Breeding fish that eat mosquitoes.** The Central American mosquito fish, South American guppies, African tilapia, carp, and other fish can be used to control mosquitoes. These fish have different common names in different places, but are often called "mosquito fish."

- **Make sure water flows and fields drain** by restoring natural waterways, making drainage channels to let water move, and filling in unused irrigation trenches and ponds. Drain rice paddies once a week for 2 or 3 days to kill young mosquitoes without harming rice production.

- **Plant trees** to provide homes for birds, bats, and other natural helpers in mosquito control. Neem trees from Africa and India keep mosquitoes away and the leaves can be used as medicine.

Using insecticides

Where mosquitoes breed only part of the year, they can be quickly destroyed with insecticides. In the past, the pesticide DDT was widely used to kill malaria mosquitoes, and was sprayed outdoors over mosquito breeding sites. But DDT is a poison that does great harm to people and animals, causing cancer and birth defects (see Chapter 16). DDT can travel great distances in the air and in water, and stays in the environment for many years, becoming more dangerous over time. Because of this, less toxic insecticides are now recommended in most countries.

One type of insecticide, called pyrethrins, causes less long-term harm to people, animals, and the land. Another advantage of pyrethrins over DDT or malathion (another common but harmful pesticide) is that much less is needed to spray the same amount of space.

Pyrethrins do not collect in the environment. But they are toxic when people are exposed to them, and must be used with care. Pyrethrins irritate the skin and eyes, and cause rashes and difficulty breathing. Avoid direct contact with this insecticide, especially children and women who are pregnant or breastfeeding. Pyrethrins are very toxic if they get into water sources. **Never use pyrethrin products near waterways or ponds.**

Recently, DDT has come back into use in different ways than before. It is now recommended only for limited use indoors, in a method called Indoor Residual Spraying (IRS). This is spraying small amounts of DDT on the inside walls of a house to kill mosquitoes that land there. This method uses less poison in a smaller area, prevents it from entering water sources, and has less chance of causing mosquitoes to become resistant.

All insecticides are poisons. When using DDT, pyrethrins, or any other insecticide:

- Follow directions and spray with caution.

- Always wear protective equipment when spraying (see Appendix A).

- Use as little of the chemical as possible. Spray only where mosquitoes enter the home, and where they live or rest.

Insecticides are a short-term mosquito control measure. If you must use them, wear safety equipment.

- Never spray near children or women who are pregnant or breastfeeding.

- Make sure children do not suck or chew on insecticide-treated bednets, and that they touch the net as little as possible.

- When washing insecticide-treated bednets, use a basin and pour the wash water into a soakaway pit (see page 82) to protect waterways and drinking water sources.

Overuse of any insecticide can cause mosquitoes to become resistant to it and the insecticide will no longer harm them. (To learn more about the dangers of insecticides and how to use them as safely as possible, see Chapter 14.)

Spraying insecticides is an emergency measure for quick mosquito control. But insecticides will only reduce mosquito-borne illnesses if they are used as part of a program that includes treatment for everyone, communitywide control of mosquito breeding, and community education.

Stopping dengue by stopping mosquitoes

Over the past 25 years, people in Managua, Nicaragua have been increasingly getting sick with dengue fever. Because the mosquito that spreads dengue lives in water in and around homes, dengue spreads widely when more people move into tropical cities without safe water storage and wastewater drainage.

People in Managua worked with scientists, NGOs, and the Ministry of Health to reduce and prevent dengue in 10 neighborhoods. The first thing they did was to collect 'evidence' of the spread of dengue. Children collected samples of water with mosquitoes in different stages of growth, scientists tested children's saliva to see how many had been bitten by dengue-infected mosquitoes, and community members visited people's homes to ask them what they knew and thought about dengue.

They used neighborhood meetings, posters, and **sociodramas** to share what they learned about dengue. Children played games where they smashed hollow dengue mosquito puppets, scattering the candy hidden inside. Young people, including gang members, wrote and performed popular-style songs about preventing dengue.

Each neighborhood developed its own mosquito control program. Because they knew that mosquitoes breed in discarded tires, one group decided to collect old tires, fill them with soil, and use them to make stairways up steep paths. That got rid of mosquito breeding sites and made it easier to get up and down the hillside. Other tires were used as planters.

A group in another neighborhood made and sold low-cost lids for water storage barrels. This got rid of mosquito breeding sites while also earning money for their community.

The community dengue prevention program continues today. Not only are fewer people getting sick with dengue , but the program has brought other benefits:

- Young people, including gang members, were involved in making positive changes in their neighborhoods, which increased the community's togetherness.

- Musicians wrote popular songs to educate people, making dengue prevention fun.

- Different religious and political groups put aside their differences to work together on a common project.

- Local health activists were asked to serve on Ministry of Health governing boards for health posts and centers.

Now, people from these 10 neighborhoods are helping other communities get organized to stop dengue and improve community life.

9 Protecting Watersheds

In this chapter: **page**

Protecting Watersheds

No matter where you are, in a rural or urban area, you are in a **watershed.**
A watershed is an area of land where all the water from rain and snow drains
downward to a single body of water, such as a stream, river, lake, or wetland.
A watershed is also called a **catchment,** because the land uphill and upstream
"catches" all the water and then the water runs downhill and downstream.

A watershed can be very large, covering thousands of kilometers of land,
or it can be as small as one valley. Within each large watershed where water
flows from high hills to low valleys (such as a whole range of mountains) there
are many smaller watersheds (such as the small streams and other waterways
that run down toward rivers and the sea).

A healthy watershed protects water supplies, nurtures forests, plants, and
wildlife, keeps soil fertile, and supports self-reliant communities. Large and
sudden changes to a watershed, such as clearing trees and brush, dumping
waste, or building roads, houses, and dams, can damage the watershed and
its water resources. This can affect the land's ability to support healthy
communities, and lead to health problems, hunger, and migration. Planning for
changes in how water flows through watersheds, and how water and land will
be developed and used, can prevent future problems.

How Watersheds Work

Everyone's health is affected if the watershed is damaged. To understand how important watersheds are to the environment, it helps to think of rivers and streams as the veins of the earth. They carry and move water through the land the way our veins carry blood through our bodies. Just as we depend on blood for life, the environment depends on water for life.

The boundaries of any watershed are the peaks and ridges of the hills.

These small watersheds...

...are parts of the larger watershed.

The water cycle

Water is always moving. Sometimes it moves by flowing along, like a river. Sometimes it moves by changing from a liquid (water) to a gas (steam or water vapor) to a solid (ice or snow). But the total amount of water in the world never changes. All the water there is moves from the sky to the earth, soaking into the ground, flowing into rivers, lakes, and oceans, and then evaporates back into the sky. This movement of water is called the water cycle.

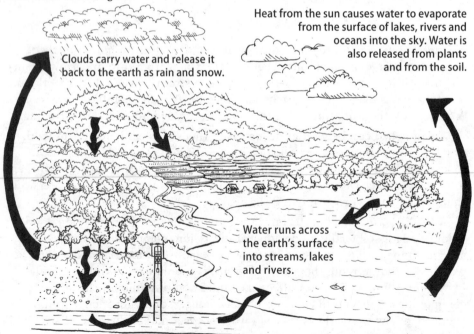

Clouds carry water and release it back to the earth as rain and snow.

Heat from the sun causes water to evaporate from the surface of lakes, rivers and oceans into the sky. Water is also released from plants and from the soil.

Water runs across the earth's surface into streams, lakes and rivers.

Water seeps into the soil where it nourishes plants and trees. It sinks underground where it is stored as groundwater, the source of water in wells and springs.

How watersheds protect water and soil

Most of the water in a watershed is not in the rivers and lakes, but in the soil itself. A healthy watershed has a supply of clean water and rich soil. Trees and plants, especially grasses, in the higher parts of the watershed and along the banks of rivers and streams, improve the quality and quantity of groundwater.

By protecting and conserving water, plants, and soil, we protect the watershed.

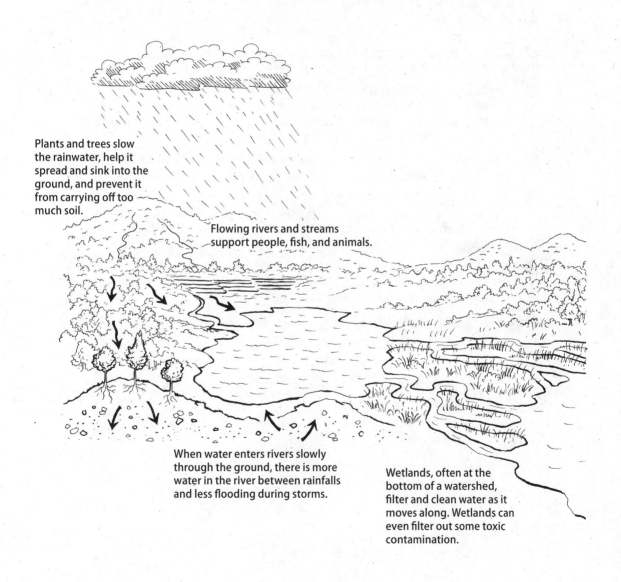

Plants and trees slow the rainwater, help it spread and sink into the ground, and prevent it from carrying off too much soil.

Flowing rivers and streams support people, fish, and animals.

When water enters rivers slowly through the ground, there is more water in the river between rainfalls and less flooding during storms.

Wetlands, often at the bottom of a watershed, filter and clean water as it moves along. Wetlands can even filter out some toxic contamination.

Make a watershed

This activity helps people understand how a watershed works and how all things within a watershed are important to the health of all the people living in the area.

Time: 30 to 45 minutes

Materials: For each group a large sheet of paper, a basin or pan, colored pencils or water-based colored pens, and water

1 Divide into groups of 3 to 5 people.

2 Each group takes their large sheet of paper, crumples it up, and then partly smoothes it out, being sure to leave some ridges and raised areas.

3 The group colors different features of the watershed on the paper, showing ridges in brown, valleys in green, rivers and waterways in blue. Then different colors can be added to show what people have added to the watershed: red for waste dumps, black for pesticides, gasoline, and other chemicals, and so on.

4 Place the paper in the pan or basin and fix the shape so that it resembles a watershed, with creased lines to show ridges and depressions to show valleys.

5 People in the group wet their fingers with water and gently flick water on top of the watershed until the colors begin to run on the paper. Within each group, discuss what happens to the colors as they run down into the lowest parts of the watershed.

6 Bring the groups together to discuss how what they have seen represents what happens in a real watershed. Note the distance that things can travel and the way different elements mix within the watershed.

Questions for discussion:

- What health problems can runoff from waste dumps (red color) and pesticides (black color) cause for people living downstream?

- What changes do you think your community would see if the watershed were damaged?

- What actions could your community take to protect or restore the watershed?

Watershed damage in the Aguan River Valley

40 years ago the hills above the Aguan River were forested. The valley was one of the most fertile regions in all of Honduras, and provided a good livelihood for people in many villages and farms. Many small, clear streams flowed down from the hills into the blue Aguan River. The river flowed through the heart of the valley and into the Caribbean Sea.

Then people started cutting down trees to use more land for farming and cattle grazing. Big fruit companies came in and cut down more trees to make banana plantations. Families started moving into the hills because the best valley land had been taken by rich landowners. Finally, most of the trees were cut down and there were many more people living on the hillsides. There was less water in the river and streams, and the water was no longer clear.

The people of the Aguan Valley knew things had changed, but it took a hurricane to make them understand how much their watershed had been damaged. Heavy rains caused landslides in the hills. Many homes and entire villages were washed away. Many people died and many more became ill.

As they worked together to recover from the storm, people began to see that the loss of trees on the hillsides, the landslides, and their health problems were all related. Cattle polluted their drinking water, causing diarrhea and other illness in their children. Harvests got worse. Because the soil no longer held water from the rainy season, the fields dried out quickly. Then when the winter rain came, it washed the soil away. Harvests were so poor that people were always hungry, and hunger made their health problems worse.

The villagers began to understand that to improve their health, they had to protect their watershed.

After the discussion of the "Health effects of damaged watersheds," the Aguan River Valley story continues on page 163.

Health effects of damaged watersheds

When land is cleared of trees and plants (deforestation), soil holds less water, drying up wells and springs. Dry periods may become longer or more frequent, causing all the health problems of not having enough water (see Chapter 5). Deforestation also causes loss of soil (erosion, see page 200) which makes growing food more difficult, leading to hunger and migration.

When wetlands are destroyed, they cannot filter toxic pollution out of the water, leading to greater contamination. Damage to wetlands and deforestation both cause flooding which leads to injury, death, and increases in diarrhea diseases.

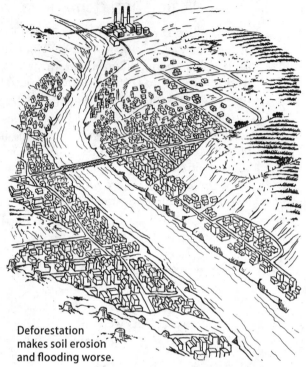

Water contamination from industry and industrial farming pollutes water.

Deforestation makes soil erosion and flooding worse.

Destroying wetlands by too much building or paving over land causes more flooding and water contamination.

Changes in a watershed increase illnesses from mosquitoes

Mosquitoes breed in slow-moving and standing water. When large or sudden changes are made in how land is used and how water flows through the watershed, they often create conditions for mosquitoes to breed. Changes from:

- Digging out riverbeds for building materials like gravel and sand, and precious minerals like gold, often leaves stagnant pools.
- Damming rivers creates standing water, and changes the way water flows (see page 170).
- Building roads can block the flow of water and create stagnant pools.

If you can keep the water moving, changes to the watershed do not have to lead to more mosquito-borne illnesses such as dengue, malaria, and yellow fever. For more about preventing problems from mosquitoes, see Chapter 8.

Protecting and Restoring Watersheds

The land in a watershed is usually owned by many different people. It can be difficult to get everyone's cooperation to restore and improve a watershed. But because the watershed includes everyone, it is important for as many people as possible to support and participate in efforts to protect the watershed.

Sustainable development protects watersheds

Some changes to watersheds, such as building roads, damming a river to provide irrigation or electricity, or draining wetlands to reduce breeding grounds for insects, are made in the hope of improving people's lives. But if these changes are made without considering how water naturally moves through the watershed, they may cause more harm than good.

Houses and businesses are built away from the river's edge

Forests slow water runoff and spread it across floodplains.

The natural curves of the river reduce flooding.

Wetlands filter contamination and absorb floodwaters.

There are many ways to make improvements to living conditions that will not damage the watershed, helping it to remain healthy for people now and in the future.

- Make sure water supply and sanitation projects are well managed for the benefit of local communities and the environment (see Chapters 6 and 7).
- Work to keep the forests healthy (see Chapter 10).
- Plant crops using sustainable methods to keep farmland rich and fertile (see Chapter 15).
- Get rid of waste safely and create less of it (see Chapters 18 and 19).
- Build houses, roads, and settlements so as not to change the natural flow of water through a watershed or cause erosion, and so they are protected from seasonal flooding.

Benefits of protecting a watershed

Protecting a watershed often involves settling disputes over land, marking clear boundaries, developing plans for the flow of water, making agreements among neighbors about the use of land and water, and gathering and sharing the resources necessary to do the work.

In many communities, these are not easy projects. Local and regional governments may become involved in settling disputes — sometimes for better, sometimes for worse.

When communities work to protect their watersheds, there is more water for everyone.

But if people can work together to protect the watershed, it will mean having more water. Since water scarcity causes or worsens conflicts, having more water will improve relations among people as well as protect community health.

Some benefits of protecting a watershed are:

- more and cleaner water in wells and springs.
- better crop yields, even during dry times.
- healthier livestock.

With more water, more crops are produced. This increases people's incomes, making them less likely to leave their homes in search of work.

The story from page 159 continues here.

Improving health in the Aguan River Valley

The hurricane that hit Honduras affected everyone in the Aguan River watershed, so everyone was willing to work together to recover. People from towns and villages all over the valley began to meet. There had been landslides everywhere and many people were without homes. With help from the Catholic church, they began talking about how to fix their problems in a lasting way.

As they rebuilt their communities, they learned that the way they farmed could either damage or protect the land. Farmers could improve the soil and prevent erosion by planting in rows across the hillsides instead of up and down. And drainage ditches, stone walls, and other barriers they made could protect their hillsides. The farmers were glad to learn new ways to protect their lands. But they also knew that the people doing the most harm were the cattle ranchers and plantation owners.

Villagers and farmers began visiting families who had large banana plantations or ranches with many cattle. The villagers spoke with the large landowners about the importance of protecting the water for everyone. "It is not only the poor who suffer from the effects of damaged land and contaminated water," they said. "It is all of us."

Over time, even the richest landowners in the valley began to help in the recovery effort. Some agreed to fence the creeks and springs to keep cattle out. Others, who owned land in the hills, let the villagers who had land below plant trees on their hillsides. Farmers from the valley approached landowners near the hilltops and offered to trade some of their land for permission to fence and protect the lands above. It was better for ranchers to have valley land for their cattle and better for the whole community to keep cattle off the hilltops, so the plan helped everyone.

After the hurricane, villagers in the Aguan River Valley began to have good relations among people who once had rarely spoken to each other. They learned that by protecting their watershed, they and their children would have cleaner water and safer homes. This is good for the watershed and good for the community.

Planning a community watershed project

The watershed team of the Aguan River Valley followed these steps in beginning to protect their watershed:

1. Find out the condition of the watershed

As a group, with community leaders, teachers and other people, visit places important to the health of the watershed. Depending on the size of the watershed, this may take 1 day or several weeks.

Visit the main waterways, and note where they connect with one another. Make notes about who lives in which parts of the watershed, and how land and resources are used in different areas. Visit the places where people collect water, places where water may become contaminated (such as near factories, pastures, and places where trash collects) and other areas of concern.

Why do you think the river is so contaminated?

The water downstream by the factory is warmer than before. The rocks where my husband used to fish are covered in slime.

Speak with people about the changes they have noticed over time. Hunters and people who fish know where the animals are, and where they used to be, at different times of the year. Your community is full of experts about your watershed.

OUR WATERSHED

river

homes   water   toilet   cattle   hills   factory
        source

2. Make a map or drawing of the watershed

After these visits, discuss what you have learned and how to best share the information with the whole community. Discuss what things can cause harm to the land and water. It can help to make a map of the watershed and mark the places of concern. Elders can help by making maps of how things used to be and how they have changed. (For more about mapping, see page 15.)

3. Organize a community meeting

Organize a meeting of people from all the communities in the watershed. It is especially important to invite health workers, people responsible for water and sanitation, landowners, business owners, and people who collect water.

Use your map or drawing to explain the problems you found. Encourage people to share their concerns about health and discuss how problems might be caused by water contamination, deforestation, soil erosion, and other watershed issues.

The goal of this discussion is to begin moving from identifying problems to the process of solving them. As each issue is raised, ask: How could we start solving this problem right now? Will we need technical support, money, or other resources? Who needs to be involved?

4. Build partnerships

Meetings and watershed walks are ways to build partnerships among people in a watershed. Organize meetings with people who live in the downstream parts of the watershed, and other meetings with those who live upstream. Then organize meetings with representatives from the different groups. Identify common goals and find ways of working toward them so everyone benefits.

Partnerships can sometimes be difficult to build, especially in a large watershed. Different groups or communities will often have their own ideas of what should happen in the watershed and may have difficulty understanding or accepting the needs and ideas of others. Differences in power, resources and influence can cause serious conflicts. But when everyone's needs and contributions are respected, not simply those of people with wealth or status, strong partnerships can develop. Openness and honesty in working relationships will help create trust. And if all partners are expected to contribute to the partnership, they should also benefit from it.

Think about some of the deals made in the Aguan River Valley. One group planted trees on other people's land. Wealthy ranchers agreed to fence creeks and springs. Some people even traded land. Determination, patience, and benefits of more and cleaner water allowed partnerships to grow and succeed.

5. Make an action plan

Set clear goals and make an action plan. One goal may be to have trees growing near all water sources in 5 years. Another goal may be to protect a river so that in 50 years it will be safe to drink.

The action plan could include the protection of some land by not using it at all, especially near streams or on hilltops. Post "Watershed Preserve: Do Not Use" signs or mark trees with paint.

The first to benefit from watershed protection are usually people at the bottom of the watershed (by having more water and improved soil). Make an action plan that includes the needs of those at the top of the watershed who will only benefit later. When everyone in the community works together, the plan is more likely to succeed.

Aguan River Valley Watershed Action Plan

1. Do not cut vegetation near water sources.
2. Help young trees grow, and reforest areas that have few trees, especially close to water sources.
3. Start community nurseries to grow plants for reforestation.
4. Organize groups to prevent and fight forest fires. Educate local farmers not to burn their fields, or how to do safe, controlled fires.
5. Fence the area around water sources and post "Protected Area" signs.
6. Encourage farmers to conserve soil by using green manures, recycling crop wastes, building retaining walls, and planting on contour lines.
7. Discourage the use of chemical pesticides and fertilizers.
8. Work with the local government and water commissions to move toilets, sewer systems, and washing areas away from water sources.
9. Organize community trash collection, and prevent trash from washing into streams and rivers.
10. Move cattle away from water sources, and mark areas where no cattle should graze.
11. Make sure people who have just moved to the community and new businesses learn about the watershed and how they can help care for it.

These steps can be a model for any community's watershed protection project. The most important part of the project is to involve as many people as possible in agreements that will benefit everyone in the long term.

Managing the Way Water Flows

When water flows into the ground or into waterways, it is called **drainage**. Good drainage reduces the dangers of flooding and erosion, and helps more water soak into the ground. Poor drainage causes soil erosion and stagnant water.

The best way to improve drainage is to make the **surface water** after a rainfall (called runoff) "walk off" rather than "run off," so that it slows down, spreads out, and sinks into the ground. To do this:

- Avoid cutting down plants and trees, especially on slopes and along streams and rivers.

- Direct surface water to plants, irrigation ditches, and low areas. Gardens can be planted or fishponds built in places where water collects (see page 309).

Regular cleaning of drainage channels helps prevent flooding and illness.

- Build live barriers, low walls, and other erosion control structures to hold and direct surface water (see page 293).

- Improve soil using sustainable farming methods, so water sinks into the ground (see pages 282 to 289).

- Direct wastewater from taps and wells into drainage ditches or soakaway pits (see page 82).

- Collect runoff from roofs in cisterns and containers for drinking water (see page 86), or direct it into ponds, fields, and gardens.

- Maintain roadside plant life or build drainage channels alongside roads and keep them clear of blockages.

Turn rainwater into a household resource.

Watersheds in towns and cities

When a town or city is built, it changes the way water flows through the watershed. Urban development brings more hard surfaces such as roads, pavements, and roofs that cause rainwater to run off rather than to soak into the ground. This can cause water to collect and stagnate, providing places for mosquitoes to breed. It may also lead to flooding.

Where people gather in large numbers and industry develops, more pollution contaminates the water. Keeping wetlands and riverbanks healthy in towns and cities can be difficult, but it is especially important because wetlands prevent polluted water from collecting, contaminating plants and animals, and damaging human health.

To protect their part of the watershed, people in towns and cities can:

- Safely dispose of human wastes and toxic chemicals to prevent them from polluting water sources (see Chapters 7, 16, and 20).

- Restore riverbanks, streams, and wetlands as parks within the city. Some communities plant gardens alongside roads to help water sink into the ground, rather than drain into sewers.

- Campaign to have city governments provide safer homes for people living in dangerous flood areas.

- Pressure businesses and industries to take responsibility for their wastes.

- Get involved through city government and civic organizations in regional planning and sustainable development efforts.

Watersheds in cities and towns are easily contaminated, but they can be protected!

Large Dams Damage Health

A dam is a wall built across a river. Dams are built to block the flow of a river and form a human-made lake called a reservoir. Water stored in reservoirs can be used to control flooding, to provide water for irrigation and drinking, to make electricity, or for recreation.

Dams have contributed to building modern cities and improving many lives. But large dams, more than 15 meters tall and sometimes as tall as 250 meters, also harm people and the land in many ways.

How a large dam made the Yaqui people sick

Many years ago the Yaqui people lived by farming in the hot, dry climate of northern Mexico. Thanks to their river, the Rio Yaqui, they had water for farming, for drinking, and to meet their needs all year.

This all changed when their river was dammed. The Mexican government agreed that half of the water from the dam belonged to the Yaquis. But the Yaquis soon found that no water arrived at their villages. The entire river had been channeled into a giant canal to irrigate many large industrial farms growing wheat and cotton. These large farms soon surrounded the Yaqui villages, and the Yaqui people were left with no water for their own crops.

To grow wheat and cotton in dry desert soil requires a lot of water, chemical fertilizers, and pesticides. Pesticides are sprayed as many as 45 times in the months between planting and harvest. All of this poison ends up in the irrigation canals. With their river diverted and no other source of water, the Yaquis drink from the canals. Over the years, the polluted water made them sick.

After years of drinking contaminated water, Yaqui children were having problems learning, thinking, growing, and playing. Many children also suffered from severe health problems such as cancer of the blood (**leukemia**) and birth defects, such as withered limbs and soft bones. These health problems are most likely caused by drinking water and breathing air poisoned with pesticides.

The Yaqui people's health problems began when their river was dammed.

Dams cause problems upstream and downstream

First, dams create problems for people who live upstream from where the river is or will be blocked.

Displacement and poverty

People are displaced by dams and forced to migrate. Many end up living on poor land or in urban slums. Displaced people may be promised money or land. But often money is not handed over by local officials. Many times, only people with legal title to land that will be flooded by the dam receive money or other land. Sometimes, the replacement land is too poor to farm.

Towns that will be flooded by a dam do not receive government funds for upkeep and development, so schools, roads, and health services fall into neglect. Some towns remain like this for many years before they are flooded.

Dams builders are oppressed. They often have unsafe work conditions, poor housing, bad food, and little access to health care. These conditions promote illnesses such as TB and HIV. After a dam is built, they must find another place to live and work.

Dams destroy communities. Families living in the reservoir area lose their homes, lands, and livelihoods. Displaced people are often not resettled together. People are usually poorer after they move.

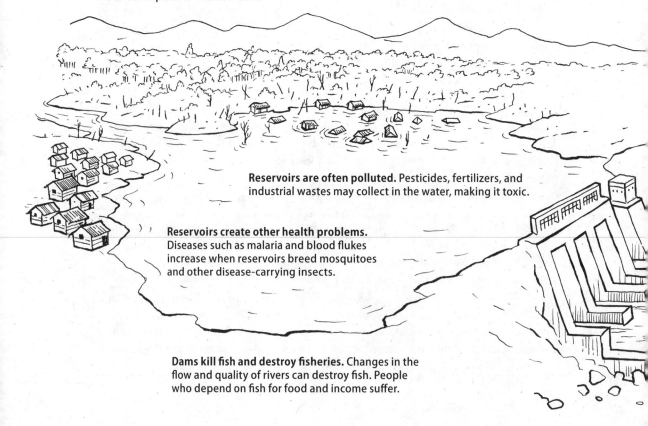

Reservoirs are often polluted. Pesticides, fertilizers, and industrial wastes may collect in the water, making it toxic.

Reservoirs create other health problems. Diseases such as malaria and blood flukes increase when reservoirs breed mosquitoes and other disease-carrying insects.

Dams kill fish and destroy fisheries. Changes in the flow and quality of rivers can destroy fish. People who depend on fish for food and income suffer.

Dams destroy the natural flow of the river. They cause either an increase or decrease in water flow, depending on the dam. The natural cycle of flood and drought may be disrupted, affecting the entire river and damaging huge areas of land.

New insect breeding grounds

Mosquitoes breed in the shallow, sunny waters of irrigation canals, and at the edges of reservoirs. Regularly raising and lowering the level of the reservoir can kill young mosquitoes. But the people who manage dams do not usually consider this important.

Black flies that spread river blindness lay their eggs in fast flowing water, like the water that flows out of a dam. The still waters in dam and irrigation projects are breeding grounds for snails that carry blood flukes (see page 56).

Erosion of riverbanks and floodplains

When a dam blocks a river, bits of soil and rock carried by the water (silt) settle on the river bottom and in the reservoir instead of on riverbanks. When water is let out of the reservoir, the water has no silt in it. Because silt is part of what makes land rich for farming, downstream lands become poor. And because water released from the dam collects silt as it moves, it further erodes the land as it digs deeper into the riverbed.

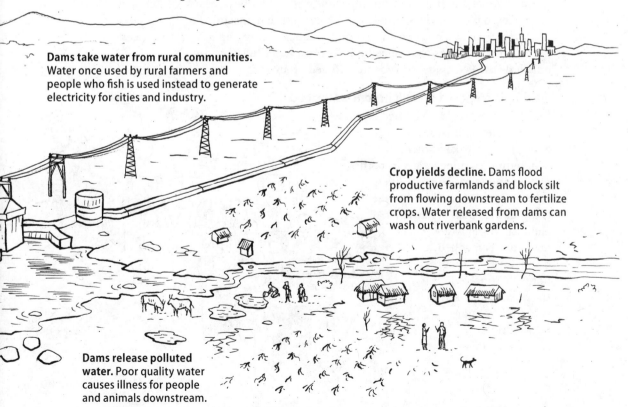

Dams take water from rural communities. Water once used by rural farmers and people who fish is used instead to generate electricity for cities and industry.

Crop yields decline. Dams flood productive farmlands and block silt from flowing downstream to fertilize crops. Water released from dams can wash out riverbank gardens.

Dams release polluted water. Poor quality water causes illness for people and animals downstream.

Alternatives to large dams

When there are plans to build a dam, the first question to ask is: Is it necessary? Dams are built for flood control, electricity, irrigation, and to provide water to growing cities. These services could be provided in less harmful ways.

The second question to ask is: Who is going to benefit? Around the world, communities that would be harmed have resisted big dams and proposed alternatives. In many cases, they are succeeding.

Flood control. If possible, avoid building in natural floodplains and wetlands. Improve warning systems to help people prepare for floods. Preserving the natural flow of rivers can prevent floods more effectively than damming them.

Electricity. Encourage governments and developers to promote wind, solar, or small-scale water power that generates electricity close to where it will be used. Locally managed and controlled energy is more sustainable for people in cities and towns, as well as in rural areas (see Chapter 23).

Irrigation. Local development provides better water security than large dams. In the state of Gujarat in India, thousands of small check dams (see page 293) have been built to collect rainwater for use in the dry season and to replenish the groundwater. The government and villagers share the cost of the check dams. Many villages that once had water to irrigate fields for only half the year, now have water all year round.

If a dam is proposed or built in your watershed

Communities worldwide have been resisting new dams, working to have old ones taken down, and demanding compensation in both money and land for harm they have suffered from dams. Some communities also demand changes in the ways dams are controlled, to help rivers flow more naturally and reduce the harm dams have caused. (For more information, see Resources.)

Intertribal partnership protects the Yukon River

In Alaska and the Yukon Territory at the border of the United States and Canada, the mighty Yukon River flows 2300 miles (3700 kilometers) through many towns and villages. Because the river is threatened by contamination, 60 indigenous communities signed a treaty agreeing to work as partners to keep the river clean for future generations. They formed an alliance called the Yukon River Intertribal Watershed Council.

The Watershed Council did not begin by trying to clean up the entire river. They started with small projects and clear goals. One of their first programs was to ban the use of plastic bags in towns along the river. By banning plastic bags, people along the river learned that taking personal responsibility could make a big difference in protecting the watershed.

After the plastic bag ban succeeded, the communities began cleaning up discarded batteries, oil, and broken down cars. Every community in the watershed built a landfill and set up a bin to collect batteries, keeping poisons out of the soil and water. Then they worked to convince all the small airlines, shipping companies, and military bases in the area to dispose of old batteries, cars, and oil safely.

Now, Yukon tribal governments are improving their sewage systems and landfills, and creating programs to recycle and reuse trash. They teach young people to test the water for pollution and to recognize signs of contamination in order to prevent it.

The Yukon River Intertribal Watershed Council built partnerships with tribal, state, local, and national governments in Canada and the United States, and with environmental and watershed groups, funding agencies, and outside advisers. By bringing many groups together, the Watershed Council was able to make a plan that included everyone in the watershed, and to gather enough resources to get the work done.

By taking small steps at first and then larger steps, the Watershed Council encourages change that is slow, but effective. One member of the Council said, "When I was a child I drank water straight from the river. In 50 years we will be able to drink from the river again."

10 Forests

In this chapter: page

Forests

Forests provide essential resources such as food, firewood, building materials, fodder, medicines, and many other things. Trees and forests also play an important role in sustaining a healthy environment. They keep the air and water clean, prevent erosion and flooding, enrich soil, make homes for birds, animals, and plants, provide shade, and make our communities beautiful.

In order for forests to continue providing resources and sustaining a healthy environment, they must be well cared for, managed fairly, and used wisely. But because forest resources are valued by industries as well as by communities, and because the land under forests is sometimes wanted for other uses, forests around the world are being cleared faster than they can grow back. Sometimes logging companies or other industries that clear forests, such as mining, offer people sources of income they desperately need.

However, there is a balance to be found between the need to use land and resources, and the need to protect these resources for the future. Whenever too much of a resource is used, it causes far-reaching and long-lasting harm. Many communities which have lived off the forest for generations know that they will be seriously harmed if too much of the forest is used up or cleared.

The Green Belt Movement

Wangari Maathai, a woman from the East African country of Kenya, says Mount Kenya used to be a shy mountain, always hidden behind clouds. This mountain is sacred to her people because many rivers flow from the forests that once covered the mountain's slopes. Now, Mount Kenya is no longer shy. The clouds that covered it are gone, and so are the forests. And with the loss of the forests and clouds, the rivers also have begun to dry up.

As she grew up, Wangari saw how deforestation led to soil erosion, loss of water sources, and a scarcity of firewood. She began to understand that deforestation caused poverty and drought. So Wangari began planting trees.

Wangari organized a group of women to plant trees around their homes and fields. Because they planted trees in rows or "belts," they became known as the Green Belt Movement. The women of the Green Belt Movement began to teach other people how their lives were affected by deforestation and to plant trees with them. They brought fruit trees to farmers, and planted them on hillsides to prevent erosion. By planting trees in both cities and villages to create green spaces, give shade, and to provide firewood, they showed how planting trees could solve many problems. The Green Belt Movement also planted vegetable gardens, built small dams to capture rainwater, and held workshops to help people understand the need for healthy forests.

In taking responsibility for their environment, the Green Belt Movement realized they needed the support of their government to care for the environment for the good of all Kenyans. Planting trees became an expression of a movement for peace and democracy in Kenya. When conflicts arose between different communities, the Green Belt Movement used "peace trees" to help bring them together.

As a woman who planted trees, Wangari became a hero in her country. But she also faced many hardships. Unable to live with such a strong woman, her husband left her. Because she organized among the poor, her government arrested her. But because of her bravery, and the work of thousands of Kenyans, the Green Belt Movement succeeded in planting millions of trees.

In 2004, Wangari Maathai won the Nobel Peace Prize, one of the most honored awards in the world. The prize was given to her for promoting peace through a sustainable development that includes democracy, human rights, and equality for women. And it all started with planting trees.

Forests and Health

Forests support the health of people everywhere. Even people who live far from forests, or in areas where forests have been degraded or severely damaged, depend on the things forests provide. When forests are degraded or destroyed, community health is threatened because the processes and functions that trees and forests carry out in support of health are not done.

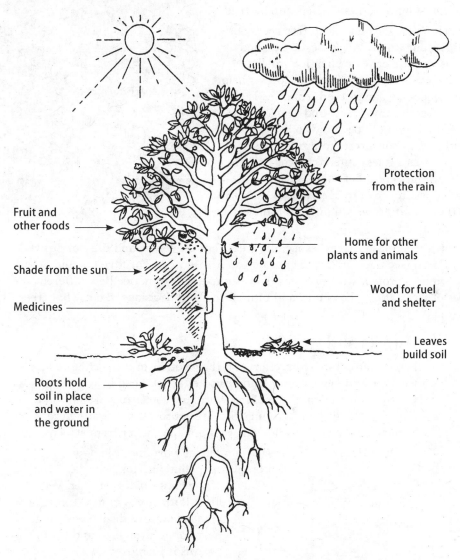

Trees and forests support community health and well-being in many ways.

Forests and water

Some people believe trees attract rain and hold water close to the ground. Others believe trees use more water than they make available, and that they compete with crops. Depending on the kinds of trees, where they grow, and other conditions, both of these beliefs can be true.

Rich forest soils and deep tree roots act as filters for water. When pesticides, heavy metals, and other toxic chemicals pollute surface water and groundwater, forests help filter them out. The filtered water feeds our wells, streams, and lakes, and keeps our watersheds and the people who live there healthy. Without forests to protect water sources, there is less safe water for drinking and bathing. For all of these reasons, it is usually best to leave trees standing rather than cut them down, especially if your water is clean and abundant.

But some kinds of trees, especially trees that grow fast and are not native to the area (see page 202), may use up water resources. For farmers and others who want to protect water resources, it is important to notice how different types of trees affect the water, and to make careful decisions about what trees to plant.

Forests and weather

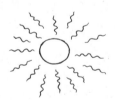

Forests have important effects on the weather and the climate (the weather in a place over a long period of time). They help make weather less extreme by making warm air cooler and wetter, and making cold air warmer and drier. Trees protect houses and crops from strong winds and hot sun, and provide shelter from strong rains.

On a larger scale, forests fight global warming (see page 33) by absorbing toxic pollution. This helps keep the climate of the entire planet milder. When we lose large areas of forest, the threat of natural disasters such as hurricanes, droughts, and heat waves is increased.

Where forests have been cleared, the weather becomes more extreme.

Forests prevent erosion and reduce flooding

By adding leaves to the soil, providing shade for plants that grow beneath the trees, and holding soil in place with their roots, trees prevent erosion and reduce flooding. They slow rainwater and spread it across the ground, so it will sink into the soil rather than run off.

When forests are cleared, soil washes into rivers and streams. When storms come, the soil is no longer able to absorb and hold the rainwater. Instead, the water flows faster across the land, causing floods. Keeping trees and forests standing is an important way to protect the natural flow of water through the watershed. (For an activity that shows what rain does to bare soil, see page 289.)

Forest diversity and health

In a forest, it is easy to see the web of life (see page 27) because a healthy forest contains many different kinds of plants and animals. This diversity of life protects people's health in many ways. Bees and other insects that live in trees **pollinate** crops so they flower and produce fruit. Wasps and ants eat insects that attack crops. Bats and birds eat mosquitoes that spread malaria, yellow fever, and other diseases. Other forest animals keep rats, fleas, flies, and ticks under control by hunting them or competing with them, and prevent them from spreading disease.

When human settlements are built in or close to degraded forests, the number and variety of animals are reduced because their sources of shelter and food become less plentiful and less diverse. Also, the animals that remain are forced to live in closer contact with people. This leads to a greater possibility that animal diseases will be passed to people. By maintaining enough forest to support a variety of plants and animals, we protect human health.

Forests, food, fuel, and medicine

How can we cook if the food and firewood from our forest are all gone!

Forests contain a large variety of fruits, nuts, seeds, roots, insects, and animals that serve as food and medicine for people. When forests are degraded, it often results in hunger, malnutrition, and illness. People who depend on these resources must find other ways to survive. When foods and medicines from the forest are lost, the knowledge of how to prepare and use them is also lost. In this way, the loss of forests leads to the loss of important knowledge and traditions.

In places where resources are scarce, people sometimes feel forced to choose between keeping forests standing and cutting down trees to plant crops for food. But even for farmers who clear the forest to plant crops, keeping some trees is important. In areas where farming competes with forests, it is important to try to keep a balance between them. (For more about forests and farming, see page 302.)

Women's burden

Women and children often do the hard work of collecting and carrying wood for fuel. The burden of this work over many years can lead to health problems. As forests are destroyed, people must travel longer distances to collect wood. This gives them less time to do other necessary work and to go to school.

Women and children may also face physical and sexual violence when they travel to collect wood. Because of this, in some places women and girls go in groups to collect firewood during daylight hours. By planting and maintaining good firewood trees close to home, the people who collect wood can stay safe and healthy.

Carrying heavy loads over long distances can cause headaches, backaches and, especially in children, damage to the spine.

Forests and Livelihood

Forests are an important source of livelihood. Some governments and international organizations say the greatest damage to forests is caused by poor people who cut down trees to farm or earn their livelihood in other ways. But when people do not have enough food, income, or other basic needs, the need to survive becomes more important than the need to preserve forests. Sometimes people have no choice but to cut trees, whether to clear new farmland or to harvest firewood and lumber. The blame for forest destruction is rarely placed on industries that take huge amounts of wood or cut down forests for mining, oil exploration, or industrial plantations.

When people's daily needs are met they are better able to think about the future, including how to care for the environment. People who live in and care for forests know there are many ways to earn a living from the forest without causing too much damage. In many cases, deforestation is caused by the demands of industry and the pressures of poverty.

Deforestation causes poverty and poverty causes more deforestation.

Farming in the forest

Farmers in many places clear spaces in the forest to plant crops, leaving the surrounding forest untouched. They farm there until weeds begin to compete with their crops. Then they clear a new plot and the forest grows back in the old plot and restores the soil. This is sometimes called "slash and burn," or swidden farming.

Swidden farming has been done for thousands of years. But as populations grow and settle new areas, the amount of forest available to farm this way is reduced. Neither is there enough land to let farm plots be reclaimed by forest. Swidden farming has become unsustainable, both for the farmer and for the forest. Communities that farm in forest areas can get better results and remain on their land longer if they use sustainable farming methods (see Chapter 15).

Protecting forests and livelihood

In the forests of Andra Pradesh, India, villagers clear patches of forest to grow crops. But in the months when there is little food from their farm plots, many people's livelihoods depend on things that grow in the forest. Some villagers gather and sell wood for fuel, while others use wood to make tools to sell. The way the villagers are allowed to use forest resources is controlled by groups called "community forest committees."

When the forest committees saw that some areas were being damaged from overuse, they made new rules to reduce the amount of wood that could be taken. The rules were very strict, and many people's livelihoods were threatened. People who survived by selling wood for fuel and making tools no longer had this income. During the months when food was scarce, these families suffered.

The members of the forest committees came from these same communities, so they wanted to find a solution that made sure no community member went hungry, but still protected the forest. After many meetings, a decision was reached. Instead of changing the new forest rules, the forest committees would help to improve farmland by building contour barriers to slow the movement of water and prevent erosion. This would make the soil richer and provide more water for crops so farms would be more productive and there would be more food for everyone without endangering the forest.

Ecotourism

Ecotourism is a way to earn money from visitors coming to see the natural beauty of an area, or to learn about the plants and animals that live there. Some ecotourism projects bring people only to enjoy the natural beauty. Others invite them to live with people in the community to learn about protecting the environment. Still other projects invite tourists to actively work on projects to protect the environment.

Carefully managed ecotourism can protect forests.

Ecotourism is a good way for forest communities to earn money. But starting and running a project can be costly, and needs careful planning. Tourists require food, comfort, lodging, guides, and lots of patience in dealing with cultural differences. They may have accidents or need health care. Getting tourists to visit requires advertising in magazines or on the internet, printing brochures, and doing other forms of publicity.

Ecotourism projects must be carefully managed so the money they bring benefits the community, not just outside agents or businesses, or a few local families. Successful ecotourism projects often limit the number of tourists who visit, in order to cause less pressure on the community and less damage to the environment.

Non-timber forest products

Non-timber forest products are anything besides wood that can be taken and sold without damaging the forest. This includes nuts, fruits, medicinal plants, and fibers. Communities that have success selling non-timber forest products have found it important to follow these guidelines:

- Set clear rules about who may harvest and sell the product, and how to best harvest it in a sustainable way. Once a product becomes successful, it is in danger of being overharvested. Collect only enough of the product that it can continue to grow and reproduce.

- Find or develop a market for the product. There is no point harvesting products if they will not sell or be used.

Harvesting medicine from the forest

Near the Bay of Bengal in India, many people go to traditional healers when they are sick. These healers make medicines from plants gathered in the forest. One day, people from a non-governmental organization (NGO) came to a village there to help people earn money by gathering these medicinal plants and selling them in the city. By using their organization to sell these medicines, they helped the community make money from the forest without cutting down trees.

The villagers were glad to have a new way to earn money, and many people began to collect and sell the medicinal plants. But they did not ask the healers how to collect the plants without damaging them, and they were not careful about how much they gathered.

In their excitement to earn money, some villagers harmed the trees they collected from. Instead of digging around a tree to collect a few roots some people cut down the whole tree. In a short time, the medicinal plants had mostly disappeared from the forest. This left traditional healers with no plants to use for healing. So the villagers had to spend a lot of money to buy medicines at the pharmacy when they were sick. In the end, the health of both the people and the forest suffered from harvesting plants in a way that did not protect them for the future.

Forest Destruction

Most forests are destroyed by logging companies and other corporations that profit from unsustainable resource use. When one forest is destroyed, the big companies simply move to another forest. But the people who live in or near the destroyed forest usually have nowhere else to go.

People who do not live off forests directly still use many forest products, such as books and newspapers, building materials, foods such as beef, soy, and palm oil from plantations cut out of the forest, and minerals dug from beneath it. Rarely do people consider the need to replace forests used up in these ways.

How forests are degraded and destroyed

If forest resources are not used and managed in ways that allow the forest to continue growing and producing, all of our forests will soon be gone. Causes of large-scale damage to forests include:

- **Clear cut logging** (when most of the trees in an area are cut for lumber) compacts and erodes soil, destroys wildlife, and fills waterways with silt.

- **Large commercial farming,** cattle ranching, and **tree plantations** often involve clearing land of forests.

- **Shrimp farms** are built by cutting down and clearing mangrove swamps and other coastal forests, often putting small fishing communities out of work, contaminating water, and leading to increased sickness, poverty, and malnutrition.

- **Paper mills** leave behind toxic waste that pollutes the land, water, and air.

- **Mining, oil, and gas companies** cut down forests and leave behind toxic waste that poisons water, land, and air.

- **Large dam projects** flood large areas of forest. People forced to move from the dam site then cut down more forest to make new homes and fields.

Corporations and governments seldom consider the effects on people's health and livelihoods when forests become products to be bought and sold.

Forest Conflicts

Because forest resources are limited, conflicts often arise among people who need to use the forest resources in different ways. Conflicts also arise between local communities that depend on the forest and industries from outside the community that want the resources the forest can provide.

Sociodramas

A sociodrama is a way to use theater to help think about conflicts and the causes of those conflicts. Sociodramas can also help people explore possibilities for action and change. (See page 17 for more about sociodramas and role plays; also see the Hesperian book, *Helping Health Workers Learn*.)

❶ **Divide into groups** of about 5 people each and give each group a short description of a situation that might lead to conflict over forest resources. Make up situations that are believable to people, but avoid local situations that might shame or anger the people involved in them. The plays will be more realistic if the participants use a few simple costumes and props to show the parts they are playing.

❷ **Ask each group** to spend 15 to 20 minutes to prepare a 5 minute sociodrama. Encourage everyone to play a part. Each group presents their play for the other participants. After each sociodrama is over, a discussion about community conflicts can lead to solutions. Or you can wait until all groups have presented and discuss them all together.

❸ **How did you feel?** After presenting the sociodramas and before the discussion (see page 189), ask each participant how it felt to play their part. Ask the people who watched how they felt during each sociodrama, and how the actors made them feel about the conflict.

> *A facilitator should be aware of conflicts in the community and be sensitive to the ways different community members may react to the discussion. During sociodramas, be careful to create a safe and open environment where people are not afraid to speak.*

Sociodramas (continued)

Choose some of the stories below to make sociodramas about forest conflicts. Or make up sociodramas based on real conflicts in your community.

Situation 1. Characters: man with cattle; herbal medicine collectors; community meeting participants.

After years away from the community, a man returns with 10 head of cattle and begins to graze them on community forest land. When other community members go to the forest to collect medicines and thatch, they find that the cattle have eaten so much there is little left for them. They call a meeting to discuss the problem. The man with the cattle insists he has a right to graze his cattle, no matter how much they eat. Others in the community disagree. What happens next?

Situation 2. Characters: young men cutting trees; government workers; women collecting firewood.

Several young men are cutting down trees on communal land without permission, and selling the lumber to local government workers, who take the lumber away on a truck. A woman goes to the place where she usually collects firewood and finds the young men cutting down trees. One of the men is her son. She returns to the community and tells the mothers of the other young men. The next day, the women go to the forest to tell the young men to stop cutting down trees. The first woman's son says he needs the money from selling trees to buy medicine for his baby daughter, her granddaughter. What happens next?

Situation 3. Characters: community members with axes and oxen; government men with chainsaws and trucks; village council officials.

For generations, people cut down trees using axes and hauled them out with oxen. Now, men from the local government have been coming with chainsaws, cutting down trees and saying the forest is state property. One day the government men show up with bulldozers and heavy equipment. They want to build a road into the forest to take out the biggest trees. A group of men from the community goes to the forest to confront them. What happens next?

Sociodramas (continued)

4 **Discuss each sociodrama**

Ask the actors to leave their props or costumes in a pile at the front of the room and return to the group. Then ask questions that help the whole group to:

Having the actors "step out" of their roles before beginning the discussion prevents people from labeling one of the participants as a villain or victim. It's important not to confuse the person with the role he or she plays.

- tell what happened in the sociodrama.

- identify the actions that led to conflict.

- identify the different needs that were the root causes for the conflict.

- suggest ways the conflict could be resolved in the long term.

Repeat this process with each sociodrama. The facilitator may want to write the important ideas on a large piece of paper or a chalkboard.

Q: What caused the conflict?

A: One man wanted to keep cattle, but they damaged the forest.

Q: Why did the man feel he had a right to graze his cattle in the forest?

A: There was no agreement about who could use the forest, and for what purposes.

Q: How did the forest damage affect the community?

A: No more medicine and thatch.

Q: So what needs are in conflict?

A: The need to have forest products and the need to graze cattle.

Q: Is there a way for both needs to be met?

A: The cattle could graze in areas with no plants that the community needs.

A: The cattle owner could build a fence.

A: The owner of the cattle could give up his right to collect forest products in exchange for the right to graze his cattle, and then trade for the forest products when he needs them.

If the discussion creates a lot of disagreement, it is important to end in a way that brings everyone together. Singing a song together or doing a cooperation activity can help people leave with a better feeling.

Sustainable Use of Forests

Sustainable forest management means using and caring for forests in ways that meet daily needs while protecting the forests for the future. Sustainable methods are not the same everywhere. Each community needs to find what works best for them and for their forest.

Making a sustainable forest management plan helps a community decide how best to use their forest. It can also help resist threats to the forest by industry or the government. Sometimes, you can get a better price for forest products if you can show they were produced sustainably. But the most important part of a sustainable forest management plan is that it helps local people work together to use and protect forests.

Some ways to both use and protect the forest at the same time include:

- **Thinning** vines, plants, and trees allows more sunlight into the forest, so that the plants you want can grow.

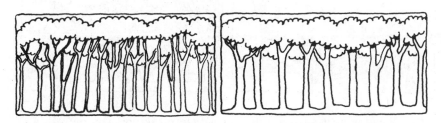

Thinning trees means cutting certain trees so the ones that remain grow wider and healthier.

- **Enrichment planting** means planting new trees or plants under older trees or in small clearings when they do not grow back by themselves.

- **Replanting after cutting** is a way to make sure there will be new trees and seeds to replace the ones that were cut.

- **Controlled burning** can reduce brush that grows under trees. This releases nutrients into the soil, and kills pests that might hurt the trees. Controlled burns need careful planning because fires can easily burn out of control.

- **Selective logging** means cutting only some trees, while saving young trees and some healthy older trees to hold soil and provide seed for the future.

Selective logging protects some trees for the future, allowing forests to continue growing.

- **Collecting and selling non-timber forest products** rather than selling wood is a way to care for the forest while also earning money.

- **Paying** ranchers to keep grazing animals out of the forest, and paying farmers not to cut trees on part of their land, can support healthy forests and prevent conflicts.

- **Preserving wildlife corridors** (areas of connected forest or wild land) lets wildlife live in and travel through an area.

- **Planting green spaces,** smaller areas of trees in places where most trees have been cut down, or where the forest is completely gone, is a way to improve the soil, water, and air even in populated cities and towns.

- **Supporting natural regrowth** of forests by limiting the use of areas where too many trees have been cut helps forests recover.

- **Using animals** to haul logs causes less damage than bulldozers or other heavy machinery.

Animals compact forest soil less than machines.

- **Trimming bark and branches** from fallen trees before taking them out of the forest causes less damage to other plants when the tree is hauled out. The bark and branches rot and make good soil.

- **Ecotourism** earns money by showing visitors the natural beauty of a forest, without having to cut trees or damage the environment.

There are many ways to use forests that keep them healthy for the future.

Use everyone's knowledge, consider everyone's needs

This activity helps a community consider how to use and care for forest resources in ways that benefit everyone. It can be done with up to 25 people, divided into 3 smaller groups. It is important to include everyone who will be affected by decisions about forest use.

Time: 3 to 6 hours (or in more than one session, as long as you save the maps)

Materials: Pens, pencils, notebook paper, 3 big pieces of paper with maps of your area, and sticky tape. The maps can be roughly drawn, as long as people can recognize what they intend to show.

1 Give 1 map to each group. Ask every person to draw pictures of what they do in the forest (cut firewood, graze cattle, gather fruit and plants, hunt, etc.) on their notebook papers.

2 Within each group, every person talks about what they drew and what it means to them. 1 or 2 people then draw pictures on the big map to show where and how each person uses the forest.

3 Bring the groups together for a discussion about what their big maps show. Are some parts of the forest used more than others? Do men, women, children and older people use the forest in different ways? Were there any surprises in the ways the forest is used?

4 The facilitator leads a discussion about the health of the forest by asking questions like these: Does the forest provide the same resources now that it always did? Are there fewer birds, animals, and plants than there once were? Are there places where all the trees have been cut down? What happens now in those places?

5 Have 1 or 2 people from each group mark their map using different colors or symbols to show places where the forest is healthy, degraded, or gone.

6 Think about the different areas of forest and discuss what changes people want to see. Draw or write them on the map. On the following page are some questions that can help guide a discussion.

Make a forest management plan

After doing the activity on page 191, consider these questions:

- **What benefits and resources does the forest give us?** What trees, plants and animals are used? How much is used in each season? Are there areas where these resources have grown scarce or have disappeared?

- **How do we support the forest?** Does the community plant trees, protect certain areas, or have other ways of making sure the forest stays healthy?

- **Should some parts of the forest be protected from use?** How will that affect people who use those parts of the forest?

- **Should sustainable methods be practiced in some parts?** What knowledge does the community have about caring for forests that can help to make these changes?

- **What skills do we need to make sustainable forest management a success?** If we do not have those skills, can we learn them? Will we need to rely on other organizations? How can we form strong alliances with organizations we trust to help us gain skills and knowledge?

- **How can our community keep control over our forest projects?** Well-organized communities that present a strong and clear message to outsiders about what they want usually receive greater benefits from sustainable forestry projects.

- **How will we get our products to market?** It is often more expensive to get products to national or foreign markets than to sell products locally. Local prices are lower, but the cost of selling is also lower.

- **How much will our forest products be worth?** If you wonder whether you are receiving a fair price for forest products, you may want to contact some fair trade organizations (see Resources).

- **What changes will the new plan bring?** Will the new management plan limit some people's ability to use the forest? How will the community help them in return?

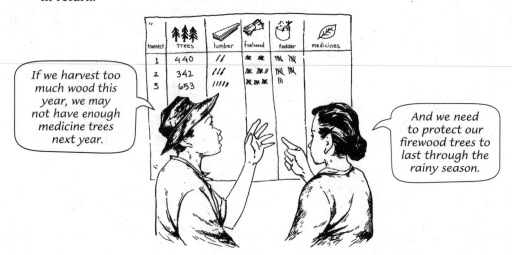

If we harvest too much wood this year, we may not have enough medicine trees next year.

And we need to protect our firewood trees to last through the rainy season.

Partnerships to protect the forest

Building partnerships with as many as possible of the groups that benefit from the forest helps make sure the forest is used in ways that meet everyone's needs. Partnerships with people outside your local area can also help protect your rights.

Working together to protect the Amazon rainforest

The people of Amazanga did not always live where they do now. An oil spill forced the members of the Quichua tribe to move from their traditional land in the Amazon. When their new homes were threatened by deforestation and industrial farming, the villagers decided that managing their lands according to the traditions of their people -- hunting, fishing, and gathering plants for food and medicine – was the best way to protect their lands.

But this required more land than they had. Amazanga demanded that the government grant them territory to live as their ancestors had lived. "We cannot live from a piece of land like a piece of bread," they said. "We are talking about territory, and the right to live well from the forest." When the government ignored their demand, they asked international environmental groups for help buying back their ancestral lands.

The villagers invited their international partners to take photographs and videotapes showing traditional ways of using the forest, and to share these with people in their home countries. After several years, Amazanga raised enough money to buy almost 2000 hectares of forest.

But buying this much land created suspicion among members of the Shuar tribe who lived nearby. When the Shuar claimed ownership of the same land, the people of Amazanga understood they had made a mistake. They had built partnerships with international organizations, but had failed to make agreements with their neighbors! The Shuar were so angry they threatened violence. After many meetings, the people of Amazanga and the Shuar agreed to share the forest according to shared rules. Because the Quichua and the Shuar have similar understandings of how to best use the forest, they were able to form an alliance.

They made the land a forest preserve and agreed to a forest management plan preventing the felling of trees and building of roads. The land was declared "patrimony of all the indigenous tribes of the Amazon" and protected for future generations. By reaching out to visitors from near and far, the people of Amazanga will protect the forest, preserve their culture, and help others to protect their own forest homes.

Forest Reserves

Creating forest parks and reserves can be a way to get support from governments and international organizations to protect forests and foster ecotourism. But governments and **conservation** groups sometimes think the only way to protect and preserve a forest is to keep people out. In many cases, they are wrong. People who live in the forest know how to use and care for it. By staying in the forest and managing forest parks and reserves, local people may be better able to protect it than any government or conservation group.

Some communities maintain access to the resources in forest reserves by making agreements with the government and other local communities to manage these resources together. This is called a 'co-management scheme.'

Co-management partnerships let people continue their traditional and sustainable uses of the forest and its products. Communities that manage forest reserves can also educate other communities about the importance of protecting the forest.

Forestry that sustains both people and trees

In the Amazon rainforest of Brazil, conflicts have often erupted between logging companies, cattle ranchers, and others who earn a profit from cutting down the forest, and people who live in the forest farming, harvesting rubber, and making crafts. After huge portions of the rainforest were destroyed, workers and indigenous people finally convinced the government to create "extractive reserves" – large areas of forest protected from destruction, but open to limited use.

Unfortunately, even people who lived in the forest for many years were denied the right to use the extractive reserves. The very forests they had fought so hard to protect would no longer protect their livelihoods.

People in the Tapajos Community Forest Reserve traditionally earn their living farming, hunting, and using forest products to make baskets, canoes, and other handicrafts. But they also need medicines, tools, fuel, electricity, and other things, which requires them to earn money. With some financial help, they built a carpentry workshop which they named the Caboclo Workshop, for the Caboclo people of mixed indigenous, African, and European descent. Using only trees cut down on land cleared for farming, they made furniture to sell in local markets and in stores throughout Brazil.

This income led them to think about making more wood products to earn more money. But they were not allowed to cut any standing trees unless they had a "forest inventory" and a "sustainable management plan" approved by the Ministry of the Environment.

To fulfill these government requirements, they would have to collect information about how much wood was in the forest and how much new wood grew each year. The government did not believe that villagers, many of whom could not read or write, could do such a thing. But the villagers were the real experts of the forest. They had been guiding environmental scientists through the forest for years, teaching them about plants and animals. Now the scientists taught them to use a simple tool to measure tree growth and calculate how much wood grew each year. The villagers made a plan to produce small, high-value products such as butcher blocks and stools, limiting their use of wood to the amount that could grow in a year.

The Ministry of the Environment accepted their plan, and now the Caboclo Workshop allows them to earn income without abusing the forest's resources.

The forest dwellers of the Caboclo Workshop have done what scores of scientists, economists, and development workers have long struggled to achieve: establish a forest management plan that is sustainable for both their community and their forest.

Reforestation

Ancient forests (old forests that have never been cleared or seriously damaged) are increasingly rare. Once an ancient forest is gone, it will never grow back to contain the variety of plant and animal life that it had before. But secondary forests (forests that have been damaged but are growing back) can provide many of the same resources as ancient forests if they are allowed to grow and maintain biodiversity. And forests planted by people and managed well can also provide many resources to support community health.

A healthy forest takes a long time to grow, but there are things you can do to give it a good start. Controlling erosion, preparing the soil, and planting native trees or trees that are appropriate to your area will help a forest grow well. Following the natural order of tree growth in forests is another way to help produce a healthier forest (see Chapter 11).

Is planting trees always helpful?

Before beginning a community reforestation project, be sure it will meet the needs of your community and your local environment. Trees may compete with crops for limited water and land. Sometimes it is too much work to care for young trees in harsh environments. Planting trees where they cannot or will not be cared for leads to failed projects and dead trees.

If your community relies on forest products, such as timber or fruit, planting trees may be a good way to quickly bring back forest resources. If your community mainly relies on the forest for providing hunting grounds or protecting soil, air, and water, then you may benefit more by protecting areas of land from being used while trees regrow on their own.

Forests are not right for all places. Few trees grow naturally in deserts, marshes, or grasslands. If people try to plant trees in these places it may disturb the balance of plants and animals. But in other places where there are few trees, such as in cities and towns, planting trees along roads, near factories, and in parks may greatly improve the health and well-being of the community.

Who owns the land, and what are the laws?

If you want to reforest land and use its products later, be sure you will be allowed to use the forest once it is grown. Knowing who legally owns the land and getting permission before planting trees can help avoid problems later. Land that once was poor and barren will become valuable once it is covered by healthy forest. Also, some places have laws that prohibit people from cutting or using certain trees, even if they planted them themselves. Find out if there are such laws where you live.

Different trees meet different needs

The kinds of trees planted should be decided based on what people in the community need and want.

If we want a place to relax and enjoy...

...we should plant shade trees in a public place, like a park.

But we also want to protect our water supply...

...so we should plant slow-growing trees along rivers and around springs.

We need to prevent erosion...

...we can plant trees with deep roots on bare hillsides where the forest was cut down.

What about firewood, lumber, or animal fodder for the community?

We can plant a mix of trees on common land for everyone to use.

I would like food, medicine, and animal fodder for my family...

...so we will plant a mix of trees close to the house.

Although it may take time and patience, by using everyone's knowledge and considering everyone's needs, a good plan can be made for the whole community.

11 Restoring Land and Planting Trees

In this chapter: page

Restoring Land and Planting Trees

Healthy communities depend on a regular supply of clean water, fertile soils, and usually on trees and the resources they provide and protect. To maintain and improve the health of communities, it is important to learn how to restore damaged land and how to use the land in sustainable ways. When land has been damaged, trees cut down, and soil lost to erosion by wind and water, there are many ways to make the land healthy and productive again.

Preventing Erosion

Loss of soil, or erosion, is caused by wind and water wearing away the soil and carrying it off. Protecting soil from erosion, especially on steep hillsides, improves the land's ability to grow crops, protects water sources downhill, and prevents landslides. Farmers follow 3 principles to prevent erosion and surface water runoff:

1. **Slow the water** by creating natural barriers from the top of the watershed down.

2. **Spread the water** by creating channels to divide it and direct where it flows.

3. **Sink the water** by improving the soil so it allows the water to filter into the ground.

The signs of erosion are sometimes difficult to recognize. They include crops that do not produce as much as they used to, rivers that are muddier than they used to be (especially after storms), and soil that has grown thin.

This erosion gully is just forming...   **... but before long, it will look like this.**

Where erosion has not begun, it can be prevented by keeping as many plants and trees as possible, and by directing surface runoff water into ditches, ponds, and natural waterways. Where erosion is already severe, it is still possible to stop it and to restore healthy soils. Even placing a line of rocks or building a low stone wall across the slope of the land can prevent soils from washing downhill, and create fertile places for trees and plants. Sustainable farming methods such as green manures, crop rotation, mulching, and planting trees along with crops are also ways to protect soil and conserve water resources (see Chapter 15).

NGO workers learn about erosion from farmers

In the Gulbarga District of Karnataka, India, an NGO worked with farmers to prevent soil erosion in their fields. Farmers traditionally built high stone barriers that collected most of the soil but had openings below to let water through, even when the monsoons came.

The NGO workers noticed that the farmers' stone barriers allowed some soil to be lost to the fields below. And when high stone barriers were built at the lower edges of the field, some of the stones toppled over and had to be collected from below and replaced. They proposed building solid stone barriers that would stop all the soil loss and would not need constant repairs.

The farmers said they did not mind replacing a few stones. But the NGO workers could not understand this. The farmers' stone barriers took more work to build and they let soil through, failing to control erosion completely. They proposed an experiment. In some fields they would build solid, low stone walls. In others the farmers would build the traditional barriers.

At the end of the season, the farmers and the NGO workers met and compared the effects. Many farmers with fields below the new, solid walls were unhappy. Cattle wandered across the low walls onto their fields, and after the monsoons, these farmers had less new soil and less water for rice paddies than before.

These problems led to arguments between the owners of the lower fields and the fields above. The experiment showed the farmers that their own traditional barriers worked better than the "improved" walls. The farmers told the NGO workers that the solid stone walls caused too many problems. Through this experience the NGO workers learned that the farmers' traditional barriers not only prevented soil erosion, they also prevented cattle from straying. Allowing some soil and water through prevented good neighbor relations from eroding, which was more important to the farmers than a little extra work!

Restoring Damaged Land

Sometimes land is so damaged that it seems impossible to restore it to a healthy state. In places where healthy land has turned to desert, or where toxic chemicals in the soil have made it impossible for plants to grow, the land could take hundreds of years to restore. But in many places, with careful work and understanding of the ways the earth restores itself, we can help the land recover.

Nobody can force land to be productive. Even chemical fertilizers work for only a little while before the land no longer produces. But if we pay attention to natural cycles, we can help create the conditions the land needs to restore itself to a healthy, fertile state.

Natural succession

Sometimes, the best way to restore land is to leave it alone or help it recover in small ways. Building fences or posting signs asking people to stay out, or reducing the number of livestock that graze the land, can go a long way toward letting land recover. When land is protected from use, and the conditions are right for life to return, plants come back in a natural order, called natural succession. This process can take many years, even several generations.

Natural succession will NOT restore land when:

- There are no sources of seeds or native plants nearby.
- Rapidly spreading plants have taken over and crowd out desirable plants.
- The land is so degraded or contaminated that nothing will grow. (For a story about restoring land after an oil spill, see page 520.)

Native and non-native plants and trees

Native plants (plants from the local area) grow easily in local conditions. They also preserve biodiversity by attracting and providing homes for native insects, birds, and animals.

Sometimes, plants and trees that are not native to the local area become popular because they grow fast, produce good lumber, or help improve the soil. Some trees, such as eucalyptus, pine, teak, neem, and Leucaena have been planted all over the world.

But planting trees and plants that are not native to your area can lead to problems. They may use too much groundwater, compete with crops and native trees for water and soil nutrients, spread beyond where you want them to grow, or cause native animals and insects to seek other places to live. When non-native plants take over, it is difficult to restore land through natural succession.

Natural Succession

1. Degraded land with poor soil and no plant life.

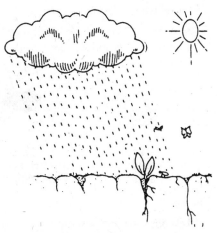

2. Small, hardy plants called pioneer plants grow back first in places where soil can collect. Pioneer plants hold water and attract insects and birds.

3. Water settles into small catchments created by pioneer plants, bringing seeds and nutrients. Birds bring more seeds.

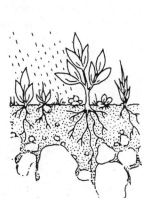

4. Larger plants and small trees grow. Plant roots break up compacted soil. Soil builds up and holds more water.

5. Bigger plants and shrubs grow back, and the land is restored.

How to make seed balls

A simple method to restore plant life to an eroded area is by using seed balls. Each year, collect wild seeds. Children are especially good at gathering seeds, and it is a fun learning activity.

Gather as many different kinds of seeds as possible from plants native to the area. With these seeds and some soil, make little balls.
Mix:

**1 part
mixed
seeds**   **2 parts
sifted compost or
planting soil**   **3 parts
clay soil sifted to
remove stones**   **a small
amount
of water**

Mix seeds with compost or planting soil, then add clay. Add just enough water to make the mixture damp. If you add too much water, the seeds will sprout too soon. Make small balls out of this mixture. Let them dry for a few days in the sun.

Just before or during the rainy season, go to the area where you want to restore plant life and toss the balls out. Building contour trenches and other barriers there first (see page 290) will direct surface runoff water and help the seeds sprout and grow.

The seeds will sprout when it rains. The compost provides nutrients, and the clay prevents the seeds from drying out, being eaten by mice or birds, or blowing away. After a year the new plants will make their own seeds, and before long many new plants will grow. Soil will build up around the plants, preventing erosion.
Soon, other kinds of plants will appear. If it is not disturbed, after many years the whole area will be restored.

Helping trees plant themselves

In Somalia, East Africa, there are few trees due to the dry, desert climate. But the number of trees has gotten even smaller because the few trees that do grow are often cut down to make charcoal. Some of this charcoal was used by the Somali people, but much of it was sold to other countries. When a woman named Fatima Jibrell saw this problem, she started a campaign to prevent the sale of charcoal to other countries. "When we have barely enough for ourselves," she said, "we cannot afford to let others exploit our resources."

Fatima's campaign was successful. But by then, there were very few trees left. So she started a campaign to promote new tree growth in Somalia. She believed that the best way to reduce the severe poverty of her people was to bring trees back to Somalia.

The land in Somalia is very hot and dry, making tree planting difficult. And because most people in Somalia move from place to place with the seasons, it was not practical to expect people to plant trees and care for them. So Fatima started teaching people to build low rock fences as they traveled around the country. Even though the land is very flat, Fatima believed that water would find its way to the lowest places and would bring life with it. During the short rainy season, these low fences helped build up soil nutrients, and plants and trees began to grow by themselves. Now there are more trees growing in Somalia than there have been in many years.

Planting Trees

Under the right conditions, planting trees helps restore damaged lands and provide firewood, timber, food for people and for animals, and medicine. Planting trees can make land that is poor and barren become rich and fertile again. But trees planted in harsh conditions need care to grow well. Tree planting has many benefits, but it is not right for all areas or all communities (see page 191 for an activity that can help decide whether to plant trees). There are several ways to grow trees:

- Plant seeds or cuttings (pieces of a branch) directly into the ground (see page 207).

- Collect and transplant wild seedlings (see page 208).

- Grow tree seedlings in a nursery and then transplant them into the ground (see page 209).

- Graft (attach) a cutting from a tree you want onto the root stock of another tree. (Grafting is usually used to grow fruit trees and is not covered in this book.)

The method you choose depends on what trees you want to plant, and what seeds or cuttings are available.

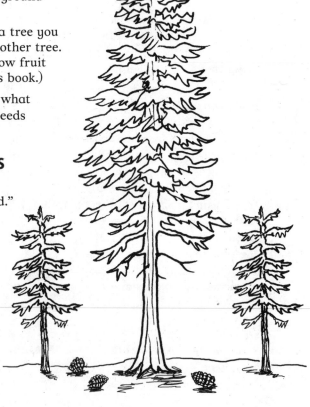

Selecting seeds or cuttings

Many people have sayings such as, "Like the parent, so will be the child." Just as a child whose parents are tall will also likely grow tall, a tree seedling whose "parent" has a straight trunk that is good for lumber, or produces useful medicine, is likely to share those same qualities. It is best to collect seeds or cuttings from parent trees that are healthy and have the qualities you want. If you cannot collect seeds in your area, you may be able to get seeds from an extension agent, or from a nursery or garden in a nearby town.

Preparing seeds for planting

Some seeds, usually those with soft coverings and which are mealy or juicy, must be planted soon after they are collected. Other seeds may need to be stored for many months before you will plant them. (For information about storing seeds, see page 303.)

Most seeds need water to sprout. When a seed is covered with a thick or hard skin it may also need to be softened or cut before the water can soak in. Some seeds may need more treatment before planting.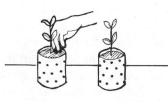

- If the seed covering is not too hard (you can dent or break it with your fingernail) and not too thick (not thicker than the cover of this book), plant it directly into moist soil.

- If the covering is hard but thin, wrap the seeds in a piece of cloth. Let them soak for 1 minute in water that is too hot to touch, but not yet boiling (80° C). Take them out of the hot water and quickly put them in cool water to soak overnight. Plant them the next day.

- Another way to treat seed coverings that are hard but thin is to soak seeds in cold water for 1 full day, then cover them with moist cloth sacks for another 24 hours. Repeat this procedure for 6 days. On the 7th day, plant the seed.

- If the covering is hard and thick, rub the seeds with a piece of rough stone or sandpaper until you see the soft, inside part of the seed. Be careful not to rub too deep and damage the seed.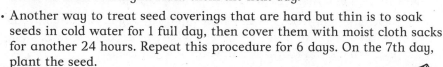

- If the seed covering is soft but thick, cut a thin strip of the covering away from the soft inside of the seed, being careful to cut the seed as little as possible.

- Some hard-coated seeds are best treated by soaking overnight in water mixed with cow dung, then dried in the sun for 1 day. Repeat this process for 3 to 4 days. The good seeds will sprout and be ready for planting. The seeds that do not sprout can be discarded.

Some seeds need more complicated treatments, such as being heated in a low fire, chilled, or being eaten and passed by animals. Experiment to find what works best. After many attempts, you will be an expert at starting tree seeds.

Preparing tree cuttings

Some trees grow best by putting a cutting in the soil and watering it until it grows roots and leaves. Trees grown from cuttings usually produce fruit or seeds sooner than trees grown from seeds.

Plant cutting at this angle

3 to 4 nodes underground

Roots grow from nodes underground

Some cuttings can be planted directly into the soil where you want the tree to grow. Others should be planted in a nursery until they have sprouted plenty of leaves and roots and can survive on their own.

Make cuttings from the middle of a branch where the wood does not bend too much but is not too rigid. Select a piece with about 6 to 10 "nodes" (bumps on the branch where the leaf grows or used to grow.) Gently remove the leaves, being careful not to damage the nodes. Cut the branch at an angle instead of straight across, to help roots form properly.

Whether the cuttings have been planted in a nursery or directly into the ground, be sure they have plenty of water and are protected from pests until they have grown enough roots to find water on their own.

Collecting seedlings from the forest to transplant

Transplanting wild seedlings

Another way to create a forest is to dig up wild tree seedlings and replant them where you want them to grow. Find healthy parent trees and choose seedlings growing near or under them.

Dig up small seedlings, careful not to damage the main, long tap root. If this root is damaged, the tree will not grow well. Dig in a circle around the seedling and as deep as you think the tap root has grown. Use your hand or a tool to bring the seedling up without shaking off the soil around the roots.

Keep the soil around the roots of the tree seedling moist until it is planted in the ground. Continue watering it until its roots have grown into its new place and it can find water for itself.

Growing trees in a nursery

Tree nurseries give trees a healthy start before they are transplanted to other places. But creating and caring for a nursery can be a lot of work. It makes sense to grow trees in a nursery when:

- The seeds or cuttings of the trees you want to plant are scarce.
- Pests would damage the young trees if they were not protected.
- People have enough time to take care of the nursery.

Planting trees directly is easier than growing them first in a nursery and transplanting them. However, many more tree seedlings die using the direct method than when you grow them in a nursery.

When to start trees

The time of year you plant will depend on how long the trees need to be in the nursery. If your area has a wet and a dry season, plant your trees just as the wet season starts so you will not have to water them as much. Most trees need 3 to 4 months in the nursery before they are big enough to plant outside.

Where to put a tree nursery

A nursery should be easy to get to and available for as long as it takes for tree seedlings to grow and be transplanted. It should also be accessible to everyone who will work there. Every nursery needs these things:

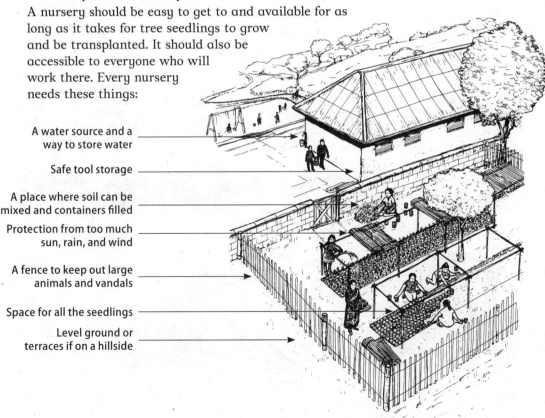

A water source and a way to store water

Safe tool storage

A place where soil can be mixed and containers filled

Protection from too much sun, rain, and wind

A fence to keep out large animals and vandals

Space for all the seedlings

Level ground or terraces if on a hillside

Growing tree seedlings in containers

Growing tree seedlings in containers makes them easy to transport and to plant. Containers should be wide and deep enough to allow the seedling to grow a root ball, but not so big that they are very heavy or soak up more water than the tree will need.

The longer a seedling needs to be in the nursery, the bigger the container should be. A good size for most trees is about 6 inches wide at the top and 9 inches deep. They should be strong enough to stand upright when filled with soil, and have holes to allow excess water to drain out.

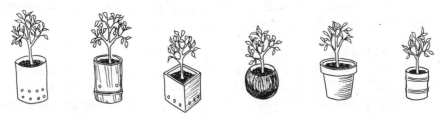

Containers that will rot (newspaper, leaves, cardboard) can be planted directly in the ground along with the seedling. Containers made of plastic, glass, or wood must be removed before planting, but can be used again many times.

Young tree seedling need to be protected against too much sun. Many grow best under some shade during the heat of the day.

Soil for planting

The soil used for planting should be loose so the roots of the young trees do not rot. It should also be rich in nutrients (see page 282) so the trees will grow well. Soil from the forest or from bends in rivers or streams is very good for young trees.

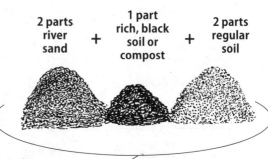

2 parts river sand + 1 part rich, black soil or compost + 2 parts regular soil

Sifting plant soil

How to plant seeds or cuttings in containers

1 Water your planting soil the day before you plant so it will be moist but not wet. Treat the seeds before planting, but not so long before that they will begin to sprout or rot (see page 304). Fill your containers with soil.

2 To plant very small seeds, scratch the surface of the soil, sprinkle 5 or 10 seeds, and cover them very lightly with dirt by scratching the soil again with a fork or stick.

To plant larger seeds, make a hole in the center of the soil about 2 to 3 times as deep as the width of the seed. You may want to plant more than one seed in each container. Cover the seeds with dirt and press down lightly. Pressing the dirt removes air pockets where fungus could grow.

3 Water the containers after planting. If the seeds are very small, this must be done carefully so the seeds are not washed away.

4 When the seeds have sprouted 1 or 2 leaves, choose the seedling that looks strongest and cut away any others, leaving one seedling in each container. By cutting the seedlings you do not want rather than pulling them out, you will not disturb the roots of the seedling you do want.

Watering tree seedlings

Watering tree seedlings is one of the most important activities in a nursery. Water your trees in a way that gently sprinkles the water like rain, instead of in a single stream like a tap that might wash away soil and uncover roots.

The amount of water a seedling needs depends on how deep its roots have grown. Water seedlings as soon as their leaves begin to droop. But it is best that they never get to this point, because it is stressful for the plant.

Until seedlings have 2 or 3 leaves, water whenever the top of the soil appears completely dry.

Then, until they have 5 or 6 leaves, water when the soil is dry as deep as the fingernail on your thumb.

Then, until the roots push against the bottom of the container, water when the soil is dry as deep as the first joint of your thumb.

Weeding and fertilizing

Weeds compete with tree seedlings for light, water, and nutrients from the soil. A few small weeds in a container will do no harm. But if there are more, cut them away at their base to not break up the soil.

If your soil is fertile, seedlings should get the nutrients they need. If fertilizer is needed, make natural fertilizer from manure, compost, or urine (see Chapter 15).

This tree needs water.

This tree has enough water.

Transplanting seedlings

When the roots of the seedlings begin to push through the bottom of the containers (usually 3 to 4 months after planting) it is time to transplant them. If you cannot plant at this time, trim the roots back once a week. This helps the tree form a full ball of roots in the container and keeps it from rooting in the ground.

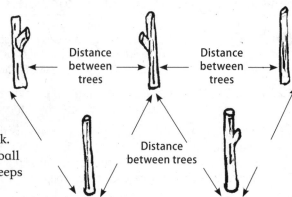

Planting in a triangular design allows many trees to grow in a small area.

A month before planting, gradually remove the shade over the seedlings until they have the same amount of sun as the site where they will be planted. This gets the seedlings used to the sunnier and drier conditions of the planting site.

The day before planting, water the seedlings so the containers will be wet. Transport them carefully, being sure not to damage the roots. Mark where you want to plant each seedling. The distance between trees depends on the type of tree and the reason for planting. As a general rule, plant trees so their branches will just touch when full grown.

Clean all weeds or brush that might shade the seedlings or compete with them for water in a 1 meter circle around the planting area. Plant in early morning or the cool hours of the late afternoon to protect the trees from sun. Avoid damaging or drying out the roots while planting.

Dig square holes 1½ times as deep as the containers. Round holes prevent roots from reaching into the surrounding soil.

Fill the hole with soil so the base of the trunk will be level with the ground when the hole is filled. You may want to add a few handfuls of compost or rich, black soil to help the tree get started. After planting, soak the soil around the tree with water.

Transplanting in difficult places

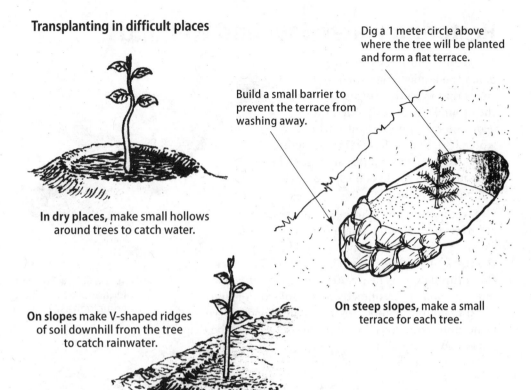

In **dry places,** make small hollows around trees to catch water.

Build a small barrier to prevent the terrace from washing away.

Dig a 1 meter circle above where the tree will be planted and form a flat terrace.

On slopes make V-shaped ridges of soil downhill from the tree to catch rainwater.

On steep slopes, make a small terrace for each tree.

Caring for young trees

A tree needs to be protected through its first year of life. Many tree planting projects fail because no one takes care of the young trees.

If the weather is hot and dry, seedlings need to be watered first once a day, and then every 2 or 3 days. After a few weeks, the tree roots should find water. But if the weather is still hot and dry, water as the trees need it.

Cut back weeds until the plant is taller than the weeds. If animals or children might damage the young trees, construct barriers around the trees.

If a tree is not growing well, or the leaves look yellow or unhealthy, it may help to spread natural fertilizer (see page 287) in a circle as wide as the tree branches.

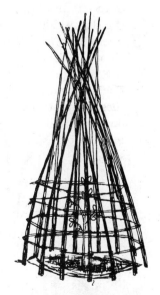

Make barriers to protect young trees.

Restoring Waterways and Wetlands

The plants and trees that grow along the banks of streams and rivers and in **wetlands** (areas where the ground is wet or flooded all year), do many important jobs in the watershed. They control floods, clean water, help surface runoff sink into the ground, and provide homes to a variety of animal and plant life.

This river will flow fast and could cause erosion and flooding downstream.

Streams and rivers in cities and towns are often made to flow in a straight line to control flooding and make it easier to build around them. But the straighter a stream or river, the faster water flows through it. When water speeds up, it causes more erosion of streambeds and banks and is more likely to cause flooding downstream. Floods carry large stones and logs downstream, so even in the dry season you can tell if a river may flood by looking at the size of the rocks and logs in the streambed. If a slow, shallow river has large stones in its bed in the dry season, this is a sign of dangerous flooding that carries these large stones downstream in the rainy season.

This river will flow slower, allowing water to sink into the ground.

Restoring plant life

Plants that grow along waterways help to slow, spread, and sink rainwater into the ground and hold soil in place.

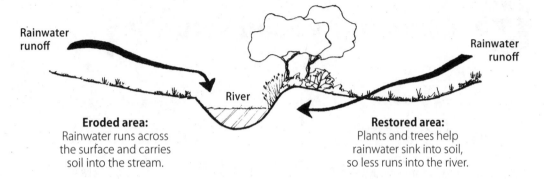

Eroded area:
Rainwater runs across the surface and carries soil into the stream.

Restored area:
Plants and trees help rainwater sink into soil, so less runs into the river.

One way to stop soil erosion along streams and rivers is to plant trees alongside them. Planting in an area 20 to 50 meters wide on each side of a waterway will usually reduce erosion.

Trees that like to have wet roots grow easily from cuttings. Plant 2 or more rows of cuttings, and then pile brush or branches between the rows. This holds the soil in place and starts to create the conditions for other plants and animals to return.

Trees, shrubs, and grasses may begin to grow on their own once the sides of the river or stream are stable. If they do not, you may want to plant them. If possible, fence the area to keep animals out and to prevent people from gathering wood in the area until trees are fully grown.

Preserving and restoring wetlands is an important part of watershed protection.

12 Community Food Security

In this chapter: **page**

Community Food Security

In order to be healthy, people need to eat nutritious food. If we cannot grow, buy, or trade enough food for our families and ourselves, we face hunger, malnutrition, and many other health problems.

Food security means that everyone has enough safe and nutritious food all year round to lead an active and healthy life. It also means food is produced and distributed in ways that promote a healthy environment, community self-reliance, and enough good food for every person and community.

Hunger has many causes. Some causes are environmental, such as poor soil, changes in climate, and a lack of water. Hunger from these causes can be addressed through sustainable farming (see Chapter 15) and better use of land and water resources (see Chapter 6, and Chapters 9 to 11).

Other causes of hunger are political, such as unfair food prices, no land to grow food, and corporate control of markets and food systems. Hunger from these and other political causes can be addressed through community organizing.

To produce food, we need land, water, tools, seeds, and knowledge of how to farm. To make sure that everybody has enough food, we need fair distribution, affordable food prices, local markets, and food safety. To achieve these, we must work for a just and sustainable world. Only by working towards a healthy environment and social justice can we guarantee food security for everyone.

Changes in farming

In Prey Veng, Cambodia, people have grown enough rice to feed themselves for as long as anyone can remember. Along with rice, they traditionally ate wild greens, fish, eels, snakes and other animals from the rice paddy, as well as fruits, nuts, and roots from the forest, and meat from animals they hunt. This diet gave them good health all year round, except in times of war or flooding.

More than 40 years ago, the government began to promote new farming methods to increase production of a few main crops, like rice, for export. These new methods were part of a worldwide change in agriculture, the deceptively named Green Revolution. The Green Revolution encouraged the use of chemical pesticides and fertilizers to produce more rice than traditional methods. It also used large irrigation systems and machinery to plant and harvest.

When they started using these new farming methods, the people of Prey Veng were able to produce large amounts of rice to sell. They used the money to improve their houses, build roads, and buy personal goods like clothes and radios. The villagers stopped using animal manure, stopped rotating rice with dry season crops, and stopped using other traditional farming methods as well.

The new methods worked very well for growing large areas of a single crop, and increased the amount of rice they had. But over time, they discovered that their land and the way they ate had changed. Herbicides killed the wild greens the villagers had eaten before. Fish and other wild foods grew scarce. Year by year they spent more money on chemicals and had nothing but rice to eat. Before long, the soil in their fields no longer supported healthy crops, and rice yields began to go down.

Coming together to discuss the growing hunger, the villagers recalled the old ways of farming that used mixed crops, field rotations, and natural fertilizers to grow crops all year round. They saw many advantages to the traditional methods, and decided to change back. They also began trying new methods like planting rice plants closer together and growing different crops in the same field.

There were hungry years while their soil recovered fertility after heavy chemical use, but now the villagers of Prey Veng have more food. They have less rice to sell, but more variety of foods to eat. As Meas Nee, one of the village elders, said, "Because we grow food in the ways of our ancestors, the ancestors are happier, the fields are happier, and we are healthier."

What Is Community Food Security?

To understand what problems a community has in getting enough healthy food, look at all the different things that together add up to food security.

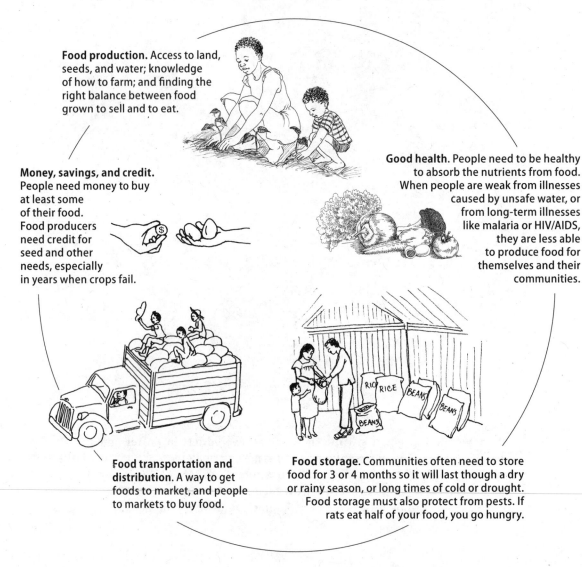

Food production. Access to land, seeds, and water; knowledge of how to farm; and finding the right balance between food grown to sell and to eat.

Money, savings, and credit. People need money to buy at least some of their food. Food producers need credit for seed and other needs, especially in years when crops fail.

Good health. People need to be healthy to absorb the nutrients from food. When people are weak from illnesses caused by unsafe water, or from long-term illnesses like malaria or HIV/AIDS, they are less able to produce food for themselves and their communities.

Food transportation and distribution. A way to get foods to market, and people to markets to buy food.

Food storage. Communities often need to store food for 3 or 4 months so it will last though a dry or rainy season, or long times of cold or drought. Food storage must also protect from pests. If rats eat half of your food, you go hungry.

Food contaminated by pesticides, toxic chemicals, germs, or genetically engineered (GE) foods (see Chapter 13), may be available, but will not provide a safe, healthy diet. Also, without a safe cooking space and enough time and fuel to prepare food, people often eat too many processed foods, which can lead to health problems.

10 seeds

This activity can help people agree on what their community's most urgent food security problems are, and then help encourage them to make changes that improve community food security.

Time: 2 hours

Materials: 10 seeds for each group, colored pens or markers, large poster paper

1 Divide into groups of 8 to 10 people. Ask each group to talk about the different things that make up food security, such as food production, food storage, credit, stores and markets that sell healthy food, good land to grow food, and so on. Rural communities that farm, hunt, and fish will have different food security issues than people in cities. Talk about the different things that make up food security where you are. On a piece of large poster paper, write or draw pictures to show the different parts of food security.

2 Give each group 10 seeds, and ask them to decide which parts of food security are causing problems in their community, putting more seeds where there are the most problems. For example: Is there hunger for some families because food storage is poor? Or because there is no transportation to get food to the market, or no market where you can buy food? Or because of crop pests, poor soil, or lack of water? This will help the groups identify the weakest parts of their food security. Different people in the community will have different problems. Make sure everyone's problems are heard.

3 After each group identifies their most urgent food security problems, discuss what local resources may help. If food production is the biggest problem, are there people with knowledge and skills to start home gardens, or to improve farming practices? If food storage is the biggest problem, what ideas could improve it? If there are no markets, is there a way to open a cooperative store to sell healthy food? Or to buy or share a truck to bring food to the community? Every idea counts.

4 After discussing possible solutions, have each group use another large poster paper to draw or write the solutions that seem most practical. Then divide the 10 seeds among these solutions, putting more seeds near the solutions that seem most possible to carry out.

5 After each group decides on problems and solutions, come together in a larger group. Using the 10 seeds again, or just voting by raising hands, choose the 1 or 2 most popular solutions. Discuss how to put these solutions into practice. Who needs to be involved, and what resources can the community provide? When can work begin? Set long-term goals, such as "after 2 years, nobody in the community will go hungry." Also set short-term goals, such as pooling community resources each month to open a store in 3 months, or preparing land for planting by the beginning of the growing season.

Nutrition and food security

When people are sick or **malnourished,** they are less active and less able to produce food, carry water, and maintain a clean home and a healthy environment. But when healthy foods are affordable, produced in a sustainable way, and available in local markets, people have access to a varied and healthy diet.

Dry malnutrition: this child is just skin and bones

Not eating well can weaken the body and cause:

- severe diarrhea, especially in children.
- childhood **measles** to become more dangerous.
- dangerous pregnancies and births, and babies born too small or with disabilities such as slow mental development.
- **anemia,** especially for women.
- **tuberculosis** to be more common, and get worse more quickly.
- **diabetes,** a disease caused when the body cannot use sugar properly, to be more common.
- minor problems like colds to be more frequent, and often more severe, leading to **pneumonia** and **bronchitis.**
- people with HIV or AIDS to get sicker more quickly, and cause their medicines to not work as well.
- **silicosis, asthma, heavy metal poisoning,** and other problems caused by contact with toxic chemicals (see Chapters 16 and 20) to be more common and more severe.

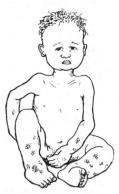

Wet malnutrition: this child is just skin and bones and water

Malnourished children grow slowly and learn poorly in school, or are too weak to go to school.

Malnutrition is particularly a problem for young children and must be treated immediately. To learn more about these health problems, and about how good nutrition can prevent them, see a general medical book such as *Where There Is No Doctor.*

Junk food is not healthy

When people do not have land to grow food, live in crowded cities, cannot buy healthy foods in the market, or lose the cultural traditions that help them eat healthy food, they often end up eating "junk" food that contains little nutritional value. Often these foods are refined in ways that remove nutrition, are processed with chemicals, are fried in oil, and contain too much sugar or salt. In small amounts, such foods may not be harmful. But when people eat them regularly instead of more nutritious food, they prevent us from getting the nutrition we need.

> We had more and better food when our grandparents were alive. Since they died, nobody in my family grows food anymore.

> I know, it's a shame. But don't these fries taste great?

As people eat more junk foods, they are more likely to gain too much weight and have health problems such as high blood pressure, heart disease, strokes, gallstones, diabetes, and some kinds of cancer. This is why people can be undernourished and overweight at the same time.

When farming changes, eating changes

Everywhere in the world, farmers are being driven off their land. Fields that produced food for local communities now grow crops for export. The growing control by corporations of land, seeds, markets, and the ways that food is distributed not only harms farmers, it harms all of us.

Healthy food is becoming harder and harder to find. In many cities, it is easier to buy "junk" foods, alcohol, and illegal drugs than fresh fruits and vegetables. This has led to big changes in our diets in only a few generations. While our grandparents ate mostly foods prepared with fresh ingredients, people now eat too many refined and processed foods lacking nutrition but containing preservatives, flavorings, colorings, and large amounts of sweeteners (sugars and corn syrup), salt, and fats. So, while many of us eat more food than in the past, the foods we eat are less healthy than ever before.

Changing diets affect Native Americans' health

Only a few generations ago, Native Americans had a healthy diet of foods they hunted, grew, and collected in the wild. When meat, vegetables, and fruit were scarce, they were still able to collect "survival foods" of roots, seeds, tree bark, and small animals.

About 100 years ago, the US government forced Native people to live on reservations and did not allow them to hunt or fish. Rather than providing them with foods they were used to, the government provided mostly white flour, white sugar, and lard (processed animal fat). Today, many Native Americans still eat these government foods. On many reservations, the only food available is fried junk food. Even the people who do not receive food from the government often eat poorly because they have few other choices.

Because they have been forced to eat a lot of foods that are low in nutrition, and because they do not have the foods their bodies need, many Native Americans are overweight and suffer from heart disease and other health problems related to poor diet. Diabetes is now one of the leading causes of death among Native Americans.

This problem has led some Native Americans to begin recovering their culture and good health by bringing back traditional foods. They are planting maize, beans and squash, gathering wild rice, fishing, and raising buffalo for meat. Richard Iron Cloud, a Native American health worker from the Lakota Nation, says, "Change in cultural traditions, lifestyles, and eating habits caused diabetes to increase. The return to our ancestors' ways of eating can make disease go away again."

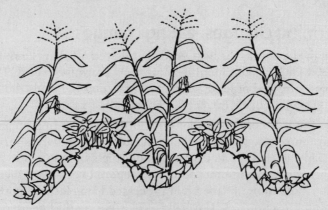

Farming traditions, like growing different crops together, can ensure good health and protect the land for future generations.

Improving Local Food Security

Every government should try to make sure people do not go hungry. National governments can make policies that promote the use of land for family farms, protect against pollution of farmlands, make affordable credit available to farmers, and help farmers solve problems.

Some national governments offer **subsidies** (money to support farmers, food buyers, or both) as a way to improve food security. Kinds of subsidies include **price supports** to help farmers by setting a higher market price for the foods they produce, and **price controls** for food buyers (**consumers**) to make sure that important foods are affordable.

Government support is often misused by giving it to corporations that own large industrial farms or produce and distribute unhealthy foods. When government support is corrupted by pressure from large corporations, the result is often more hunger and malnutrition.

But with or without government support, there are many ways people can improve local food security. From planting a small garden to organizing a farmers' market, changes that improve food security can often bring results quickly and motivate people to do more.

Local food is healthy, fresher, and supports the local culture and economy.

Community food projects

Food security is strongest when food is produced and distributed locally. Locally grown food is fresher and so more nutritious. It builds the local economy as money circulates to farmers and businesses in the area. And it helps build relationships among people, making communities stronger and healthier places to live. Because poor communities often have little land and few food markets, regaining control of food production and distribution is especially important for them.

Community food programs help keep the culture in agriculture.

Ways to grow more food locally

Most of these projects can be started with little land or money, and help communities get more fresh food.

- **Family gardens** add healthy vegetables and fruits to the family meal.

- **School gardens** can provide fresh food for children and help keep children in school by providing nourishment. And they teach children to grow food, making sure this important knowledge stays alive!

- **Community gardens** provide food and places for people to get together, even if they do not own land. Community gardens can also help people learn about food production, develop skills, and start new businesses such as restaurants and markets. Even small gardens can make a big difference to food security.

- **Community supported agriculture** is when farmers sell their food directly to consumers. People pay the farmers before the crops are planted, and then receive fresh fruits, vegetables and other foods each week throughout the harvest season. By making this investment, consumers help farmers stay on the land and in business while getting a dependable supply of nutritious food.

- **Seed saving programs** help make sure that traditional seed supplies are available. A variety of seeds is the basis of sustainable farming and self-sufficient communities (see Chapter 15).

Making healthy food available at fair prices

The world now produces more than enough food for everyone, but people still go hungry. This is partly because food prices are often higher than people can afford, and healthy food is often not available to the poorest people. Government support is important to make sure prices are fair for both buyers and sellers of food. Some ways people work locally to make sure healthy food is available at fair prices include:

- **Farmers markets** reduce transportation costs and the need for merchants in the middle, so farmers can earn more and consumers pay less. Farmers' markets also let consumers meet and talk with the people who grow their food. This helps farmers learn what consumers need and helps consumers know what farmers do to bring them food.

- **Food cooperatives** are markets partly or entirely owned by the workers and people who buy food there. Food coop members pay part of their food bill by working at the market. Most food coops try to buy and sell locally grown food.

- **Farmers cooperatives** help farmers get better prices for what they grow, and still offer better prices to consumers (see page 313.)

Safe food storage

Safe food storage is as important as the ability to grow food or have access to food. Drought, storms, flooding, pests, or illness can all leave a family or community with not enough to eat and nothing to sell. Community food storage programs can help overcome these problems. (For information on storing food and protecting it from pests, see page 305. For ways to prevent food from spoiling in the home, see page 375.)

For example, on the Pacific island of Temotu, hurricanes frequently destroy many crops. To improve food security, communities build big, communal pits to store fermented cassava, unripe plantains, bananas, and breadfruit. Everyone contributes to making and filling the pits. When crops are destroyed and people are hungry, they use this stored food.

Food banks are places where food is collected and then given away to those in need. Food banks help during a hunger crisis. But because people may come to depend on them, they are not a good solution to long term food security.

When entire regions suffer from hunger, food aid from international agencies can help them get through the crisis. Food aid is a short term solution to food security, but it does not solve the long term need for **food sovereignty** (see page 235).

Junior Farmer Field School for HIV/AIDS orphans

In Mozambique, as in much of Africa, thousands of children are orphaned because their parents died of HIV/AIDS. Children orphaned in rural areas are especially at risk from malnutrition, disease, abuse, and sexual exploitation. After the deaths of their parents, many children become heads of the household and have to search for ways to earn money, a difficult task in rural areas with few job opportunities. Although they are from farm families, many of these children cannot farm because their parents were too ill to pass on their knowledge before dying.

With the help of the United Nations World Food Program and the Food and Agriculture Organization, Junior Farmer Field and Life Schools were begun to care for the growing numbers of AIDS orphans. In these schools, youth between 12 and 18 years old live and work together, and learn about farming, nutrition, medicinal plants, and life skills.

The young people learn traditional and modern farming methods, including field preparation, sowing and transplanting, weeding, irrigation, pest control, use and conservation of resources, processing of food crops, harvesting, and food storage and marketing skills. Dancing and singing help them gain confidence and develop social skills. Theater and discussion groups are used to talk about other important life skills, such as the prevention of HIV/AIDS and malaria, gender equality, and children's rights.

There are now 28 Junior Farmer Field and Life Schools in Mozambique and there are more in Kenya, Namibia, Zambia, Swaziland, and Tanzania. Thousands of orphans have been trained as farmers. After graduating, the children go on to start their own small farms with money earned from selling their crops. One school worker says, "When we started these schools, the children had no future. Most of them wanted to grow up to be truck drivers, because it was the only option they saw. Now they want to be teachers, agronomists, farmers, and engineers."

Food Security in Cities

Most people in the world now live in or around cities. Many live in refugee camps or other communities with poor housing and sanitation, and little access to jobs, clean water, or healthy food. Food security is better for city people when they have jobs, money, and safe and healthy housing. Then they can buy and eat better food, cook and store food, and even grow their own food in urban gardens.

The People's Grocery

Like many urban areas in the United States, West Oakland (in California) has more stores that sell alcohol and junk food than ones that offer healthy, fresh food. With stores that do sell healthy food setting prices too high for most people in the community, many people in West Oakland are malnourished or overweight. Problems of alcoholism, drug abuse, and violence make the community a dangerous place to live. Almost 1 of every 4 people in West Oakland depends on emergency food programs.

Seeing this problem, some people got together to bring healthy food to the community at prices people could afford. They began by raising money to buy a truck. They painted the truck in bright colors and put in a stereo system that played popular music. Every week they drove to farmers' markets in other parts of the city and brought back vegetables and fruit. They parked on street corners where people gathered, played music to attract more people, and sold the fresh food at low prices. As they sold food, they talked to people about the importance of a healthy diet.

They called their mobile market The People's Grocery and invited people from the community to join them. Some people decided to start a community garden to grow fresh produce that could be sold by the People's Grocery truck. Young and old people worked together and learned how to grow food. Other people planted gardens of their own. Soon a nearby school and community center also planted gardens. Most of the food from these gardens was sold by the People's Grocery truck.

After success in the community, the People's Grocery asked the city government for land, funds, and advertising. With some government support, they thought their project could feed many more people.

People's Grocery continues to build the local food system and economy, improving food security for everyone in West Oakland. People's Grocery says no one should live without healthy food just because they are poor or live in the city. They say: In order to have food security, we need food justice!

To build food security in cities, governments must help

The story of the People's Grocery shows how people in a poor urban community are working to solve their own problems of food security. The program they developed has helped many people, but it has not completely solved the problems of food security.

- Why did people in West Oakland not have healthy food?
- How did the People's Grocery get local people interested in healthy food?
- How could local government become involved in supporting this kind of project?
- What other groups or institutions could the People's Grocery work with to help the project?
- How can you help promote food security in your community?

Sustainable food policy for cities

To have lasting food security, all aspects of city life and development must be discussed. People responsible for planning transportation, education, employment, and development of new homes and settlements should think about how people in the city get their food. Providing land for community gardens, transportation to markets, and teaching about food security and nutrition in schools are all ideas local governments can use to help people today, while making sure there will be better food security tomorrow.

Stores that sell healthy foods at affordable prices support community health.

Social and Political Causes of Hunger

Hunger may be caused by many things, such as poor soil, changes in climate, lack of access to water, and so on. But in most communities, hunger is also caused by poverty. When there is little or no income for farmers, or little money to buy food, people go hungry. To understand the root causes of poverty and hunger in one community, it helps to look at the problems with food security that affect every community.

The social and political causes of hunger

Corporate control harms food security

When food is treated as just another product to be bought and sold instead of something all people need and have a right to, profit from selling food becomes more important than feeding people, and community health suffers. Many people now shop for food in stores owned by large corporations. They buy foods made by large corporations, grown on land owned by large corporations, using seeds, fertilizers, and pesticides produced by large corporations.

Corporate control of all parts of food security forces farmers out of business and off their land. When corporations use land to grow food to sell outside the region, people living and working in those communities must eat food brought in from elsewhere, if they can afford to buy it.

Corporations profit from this food "insecurity" as communities, and whole countries, become dependent on the global market for food. When the market fails to meet people's food needs, people go hungry and corporations profit further by selling food to governments to be distributed as food aid.

Until people have control of their food security, hunger will be the biggest product of the corporations that control the production and distribution of food.

Recovering lost seeds to resist drought

In Zimbabwe, farmers once planted many kinds of grains. During the Green Revolution of the 1960s, the government and international agencies brought a new kind of maize for farmers to plant. Farmers liked the hybrid maize because it had large grains, grew quickly, and was easy to sell. The government bought much of their crop, and then resold it to other countries and to cities in Zimbabwe where food was scarce. Over time, maize became the most common food to eat in Zimbabwe, and most farmers grew it in large quantities.

Then came years of drought. Very little rain fell over the fields of Zimbabwe and other countries in southern Africa. The maize grew poorly, and there was little else to eat. Many families had stored grains for times of hunger, but much of their stores of maize had rotted. This was a surprise, because the millet and sorghum they used to grow had lasted many seasons in storage.

When the rains finally started, they came in huge storms that uprooted crops and washed away precious soil from the dry fields. Hunger grew so severe in Zimbabwe that the government was forced to ask for food aid from the United Nations. Large shipments of maize came in by airplane and were handed out to hungry people across the country. But food aid and the new hybrid seeds could not solve the long term problem of hunger and food security.

The farmers realized they could not bring more rain, but they could change how they farmed to make better use of the rain. Farmers began to collect and plant seeds from small grain crops such as sorghum and millet that had always grown well in Zimbabwe. Farmers planted every kind of seed they could get. If drought destroyed one crop, others would surely survive. Some farmers left their crop stubble to rot in the field after harvest, protecting their soil from washing away during the hard rains. The next season, their soil was still soft and good for planting. Some farmers planted lab lab beans after the grain harvest so something was always growing. They could feed these beans to livestock, and the bean plants also helped to hold and enrich the soil.

It still rains less in Zimbabwe than it once did. But some farmers there no longer rely on non-native seeds or international food aid, and have become better able to prevent hunger, by growing crops that can survive the drought.

Green Revolution farming methods

Ever since the "Green Revolution" of the 1960s, corporations and international agencies have claimed they can "feed the world" with "improved seeds," chemical fertilizers, and pesticides. While they have succeeded in gaining control of farm land, seed supplies, marketing and distribution systems, and so on, they have failed to stop world hunger, and have often made hunger worse.

Poor access to water

Crops need water to grow. As large farms use more and more water, less and less is available for smallholder farmers. When water is polluted or privately owned, the right to water is threatened (see Chapter 6). There are many ways to manage soils and water to preserve water resources (see Chapters 9 and 15), but these methods must be protected and promoted by governments and international agencies supporting people's right to water.

Loss of land

When most of the land is owned by a few people or corporations, this causes many food problems. Many smallholder farmers are forced to leave their land and migrate to the cities, or work on plantations or in factories. Because they no longer have land to grow their own food, or money to buy healthy food, they become victims of hunger and malnutrition.

Usually larger farms and corporations will plant just one crop, employ fewer people, use more machinery, more chemical fertilizers, pesticides, and herbicides, and sell produce far from where it is grown, often sending it to other countries. This creates less variety of food, poorer nutrition, less income for farm workers, more environmental damage, and less food available locally. This also harms local cultures because people can no longer maintain their traditions of growing food and taking care of the land.

Poor access to credit and markets

Because farming depends on the weather and on market prices, farmers sometimes need to borrow money until harvest time or until the market improves. Banks often refuse to lend money to smallholder farmers while lending money to larger, more powerful farms. This causes smallholder farmers and their families and communities to go hungry. In many cases, it also forces them to give up their land.

Migration

When people are forced off their land, they may also lose their knowledge of how to produce food. If young people leave for the city before learning to farm, they will never be able to teach their own children how to farm and the family's loss of land will be permanent.

Epidemic diseases

As diseases like HIV/AIDS, TB, and malaria kill millions of people worldwide, hunger and malnutrition increase. Families and communities are losing whole generations of people, usually the people who would be most active growing food. Food production goes down as farmers die, and their knowledge of how to grow food dies with them. Preventing and treating these diseases not only prevents the hunger and malnutrition that go with them, but is important for the entire community's food security.

Lack of knowledge

In many places, people have lost traditional knowledge of how to produce food. And because of rapidly changing conditions, such as overcrowded communities, less fertile land, and changing weather, old methods often no longer work. When people do not know how to produce food, hunger and a lack of food security is the result. One solution to this problem is to maintain, pass on, and improve knowledge through farmer field schools, farmer to farmer education programs, and agricultural extension services (see page 316, and Resources).

Hunger is caused by a lack of food. A lack of food is often caused by a lack of justice.

Food Sovereignty is a Human Right

All people have the right to food that is safe, healthy, and culturally acceptable to them. **Food sovereignty** is the right to determine our own food systems, and make sure every community has food security.

Vía Campesina promotes people's control of food

Many smallholder farmers do not earn fair prices for their crops. One reason for this is that the rules of international trade benefit rich nations and large landholders. Often, farmers cannot get fair prices, even in local markets, because imported foods are cheaper. This forces farmers to sell at lower prices and drives them deeper into debt, poverty, and hunger.

In response to this problem, farmers in many countries joined together to form a movement called *Vía Campesina* ('The Peasant Way' in Spanish). Vía Campesina brings many farmer organizations together to strengthen farmers' ability to earn fair prices, to preserve land and water resources, and to have control over how food is produced and distributed. For Via Campesina, food security can be achieved only through food sovereignty – when farmers and peasants have the right to decide what foods they produce and how much to sell them for, and when consumers have the right to decide what they consume and who they buy it from.

In some places, Vía Campesina pressures politicians and corporations to respond to the demands of local farmers' unions. In other places they support landless farmers working to reclaim unused farmlands. They also help build local institutions that distribute food fairly to those most in need.

When a huge earthquake and tsunami (a massive tidal wave) struck Indonesia in 2005, most of the people affected by the disaster were farmers and fishers. Vía Campesina provided aid, but rather than simply bringing food and other materials from outside the area, they worked with local organizations to buy food, tools, and other materials from local small producers. They raised important issues such as the origin of food aid (whether it was local or imported), the way farm reconstruction would happen (whether it promoted family based production or large food corporations), and how to strengthen local organizations (not make them dependent on aid).

Most of the money Vía Campesina raised was used for long-term reconstruction, such as rebuilding houses and fishing boats, making new tools for farmers and fishers, and restoring farm lands to production. By focusing on the self-reliance of the people affected by the disaster, Vía Campesina promoted not just short-term recovery, but long-term food sovereignty.

13 The False Promise of Genetically Engineered Foods

In this chapter: page

The False Promise of Genetically Engineered Foods

Tomatoes that do not go bad after they are picked... wheat and soybeans and maize that can resist large amounts of pesticides... seeds that kill pests in the ground. None of these things are natural. And yet they exist.

These new kinds of plants are called genetically engineered (GE) foods or genetically modified (GM) foods. Not everyone agrees that these new crops are healthy. The corporations that make them say they will improve food security, help feed the world, and, in the case of biofuels (see page 533), end our dependence on oil. Other people say they are harmful for people and the environment. No matter what you believe, the present and future of farming, and food security for all of us, is being changed by these new crops.

Most GE crops do not provide greater crop yields, better nutrition, or any of the health benefits that their inventors claim. And so far, GE crops do not help the poor or solve the problem of hunger. Most GE crops have been invented to sell more of the pesticides and fertilizers made by the same companies that produce and sell GE seeds.

GE foods offer a technical solution — costly, man-made seeds — for a social problem: hunger. But as farmers come to depend on buying these seeds and the pesticides and fertilizers they need to produce these crops, hunger increases, not decreases. There is less food security and less food sovereignty.

Farmers resist GE cotton

Basanna is a cotton farmer in Karnataka state, in India. Several years ago, when GE crops were very new, he was approached by men from the Monsanto Corporation, who offered him a new variety of cotton seeds. They gave him the seeds free of cost, along with fertilizer to help them grow. They told him they would come every few weeks to inspect the crop and to spray his field. To Basanna, this seemed like a very good deal. He would have a cotton harvest at no cost, and the company would do most of the work.

Basanna did not know this was part of Monsanto's genetic engineering experiment. Men from Monsanto came to spray pesticides on the field regularly, but the crop still suffered from bollworm and other pests. Basanna wondered what kind of cotton would need so much pesticide, and still not grow well.

Basanna soon learned that other farmers were growing the new cotton too. He also learned that the Karnataka State Farmers' Association did not like the cotton, or the company promoting it. Basanna went to a meeting held by these farmers to learn more.

Basanna learned the new cotton needed more chemicals than he had used before, and that these chemicals would decrease the fertility of his soil. He also learned that this cotton might not yield any more than his old cotton did. Basanna heard that he would not be allowed to replant the cotton seeds because the company owned the rights to them. Worst of all, he learned that pollen from the plants could travel on the wind and affect his neighbor's crops. If the neighbor's crops pollinated this new cotton, they would not be allowed to replant their seeds the next year.

When Basanna realized the GE cotton was a threat to his farm and to his entire community, he joined the Karnataka State Farmers' Association. Together, thousands of farmers came up with a plan to tell the world what they thought of GE cotton. They planned an activity and then, the day before they gathered, they sent a letter to newspapers throughout the country that said:

> *Three fields in Karnataka will be reduced to ashes on Saturday. Activists have already contacted the owners of these fields to explain to them what action will be taken and for what reasons, and to let them know we will cover any losses they will suffer. Saturday at midday, thousands of farmers will occupy and burn down the fields in front of the cameras, in an open, announced action of civil disobedience.*

The next day they did what they promised. The first field burned belonged to Basanna. He supported the burning because he was angry that the Monsanto Corporation had not been honest with him and that the GE cotton would do so much harm to his fields and his neighbors. With the money the Farmers' Association paid for his burned crop, he bought traditional cotton seeds, and went back to planting the variety that had served him well in the past.

Questions for discussion

- Have you ever known a farmer to destroy his own crops? What would make a farmer, or you, do that?
- Can you think of any other ways the farmers of Karnataka could have shown how much they were against GE crops?
- What are the benefits of growing "improved" GE seeds?
- What are the "hidden" costs of using GE seeds?
- What else do you know about GE seeds?

Traditional plant breeding

All living things contain tiny parts called **genes.** Genes determine how each plant, animal or person grows, and what it becomes: from a seed to a plant, from an egg to a chicken, from a child to an adult.

As they interact with conditions such as heat, cold, wind, soil quality, and so on, the genes in plants determine how plants will grow. Qualities such as the color, shape, and size of plants, if they will grow quickly or slowly, when they produce flowers and fruit, or what nutrients they have are determined by each plant's genes.

When farmers select and save the biggest maize seeds after each harvest to plant the next year, the gene for large seeds is passed from one crop to the next over many years, and the gene for small seeds disappears. This is how **plant breeding** works. It is a slow process of selecting and favoring the development of the characteristics in a plant that a farmer wants.

By selecting the seeds of the healthier plant, you can help the next season's crops be stronger.

How are GE plants different from traditional plants?

Genetic engineering is different from plant breeding. Scientists use laboratory methods to change the genes of plants or animals in more extreme ways than traditional plant breeding does. To get the plant qualities they want, they can bring together genes from 2 completely different kinds of plants (such as rice and maize). They can also mix plant genes with animal genes. For this reason, it is called "genetic engineering." Like an engineer, a plant scientist "builds" new kinds of plants and animals that would never develop naturally.

GE plants are not simply new varieties with better qualities. They are a new kind of plant that never existed before. Corporations spend billions of dollars every year to invent new combinations, such as trees that grow quickly and have soft wood for making paper, tomatoes that stay fresh when they are stored for a long time, soybeans, wheat, and cotton that can survive large doses of pesticides, and animals such as fish and pigs that grow much larger than normal.

The high cost of GE crops

Growing GE crops is more expensive than growing traditional crops in a sustainable way. Instead of saving the seeds from the previous crop, farmers must usually buy GE seeds each year along with costly fertilizers and pesticides. GE crops also have many other hidden costs. They can be poor in nutrition and can damage the environment (see page 243). Before planting GE crops, consider these other, often "hidden," costs.

GE Foods and Health

Some of the health effects of GE foods are known because people have become sick from eating them. Other health problems are suspected but not yet proven.

Government agencies in the United States and other countries that develop GE crops have refused to test their possible health effects. Corporations that develop these crops do everything possible so their crops will not be tested. GE crops and the foods made from them are often not labeled, and are mixed with ordinary crops and foods. All this makes it difficult to know if a GE food is dangerous or if someone has become sick from eating GE crops.

How can I know if the formula we are feeding our baby contains GE crops or not?

There is no way to know because the companies will not tell you on the label. But most formula is made from soy, and soy is one of the most GE crops around!

It would be better for the baby to be breastfeeding anyway. Would you like me to speak with your wife?

Health problems from GE crops

To know for certain what the health effects of GE crops are will require many years of study. Scientists have already done some studies that show GE crops probably do cause health problems:

Allergies

Foods made from GE crops contain things that have never been eaten before. This may cause people's bodies to have bad reactions to these foods. Because we cannot know in advance what substances in GE crops will cause **allergies,** people may become allergic to many of the foods they commonly eat.

Increased pesticide poisoning

Most GE crops grow well only when large amounts of chemicals are added. Some GE seeds have even been designed to contain pesticides. Limited use of some pesticides may benefit farmers. But using too much leads to more pesticide poisonings of both people and the environment (see Chapter 14).

Cancer and organ damage

Animals fed GE potatoes and tomatoes had changes in their stomachs that could lead to cancer, damage to the kidneys and other organs, and poor brain development. But when GE foods are not tested or labeled, it is almost impossible for doctors to know if a person's cancer or organ damage is caused by GE foods.

Resistance to antibiotics

Some GE foods include genes resistant to **antibiotics** as a result of genetic engineering. Some scientists believe when people eat foods containing these genes, **antibiotic resistance** in bacteria will be created in the stomach. Then, if that person needs to take antibiotic medicine to solve a health problem, the medicine may no longer work.

Golden rice in Asia

Around the world, millions of people suffer from blindness caused by a lack of Vitamin A in their diets. As a solution to this problem, a new kind of GE rice containing Vitamin A was developed and named Golden Rice. The company that makes Golden Rice plans to sell it to farmers all over Asia where rice is the main food, and where blindness from a lack of Vitamin A is a serious problem. The company hopes farmers will grow Golden Rice instead of traditional varieties of rice.

However, Golden Rice will not prevent people from going blind. The blindness Golden Rice is trying to cure is not caused only by a lack of Vitamin A. It is caused by the lack of a sufficient variety of healthy foods that naturally contain Vitamin A. Even if a person eats Golden Rice, the Vitamin A will not nourish them unless there are enough nutrients from other foods eaten at the same time.

A healthy diet includes vegetables and fruits as well.

Instead of trying technical solutions like GE rice to prevent blindness and other problems of widespread hunger, it would be better to improve food security. Because the inventors of Golden Rice did not challenge the real problems of poverty and malnutrition, they will not prevent people from going blind.

A better way to end problems from poor nutrition

Golden Rice is an example of trying to solve a social problem — blindness due to poverty and malnutrition — with a technical solution: genetically engineered crops. But there is another solution.

There are large amounts of Vitamin A in fresh fruits, dark green leafy vegetables, and other foods. (See a general health book such as *Where There Is No Doctor* for information on good nutrition.) Green vegetables used to grow wild in rice paddies and farmer's fields until the increased use of herbicides killed them.

In the country of Bangladesh, people organized to plant home gardens to make sure that children have enough nutritious food. With the help of an organization called Helen Keller International, people planted 600,000 home gardens to help prevent blindness and other health problems from malnutrition. Home gardens are one way to improve nutrition and food security without looking for expensive technical solutions such as GE food, which may not work anyway.

Environmental Problems from GE Crops

When large corporations make and sell only a few kinds of seed, and then convince farmers worldwide to use only these seeds, many different types of plants may be lost and food security is harmed. But the most harmful effect of GE crops on the environment is the loss of biodiversity (see page 27) essential for a healthy environment.

Loss of natural pest controls. Some GE crops are made with pesticides inside them. When pesticides are used without careful controls, the pests they are meant to kill can become resistant to them (see page 273).

Harm to wildlife and soil. Pesticides in GE crops kill helpful insects and bacteria that live in the soil. They may also harm birds, bats, and other animals that help pollinate plants and control pests.

Effects on nearby plants. Pollen from GE crops blows in the wind and spreads to other plants that are similar to them. But because GE plants are new, nobody knows for sure what long-term effects this may have.

Farmers suffer when GE crops harm the environment.

Better safe than sorry

An African proverb says, "If you have to test the depth of a river, put one leg in the water first. This way you do not risk drowning." This is another way to say it is wise to act with precaution, and to follow the **precautionary principle** (see page 32.) When we are thinking about using new inventions and substances, it is best to know they are safe, rather than risk being harmed unnecessarily.

But corporations and governments are testing GE foods on us every day by having us plant and eat them without knowing what harm they may cause. They are forcing us to "test the depth of the river" with 2 legs, instead of one!

How do you know if seeds and food are genetically engineered?

Most genetically engineered seeds do not look, feel, smell, or taste any different than ordinary seeds, so they may be planted by farmers who do not know what they are. Monsanto, the company that makes most GE products, has refused to label them as GE foods, so the people who eat them can not know if they are GE foods. The only way to know if seeds and food are GE is to test their genetic structure. Testing kits are available, but expensive, in the United States and Europe.

Mother Seeds of Resistance

In Chiapas, Mexico, farmers are concerned that pollen from GE crops may affect their maize crops. With the help of international supporters, they found a way to test their crops to know if they are affected in any way. The project is called "Mother Seeds of Resistance."

Seeds are tested with testing kits bought from companies in Europe or the United States. By finding out if their crops have been contaminated by GE maize, they can tell their communities and their government about the problem, and work to prevent it from spreading further. Because they are testing the seeds themselves, farmers gain control over the process — a kind of control that is lost by not knowing what is in the crops they are growing.

By taking back control of their crops, farmers in Chiapas are protecting their food security while practicing long-term food sovereignty.

GE Food is Dumped as Food Aid

Many countries do not allow GE foods to be grown or brought into the country. But even in these countries, GE foods may find their way into the food supply. In poor countries, one way GE foods get into the markets and fields is through food aid.

When countries face severe hunger, they often receive aid in the form of grain from the United Nations or from individual countries. Countries where GE grain is produced often give it as food aid. This forces farmers, hungry people, and their governments to choose between GE foods and starvation.

But sometimes, even in the face of disaster, governments take a stand. For example, Zambia and Zimbabwe were offered GE maize as food aid in the winter of 2002, a time of severe famine. Zambia refused the GE food aid. After their decision, foreign donors supplied Zambia with cash to buy food from other countries in Africa that had produced extra food. Some European countries, where GE food is illegal, responded by offering food aid free of GE grains.

The government of Zimbabwe also felt the pressure of many hungry people. Zimbabwe accepted the GE food aid, but only after making an agreement that the maize be milled so it could not be planted later and cause future problems.

Learning Resources
Centre

Community seed savers

Around the world, communities are responding to the threat of GE crops. Some people demand that governments label GE foods so they can avoid buying or eating them. Others refuse to allow GE crops to be planted in their regions. Many communities have returned to the ancient practices of seed saving and **community seed stewardship.**

RICE

*contains genetically engineered ingredients

Community seed stewardship is when communities take control of the seeds they have, save a variety of seeds to plant in the future, and keep careful records of these seeds. In this way, communities keep important seed resources alive and protect biodiversity. Also, they can prevent outsiders from claiming ownership over their traditional seeds.

Governments can and should maintain national seed banks to make sure there are plenty of different crops, and to prevent varieties of each plant from growing scarce or disappearing. Keeping control over the seed supply is essential to food security and food sovereignty.

Villagers organize a seed swap

The people in the Mexican village of Vicente Guerrero were worried about losing their traditional seeds. Older people in the village remembered when there were many different kinds of maize and even more kinds of beans. Now there were only 2 kinds of maize and 4 kinds of beans. They knew that seed companies were making new kinds of seeds that could be used for only 1 year, or needed expensive chemicals to grow. So the villagers decided to do something.

The villagers invited people from the region to a big party, and asked everyone to bring food to cook and their favorite kinds of seeds. People would trade seeds with each other, cook meals with their favorite crops, and tell stories about where these crops came from and how they grew. The meeting was called a seed swap.

Some farmers arrived with varieties of maize and beans that others had not seen in many years. They gave away seeds for others to plant. That year there were 5 kinds of maize and 8 kinds of beans at the seed swap. By the next year, news of the seed swap had spread throughout the region, and farmers brought seeds even the grandparents had not seen since they were children.

After a few years, the village had collected over 20 kinds of maize and over 40 kinds of beans. The variety of plants makes sure that some maize and beans will grow every year, because some kinds grow best on dry hillsides, others in wet valleys, and others grow well on flat land, and so on. Many people in Vicente Guerrero started planting these crops, and now the villagers do not fear losing control over their seeds. By eating a variety of plants, they have also improved their diets.

Now other villages in the region are having seed swaps, and many old crops are coming back. The farmers in Vicente Guerrero say planting the old crops not only improves their food security, it also gives them a great reason to have a big party!

14 Pesticides Are Poison

In this chapter: page

Pesticides Are Poison

Pesticides are chemicals used to kill insects, rodents, and weeds that might harm our crops and health. But pesticides also poison and kill other living things, including helpful plants and insects, and animals and people. Pesticides can drift far from where they are used and pollute the soil, water, and air.

In this chapter we use the word **pesticides** to describe all chemicals used to control pests. They include:

- **Insecticides** used to kill insects.
- **Herbicides** used to kill weeds and unwanted plants.
- **Fungicides** used to control plant molds.
- **Rodenticides** used to kill rats, mice, and other rodents.

Farmers did not always use pesticides, and many farmers have great success farming without them. If you have a choice, it is safer for your health and the health of the land not to use pesticides. **Pesticides are never safe.** But for farm workers, plantation workers, and anyone who feels they must use pesticides, there are ways to reduce harm and to be as safe as possible.

Why are pesticides used?

Pesticides are not healthy for the food, the farm, the farmer, the farm worker, or the environment. So why do people use them?

Pesticides are often used together with farm machines, giant irrigation systems, low-paid workers, and government **subsidies** to produce crops that can be sold cheaply. Pesticides can kill everything that might reduce crop yields or make the food look less attractive, so large farm corporations use them as part of a system to sell more food.

Farm owners call pesticides "medicine." But are they really medicines?

No. They are poisons that kill weeds and insects. They can even kill people.

For family farmers to compete with large corporate farms, they often believe they too must use pesticides. When a struggling farmer needs to feed his family today, he may not think about what will happen to his own health or his family's health tomorrow. But this way of producing crops has high costs for people's health and the environment.

Over time, pesticides cause great harm. After years of spraying, pests may become **resistant** to chemicals (see page 273). Pesticides also kill many insects and birds that are not pests and that actually control crop pests. When this happens, pesticides no longer reduce crop loss from pests, crop yields go down, and family farmers are forced into poverty. Worse, pesticides kill thousands of people every year and make many more sick.

The companies that make pesticides say their products will help farmers "feed the world." But what these companies really want is to feed their profits without considering the long-term harm they cause. Pesticides are one part of an unjust and unhealthy system that makes a few people richer and makes everyone else sick.

There are many kinds of pesticides

There are many types and brands of pesticides, and they are called different names in different countries. Some pesticides may be banned in one country for being too dangerous, while still being sold in other countries.

Pesticides are made in different forms: powders for mixing with water and spraying, granules and dusts for dusting, liquids for spraying, coatings on seeds, pellets to kill rodents, and others. Mosquito coils and rat poisons are common for killing pests at home.

Pesticides are sold in different packages: cans, bottles, buckets, bags, and others. Pesticides are often put in other containers than the ones they originally came in. No matter what kind of pesticide it is, no matter what form it is in, no matter what kind of package it is in, **pesticides are poison!**

I understand that pesticides are poison. But I still need to go to work on the banana plantation. Sometimes I feel sick when I go home. How can I know if it is from the pesticides we use?

Pesticides Cause Many Health Problems

A person exposed to pesticides may have more than one sign of illness. Some signs show up at the time the person is exposed. Other signs do not show up until hours, days, or even years later. (For more on health effects of toxic chemicals, see Chapter 16.)

Many people are exposed to pesticides but may not know it. Laundry workers, garbage and recycling workers, and others who have direct contact with pesticides may be in just as much danger of poisoning as farm workers. They should be aware that there are pesticides in their environment, and they should follow the same precautions as farm workers.

Signs of pesticide poisoning

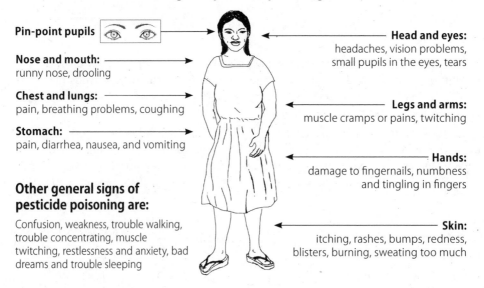

Pin-point pupils

Nose and mouth:
runny nose, drooling

Chest and lungs:
pain, breathing problems, coughing

Stomach:
pain, diarrhea, nausea, and vomiting

Head and eyes:
headaches, vision problems, small pupils in the eyes, tears

Legs and arms:
muscle cramps or pains, twitching

Hands:
damage to fingernails, numbness and tingling in fingers

Skin:
itching, rashes, bumps, redness, blisters, burning, sweating too much

Other general signs of pesticide poisoning are:

Confusion, weakness, trouble walking, trouble concentrating, muscle twitching, restlessness and anxiety, bad dreams and trouble sleeping

If you have any of these problems while working with pesticides, leave the worksite immediately. Do not wait until you feel worse. Get away from the pesticides and **go to a hospital or clinic right away!**

Signs of severe poisoning:
Unconsciousness, loss of control over bladder and bowels, blue lips and fingernails, shaking

Severe pesticide poisoning can kill.

Children and Pesticide Poisoning

Pesticides are more dangerous to children than they are to adults. Because children are smaller and are still growing, they get sick from amounts of pesticides that may not hurt adults. Amounts of pesticides that will make adults sick may kill babies and children.

Signs of pesticide poisoning in children

Even small doses of pesticides can affect a child's ability to learn and grow, and may cause allergies and breathing problems that last his whole life.

Common signs of pesticide poisoning in children are:

- tiredness
- diarrhea
- pain in the stomach
- skin rashes
- coughing fits
- seizures ("fits") and shaking
- unconsciousness

Signs that may show up months or years after a child is exposed to chemicals include:

- allergies
- breathing problems
- difficulty learning
- slow growth
- cancer
- other health problems may be made worse

Pesticides can also cause birth defects (see page 324). For more on how toxic chemicals affect children, see page 322.

Protecting Children from Pesticides

Children should by kept away from pesticides. Children:

- should not play with, use, or even touch old pesticide containers.
- should not play on farm equipment that is used to spray pesticides.
- should not wade or swim in irrigation or drainage ditches.
- should not enter or play in recently treated fields.

Wait a moment until I change my clothes and wash, Olanike.

Adults can protect children from pesticides:

- wash work clothes, shoes and your hands before entering the house and before touching children.
- wash children's clothes apart from parents' clothes.
- wash fruits and vegetables very well before anyone eats them.
- avoid the use of pesticides at home, especially indoors.
- store pesticide containers and equipment out of children's reach.

A village struggles against pesticide poisoning

People in Padre Village in Kerala, India used to think they were cursed. Young people suffered from serious health problems such as **epilepsy,** brain damage, and cancer, and did not grow as they should. Many women were unable to give birth, and many babies were born with missing arms and legs. What could cause all this illness besides a curse?

Padre Village was famous for its rich cashew plantations. Years ago, the company that owns the cashew plantations began spraying a pesticide called endosulfan. After spraying began, villagers noticed that bees, frogs, and fish vanished from the area. Many people thought they were killed by endosulfan, but they could not prove it.

Shree Padre, a local farmer and journalist, saw his calves born with deformed limbs. Since endosulfan had been sprayed near his farm many times, he wondered if the birth defects were caused by the pesticide. Shree Padre spoke with a doctor who had noticed similar health problems in people. After writing to people all over India, they learned that almost all the problems they noticed were known to be caused by endosulfan.

Visits from other organizations confirmed what Shree Padre and the doctor had learned. Word spread that the ill health of the people was caused by endosulfan.

Villagers gathered at the plantation offices and demanded that the spraying be stopped. The plantation officials, the pesticide industry, and some local authorities denied that endosulfan caused the problems. The police were called in and protests were broken up.

Soon, the local press and television picked up the story. Before long, people across India and around the world learned about the health problems caused by endosulfan. The state government banned endosulfan in Kerala.

But the pesticide industry argued that endosulfan was safe. They paid doctors and scientists to say that the health problems had no connection to endosulfan. Soon, due to pressure from the pesticide industry, the ban was dropped. Plantations in Padre began spraying again.

Farmers, doctors, and villagers from the area demanded that the government study the problem. Finally, the government agreed with the people of Padre Village: endosulfan was a deadly poison. A law was passed to ban it once and for all in that part of India.

But endosulfan is still sprayed in other parts of India, and in other countries. Laws say it is poison in some places, while it is considered safe in others. Poisons like endosulfan are only banned when people work together to pressure industry and governments for change.

Treatment for Pesticide Poisoning

Like other toxic chemicals, pesticides can poison people in different ways: through the skin and eyes, through the mouth (by swallowing), or through the air (by breathing). Each kind of poisoning needs a different kind of treatment.

When pesticides get on the skin

Most pesticide poisonings happen when pesticides are absorbed through skin when they spill while they are being moved, when they splash during mixing, or when you spray or touch crops that have just been sprayed. Pesticides can also get on your skin through your clothes, or when you wash clothes with pesticides on them.

Rashes and irritation are the first signs of poisoning through the skin. Because skin problems may be caused by other things, such as a reaction to plants, insect bites, infections, or allergies, it can be hard to know if the problem is caused by pesticides. Talk to other workers to find out if the crop you are working with causes this kind of reaction. If you work with pesticides and get any unexpected skin rashes, it is safest to treat them as if they are caused by pesticides.

Treatment

If you or someone else gets pesticides on the body:

- Quickly remove any clothing the pesticides spilled onto.
- Wash the pesticides off the skin as soon as possible with soap and cool water.
- If it got into the eye, rinse the eye with clean water for 15 minutes.

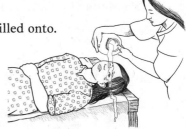

If the skin is burned from pesticides:

- rinse well with cool water
- do not remove anything stuck to the burn
- do not apply lotions, fats, or butter
- do not break blisters
- do not remove loose skin
- cover the area with a sterile dressing if available

- **If pain lasts, get medical help!** Bring the label from the pesticide containers or the names of the pesticides with you.

Pesticides can stick to your skin, hair, and clothes, even if you cannot see or smell them. Always wash with soap after using pesticides.

When pesticides are swallowed

People can swallow pesticides by eating, drinking, or smoking cigarettes in the fields while working with pesticides, or by drinking water polluted with pesticides. Children can drink or eat pesticides, especially if they are stored in containers also used to hold food, or left in the open or low to the ground.

Treatment

When someone swallows pesticides:

- If the person is unconscious, lay her on her side and make sure she is breathing.

- If the person is not breathing, quickly do mouth-to-mouth breathing (rescue breathing). Mouth-to-mouth breathing can also expose you to the pesticide, so cover your mouth with a pocket mask, a piece of cloth, or thick plastic wrap with a hole cut in the middle, before you start mouth-to-mouth breathing (see page 557).

Eating foods sprayed with pesticides might make you sick later.

- Find the pesticide package and read the label right away. The label will tell you if you should make the person vomit up the poison or not.

- If the person can drink, give her lots of clean water.

- **Seek medical help.** If it is available, always take the pesticide label or name with you.

Do not vomit if the label says not to. Never vomit after swallowing a pesticide that contains gasoline, kerosene, xylene, or other petroleum-based liquids. This will make the problem worse. Never make the person vomit or drink if she is unconscious, confused, or shaking badly.

If you are sure vomiting is OK,
give the person:

- a glass of very salty water **or**
- 2 tablespoons of pounded strong-tasting edible plant (such as celery, basil, or another local herb) followed by 1 or 2 glasses of warm water

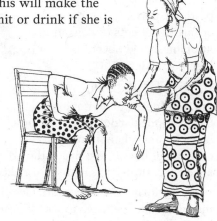

Keep the person moving around. This can help her vomit sooner.

After vomiting, activated or powdered charcoal (see next page) can help absorb any poison still in the stomach.

Mix ½ cup of **activated charcoal** or
1 tablespoon of finely **powdered charcoal**
with warm water in a large glass or jar.

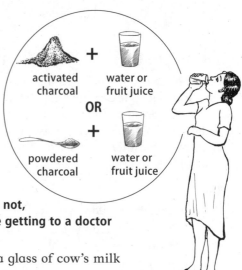

activated charcoal + water or fruit juice

OR

powdered charcoal + water or fruit juice

Make powdered charcoal from burnt
wood, or even burnt bread or tortilla.
This is not as good as activated charcoal,
but it still works. NEVER use charcoal
briquettes. They are poison!

**After the person vomits, or even if she does not,
you can slow the spread of the poison while getting to a doctor
by giving her a drink of:**

• 1 raw egg white,   or   • a glass of cow's milk

Drinking milk does NOT prevent pesticide poisoning.
It just slows the spread of the poison.

If someone swallowed pesticides and does not have sharp stomach pain,
they can take **sorbitol** or **magnesium hydroxide** (Milk of Magnesia). These
medicines cause diarrhea, which can help to get poisons out of the body.

When to use atropine

Atropine is a medicine for treating poisoning from certain
pesticides called **organophosphates** and **carbamates.** If the label on
the pesticide container says to use atropine, or if it says the pesticide is
a "cholinesterase inhibitor," use atropine as directed. If the label does
not say to use atropine, do not use it.

Atropine is used only for organophosphate or carbamate poisoning.

Atropine does NOT prevent
pesticide poisoning. It only
delays the effects of poisoning.
**Atropine should never be taken
before spraying.**

IMPORTANT: Do NOT give these
drugs for pesticide poisoning:
Sleeping pills (sedatives), morphine,
barbiturates, phenothiazines,
aminophylline, or any drugs that slow or
lessen breathing. They can make the person stop breathing completely.

Every farm that uses pesticides should have an emergency kit with
medicines and supplies to use in case of poisoning. See page 546 for
what to include in an emergency kit.

When pesticides are breathed in

When pesticides are released into
the air, we breathe them
in through our nose and
mouth. Once in the lungs,
the pesticides quickly enter
the blood and spread poison
through the whole body.

Because some pesticides
have no smell, it is often hard to know if they are in the air. The most common
forms of air-borne pesticides are fumigants, aerosols, foggers, smoke bombs,
pest strips, sprays, and residues from spraying. You can also inhale pesticide
dust in a storage area, when it is being used in an enclosed area, such as a
greenhouse, or when it is being transported to the fields.

Pesticide dust in the air can travel miles to
pollute an area far from where it was used. It is
easy for pesticide dust to get into houses.

If you think you have breathed in pesticides,
get away from the pesticides right away! Do not
wait until you feel worse.

Treatment

If you or someone else breathes in pesticides:

- Get the person away from the area where
  she breathed in the poison, especially if it
  is an enclosed area.

- Get fresh air.

- Loosen clothing to make breathing easier.

If you have doubt, get out!

- Sit with head and shoulders raised.

- If the person is unconscious, lay her on her side and watch her to make
  sure there is nothing blocking her breathing.

- If the person is not breathing, quickly do mouth-to-mouth breathing
  (see page 557).

Seek medical help. Take the pesticide label or name of the pesticide with you.

Drawing for discussion: **How do pesticides enter the body?**

Discussion questions:

- In what ways could this man be harmed by what he is doing?

- What can he do to protect himself?

- Who else may be affected by his actions?

- What are some reasons why he is not doing everything he can to protect himself?

Long-term Health Effects of Pesticides

Most pesticide poisoning comes from contact with pesticides over weeks, months, or years, not from using them only once. People may not get sick from pesticides until many years later. In adults, it can take 5, 10, 20, 30 years or more to get sick from regular exposure. How long it takes for illness to show up depends on many things (see page 321). In children, it usually takes less time. Illness from pesticides can start in a baby before the baby is born, while the mother is pregnant and in contact with pesticides.

When a person is exposed to pesticides over a long period of time, it is hard to know if his health problems are caused by pesticides. Long-term exposure may cause long-term harm, such as cancer, damage to the reproductive system, to the liver, brain, and other parts of the body.

Many long-term effects of pesticides are hard to see because people in farming areas are exposed to many different chemicals and because farm workers may move from place to place.

When people get cancer and other diseases, doctors and scientists may say the illness is due to chance, or to problems other than pesticides or contamination. They may tell us we cannot blame pesticides or other toxic chemicals. And sometimes people who sell pesticides or promote pesticide use will lie about it because they do not want to be responsible for other people's health problems. They can say this because it is often impossible to prove without a doubt that an illness which takes a long time to develop was caused by a particular pesticide or other toxic chemical.

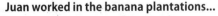

Juan worked in the banana plantations...   **...and 10 years later, he developed cancer.**

Signs of long-term illness from pesticides

Pesticides and other toxics can cause many long-term (chronic) illnesses. Some signs of chronic illness are: weight loss, constant weakness, constant or bloody cough, wounds that do not heal, no feeling in the hands or feet, poor balance, loss of vision, very fast or very slow heartbeat, sudden mood changes, confusion, memory loss, and trouble concentrating.

If you have any of these signs, tell your doctor or health worker. Be sure to tell them all the ways you may have been in contact with pesticides and, if possible, which ones.

Some long-term health effects of pesticides

Damage to the lungs: People exposed to pesticides may get a cough that never goes away, or have a tight feeling in the chest. These can be signs of bronchitis, asthma, or other lung diseases. Damage done over time to the lungs may lead to lung cancer. If you have any signs of lung damage, do not smoke cigarettes! Smoking makes lung disease worse.

Cancer: People exposed to pesticides have a higher chance of getting cancer than other people. This does not mean you will get cancer if you work with pesticides. But it means that working with pesticides gives you a higher risk of getting the disease. (For information about cancer, see page 327.)

Hundreds of pesticides and pesticide ingredients are known or believed to cause cancer. Many more have not yet been studied. The most common cancers caused by pesticides are blood cancer (leukemia), non-Hodgkins lymphoma, and brain cancer.

Damage to the liver: The liver helps clean the blood and get rid of poisons. Because pesticides are very strong poisons, the liver sometimes cannot get rid of them. Severe liver damage can happen after a serious poisoning or after working with pesticides for many months or years.

Because alcohol can damage the liver...

Toxic hepatitis: It is a liver disease people get from being exposed to pesticides. Toxic hepatitis can cause nausea, vomiting and fever, yellowing of the skin, and can destroy your liver.

Damage to the nervous system: Pesticides damage the brain and the nerves. Long-term exposure to pesticides can cause loss of memory, anxiety, mood changes, and trouble concentrating.

...drinking alcohol makes pesticide poisoning worse.

Damage to the immune system: Some pesticides weaken the immune system, which protects the body from disease. When the immune system is weak from poor nutrition, pesticides, or from illnesses like HIV/AIDS, it is easier to get allergies and infections and it is harder to heal from ordinary illnesses.

Reproductive health effects of pesticides

Pesticides have many of the same reproductive health effects as other toxic chemicals (see page 325). They can harm people's ability to have babies, or for babies to grow up healthy.

Chemicals can enter a woman's body and appear in her breast milk later. There are so many pesticides in use all over the world that even mothers who have never used pesticides have some toxic chemicals in their breast milk.

Breast is best!

Even if you think your breast milk may have pesticides in it, **the benefits of breastfeeding are stronger than any possible harm from pesticides in breast milk.** Breast milk is the best food to help a baby grow healthy and strong.

Some effects of pesticides on reproductive health are:

Sterility: Many male farm workers around the world have become unable to have children after they worked with certain pesticides because they can no longer make sperm.

Birth defects: When a pregnant woman is exposed to pesticides, the baby inside her is also exposed and can be damaged. Being exposed to pesticides when pregnant does not always mean the baby will have birth defects. But the baby will have a higher risk of having birth defects, learning difficulties, allergies, and other health problems. (For more about birth defects, see page 324.)

Damage to hormone-producing glands: Hormones control many of our body activities, such as growth and reproduction. When pesticides damage the glands that produce hormones, this can cause problems with childbirth and reproduction.

Even if a woman is exposed to pesticides before she is pregnant, she can have a miscarriage or the baby may be born dead because of the exposure.

Pesticides on clothing can affect anyone who comes into contact with them.

Pesticide Poisoning Can Look Like Other Illnesses

There are many different signs of pesticide poisoning, and they are easily confused with the signs of flu, malaria, an allergic reaction, or lung diseases. It is unusual to have only one sign. Most of the time several signs come together. You might not even know someone was poisoned because the signs can develop slowly.

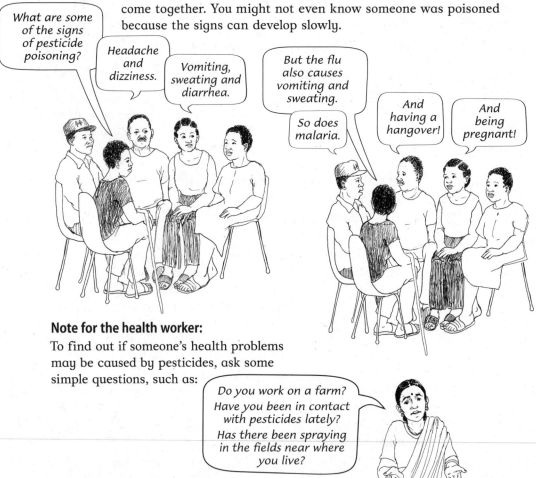

What are some of the signs of pesticide poisoning?

Headache and dizziness.

Vomiting, sweating and diarrhea.

But the flu also causes vomiting and sweating.

So does malaria.

And having a hangover!

And being pregnant!

Note for the health worker:

To find out if someone's health problems may be caused by pesticides, ask some simple questions, such as:

Do you work on a farm?
Have you been in contact with pesticides lately?
Has there been spraying in the fields near where you live?

How do you know if a health problem is caused by pesticides?

Sometimes you can find out if a sickness is from pesticides by talking to people who have the same sickness or work with the same pesticides. When people share the same signs of poisoning, and there are pesticides used nearby, there is a good chance they are all sick from the pesticides.

Doctors do not always have the answers

Carolina worked on a large strawberry farm. One day her stomach hurt and her eyes burned. She stopped working and went to talk to her boss. Her boss told her to go see the company doctor.

When she got to the doctor's office, he was not very friendly or helpful. Carolina thought pesticides might have made her sick, but she was too shy to say this to the doctor. The doctor did not ask her about her work or why she thought she was sick.

The doctor asked Carolina questions that made her feel like being sick was her fault: What did you eat today? Do you smoke cigarettes or drink a lot of alcohol? What did you do after work yesterday? Did you sleep enough?

In the end the doctor told her she was just lazy and only wanted a note to get out of work. He even said she might be sick from being drunk!

Finally the doctor gave her some pills for headaches. She was not sure the pills would help, but she took them anyway. As she went home, she wondered about going back to work the next day. She felt worse after seeing the doctor than she did before.

How could Carolina have gotten better care?

Perhaps if she brought the label of the pesticide she worked with and told the doctor it was what made her sick, he would have considered pesticide poisoning as a cause for her illness.

But even if she had done this, it might not have helped. The doctor worked for the company that owned the strawberry farm. Often company doctors will not admit that pesticides make farm workers sick. Pesticide illness can be difficult and expensive to treat. The company may prefer to hire new workers rather than treat treat their sick workers.

Perhaps Carolina could have gone to another doctor. But this would have been expensive, and she would have to take more time off from work. And most doctors do not know much about pesticides.

This is a very difficult problem for Carolina, and for all farm workers. The best way for farm workers like Carolina to take care of their health is to work together to change the conditions that make them sick in the first place.

Body mapping

This activity can help people share their experiences of how pesticides affect them. By drawing an outline of a body and marking where they have been affected by pesticides (a body map), people can begin to discuss common dangers they face in their work. This is a drawing activity and a group discussion.

Time: 1 to 2 hours

Materials: Large drawing paper, pens or pencils, tacks or tape

❶ **Make a large drawing of a person's body.** Use sheets of paper that are as large as a person, or several smaller sheets taped together. Have a person lie down on the paper while another person traces her outline. Next, tape or tack the drawing to the wall so that everyone can see it. If you want you can make 2 drawings, 1 for the front of the body and 1 for the back of the body.

❷ **Show which parts of our bodies have been affected by pesticides.** Each person in the group marks the paper with an X on a part of the body where he or she has been affected by pesticides. If the group is small, each person can say what the health effect was. For example, was it stomach pain, skin rashes, dizziness? He or she might also say what caused the health problem. Was it a spill, a mixing accident, drift, just normal work, or something else?

If the group is large, it may be easier for someone to guide the discussion of health effects after everyone makes their marks. The activity leader can point to each mark and ask what effect the mark represents. The important thing is that everyone includes their own experience of being affected by pesticides on the body map.

❸ **Ask questions to help people talk about pesticides.** It can be helpful for another person to take notes on a large sheet of paper that everyone can see. The talk may be most focused if at first it is limited to 3 main questions, such as: What effects have people felt from pesticides? What activities or kinds of exposure have caused the effects? What pesticides have caused the effects?

The body map shows where people feel the harmful effects of pesticides. The discussion and the notes are a good way to record how many people suffer from the same problems with pesticides and what exposures are most common. Further discussion can cover ways to prevent more exposures.

How to Reduce Harm from Pesticide Use

If you work with pesticides, use them with great care. Whether you are a farmer or a laborer, be responsible for your own well-being, the well-being of other people, and the environment. To protect yourself and those around you:

- Control pests without pesticides (see Chapters 15 and 17).
- Do not work alone with pesticides.
- Use the pesticide only on the crop it is meant for.
- Use the smallest amount you can. More is not always better.
- Do not mix different pesticides together.
- Keep pesticides off your body and off other people.
- Keep pesticides away from water sources.
- Do not use pesticides when it is windy, raining, or about to rain.

- Make sure your clothing covers you completely.
- Try not to wipe your eyes, face, and neck when you handle pesticides.
- Wash your hands before eating, drinking, or touching your face.
- Keep your fingernails and toenails short so pesticides cannot collect under them.
- Use protective clothing and equipment.
- Do not enter sprayed fields until it is safe to do so (see page 269).
- Wash well after using pesticides.

It's too hot to wear all this!

Yes it is uncomfortable, but without protective clothing you can get poisoned.

Protective clothing may be uncomfortable, but it can save your life.

To make wearing protective clothing more comfortable, spray early in the morning or late in the afternoon when the sun is not so hot. Rest in the shade and drink a lot of clean water to prevent heat sickness. For more on protective clothing and equipment, see Appendix A. To prevent or treat heat sickness, see *Where There Is No Doctor* or another medical book.

When you work in the fields

Make sure your equipment works properly

Check equipment for safety before you use it. Make sure pesticide applicators are not damaged and will not leak on you. Do not wear a cracked or broken backpack sprayer or ripped or cracked gloves. If you have a respirator, use it and change the filters every day. Breathing any pesticide without a respirator can affect your health.

Most farmers and farm workers cannot get good protective equipment. This is one reason why using pesticides is not safe.

> *Respirators and gloves are made for men. They do not fit women's bodies or young people. Women use pesticides as much as men, so protective equipment should protect them too. If it does not fit, it does not protect.*

Farm owners must provide washing facilities

If farm laborers use pesticides, it is the responsibility of farm owners to make sure there are places for workers to wash themselves and their clothing and equipment, as well as enough soap and clean water.

Wash yourself well and often

Wash your hands with water and soap before eating, smoking, drinking, chewing gum or tobacco, touching your eyes, nose, or mouth, and before going to the toilet.

After working, first clean under your fingernails and toenails. Then wash your whole body with soap and cool water.

Wash your clothes with care after working with pesticides

Washing work clothes is one of the most important things you can do to prevent pesticide poisoning. When work clothes are put back on without being washed, the skin is exposed to pesticides.

After work, change clothing and put work clothes in a plastic bag to protect the person who has to wash them (even if it is you).

Use clean water and soap, and wear gloves to protect your hands. Do not wash pesticide-covered clothes in rivers. **Never bathe or wash anything in irrigation or drainage ditches.** Try not to touch the clothes without gloves, and wash your hands afterward. Throw dirty water back onto fields, away from drinking water sources.

Wash small amounts of clothes at a time and repeat until the pesticide stain or smell goes away. Also wash boots, gloves, and hats in soap and water.

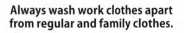

Always wash work clothes apart from regular and family clothes.

Dry clothes away from where pesticides are sprayed. Do not dry clothes outside when pesticides are being sprayed nearby or from airplanes.

Before washing other clothes in the washing basin, clean it with fresh water and detergent.

Store work clothes separately from other clothing.

Do not enter a field right after spraying

Wait until sprays have dried and dusts have settled before entering a field. Find out what pesticides have been used and do not enter the field until it is safe. See the pesticide label to find out how soon after spraying it is safe to enter a field (see page 276).

Storing pesticides

Pesticides must be stored in a safe, dry place. Pesticides are often left in storage for a long time, causing their containers to leak. Finding dead cats, birds, and other animals around buildings where pesticides are stored is often the first sign that chemicals have begun to seep into the ground and water.

Keep pesticides in their proper containers

Do not put pesticides in animal feed sacks, drink bottles, or water buckets. Make sure pesticide containers are tightly closed and stored upright. Check them regularly for breaks, leaks, and weak spots.

Label pesticide containers

If you buy small amounts of pesticides and put them in other containers, label the containers with the name of the pesticide and a picture that means "danger," for example a skull and crossbones. Do not use those containers for anything else.

Store pesticides out of the reach of children, in a locked cabinet or container, away from food or feed.

Transport pesticides carefully

When you transport or move pesticides, put them in the back of the truck or in the car trunk. Tie the containers down securely so they cannot move or fall over. Do not carry pesticides in your food basket or on your head. Do not let children buy or carry pesticides.

Get rid of empty pesticide containers safely

Never use pesticide containers for drinking, washing, storing food, or anything else. Do not use plastic pesticide wraps for raincoats or any other personal use. The best thing to do with empty pesticide containers is to make holes in them so no one will reuse them, and then to bury them.

Never use pesticide containers to carry water for drinking or washing.

When you mix and load pesticides

Wear protective clothing

When you mix pesticides and load them into applicators, wear eye protection, rubber gloves, and an apron, as well as the other protective clothing you would normally wear (see Appendix A).

IMPORTANT: Never mix pesticides with your hands.

Be careful

Open bags of pesticides with a sharp knife or scissors so pesticide dust will not spill out. Label the knife or scissors, wash them, and keep them for pesticide use only.

If you add water to pesticides, **never put a water hose directly into a pesticide mixture.** Keep the hose clean in case people use it for drinking or washing.

FOR PESTICIDES ONLY

Follow the directions for measurements. Use the amount directed on the label. **Never mix, load, or clean equipment near waterways or drinking water sources!**

Keep pesticides out of your mouth

To clear out a clogged nozzle, blow through a drinking straw and then mark the end that touches the nozzle so you do not put that end in your mouth if you use it again. To draw pesticides out of an applicator, or to transfer pesticides or fuels from one container to another, never start a siphon with your mouth. And always be careful not to breathe in the poison.

Do not touch or taste pesticides or pesticide-coated seeds. Do not eat anything from the fields until you wash it carefully.

Do not smoke, drink, or eat while mixing or applying pesticides. Leave food, gum, and tobacco in sealed containers in areas that have not been treated with pesticides. Tobacco and food absorb pesticides, so do not carry them while working.

If you spill pesticides

Before you clean up a pesticide spill, protect yourself, the people nearby, and water sources. If there are people more prepared than you to clean up a spill (trained to do this work), call them for help. Always wear protective clothing to clean up spills. (For information on cleaning up pesticides or other spilled chemicals, see Appendix A.)

Pesticides on Food

Fruits and vegetables grown using pesticides usually still have pesticides on them when we buy them. Meat, milk, and eggs are often contaminated with pesticides used in animal dips and sprays, or if livestock eat feed or grass that contains pesticides and other chemicals.

When people eat or drink small amounts of pesticides on their food day after day, poisons collect in their bodies over time. These small amounts can add up and cause long-term health problems.

Foods that have waxy skins, like cucumbers and apples, should be peeled before eating.

To clean off most of the pesticides, wash fruits and vegetables in soapy water (do not use detergents), in salt water (5 spoonfuls of salt to 1 liter of water), or in water with baking soda (2 teaspoons of baking soda in 1 liter of water), then rinse in fresh water.

Do not eat the outer leaves of leafy greens like cabbage and lettuce, because these parts collect the most pesticides.

Food grown without pesticides is much safer and healthier, both for the people who eat it and the people who grow it. Unfortunately, in many places it costs more and can be hard to get. (For information on how to grow food without toxic chemicals, see Chapter 15.)

Pest Control at Home

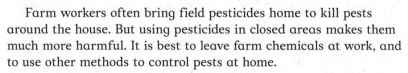

People everywhere use poisons in their homes to kill mosquitoes, ants, flies, cockroaches, termites, fleas, rats, and other pests. But many of the poisons used on these creatures can also harm people.

Farm workers often bring field pesticides home to kill pests around the house. But using pesticides in closed areas makes them much more harmful. It is best to leave farm chemicals at work, and to use other methods to control pests at home.

There are many ways to control pests without chemicals. These ways are safer and less costly than pesticides and may work just as well. (For other ways to keep chemicals out of your home, see Chapter 17.)

If you use pesticides at home:
- Read the label and follow the directions.
- Do not use pesticides in closed areas. Open windows and doors.
- Use pesticides only for the pests they are meant to kill.
- Keep pesticides away from children.
- Never spray pesticides on a mattress or sleep on a sprayed mattress.
- Do not spray near dishes or eating utensils.
- Never put pesticides in unmarked containers.
- Get rid of unwanted pesticides safely.

Pesticides Harm the Environment

Pesticides not only poison people and pests. They also harm other parts of the environment.

Pesticides poison animals when they eat, drink, and breathe them, just as pesticides poison people. The pesticides collect in their bodies and when larger animals eat smaller ones, the stored amount of poison gets larger too.

One day on the cotton farm I sprayed some termites with endosulfan. Later a frog ate the dying termites.

An owl swooped down on the frog and then sat in a tree to enjoy its meal. Ten minutes later, the owl fell down and died.

Pesticides poison the soil when they kill the insects, worms, fungi, and bacteria which create nutrients that keep soil alive and fertile.

Pesticides poison water when they run off into streams. They kill fish and harm animals and people that drink the water.

Pesticides poison air when they drift in the wind. Pesticides can travel many miles from where they were used.

Resistance to pesticides

There are always a few pests that do not die when they are sprayed because they are stronger or have chemicals in their bodies that block the pesticide. They give birth to other pests that have the same strengths and are not harmed by pesticides. This is called pesticide resistance. More and more pests are born with resistance, and that leads to a whole population of resistant pests that can no longer be killed with the same chemicals.

Pesticide companies then create new or stronger pesticides to kill resistant pests. Farmers buy the new chemicals, spending more money each season. Each year the environment is poisoned with more chemicals, more pests become resistant, and the pesticide companies make more profit.

While pesticides may reduce crop losses from pests for a few seasons, in the long run they poison people, animals, the ground, and the water. The only long-term benefit goes to the chemical companies that make and sell them.

Pesticides kill helpful insects

Not all insects are pests. Many insects are helpful to farmers. Bees pollinate plants and make honey. Ladybugs attack insects that damage crops. There are more helpful insects than there are "pests." But pesticides usually kill both the "good" insects and the "bad" insects.

For example, when a field is sprayed to kill aphids, the poison also kills the spiders and ladybugs that eat aphids. Without spiders and ladybugs to control them, more aphids come back.

**How pests become
resistant to pesticides**

**The pesticide kills most pests,
but some survive because
they are resistant.**

**The pests that survive give
birth to more resistant pests.**

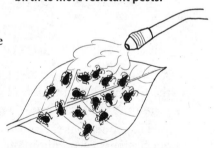

**Soon, all the pests are resistant,
and pesticides no longer work.**

Pesticide Education

If everyone stopped using pesticides tomorrow, we could end the epidemic of pesticide poisonings and begin to restore our land, air, and water to health. Educating ourselves and our communities about the harm pesticides cause, and learning how to grow food without chemicals, can help make this happen. A first step might be to bring people together in your village, town, or neighborhood to talk about their experience with pesticides.

Once people are gathered, decide what things are most important to your community. Is it personal health? Is it water pollution from pesticides? Is it the cost of pesticides? After there is some understanding of the problems, the next step will be to decide on a goal or goals. Maybe people will want to organize pesticide safety trainings, or learn how to farm without pesticides.

We know pesticides are dangerous. But we still use them every day. What can we do?

We can just refuse to use pesticides!

Then we would lose our jobs! I need to feed my children.

We should learn more about how pesticides hurt us and try to come up with some solutions together.

Farmers organize to stay independent

DOWN WITH MONSANTO

A group of farmers in Bangladesh started a program to talk about the pesticides they used and who they bought them from. Their goals were to use pesticides safely and to save money on their farms.

They found out their local bank was working with the large agribusiness corporation Monsanto. The bank and the company had made an agreement that loans could be used only to buy products from Monsanto. This forced farmers to use pesticides and seeds made by Monsanto, and did not allow them to take out loans to buy other things, such as farm animals or organic seeds.

When these farmers found out about the partnership between Monsanto and the bank, they began to organize and speak to many other farmers.

The farmers protested at the bank and refused to take out new loans. After many protests, the bank stopped working with Monsanto.

Drawing pesticide solutions

Time: 2 to 3 hours

Materials: drawing paper, colored pens or pencils, tacks or tape

If people already know that pesticides are harmful, this activity can help them think of solutions. It is helpful to have a person lead the activity.

❶ Talk about pesticide problems

Discuss the common ways people in the community come into contact with pesticides.

❷ Draw pesticide problems

Each person draws a picture of 1 way people are exposed to pesticides. These pictures are then taped or tacked to a wall. The group then looks at the drawings and decides on the 3 to 5 most common problems. Next, the group begins to talk about what might cause these problems. What makes these exposures to pesticides so common? Why are they so difficult to prevent?

❸ Draw solutions

In groups, people discuss possible solutions and draw pictures of their ideas. For example, if the problem is exposure from leaking backpack sprayers, short-term solutions include fixing the leaks and wearing protective clothing. Long-term solutions might include buying new equipment or changing to organic farming. A group might draw any or all of these solutions. Often a solution will solve more than one problem.

Tape or tack the solution drawings to another wall.

❹ Talk about solutions

Talk about the different solutions people drew. Which solutions can be achieved soon? Which solutions will take longer to achieve? The drawings can be rearranged so the most practical short-term solutions are at the top. Have people talk about how to achieve these solutions and work toward the longer term solutions too. Discuss what the group can do to make these solutions happen.

How to read and understand pesticide labels

An important part of pesticide education is helping people understand pesticide labels. All workers have the right to know what chemicals they are exposed to, what the risks are, and what protection they need. Pesticide packages are supposed to have labels so that people know how to use them safely and correctly. These labels tell what poison is being used, how to mix and measure it, how to treat poisoning, how toxic the pesticide is, and how long to wait after using it before entering fields.

Many pesticide labels are hard to read. They may use language that is hard to understand. Or they may not be printed in your local language. Since most field-workers do not even know what pesticides they are using, labels often do little to promote the safe use of pesticides.

Here is an example of a pesticide label. Other labels may look different, but they should have the same kinds of information. Remember, even if you follow the instructions perfectly, pesticides can still harm you and your environment.

Active ingredients are the chemicals that kill the pests.

This shows how poisonous the pesticide is. Words you may see here include:

DANGER, POISON - these are the most poisonous pesticides. This picture: near the word **Warning, Poison,** or **Danger,** means even a small amount is deadly.

WARNING - very poisonous.

CAUTION - these are the least poisonous pesticides, but they can still cause serious health problems!

This tells what kind of protection you need when you use this pesticide.

This tells what to do in case of poisoning. This is important because it will say whether or not to make the person vomit.

NO PEST
ABC ChemCorp
INSECTICIDE

Reg. No. M7485

ACTIVE INGREDIENTS
deltathion (1,2 phospho-(5)-4 chloromethane)
.... 50%

INERT INGREDIENTS 50%

TOTAL 100%

KEEP OUT OF REACH OF CHILDREN

DANGER   **POISON**

PELIGRO

PRECAUTIONARY STATEMENTS

Wear long-sleeved clothing, full length trousers, eye protection, and protective gloves when handling. Wash hands and face before eating or using tobacco. Bathe at the end of work day, washing entire body and hair with soap and water. Change clothing daily. Wash contaminated clothing thoroughly before reusing.

STATEMENT OF PRACTICAL TREATMENT

Hazards to Humans and Domestic Animals

If Swallowed: Do not induce vomiting. Contains aromatic petroleum solvent. Call a physician or poison control center immediately. **If in Eyes:** Flush with plenty of water for at least 15 minutes. Get medical attention. **If on Skin:** Wash with plenty of soap and water. Get medical attention if irritation persists. **If Inhaled:** Remove to fresh air immediately. Get medical attention.

Why are pesticide labels so hard to understand?

Would you buy it if the label said, "this is poison! Use it wrong and it will kill you!"?

This means that only people with training should buy or use this pesticide. But agricultural supply stores will sell them to anyone with money.

RESTRICTED USE PESTICIDE

For retail sale only to and application only by certified applicators or persons under their direct supervision, and only for those uses covered by the Certified Applicator's certification.

NOTE TO PHYSICIANS:

"No Pest" is a cholinesterase inhibitor. Treat symptomatically. If exposed, plasma and red blood cell cholinesterase tests may indicate significance of exposure (baseline date are useful). Atropine, only by injection, is the preferable antidote.

ENVIRONMENTAL HAZARDS

This product is extremely toxic to fish and wildlife. Do not apply directly to water or wetlands (swamps, bogs, marshes, and potholes). Do not contaminate water by cleaning of equipment or disposal of wastes.

REENTRY STATEMENTS

Do not enter or allow worker entry into treated areas during the restricted entry interval (REI) of 12 hours.
Written or oral warnings must be given to workers who are expected to go in a treated area.

DIRECTIONS FOR USE

Use specified dosage of NO PEST according to crop type described on table. Add ½ the amount of water indicated on table to the spray tank and begin agitation. Add the required amount of NO PEST to the spray mix. Add the remainder of the water and continue agitation until all solution has been applied.

STORAGE AND DISPOSAL

Store in original container only. Keep container tightly closed and upright. Avoid exposure to extreme temperatures. In case of spill or leakage, soak up with absorbent material such as sand, sawdust, earth, etc. Dispose of with chemical waste.

For container disposal, triple rinse and add rinsate to spray tank, then puncture and dispose of according to local authorities.

Information for a doctor about signs of poisoning and treatment. This is why the pesticide label should **always** be taken along when seeing a doctor.

If the label mentions **atropine,** this is another sign it is a very dangerous pesticide.

The **REI** or **Restricted Entry Interval** is the amount of time that must pass after the pesticide is applied before people can safely enter the field. This time is usually between 4 hours and 3 days.

How to mix, load, apply, store, and dispose of this pesticide.

Color Coding:
In many places, pesticide packages have different colors to show how poisonous they are. These color codes are different in different parts of the world. Learn the color codes in your area.

15 Sustainable Farming

Sustainable Farming

Sustainable farming means farming for the long-term health of people and the land. Farmers who use sustainable methods try to meet the needs of their families and communities for nutritious food while also conserving water, improving soil, and saving seeds for the future.

Most food comes from the land. But many people do not have enough land, or any land at all, to meet their needs for healthy food. Sustainable farming, cooperative food marketing (see page 313), and fair distribution of food can help to overcome these difficulties.

Farmers are caretakers of the land, and they are experts at what they do. Farmers develop methods of sustainable farming, and change and adapt these methods to serve the needs of their communities and the conditions of the land they work. Sustainable farming in cities and towns, or in areas that have been farmed for generations, helps solve problems of hunger, migration, loss of valuable soil, and contamination of water supplies.

Sustainable farming methods are not only for farmers. They are also valuable for home gardeners, health and development workers, and anyone who wants to begin a community garden or a city farm to improve nutrition, food security, and community health.

Juan, Pedro, and Hurricane Mitch

Juan's grandfather once grew plenty of food in the valley where he lived in Honduras, Central America. But when a fruit company bought his land, he moved up into the hills. There he taught his son, Juan's father Aurelio, how to clear the hillside of trees, and burn out the stumps. After each harvest, they burned the cornstalks and bean vines to make more ash to fertilize the soil.

Aurelio taught Juan to farm in the same way. But by the time Juan was a young man, the soil was tired and the harvests were poor. Juan could not clear new land because other farmers, fruit companies, and cattle ranchers owned all the nearby land.

Juan cut down all the trees on the hillside and planted as much corn, beans, and vegetables as he could. But the corn gave only one small ear and insects damaged the beans. Like many of his neighbors, Juan bought chemical fertilizer to help his crops grow, and sprayed pesticides to kill the insects. Finding the money for these was hard, especially when the land still produced barely enough to feed his family.

When a big storm brought 4 days of hard rain and strong winds, hillsides became rivers of mud and houses fell down all over the countryside. Juan's crops were ruined. His soil washed away, leaving behind nothing but rocks. His farm was destroyed, and he had to start all over.

Juan's neighbor Pedro survived the storm better. Pedro grows his corn, beans and vegetables between trees that produce fruit, shade, and fodder for his animals. Pedro does not burn his cornstalks and bean vines, but chops them up after the harvest and leaves them on top of the soil. Pedro also planted live barriers of agave cactus and other plants to keep soil from washing off his fields. After the storm, tree roots held most of the soil in place, and the barriers he made collected the rest.

"The different plants help each other and make the soil rich," Pedro says. "You would not even know we had a storm here. The water just soaked in better because my soil is like the soil in the forest."

With help from Pedro, Juan began to restore his field. He began by planting a bean crop as a green manure to restore soil fertility. He also planted live barriers and a variety of trees. Soon, other neighbors began trying these methods as well. Juan and the other farmers in the area have hope these sustainable methods of farming will help their families survive future storms.

As he watches his young plants and trees grow, Juan thinks of his children who will use this small piece of land to support their children for many years to come.

Farming for Health and a Better Life

Sustainable farming methods not only provide food, but they also build fertile soils, protect water, preserve valuable seeds, maintain **biodiversity,** and make sure the land will be able to sustain life for future generations. Using sustainable methods to grow food allows farmers and gardeners to grow more in less space, with few or no chemical pesticides and fertilizers. This can result in more and better food to eat and sell, less cost for producing food, and less pollution of the air, water, land, and our bodies. Sustainable farming improves people's health because it:

- reduces the threat of drought by conserving water.

- reduces dependence on chemicals, saves money, and builds self-reliance. Farming without chemicals prevents the health problems chemicals cause for farmers, farm workers, and everyone who eats the food that is produced or drinks the local water.

- decreases the amount of work needed to produce food when sustainable methods, such as green manures, are used. This is especially important when migration, HIV and AIDS, and other problems make it harder for people to work the land.

Sustainable farming makes the land more productive, so fewer people are forced to leave for the cities. Improving soil, conserving water, and saving seeds sustains farms and farming communities.

Principles of sustainable farming

Sustainable farming works best when farmers learn how to work with local conditions, and share what they learn with other farmers. Some general guidelines for sustainable farming are:

- **Healthy plants need healthy soil.** To use natural fertilizers to improve soil quality, see pages 282 to 288. To protect soil from erosion, see Chapter 11 and pages 289 to 293.

- **Save water and protect water sources.** Methods for conserving water are described on pages 294 to 295.

The green manure we planted last season really helped the soil.

The maize plants grew bigger, with larger ears, than ever before!

And there was less weeding to do because the field was covered in crops all year.

- **Save seeds** from each season's crop to plant the next season. For information about saving seeds, see pages 303 and 246 to 247.

- **Control pests and plant diseases naturally.** To learn about natural pest and disease management, see pages 296 to 301.

- **Plant a variety of crops.** Plant mixed crops and change where they are planted each year. This keeps nutrients in the soil and improves people's health by providing a variety of foods to eat. It also controls pests and plant diseases (see page 300).

- **First make small changes.** Most crops have been improved over hundreds and even thousands of years by farmers trying new methods. But not all new methods succeed. Try new ideas in a small field or garden first. If they fail, you will still have food from the rest of your land.

Improving Soil

Farmers know that healthy soil is necessary for good crops. Many farmers enrich soil with natural fertilizers, such as animal manure, green manure, and compost. Natural fertilizers are healthier for soil, plants, water, air, and people than chemical fertilizers. They add all the nutrients plants need at little or no cost.

Sustainable farmers not only grow crops — they grow fertile soil that has all the nutrients plants need.

Know your soil

Soil is a mix of sand, silt, clay, and organic matter (for example, insects, bacteria, green leaves, rotting plants, and manure). The amounts of each of these things, and the way you work the land, affect the soil texture (how coarse or fine it is), fertility (how rich it is for growing crops), and soil structure (how the soil holds together). A soil that has good texture, structure, and fertility allows air, water, nutrients, and plant roots to move through it. This improves the soil's ability to grow crops and resist erosion.

In addition, some soils are alkaline (also called "basic" or "sweet") while others are acidic (also called "sour"). You can learn the "pH" of your soil (how sour or sweet it is) by having it tested or simply by tasting it to see if it is sweet or sour. Most plants grow best in soils that are neither too sweet or too sour. Adding specific nutrients can make soils sweeter or more sour (see page 288). Adding organic matter tends to improve all soils.

Using heavy equipment to plow, till, turn over, or dig soil can make it become **compacted** (pressed down so tightly that no air or space remains). It is difficult for water or plant roots to get into compacted soil. It is also difficult for plants to get the nutrients they need from soil that is compacted.

To prevent compacting soil, clear and turn over soil when it is not too wet or too dry, but moist like a wrung-out cloth. Many farmers turn their soil as little as possible, add animal manure and crop wastes, and use methods such as planting pits (see page 295) or green manures (see page 285) to make the soil loose for planting.

Chemical fertilizers may help now, but can harm later

Chemical fertilizer

Chemical fertilizers are costly to both the farmer and the farm because they damage soil, pollute water, and create the need for more chemicals. If you look at a bag of fertilizer from the store, it will have the letters N-P-K. These letters stand for the main nutrients that plants need (N is Nitrogen, P is Phosphorous, and K is Potash, or Potassium). Chemical fertilizers have these chemicals in **concentrated** (very strong) amounts. When these concentrated nutrients are washed from fields into groundwater and waterways, they can make the water unhealthy for drinking, washing, and bathing.

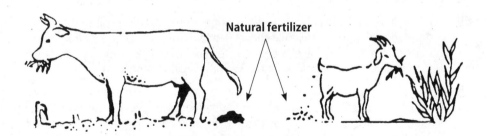

Natural fertilizer

The biggest problem for growing crops with chemical fertilizers is that farmers who use them often stop adding organic matter, such as animal manure, to the soil. This very quickly causes soils to lose nutrients and become compacted, leading to pest problems, poor harvests, water loss, and more dependence on chemical fertilizer. If you use chemical fertilizers, it is important to add natural fertilizers along with them.

Learning about soil

Purpose: This activity helps show how different farming practices affect the soil

Time: 3 hours

Materials: digging tools, 3 boards or pieces of cardboard, water, paper, and a pencil or marker

❶ Choose 3 parcels of farmland that have been used in different ways. For example, choose a field of maize or dry farmed rice, an orchard or home garden, and a plot that has been used for pasture for many years. The plots should be within easy walking distance from each other.

❷ With a group of farmers, walk through each of the areas. Cross back and forth, looking at everything that may have affected the soil. What signs show how the land has been used? Are there signs of erosion (for example, gullies, bare or rocky spots of ground, richer soil at the bottom of hills than at the top)? Do the plants look healthy?

❸ Talk to the person who farms each area to find out what practices they have used over the past 5 to 10 ten years. Do the group's observations match what you learn from talking to the farmers?

❹ Dig a small pit about 50 cm deep in each parcel. Cut 1 wall of the pit so that it is straight down and flat. Using a flat shovel or a long machete cut a slice about 3 cm thick from the flat side of the pit. Lay this slice of soil gently on a board or flat surface. Label the soil sample to identify which parcel it came from.

❺ When you have taken soil samples from all 3 areas, bring them to a meeting place where the group can examine them. What differences are there between the different soil samples? Look closely for differences in color, texture, structure, smell, and the presence or absence of worms and insects. Perhaps taste a small bit of each soil to compare the pH. Is it sweet or sour? Have different people take a little soil in their hands from different samples. Work in a small amount of water to each and say if it feels sticky, rough, smooth, or falls apart.

❻ Discuss which of these differences may have been caused naturally by wind and weather, and which may have been caused by the way the land was used.

Using knowledge from the group, from this book, or from other sources, discuss ways to protect and improve the soil in the areas that will be used for farming. These ways may include adding natural fertilizers (see pages 285 to 289), protecting the soil from erosion (see pages 289 to 293), using sustainable grazing practices for livestock (see page 307 to 308), and trying other farming practices.

Green manures and cover crops

Green manures are plants that help fertilize the soil. These same plants work as cover crops to choke out weeds. Since many plants do both these jobs, they are called by both names: green manures and cover crops.

Fava bean
Vicia faba

Many green manures are from the "legume" family (plants with seed pods, such as peas, beans, and tamarind trees). Plants in the legume family add nitrogen to the soil. If you pull up a bean plant, or look at some tree roots, you will often see small balls formed on the roots. These little balls collect nitrogen from the air and put it into the soil. This makes the soil more fertile.

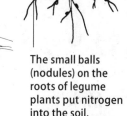

The small balls (nodules) on the roots of legume plants put nitrogen into the soil.

Alfalfa
Medicago sativa

Runner bean
Phaseolus coccineus

Sorghum
Sorghum

Lablab bean
Dolichos lablab

Velvet bean
Mucuna pruriens

Green manures have many benefits:

- They cover the soil, protecting it from erosion and helping it hold water.
- They add organic matter to the soil, making it more fertile.
- After using green manures for several years, the soil becomes easier to work.
- There are no costs for labor or transport because green manures grow right in the field where they are used.
- Planted with other crops, they control weeds and insect pests.

Green manures have other uses besides improving soil. Some provide food, such as oats, amaranth, rye, and beans. Others provide fodder for animals, such as alfalfa and clover. Plants such as Sudan grass and others in the mustard family prevent crop diseases. Trees used as green manures can provide firewood.

3 common ways to use green manures

- Grow them together with main crops such as maize, millet, and cassava.
- Plant them when the land is going to be left to rest (fallow). A 1-year fallow with green manure will improve soil and kill weeds just as well as a 5-year fallow with no green manure.
- Grow them during the dry season, after the main crop is harvested.

The best cover crop is a mix of plants. A grain that grows fast and tall will add organic matter to the soil, while a bean crop will add nitrogen and will cover the ground. Talk to other farmers in your region to learn what works best on your soils.

Grow the crop until harvest. Use the beans or grain for food or fodder, and then cut down the stalks.

Clear spaces in the cover crop and plant your next crop right into the ground.

Mulch

It is best to keep soil covered, even during the growing season. **Mulch** is anything used to cover the soil. Mulch helps hold water, control weeds, and prevent erosion. Plant wastes, such as maize stalks, bean vines, or grasses make the best mulch, because they can be simply left to rot in the field, and they add organic matter to the soil. Weeds can be used in the same way, but they must be cut before they make seed to prevent them from growing back.

Mulch should not be more than 10 cm thick. A very thick mulch can hold too much moisture and cause plant diseases.

Straw and grass cuttings make good mulch because they break down slowly.

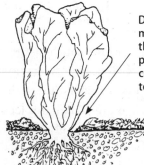

Do not let mulch touch the stems of plants. It can cause plants to rot.

Animal manure

Animal manures provide all the nutrients plants need, and over time improve soil texture, soil structure, and soil fertility. Chemical fertilizers, on the other hand, give crops only 2 or 3 nutrients and do not improve the soil.

Some care must be taken with manure. Using too much manure will cause too many nutrients to build up in the soil and can pollute waterways. Fresh manure also carries germs that can cause illness. Do not put fresh manure near drainage ditches or waterways. Always wash your hands and your clothing well after handling manure.

Fertilizing with human waste

Human urine can be turned into fertilizer, and human feces when properly treated can add organic matter to the soil. But human waste carries harmful germs and causes illness if it is not properly handled. (To learn how to safely use human waste to improve crop yields, see Chapter 7.)

Compost

Compost is a natural fertilizer made of food scraps, crop waste, weeds, and animal manure. Adding compost to the soil is a way of adding crop nutrients back to the earth. It would take a lot of work to make enough compost for a large field, so compost is most often used on smaller plots. (To make compost, see pages 400 to 403.)

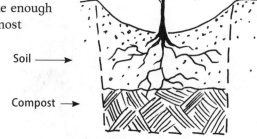

Soil ⟶

Compost ⟶

Compost can be used in many ways:

- Add a shovel full of compost in the bottom of planting holes before planting fruit trees.

- Mix a handful of compost with soil in planting holes when you plant seeds.

- Spread a layer of compost on top of your soil before turning it.

- While plants are growing, make a circle of compost around the plant stem. For a tree, make the circle where the edge of the tree's shade falls in the middle of the day. Cover it with a little soil. It will slowly feed the plant as water carries nutrients to the roots.

Compost tea

Compost can be used to make a liquid to fertilize plants and help control pests. Wrap some compost in a piece of cloth and tie it up. Put the cloth in a bucket of water for 7 to 14 days. When the water turns brown, take the cloth sack out. Spread the leftover compost in your field. Spray or sprinkle the compost tea on the leaves of your plants. Be sure to wash your hands after working with compost tea.

Other ways to add nutrients to soil

Other materials can be added to change soil pH (see page 282) and to add nutrients to the soil. Limestone, wood ash, and ground animal bones and seashells make soil less acid. The ground up animal bones also adds phosphorous and the wood ash adds potassium. Dried leaves and pine needles make soils more acid. Sugar cane that has rotted for at least a year and coffee pulp that is ground and dried add nutrients to soil, turning crop waste into fertilizer.

Ashes from wood fires can be dug into your garden soil to make it less acid.

Improving soil helps control weeds

All of the methods of improving soil with organic matter, such as green manures, compost, and mulch, also help control weeds. When the soil is healthy, small amounts of weeds do not harm crop yields.

Weeds can also be controlled by planting crops close together so there is no room for weeds to grow, and by allowing animals to eat the weeds. Also, crops that are native to the area tend to be harmed less by local weeds. Over many years, locally bred crops adapt to weather, weeds, and pests, and do well where other crops or other varieties of the same crop may not.

Protecting Soil From Erosion

When soil is not protected, wind and water can erode or damage the thin layer of soil on top (**topsoil**) and also cause the soil to lose water. The soil that remains is often compacted, lacks nutrients, and is not good for growing crops. Preventing erosion and conserving soil and water are some of the farmer's most important jobs. (To learn more about preventing erosion, see Chapter 11.)

When rain hits bare soil, it washes it away.

What rain does to bare soil

Purpose: To show the importance of keeping soil covered so it does not wash away

Time: 15 minutes

Materials: 2 pieces of clean paper or cloth, a watering can, or an old can with small holes in the bottom that makes water sprinkle like rain.

❶ Have the group meet on a piece of ground with no plants or weeds growing on it, just bare soil.

❷ Place a piece of clean paper or cloth on the ground. Pour water from the sprinkler to make rain on the ground beside the paper or cloth.

❸ See how many muddy spots were made on the paper or cloth when the water splashed on the ground. This is what happens when rain hits bare ground. The bare soil cannot hold the rain, and it washes away.

❹ With a new piece of clean paper or cloth, repeat the activity in a place where the ground is covered by grass, weeds, or mulch. The second paper or cloth should have fewer muddy spots on it than the first one because the plants hold the water and help it sink into the ground.

❺ Lead a group discussion of what happened and the importance of keeping the soil covered.

You may want to follow this activity with a farm experiment to show how mulch protects soil. Make a small demonstration plot and cover it with mulch after planting. Plant another plot with the same crop, but no mulch. At the end of the growing season, compare the results.

Contour Barriers

If you could make a path across
a slope that would let you
travel from one end to the
other while always staying
at the same level, you would
be following the slope's
contour line. Barriers built to
follow **contours,** such as walls,
mounds, lines of grass or brush, or trenches, prevent soil from being carried
away by wind and rain. They also help slow the downhill movement of water,
spread it over the soil, and sink it into the ground. Plowing along contours,
rather than up and down the slope, slows surface runoff and directs water
toward your crops. A tool called an A-frame level can help you find your land's
contour lines so you can build contour barriers.

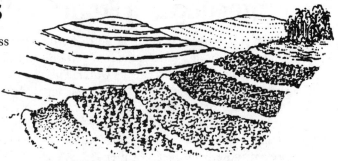

How to make an A-frame level

An A-frame level is a tool that can help you find contours. Use these materials:

- 2 sturdy sticks about 2 meters long and 2 cm thick to form the legs,
  and 1 stick about 1 meter long for the crossbar.

- 3 nails long enough to go through 2 sticks with a little sticking out.

- A bottle with a twist cap or cork, or a stone to use as a weight
  (about ½ kilo, or 1 pound).

- A string 2 meters long with a knot tied at one end.

- A pencil or pen, a hammer or stone, a machete or saw, and a tape measure.

❶ Fasten the 2 legs together in a triangle shape. If you nail them
together, leave the head of the nail sticking out because you will use
it later.

❷ Fasten the crossbar to the legs.

❸ Attach the weight (bottle or stone) to the string.
Tie the other end of the string to the head of
the nail so the weight hangs about
2 cm below the crossbar. If the bottle
is plastic, fill it with water, sand, or soil
and put on the cap or cork. The string
with a weight on the end is called a
plumb line.

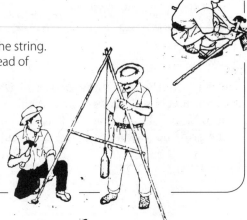

How to ready an A-frame by marking its center

1 Set the A-frame on a nearly flat piece of land. Mark where each leg stands. Make sure the plumb line can move freely, and then hold it still. Once the string stops moving, make a mark where the string touches the crossbar.

2 Turn the A-frame so the first leg is where the second leg was and the second leg is where the first leg was. Mark where the string crosses the crossbar. You will now have 2 marks on the crossbar.

3 Stretch a string between the 2 marks and fold the string in half to find the middle. Make a third mark there.

4 Set the A-frame on a flat place where the plumb line hangs right over the center mark on the crossbar. When the plumb line hangs at the center mark, the 2 feet of the A-frame are level (at the same height). Turn the A-frame and put each leg where the other was. It should still hang over the center mark. If the string does not hang over the center mark, repeat this process until it does.

Decide where to place each barrier

Once the A-frame is built, decide roughly how close together to place your barriers going down the slope. Your first barrier should be near the top of your field, to stop water from the fields above. Where you place the other barriers depends on the slope. For steep slopes, barriers should be about 10 meters apart. For moderate slopes, they should be 15 meters apart. For easy slopes, they can be 20 meters apart. If you must work on a very steep hill, it is best to make individual terraces for trees, or individual planting holes or small terraces for crops, rather than plowing or digging trenches.

Steep

10 meters

Moderate

15 meters

Easy

20 meters

You can measure with an A-frame, a tape measure, or your steps.

Also, consider the soil. Clay soil will not absorb water easily, so barriers should be a little closer together. If the soil is sandy or has a lot of organic matter, it will absorb water easily and barriers can be farther apart. When you have an idea of the distance you want between barriers, put stakes in the ground to mark them.

How to mark contour lines

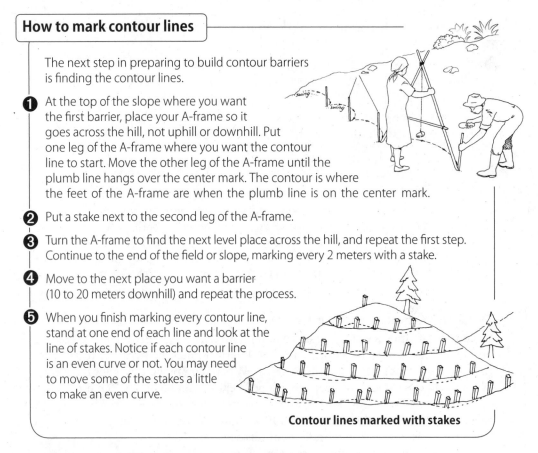

The next step in preparing to build contour barriers is finding the contour lines.

1 At the top of the slope where you want the first barrier, place your A-frame so it goes across the hill, not uphill or downhill. Put one leg of the A-frame where you want the contour line to start. Move the other leg of the A-frame until the plumb line hangs over the center mark. The contour is where the feet of the A-frame are when the plumb line is on the center mark.

2 Put a stake next to the second leg of the A-frame.

3 Turn the A-frame to find the next level place across the hill, and repeat the first step. Continue to the end of the field or slope, marking every 2 meters with a stake.

4 Move to the next place you want a barrier (10 to 20 meters downhill) and repeat the process.

5 When you finish marking every contour line, stand at one end of each line and look at the line of stakes. Notice if each contour line is an even curve or not. You may need to move some of the stakes a little to make an even curve.

Contour lines marked with stakes

Guidelines for building contour barriers

Once contour lines are measured and marked, and as you decide what kind of barriers are best for your land, keep these general guidelines in mind:

- **Preserve or plant trees and plants.** If the slope is very steep, the trees already growing there or trees you plant will protect it from collapsing. Grasses and plants with strong roots will help to hold soil and water.

- **Slow down water, but keep it moving.** It is important to keep water moving, whether down the slope or into the soil. Poorly planned barriers can lead to standing water, which lets mosquitoes breed and spread malaria and other illnesses.

- **Fix problems as soon as they happen.** Heavy storms may cause a contour trench to collapse or a wall to break. Fix it right away to prevent further erosion.

- **Start from the top.** Water runs downhill. By starting at the top, you protect everything below, and can use many small barriers.

Different types of contour barriers

Use the contour barrier that is easiest to build and works best for your land.

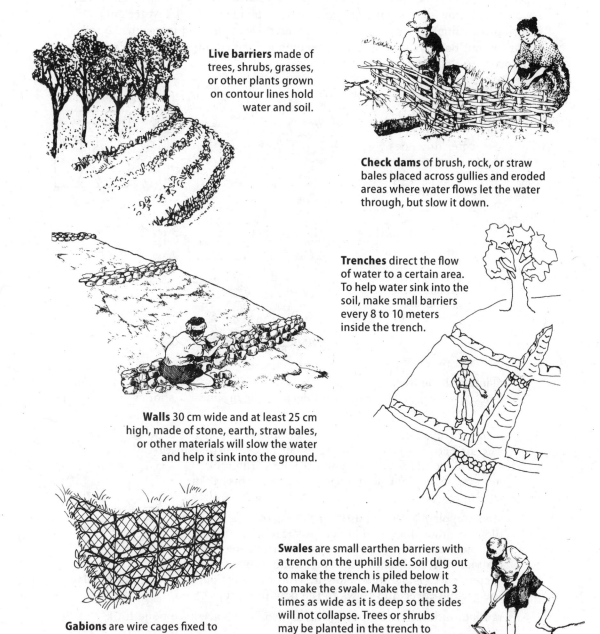

Live barriers made of trees, shrubs, grasses, or other plants grown on contour lines hold water and soil.

Check dams of brush, rock, or straw bales placed across gullies and eroded areas where water flows let the water through, but slow it down.

Trenches direct the flow of water to a certain area. To help water sink into the soil, make small barriers every 8 to 10 meters inside the trench.

Walls 30 cm wide and at least 25 cm high, made of stone, earth, straw bales, or other materials will slow the water and help it sink into the ground.

Gabions are wire cages fixed to the sides of a gully and filled with stones that catch and hold soil.

Swales are small earthen barriers with a trench on the uphill side. Soil dug out to make the trench is piled below it to make the swale. Make the trench 3 times as wide as it is deep so the sides will not collapse. Trees or shrubs may be planted in the trench to take advantage of the water, and on the swale to hold it in place.

Use Water Wisely

Every farmer needs water. If you live in a dry place, the best way to conserve water is to grow plants native to your area or plants that need water only during the rainy season. Green manure and mulch help hold water in the soil, and contour barriers save water by keeping it from running off. Other methods to save water on the farm are:

- **drip irrigation** from pipes laid on or under the ground, which uses much less water and does less damage to soil than water poured onto the ground from above.

Small holes in pipes or hoses allow water to drip into the ground slowly.

- **planting shade trees** to protect plants and soil from drying out in the sun. Some trees bring water up from deep in the ground for shallow-rooted plants to use.

- **planting crops close together** to shade soil so it does not dry out. The air between plants close together holds a little moisture so plants do not wilt. This can be done with green manure or by planting a variety of crops together in the same field.

- **strip-cropping** (growing different crops together along contour lines) to help crops share moisture. A ground-cover crop is planted uphill from the contour line, and a crop that gives only a little ground cover is planted below it. Water collects on the ground cover and flows to the downhill crops.

Strip-cropping

- **reusing wash water** to water gardens near the house (see page 100).

- **protecting water catchment areas** to provide more water for people and crops (see Chapter 9).

Make planting pits

Planting pits collect rainwater to help plants grow even in very dry conditions. Planting several crops in the same pit makes the best use of water. The crops that need the most water grow best at the downhill end. Crops that can live with less water grow well on the higher side of the slope.

In the second year, plant in the same pits, or dig new pits between the old ones. If you dig new pits, over the years the whole area will be fertilized.

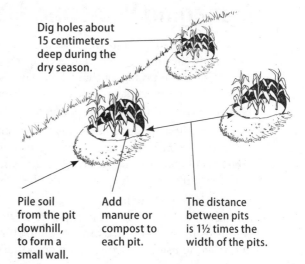

Dig holes about 15 centimeters deep during the dry season.

Pile soil from the pit downhill, to form a small wall.

Add manure or compost to each pit.

The distance between pits is 1½ times the width of the pits.

Stone walls prevent erosion and save water

The central plateau of Burkina Faso is a mix of flat ground and gentle slopes. Rainfall has always been low, but there has been even less in recent years, and the land and people have suffered. To conserve water and prevent erosion, farmers build low stone walls across fields. The walls slow down the flow of water, allowing time for it to soak into the ground. The walls also prevent soil from blowing or washing away and catch soil that erodes from higher slopes.

Farmers also dig large planting holes. They fill the holes with compost or manure to fertilize the crops and hold water.

Where gullies have formed, people fill them with stones. If a gully is too big to fill, they build a stone wall across it. Just as on the field, the stone wall slows water down and keeps the gully from getting worse. Over time, soil may fill the gully.

By using these methods, farmers in Burkina Faso are able to make the land richer and improve crop yields even with less rainfall. And with more food, people's health has improved.

Managing Pests and Plant Diseases

Pests, plant diseases, and weeds can be serious threats to crops. Chemical companies say the only solution is to spray pesticides regularly. But chemicals may cause more problems than they solve (see Chapter 14). Sustainable farming works with nature to keep crops, pests, diseases, weeds, and soil life in balance. This is called **natural pest management** or **integrated pest management (IPM)**.

Natural pest management prevents problems with pests and plant diseases, and keeps harmful chemicals out of our bodies and environment. It also avoids problems of chemical dependence and pesticide resistance (see page 273). (For some immediate methods to resolve pest problems, see pages 298 and 299.)

Even if you are willing to use pesticides, it is still important to know if pests are harming your crops, how much damage is being done, and whether creatures in the fields are already controlling the pest. Then you can decide if and when to use chemicals, and what kinds to use.

The best way to control both pests and diseases is to keep plants healthy.

- **Build healthy soil.** Healthy soil provides a home to friendly insects and helps prevent many plant diseases.

- **Plant resistant varieties.** Ask farmers or extension agents about seeds to make sure the ones you choose are resistant to common pests and diseases.

- **Space plants correctly.** Planting crops too close together limits the sunshine and air that reaches the leaves, and allows diseases to thrive. But planting crops farther apart leaves room for weeds, dries the soil, and may reduce the harvest. Experiment to see what spacing works best for each crop.

- **Plant at the right times.** Pests and diseases often respond to the weather, such as the first rains or the first warm day. Watching how each crop grows and talking with other farmers about these patterns can help you decide the best time to plant. Planting earlier than usual can make sure crops are big enough to resist pests or diseases that come at a certain time. Planting later can cause most of the pests or diseases to die out for lack of food.

- **Plant a variety of crops and change crop patterns.** Large areas with only 1 kind of plant attract pests who like that plant (see page 300).

- **Water from below.** Watering from above can cause diseases that live in soil to splash onto plants. And wet leaves and stems are good places for diseases to grow. Using drip irrigation (see page 294) or flood irrigation can keep plant leaves and stems healthy.

Look for pests

Plant-eating insects are a normal part of
farming. They cause little harm to crops as long
as they remain in balance with other types of
insects, especially those that eat pests.

**Watch what insects do to
see if they are damaging or
helping your crops.**

Examine your crops regularly. This will help you
understand when to allow friendly insects to do their
work, and when you might need to spray with natural
pesticides or use other pest control methods. When you
look for pests and diseases, ask questions such as:

- Are pieces of the plant being eaten by an insect?
- Is damage increasing? Will it affect the crop yield?
- Are friendly insects keeping pests under control?

Is it a pest, a friend, or harmless?

Sometimes the insects easiest to see are protecting plants by eating the pests.
Or, the plant may be at a stage of growth where it can withstand some pest
damage and remain healthy.

Worms are important for healthy soil. Bees, spiders, and most insects
that live in water (such as in rice paddies) are friends, and help control pests.
Also, small wasps or flies with long, thin tubes at their backside are probably
friends. It is best to leave insect friends alone so they can help your crops.

Watch the insects in your fields to know if they are pests, friends, or
harmless. If you are unsure about some insects, collect them in a container
together with some plant parts, and watch them for several days. If you
find insect eggs, watch what they hatch. If tiny worms or grubs (larva) are
released, they may be pests. If they release flying insects, they are often friendly.

The main ways pests damage crops are by sucking the liquid from them
and by eating them.

- **Sap-suckers** include aphids, scale insects and mealy bugs, leaf and plant
  hoppers, white flies, thrips, mites, and nematodes.
- **Plant-eating insects** include caterpillars, slugs, snails, plant and pod borers.

If it is a pest, how can you get rid of it?

Once you know how the pest damages crops, you can use natural pesticides
(see next page) made for that kind of pest.

Once you know when the pest appears and how it relates to its
environment, you can use physical methods of pest control (see page 299).
Answers to these questions can help know how to control a pest: Where does
it come from? When does it damage crops? Does it appear in one form and
then change to another form (for instance, caterpillars turn into moths and
butterflies)? Is it food for birds, other insects, or field creatures?

Spray with natural pesticides

Natural pesticides prevent crop damage with much less harm to people and the environment than chemical sprays. They are easy to make and cost less than chemicals.

But even natural pesticides must be used with care. Never use more than you need. Always wash your hands after handling them. Always wash food before eating or selling it. A natural pesticide may work well in some conditions but not in others. If one kind does not work, try other kinds.

Natural pesticides for plant-eating insects

Plant-eating insects are best controlled by pesticides made from strong-smelling plants such as garlic, onion, chili pepper, marigold, and citronella leaves.

1. Collect the plant you want to use, let it dry, and grind the dried plant to a powder.

2. Soak the powder in water overnight (1 handful of powder to 1 liter of water).

3. Pour the mixture through a screen or cloth to remove solids.

4. Add a little bit of mild soap to help the pesticide stick to plants.

5. Spray or sprinkle the mixture on plants. Test your mixture on 1 or 2 plants first. If it seems to hurt the plants, it may be too strong. Add more water and test it until it seems good.

6. Repeat as needed, and after it rains.

Natural pesticides for sap-sucker insects

Sap-sucker insects are killed by coating them with mild soap or oil that blocks their breathing holes. Spraying plants with mild soapy water or water mixed with vegetable oil will kill these pests. Do not use detergents or strong soaps because they damage plants, soil, and insects.

Other natural pesticides

Urine diluted in water and sprayed on plants kills pests. Mix 1 cup of urine with 10 cups of water. Let it sit in a closed container for 10 days. After 10 days, spray the mixture onto your crops.

Tobacco kills many pests. Boil 1 cup of tobacco leaves or cigarette butts in 5 liters of water. Strain out the leaves or butts, add a little soap, and spray it on plants. Do not use tobacco on tomatoes, potatoes, peppers, and eggplant. It will damage these plants and will not kill most pests that attack them.

IMPORTANT: Tobacco juice is poison! Avoid getting tobacco juice on skin or clothes. Avoid breathing the steam while boiling tobacco leaves.

Physical methods of pest control

There are many ways to control pests, or to encourage predators and parasites, based on their habits and life cycles. Talk to other farmers to learn about methods they use.

Watch the animals in your fields to know if they control pests.

Animals and insects

Many birds, bats, snakes, and insects eat pests and pollinate crops. You can tell what a bird eats by the type of beak it has and by watching how it acts in your fields. To scare off birds that are eating crops, some farmers hang shiny things such as shiny paper, tape from old cassette tapes, and scraps of metal near crops.

Most bats eat mosquitoes. But some bats eat fruit and a few others bite animals. By watching them eat, or by looking at the remains of their food under the place where they sleep at night, you can tell if they are eating the fruit off your trees or are eating the insects that bite you or eat your crops.

Some physical methods of pest control

To control fruit flies, put some rotting fruit in a plastic bottle with fruit-fly-sized holes in it. Hang it from the fruit tree you want to protect about 6 weeks before the fruit will be ripe (when the flies start laying their eggs on the fruit). The flies will fly in but will not be able to get out.

Many small wasps feed on pollen and attack pests. Growing flowering plants that make lots of pollen will attract these wasps, and the wasps will protect crops from pests.

Tall trees planted around your field can stop locusts or make them pass over your field. Trees also provide shelter for useful insects.

Ants are fierce predators. If your crops are attacked by grubs, sprinkle sugar water on the stems or harvested tubers. Ants will come for the sugar water and stay to eat the grubs!

Many flying insects lay their eggs on crops. The eggs then hatch into grub and caterpillar pests. Hanging a torch or a lamp above a bucket or lined hole full of water will attract flying insects, which then fall into the water and drown. This solves the problem before any eggs can be laid or hatched.

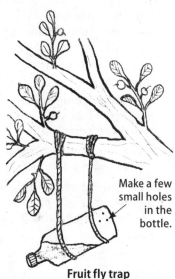

Make a few small holes in the bottle.

Fruit fly trap

Change crop patterns

Crops in the same plant family can get the same pests and diseases.
For example, if you always plant potatoes in the same field, potato beetles may
come to live and breed in that field. But if every 3 years you plant something
they cannot eat, the beetles will leave or die. The third year crop must not be
a relative of potato, like tomato or pepper. It should be something completely
different, like maize. This is called **crop rotation.** 2 ways to prevent disease and
pests are to rotate crops and to plant a variety of crops together.

Rotate crops

Rotating crops (changing the crops you grow in a particular field) controls
diseases and pests by depriving them of food. It will also improve the soil by
adding different nutrients. For example, rotating grains in one season with
beans in the next will make the soil richer. Grains grow tall and provide
organic matter, while beans add nitrogen to the soil.

Plant a variety of crops together

Planting different types of
crops provides places for
useful insects to live and
makes it harder for pests to
find the crop they like to eat.
Growing many types of crops
also improves food security,
because if one crop fails, there
are others to use. Planting
different crops next to each
other protects against pests in
these ways:

Milk thistle plant attracts harmful aphids.

Food crops nearby have few aphids.

Trap plants attract pests away from your crops.

- Some strong smelling
  herbs and vegetables keep
  away pests.

- Some flowers attract
  predators that eat pests.

- Some plants "trap" pests. This is the opposite idea from keeping pests
  away. If you plant something that pests like better than your crop, they
  will stay on the "trap plant" and leave your crop alone.

Farmers also combine trees with animals and crops to increase the benefits of
each of them (see page 302).

Plant Diseases

Plant diseases can be recognized
by their effects on plants, such
as making leaves change in
color, causing leaves to wilt, or
making parts of the plant grow
in unusual ways. Plant diseases
may be caused by a fungus, a
bacteria, or a virus. All of them
can be controlled with natural
methods.

Plant diseases are best prevented by
maintaining healthy soils and following the
other guidelines for sustainable farming
(see page 281). When you are certain a disease is affecting your crop,
you can prevent the disease from spreading to other plants.

- **Destroy diseased plants.** Infected plants can pass diseases or pests to
  future crops. For diseases that kill the entire plant or severely reduce
  production, the entire plant should be removed and burned at the first
  sign of disease. Do not compost it, because some plant
  diseases survive composting.

- **Clean tools used on diseased plants.**
  Plant diseases can be spread when your
  body, tools, and clothing touches infected
  plants and then touches healthy plants.
  Wash everything with warm soapy water
  before touching healthy plants.

- **Control sap suckers.** Many plant diseases
  are carried between plants by sap
  sucking insects. See page 298 for natural
  pesticides to use against sap suckers.

- **Milk** kills fungus diseases, caterpillar eggs,
  and spider mites. Mix 1 liter of milk with 15 liters of water and spray
  on your crops. For fungal diseases, repeat after 10 days. For caterpillar
  eggs, repeat after 3 weeks.

- **Ashes** kill fungus diseases. Planting ashes together with seeds will
  prevent some fungus. For late blight of tomato and potato crops, spray
  crops with a strained mix of ashes and water.

Planting Trees and Crops Together

When land is scarce, some farmers cut down trees in order to plant crops. But planting trees and crops together (agroforestry) can make farmland more productive and provide more and different crops.

Agroforestry requires care in choosing trees and in planting them where they will be of most use. Some farmers use these guidelines:

- Trees should not compete with crops for water, sunlight, or space.
- Each tree should provide for more than one need, such as food, fodder, medicine, shade, firewood, thatch, or lumber.

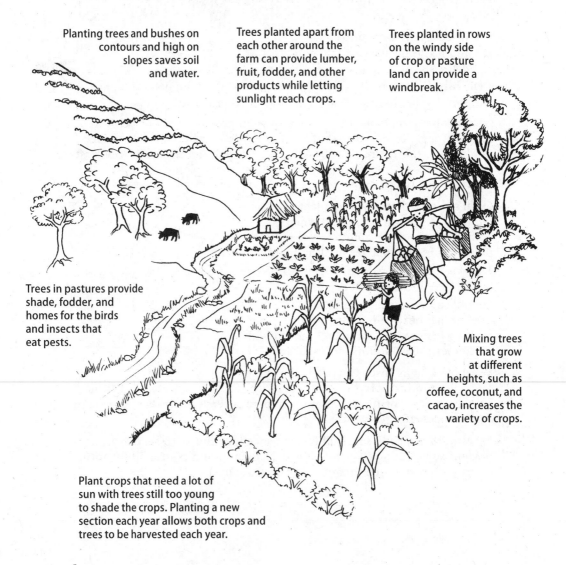

Planting trees and bushes on contours and high on slopes saves soil and water.

Trees planted apart from each other around the farm can provide lumber, fruit, fodder, and other products while letting sunlight reach crops.

Trees planted in rows on the windy side of crop or pasture land can provide a windbreak.

Trees in pastures provide shade, fodder, and homes for the birds and insects that eat pests.

Mixing trees that grow at different heights, such as coffee, coconut, and cacao, increases the variety of crops.

Plant crops that need a lot of sun with trees still too young to shade the crops. Planting a new section each year allows both crops and trees to be harvested each year.

Saving Seeds

Many farmers produce their own seed by allowing some plants to mature and then collecting the seeds. Saving seeds allows farmers to grow plants with the qualities they want. Local plant breeding and seed saving are important to preserve biodiversity and promote food security.
(For more about plant breeding, see Chapter 12.)

Selecting seeds

To make sure you have good seeds, collect them from:

- strong plants, free of pests and disease.
- plants adapted to the area. For example, if you live in a cool area where a certain type of plant grows, but you collect seeds from the same type of plant that grows in a warmer area, the plants may not survive the cool weather.

Put hard coated seeds in a container of water. The seeds that float will not sprout. The seeds that sink can be planted.

- plants with the qualities you want, such as size, taste, resistance to drought, and so on.
- plants that grew some distance away from other varieties of the same type of plant, to make sure the different varieties of plant did not breed together.

Do not collect seeds that have fallen to the ground by themselves. Sweep under plants to remove fallen seeds, and then shake the plant or tree to remove fresh seeds. Then clean the seeds as soon as possible after collecting them, and sort them to remove any seeds that are rotted or damaged.

Storing seeds

To judge how long each kind of seed can be stored, think about the conditions they need to grow. For example, seeds from areas with a cold or dry season usually can be stored for months or years, because they need the right conditions to sprout. Seeds from areas that are hot and rainy most of the year will not store well, because they can sprout any time. Seeds with hard shells usually can be stored more easily and for longer times than seeds with soft shells.

Most seeds should be stored in a cool, dry, dark place, with some air flowing through them, or they will rot.

Sprouting seeds

Some seeds need special treatment in order to sprout (see page 207). But all seeds need:

- **water.** Soak seeds in water overnight before planting. If you use very hot (but not boiling) water, it will kill many plant diseases and pests carried by seeds. This will also help sprout seeds that usually do so only after passing through the stomachs of animals. Experiment first with a few seeds and then plant them to be sure they will sprout.

- **air.** If the soil is compacted or waterlogged, seeds will not sprout because there is not enough air.

- **daylight.** Some seeds, especially those from northern areas where there is very different weather at different times of year, will only sprout when there is just the right amount of light.

- **correct temperature.** Because each crop has its own season, different seeds sprout best at different temperatures and at different times of year.

Planting seeds

The 2 common ways to plant are by starting seeds in a nursery or by planting right into the ground. Which method you use depends on what crops you want, the weather conditions when you are ready to plant, and whether or not you have room for a nursery (to make a nursery, see page 209).

Direct planting

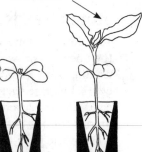

True leaves

Larger seeds are best planted directly in the field because their roots grow quickly and are easily damaged if they are transplanted. Make planting holes 2 or 3 times as deep as the size of the seed. Drop 1, 2, or 3 seeds in each hole and cover the seeds.

Very tiny seeds should be tossed out over the soil to spread widely over the planting area. Mixing seeds with sand when you toss them out will prevent the seeds from sticking together. Then cover the planting area with a thin layer of mulch or soil. Also, using a roller to lightly press the seeds into the soil will help them sprout.

Most vegetables can be transplanted once they have their first set of true leaves.

Starting seeds in a nursery

Starting seeds in a nursery helps seeds sprout by controlling temperature, water, and pests. Transplanting seedlings from the nursery into freshly weeded fields helps young plants make better use of the soil and water.

Safe Food Storage

One of the tragedies in communities that produce food is that much of the food goes bad because of weather, pests, or other causes. Safe food storage is as important as the ability to grow food in the first place.

Protect stored grains from pests

After harvest, much grain is lost to rodents, insect pests, or rot. To protect grains in storage:

- Dry and store the grains as soon after harvest as possible to avoid loss in the fields. Well-dried grains should be soft enough to break with your teeth and dry enough that they make a good cracking noise.

- Store dried grains in well-sealed, clean containers in a place protected from moisture and pests.

- Smoke the grain before it is stored to kill pests.

- Repel insects, but not rodents, with wood ash and plants such as hot chilies, eucalyptus, and other strong smelling plants. (If grain is already infected with pests, the protection will not work.) Dry the eucalyptus leaf, chili seeds, or other plant and grind it to a powder. Mix 1 handful of the powder with each kilo of grain or beans to keep insects out.
  Be careful not to breathe in the powder. More time and effort are needed to wash the grains before eating, but there will be more grain to eat.

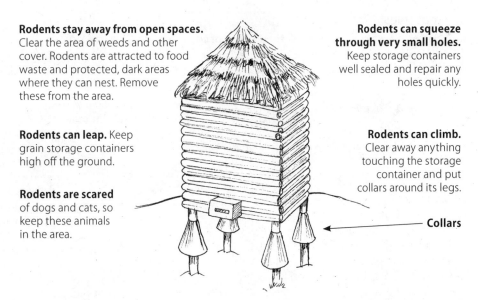

Rodents stay away from open spaces. Clear the area of weeds and other cover. Rodents are attracted to food waste and protected, dark areas where they can nest. Remove these from the area.

Rodents can leap. Keep grain storage containers high off the ground.

Rodents are scared of dogs and cats, so keep these animals in the area.

Rodents can squeeze through very small holes. Keep storage containers well sealed and repair any holes quickly.

Rodents can climb. Clear away anything touching the storage container and put collars around its legs.

Collars

Grain storage containers keep out rodents such as rats, mice, and squirrels.

Storing fruits, vegetables, meat, and milk

Fruits, vegetables, meat, and milk are full of moisture. Moisture is needed by the bacteria and fungus that cause rot. Keeping foods cold or frozen will slow down the rotting process. When there is no way to store foods cold, they can still be preserved by:

Sun, and heat from cooking, will dry maize placed on a roof.

- **drying.** Foods can be dried in the sun, in an oven on very low heat, or by putting them in salt. If kept away from pests and moisture, dried foods can be stored for a very long time.

- **smoking.** Foods put over a smoky fire will be preserved both by the drying that happens and by the smoke. Meats are commonly preserved by smoking.

- **fermenting.** Fermenting, like rotting, is the process of letting bacteria and fungus change food. But unlike rotting, fermenting allows only certain kinds of bacteria and fungus to grow. Cheese and some kinds of sour breads are fermented foods. Fermented foods can be more nutritious and easier to digest than the food they are made from.

- **pickling and jarring.** Fruits, vegetables, and meats are soaked in vinegar and kept in covered or sealed containers. The sourness of the vinegar keeps bacteria and fungus from growing. Fruits can be cooked in sugar syrup and sealed in boiled jars to preserve them.

Storing root crops

Root crops can last a long time if they are stored in places that are dark, fairly dry, cold, and safe from pests. Layering root crops in straw or sawdust so they do not touch each other keeps them fresh.

How to make a natural refrigerator

A Nigerian teacher named Mohammed Bah Abba developed a method called the "Pot-in-Pot" to store food where there is no electricity.

Leave the Pot-in-Pot in a dry, open place. As dry air surrounds it, water in the sand passes through the outer surface of the larger pot, making it stay cool. When the water passes from the sand, the inner container is cooled, destroying harmful germs and preserving the food inside. The only maintenance is washing and replacing the sand every so often.

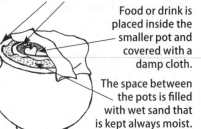

Two clay pots of different sizes, one placed inside the other.

Food or drink is placed inside the smaller pot and covered with a damp cloth.

The space between the pots is filled with wet sand that is kept always moist.

This natural refrigerator works best in a dry, hot climate.

Raising Animals

Animals bring many benefits to the farm besides the food they produce. Just like plants, a variety of animals is better for the farm and the farmer.

Bees make honey to eat, and they also pollinate flowers.

Chickens, geese, and ducks eat weeds, weed seeds, and pests, and leave manure to fertilize the soil. They also turn the soil when they scratch for food. Let chickens run in one section for a month. Then move the chickens to the next section. Rake and plant the first section. The chickens will weed and turn the soil as they go.

Pigs turn the soil when they dig, and eat the deep roots of spreading weeds. Make small pens to move them through your garden, just as with the chickens.

Goats clear land by eating brush. Because goats eat everything, you may need to tie the goats next to the brush you want them to eat.

Grazing animals

Grazing animals such as cows, sheep, and goats, can either help or hurt the land, depending on how they are managed. When animals graze in overgrown pastures, they reduce weeds and add manure. But if grazing animals eat all the grass, the soil dries out and forms a hard crust. When rain comes, water runs off and takes the soil with it. When soil is eroded from overgrazing, nothing grows.

Keep animals enclosed near the house to make it easier to protect them and to use their manure. But if their space is too small, they get sick easily when flies, parasites, and diseases grow in their manure. Clean pens regularly, especially in the wet season, to prevent animals and people from getting sick. The manure can be composted and used as fertilizer.

Whether your animals are fenced in or graze freely, keep only as many animals as the land can support.

Move animals from pasture to pasture

If you let your animals graze wherever they want, they will eat the grasses down to the roots. Next year, those plants will not grow back well. Move grazing animals between pastures when half the leaves of grazing plants are eaten.

Make a watering hole instead of letting animals graze next to streams or ponds.

If you can make fences, divide your grazing land into small pastures according to the type of plants that grow there. Move the animals between the different areas. If you graze cattle, even low stone walls will keep them from moving between pastures. If you herd your animals, you do not need fences.

Take care that livestock do not graze in and around water sources used by people. If manure gets into water people drink, or where they bathe, swim, or fish, disease can spread. Make a ditch from the stream to a watering hole for your animals.

How often to move animals

How much time animals stay in one pasture before they are moved depends on the number of animals, and the size and quality of the pasture. Each year, let one part of the grazing land rest completely, with no grazing at all. This will prevent soil from being compacted and allow grasses to grow back.

For example, if you divide the land into 3 or more pastures, move the animals through all but one of the pastures. Leave that one to rest. The following year, let a different pasture rest. Or, after each harvest, let your herd eat the crop stalks, weeds, and grains that fall on the ground. They will clean up the field and spread their manure.

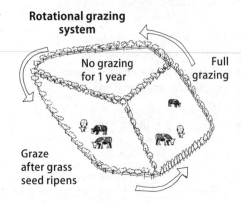

Rotational grazing system

No grazing for 1 year

Full grazing

Graze after grass seed ripens

How many animals can your land support?

Animals provide security when times are hard because people can sell or eat them. They also bring respect. But when people try to earn more respect and security by having more animals than the land can support, both the animals and the land become unhealthy. The amount of land needed for animals depends on how green and wet the area is. In dry lands, much more land is needed for grazing than in very green areas.

Fish Farming

A small fish pond can produce a lot of food in a little space, and can store irrigation water. In a pond or rice paddy, you can grow:

- fish or shellfish for food, such as carp, tilapia, crawfish, and freshwater shrimp.
- plants for food, such as pond lily, lotus root, taro, rice, and water chestnut.
- plants for making things, such as reeds and bamboo.
- **algae** (pond scum) for food, animal feed, and fertilizer.
- rich soil for your garden.

Ponds with fish and birds will prevent mosquitoes from breeding while providing food and water for you and your land.

How to build a fish pond

❶ Before you start, be sure your land has the right conditions to support a fish farm. You need enough water to make sure that some will always move through the pond. If water does not move, mosquitoes will breed.

You also need soil that will not let the pond water drain away. Clay soil is best. If you do not have clay soil, a pond liner to keep the pond from leaking can be made of clay brought from elsewhere, from concrete, or from plastic. Pond liners can also be woven grass or bamboo, sealed with pitch or other plant gums.

The best place for a pond is at the bottom of a hill (so runoff water goes into the pond) and at least 10 meters away from drinking water sources. If the pond will have water flowing in from a stream, build a temporary dam to stop the water while you prepare the pond.

❷ Dig a hole at least 1 meter deep and as big around as you can. Even a very small pond, 1 or 2 meters across, can grow algae and small fish to enrich your diet. If you have enough space, make several ponds, each less than 3 meters across. This will make digging the ponds and harvesting the fish easier.

❸ Press down the clay bottom of the hole by walking on it. If it is a big pond, ask neighbors to help. Even cows or other large animals can be used to compact the clay. Their manure will help seal the bottom.

Once the pond is filled with water, algae and other plants will grow. If there are streams or other ponds nearby, collect plants and animals to breed in your pond. To grow fish, you may need to buy some live fish so they will breed in your pond.

Sustainable Farming in the City

More and more, people are creating farms and gardens in cities to feed themselves, to create jobs, and to keep alive their knowledge and traditions of working the land. Creating green spaces with crops and trees also improves the air in cities, and reduces illnesses caused by air pollution, such as asthma. Turning the empty spaces that often become trash dumps into farms and gardens makes a city healthier and more beautiful.

Adapt farming methods to smaller spaces

- Grow plants upward on stakes, walls, or other supports. The sides of buildings can be good places for climbing plants.

- Grow food crops on rooftops and balconies, in buckets, bags, tires, tin cans, and old baskets. You can use any container that has a hole for water to drain out. Leaf crops such as spinach and lettuce, and vegetables like tomatoes, peppers, and eggplant, grow well in containers. Bananas, figs, pygmy date palm, pineapple, dwarf citrus, and dwarf mango also grow well in containers.

- Garden beds as shallow as 20 cm deep can be filled with organic matter such as corn husks, rice or cocoa hulls, leaves, or even shredded newspaper. Plant seedlings with a small amount of soil into holes in the organic matter and their roots will spread. Over time, the organic matter will turn to soil.

- Make raised planting beds by double digging (see next page) or by piling soil 1 meter deep on top of concrete surfaces and enclosing it in large containers.

- Sow seeds or seedlings closer together than usual. Plants grown this way will adapt to the close spacing over time.

- Grow more than one crop together in a small space.

- Replant a new crop immediately after harvesting the previous one.

A rooftop garden

How to double dig a garden bed

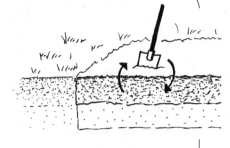

To grow as much as possible in a small area, or to plant on hard soils or soils with little organic matter, double digging is a good method.

❶ The edges of the planting bed should be just wide enough across so that 2 people can kneel at the edges of the bed and touch hands in the middle. The bed can be as long as you need.

❷ Loosen the top of the soil and spread finished compost or manure on top of the whole bed.

❸ Starting at one end, dig a ditch across the bed 30 cm deep and 30 cm wide.

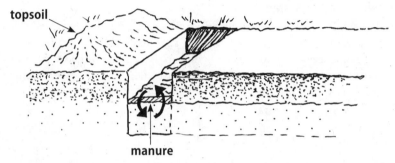

topsoil

manure

❹ Use a digging fork or shovel to loosen the soil at the bottom of the ditch and add some compost or manure to it.

❺ Dig a second ditch across the bed. Put the soil from the second ditch into the first ditch. Loosen the soil at the bottom, and spread compost or manure.

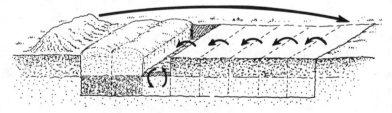

❻ Continue until you have dug the entire bed. The loose soil will rise above the surrounding soil. Make the bed smooth and flat, with the edges angled so that water and soil do not run off. Add a layer of sifted, finished compost to the top of the bed. Now it is ready for planting.

After you have prepared the beds, you should not walk on them because this compacts the soil. If you double dig a plot once and add natural fertilizer every season before you plant again, your soil will stay healthy and loose for many years.

Contaminated soils

Soil in cities may be contaminated with toxic chemicals, such as lead from paint, gasoline, and old batteries. These can all cause serious health problems (see Chapter 16). To know if your soil is contaminated:

- Find out how the site was used in the past. If it was a factory, gas station, parking lot, or waste dump, the soil is probably contaminated.
- If the soil smells like chemicals, it is probably contaminated.
- Areas underneath painted walls are most likely contaminated with lead.

Soil samples can be tested at a university, extension agency, or private laboratory. Lead tests are not expensive, but testing for other contaminants is often difficult and expensive.

Planting safely in contaminated soil

You can still grow food safely on contaminated soil. One way is to cover the soil with a layer of hard packed clay or concrete. This seals the contaminants in. Grow crops in containers or shallow beds on top. It is safer to grow fruit crops (such as tomatoes) on contaminated soils because they absorb fewer toxins than leaf crops (such as spinach) and root crops (such as carrots and potatoes).

Urban farming blossoms

Cuba is an island nation that once produced large sugar and tobacco crops for export. It had an industrial system of farming, relying on petroleum fuels and petroleum-based agricultural chemicals. When the Soviet Union collapsed, Cuba lost both its largest petroleum supplier and its largest buyer of sugar and tobacco. Because of political disagreements, most countries would not sell chemicals to Cuba or buy Cuban products. Cuba was forced to find a new way to grow food.

Cuba made sustainable farming their new national policy. It promoted sustainable methods through land grants, education, and by setting up local markets. As the new methods developed and spread, there was more healthy food for everyone.

As in other countries, many Cubans moved from the countryside to the cities. Now the government encourages people to grow food in the cities using sustainable methods. Urban farming promotes good nutrition, and provides jobs and education. Most of the fresh produce (vegetables, poultry, flowers, and medicinal plants) used in Cuba's capital city of Havana is now grown in or close to the city. Plant medicines grown in Havana are sold at low cost in shops called 'green pharmacies.' Although brought on by a crisis, susatainable farming has changed Cuban people's lives for the better.

Marketing Farm Products

To sell their products, farmers need reliable roads, transportation to markets, and fair prices. Changing government policies to support small farmers may take a long time. But there are many ways farmers can organize for fair prices, while working to gain more government support.

Local markets and international markets

Small farmers often sell to a middle buyer and get very little money for their product. Governments may offer support to stop growing traditional crops like maize and rice, and instead grow cash crops like sugar, coffee, or cacao for international markets. But the earnings from cash crops are uncertain. If the international price drops, you may have no money and nothing to eat.

For many farmers, producing food crops for local and regional markets can offer a steady source of income.

Cooperative marketing

One way to make sure there are good prices and food security is to form a cooperative or a marketing association with other farmers. When farmers sell their products together, they can better control the prices they get for their crops, and reduce the costs of transportation and marketing. Most countries have rules about how to form a cooperative or association.

Marketing associations share the labor and expense of getting produce to consumers, and lower costs for all members.

It is important to work with people you trust to make sure everyone carries out her or his responsibilities. It is also important to agree on rules that give everyone a voice in making decisions and a fair share of the earnings.

Value-added products

Companies that process foods and farm products make a lot of money that could be made by farmers instead. When farmers process crops into products for sale, such as dried fruit, dried and packaged plant medicines, jams and jellies, honey, cheese, baskets, furniture, and so on, this is called **value-added production** because you are adding value to the crops you have grown.

Buying the equipment needed to process foods and finding a market for value-added products can be difficult. A cooperative can make this easier.

Specialty products and certification

Large farm corporations are able to keep prices low and still earn a profit because they produce so much and often get support from the government. But farmers who grow on smaller plots of land can also benefit from programs that promote products grown using certain methods.

Several **certification programs** help farmers earn better prices for their products. A certification program lets the buyer know crops were grown without chemicals, or that the farmer gets a fair price. Two programs for the international market are **organic certification** and **fair trade certification**. Before making the decision to seek certification, consider the changes you will need to make in how your farm is organized. Think about how much time and money it will take to make the changes, if there is a market for the certified products you will produce, and what you will gain from having your crops certified.

Organic certification

Organic products are grown using sustainable methods, without chemicals or GE seeds (see Chapter 13). Organic certification also requires that after harvest, the products are kept separately from foods grown with chemicals. Every country has different rules for certification. Most require farmers to keep records of how they grew their crops.

Fair trade certification

Fair trade certification is given to farm cooperatives or to farm workers who belong to unions. To be fair trade certified, farmer groups show that they use fair labor practices (no forced labor, no child labor, and fair wages for workers) and promote good environmental practices. To stay certified, the group needs to show that labor and environmental conditions improve over time. There are scholarships for farmer groups who cannot afford the cost of certification.

Fair trade certification is currently provided for small producers of coffee, tea, cacao, bananas and other fresh fruit, and may include other crops by the time you read this book. (To learn about organic and fair trade certification programs, see Resources.)

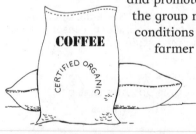

Organic and fair trade certifications help farmers earn more money.

Farmers market products cooperatively

Farmers in the Talamanca region of Costa Rica grow cacao beneath the shade of banana and other fruit trees. In the past, they sold their bananas and fruit at local markets. When they realized they could earn more money by selling cacao on the international market, many farmers decided to work together to do that.

They formed a cooperative, the Association of Small Producers of Talamanca (APPTA). At first they had trouble finding buyers for their cacao. A few buyers paid prices that covered the costs of production, but did not cover the costs of processing and transporting the cacao. APPTA needed money to build a cacao processing plant.

After several visits to the city to talk to cacao buyers, the farmers learned about fair trade and organic certification programs that would bring higher prices for their crops. Because they were a cooperative of smallholder farmers, they were already eligible for fair trade certification. If they also had organic certification, they could raise their prices enough to generate funds to build a processing plant. But even though they did not use chemicals, none of them could afford to have their land certified.

APPTA negotiated with the organic certification organizations of Europe and the United States to suggest they certify the whole cooperative. The cooperative made sure that no chemicals were used and that each farm followed the same standards for quality and health. Several cooperative members were trained to visit each cacao farm and report on their standards. The cooperative paid only 1 fee for certification, checked the farmers' records themselves, and then filled out just 1 report for each of the certification organizations.

Once the cooperative was certified organic and fair trade, they received better prices. They got a loan to build a cacao processing plant. Soon they were selling organic bananas and other fruit for very good prices, both locally and internationally, and making organic chocolate to sell in the city.

By forming a cooperative, the farmers and their families not only gained better prices for their products, they also gained more control over their work and more possibilities for their futures.

Farmer Field Schools

Farmer field schools are teaching programs that help farmers find solutions to common problems. Together with a trained facilitator, farmers ask questions, experiment, and talk about what they are learning. Farmer field schools also help farmers develop skills in solving problems, organization, and leadership. When they are encouraged to value their own knowledge and skills, farmers are better able to build on traditional farming methods to make farming more sustainable.

Farmers find solutions to their problems in their own experience and in their fields.

Farmer field schools build skills and confidence

Hoa and Khanh live in Dong Phi Village, Vietnam. Their husbands help prepare the land for sowing, and they harvest crops at the end of the season. The rest of the year, Hoa and Khanh manage their family lands alone because their husbands work outside the village. When Hoa noticed she was harvesting less rice each year for several years in a row, her husband suggested buying more fertilizer. But Hoa knew there was no money for fertilizer. When a government agricultural agent told the villagers about farmer field schools, Hoa and her neighbor Khanh decided to join.

As soon as they began attending sessions, they saw this school was different from any school they had known. Together with other farmers, Hoa and Khanh talked about crops, insects, weather, and soil. They experimented with different farming methods and decided which ones they liked and which ones they did not like. Hoa invited all the farmers to her land to help her understand why her rice harvest had gone down.

Khanh was shy and had never spoken in front of a group before. But after the first season at the farmer field school, she felt more confident and she tried leading some experiments. When Khanh tried new things in her field, she had the other farmers visit. She explained what she was doing and why. The other farmers listened, asked questions, and shared their opinions and experiences.

As Hoa and Khanh began changing the way they farmed, they realized they had to teach their husbands as well. "I had to make sure my husband would not be afraid because I stopped using chemical pesticides," Hoa said. "When he came home from work, I took him to the field to show him the different insects and talk to him about natural pest controls." When Hoa's husband saw there was more rice, he did not question his wife's wisdom. And when she used money saved from fertilizers and pesticides to buy a motorcycle for the family, he was convinced that farmer field schools helped.

Now Hoa and Khanh have started training women farmers all over their region. "I think we women work better as a group apart from the men. Our discussions are more open and we make sure everybody gets to say what she sees in the field and what she thinks about it. Knowing about pests, fertilizers, and how to care for our crops helps us take control of our lives. This makes me sleep easier," said Khanh. "If it helps me, I'm sure it can help everyone."

16 Harm from Toxic Chemicals

In this chapter: page

Harm from Toxic Chemicals

With the growth of industry and industrial farming over the past century, toxic chemicals have become a part of our daily lives. Most of these chemicals came into use with little understanding of the harm they cause to people and the environment.

We may be aware of these chemicals because we work with them, or because we can see and smell the pollution they cause around us. Factories, **oil refineries,** and vehicles produce smoke and fumes that make people cough and choke. Waterways near industrial areas and large farms are often full of ugly, smelly waste. Petroleum production, chemical spills, and dumping sites contaminate water, soil, and air, often in ways that we can see and smell.

Other times, pollution cannot be seen or smelled. Some chemicals travel far from where they are used. They move through the air and water, in the foods we eat, and in the bodies of people, animals, and fish. Many chemicals used in ordinary products such as plastic bottles or motor vehicles, are so much a part of everyday life we do not even think about the ways they are dangerous.

Toxic pollution at Love Canal

Love Canal is a neighborhood in Niagara Falls, New York, USA. Love Canal was named after William Love, the man who began digging a canal to connect two rivers. The canal was never completed. Instead, a chemical company used the unfinished canal as a waste pit for 21,000 tons of toxic chemicals. Once the canal was full, the company covered it with soil and then sold the land to the city for one dollar, with the condition that the company was not responsible for any health problems that might arise.

Over the years, homes and a school were built next to the buried waste. Before long, people living in Love Canal began to have serious health problems. Lois Gibbs, one of the residents, knew something was wrong. "We knew there were too many miscarriages, too many birth defects, too many nervous system problems, and too much asthma and other breathing problems among us," she said.

Mrs. Gibbs organized the community to demand a government investigation into these problems. When the government found toxic chemicals leaking into the ground around people's homes, the community demanded money from the government to relocate all the residents. The residents were moved, but not before many of them suffered serious health problems. Today, an empty neighborhood and many people suffering lifelong illnesses are reminders of the dangers of toxic waste at Love Canal.

Lois Gibbs went on to fight against the harm caused by toxic pollution in other places. Her work helped pressure the US government to pass laws requiring companies to clean up their toxic wastes. Most importantly, Mrs. Gibbs helped people believe they have the power to stand up to the chemical industry, demand a healthy environment, and win! In her book *Dying from Dioxin*, she wrote:

We can blame the victim and get everybody to stop eating milk, fish and meat, and stop breastfeeding their babies. Or we can explore how people became powerless as the corporations became powerful. We have to discuss why our government protects the right to pollute more than it protects our health.

How Toxic Chemicals Harm Us

Whether or not a person will be harmed by toxic chemicals, and the kind of health problem that may be caused, depends on many things:

- what kinds of chemicals and the amounts he or she is exposed to
- how long the **exposure** lasts
- his or her age, body weight, height, and sex
- his or her general state of health at the time of the exposure

The danger from toxic chemicals is strongest at times when our bodies are growing or changing rapidly:

- when a baby is forming in the womb
- when a child is young and growing quickly
- when a teenager's (adolescent's) body is going through rapid changes
- when an older person's body slows down and is less able to filter poisons

Every member of this family is affected by the chemical factory in their town — some more, some less.

The effects of toxic chemicals on a person may be severe, such as serious birth defects or cancer. Other effects may be harder to see, such as difficulty learning, slow growth, allergies, difficulty having children, and more frequent illness.

It is often difficult to know whether a certain health problem was caused or was made worse by toxic chemicals. Although toxic chemicals have been proven to cause many different illnesses, because we are exposed to so many chemicals at so many different times, proving that one particular exposure was responsible for an illness is difficult. But many illnesses are more common in places where people are regularly exposed to toxic chemicals.

Even very small amounts cause harm

Traditionally, doctors and scientists follow the rule, "the dose makes the poison." This means that more of a substance has a stronger effect, and less of it has a weaker effect. For example, poisons such as arsenic or cyanide are only toxic if a person eats too much of them. Even most medicines, like aspirin, are helpful when taken in small amounts, but can be harmful in large amounts.

But even very small amounts of some toxic chemicals can be very harmful. Some chemicals, such as **POPs** and **PCBs**, are not safe in any amount (see pages 333, 334, and 340 to 342).

How Chemicals Harm Children

Children, especially babies, are more easily and seriously harmed by chemicals than adults.

- Young children are closer to the ground and are more likely to eat, breathe, or touch chemicals that drift close to and collect on the ground.
- Children breathe much faster than adults and can get sick more easily from air pollution.
- Children often put their hands, toys, and other things in their mouths, and so are more likely to eat things that will harm them.
- Some parts of the body that protect adults from toxics are not yet well-developed in babies and children.
- When a baby's organs are developing, they are more vulnerable to damage from chemicals.

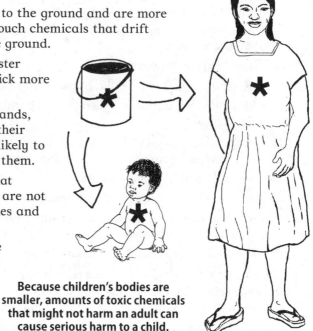

Because children's bodies are smaller, amounts of toxic chemicals that might not harm an adult can cause serious harm to a child.

I wonder if we'll have a healthy baby.

Toxics at different stages of children's growth

When the body is growing and changing quickly — during infancy, childhood, and adolescence — even very small amounts of chemicals can cause long-lasting and harmful changes in children's bodies.

Before conception

If the reproductive systems or **genes** of the mother or father are harmed by chemicals, babies can be affected even if the exposure happened before the baby was conceived.

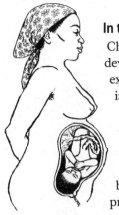

In the womb

Chemicals already in the mother's body can be passed to a developing baby during pregnancy. For example, a woman who was exposed to lead as a child may still have lead in her bones. When she is pregnant, the lead is passed to the baby in her womb.

Many toxic chemicals that a pregnant woman may be exposed to, such PCBs, lead, and mercury, can pass through the **placenta** into the growing fetus and cause harm.

Cigarette smoke, drugs, and alcohol can also harm a baby in the womb and should be avoided during pregnancy as well.

Birth to 2 years

A baby's skin and digestive system allow more chemicals to pass into the baby's body.

Some chemicals that a mother is exposed to can also collect in her breast milk and pass to the baby during breastfeeding. Toxics can also pass to babies in contaminated water used to mix formula and artificial milks. Breast milk is still the best food for a baby. Instead of avoiding breastfeeding to keep harmful chemicals out of babies, women are organizing to keep toxic chemicals out of breast milk.

Breast is best!

Infants and toddlers put everything in their mouths. This makes it easy for them to swallow harmful substances.

2 years to 12 years

When children begin going to day care (creche) or school, they may be exposed to many new chemicals, for example, if their schoolyards are sprayed with pesticides. Children who work shining shoes, scavenging through waste dumps, or in other ways to make money are often exposed to toxic chemicals. Besides causing illness, toxics can also harm a young person's ability to learn.

Children exposed to toxics may learn slowly, be irritable and restless, or show other signs of slow development.

12 to 18 years old

Adolescence (teen age) is a time of fast physical growth and change caused by **hormones** (see page 325). Toxic exposures can seriously harm a young person's ability to have healthy children later.

Birth defects

Birth defects are caused by damage to a person's genes. Because genes are passed from parents to children, harm from toxic chemicals may affect not only the person exposed to a toxic, but that person's children and the children's children. Not all birth defects are caused by toxic chemicals, but birth defects are more common in areas where industry uses or produces toxic chemicals or wastes. Birth defects can take many forms, some very mild (such as a birth mark) and others very severe (such as when the brain does not grow).

If your child is born with birth defects

If your child is born with birth defects, you may feel overwhelmed and uncertain about how you will care for your child. You are not alone!

Recognize your emotions. Parents experience shock, denial, grief, and even anger. Allow yourself to mourn the loss of the healthy child you thought you would have. Talk about your feelings with people who can understand and support you.

Seek community support. Ask your health worker or a social worker if they know other parents in the area who have children with the same condition. Join or start a support group with other parents. You and your child may discover a large and caring community.

Celebrate your child. Remember to let yourself enjoy your child the same way any parent would — by cuddling, playing, and watching the child grow and develop in his or her own way. Share your joy with family and friends.

Learn with your child. Seeking information about birth defects can be empowering, as can experiencing the changes the child goes through as he or she grows.

Physical exercises may help. Many disabilities can improve with the use of exercises and other methods. (To learn about physical exercises and other ways of helping children with birth defects and other disabilities, see the Hesperian books *Disabled Village Children, Helping Children Who Are Blind*, and *Helping Children Who Are Deaf.*)

Within and outside your community, there are people and resources to help you.

Reproductive Health Problems

Toxic chemicals can damage our ability to give birth to healthy children. Reproductive health problems affect women of childbearing age most, but they can also affect men and women at any time in their lives.

Some chemicals cause miscarriages or **sterility** (inability to have children) in men or women. They do this by interfering with **hormones,** the natural chemicals the body makes to control growth and other processes such as women's monthly bleeding and reproduction. Other chemicals act just like hormones when they get into our bodies. They can confuse our natural hormones by sending false signals. For this reason, these chemicals are sometimes called **hormone disruptors**.

How reproductive hormones work

Female hormones called estrogen and progesterone cause the changes in a girl's body known as puberty. They cause her ovaries to release one egg every month, stop her monthly bleeding during pregnancy, and after childbirth they cause her breasts to make milk. Hormones also determine how the baby grows inside its mother's womb.

Toxic chemicals disrupt hormones

Chemicals that are hormone disruptors can cause girls to start monthly bleeding early, have irregular bleeding, or have no bleeding at all. Disrupting the normal functions of hormones can also cause women to have a pregnancy start growing outside the womb, a very dangerous problem that can kill the woman.

The health of future generations depends on protecting ourselves today.

Even small amounts of some chemicals, such as PCBs, dioxins, and some plastics (see pages 323 and 340), can cause serious damage to reproductive health. Many of these chemicals cannot be seen or smelled. They may not cause problems at the time of exposure, but cause serious health problems many years later or in the next generation.

Endometriosis

Endometriosis is a serious illness that causes the lining of the womb to grow outside of the womb. No one is sure what causes endometriosis. But because it is so common in industrial areas and places with a lot of pollution, one of its causes may be industrial pollution. Endometriosis can be very painful. Endometriosis can also make it difficult to get pregnant.

Signs

The main signs of endometriosis are pain during monthly bleeding and pain in the lower back and abdomen. Other signs are:

- heavy monthly bleeding or bleeding from the vagina at other times
- pain during sexual intercourse
- painful bowel movements, often with diarrhea or constipation
- bloating, vomiting, nausea, lower back pain, and tiredness

These could all be signs of other health problems. To know if it is endometriosis or some other serious illness, see a trained health worker right away.

Many health workers, however, are not familiar with endometriosis, so if you have several signs of this illness and a health worker tells you that you do not have endometriosis, seek out another health worker's opinion if you can.

Prevention and treatment

You may be able to use birth control pills to reduce the pain and heavy or irregular bleeding. Speak with a health worker. You can also reduce pain by taking medications such as ibuprofen. See a health book such as *Where Women Have No Doctor* for ways to treat pain.

For some women, changing what they eat seems to help reduce pain and signs of this illness. Since endometriosis is caused by problems with estrogen, avoid foods containing estrogen or estrogen-like substances, such as:

- meat and dairy products from animals that have been given hormones or that have been fed with grains that contain pesticides.
- vegetables and fruits that have been sprayed with pesticides.
- soybeans and foods made from soy, peanuts, and other legumes.

It may also help to avoid foods that cause the body to produce more estrogen or estrogen-like effects, such as foods in the nightshade family (eggplant, potatoes, tomatoes, and peppers), and coffee, chocolate, tea, and cola drinks.

Some foods may help the body fight endometriosis, including:

- foods that contain fiber, such as whole grains, beans, and brown rice.
- foods with a healthy fat called Omega-3 fatty acids, such as walnuts, pumpkin seeds, salmon, and other fatty fish.
- dark green vegetables, cabbage, broccoli, cauliflower, sesame, figs, and almonds.

Cancer

Cancer is a serious illness that can affect many parts of the body. Cancer starts when some **cells** begin to grow very quickly in an abnormal way, causing growths (**tumors**). Sometimes, tumors go away without treatment. But many tumors get larger or spread, causing health problems in several parts of the body. This is cancer. Most growths do not become cancer, but some do. Once upon a time cancer was unusual. Today it is very common.

What causes cancer?

One cause of the increase in cancer throughout the world is the increasing amount of industrial pollution and toxic chemicals in our environment and in our bodies. The increasing number of cancers in people living in or near highly polluted areas should lead our governments to act quickly to protect people's health. Cancer could be reduced by better regulating the kinds and amounts of chemicals industries are permitted to use, how they are used, and how they are disposed of.

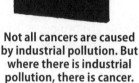

Not all cancers are caused by industrial pollution. But where there is industrial pollution, there is cancer.

Several types of cancer are known to be caused by toxic chemicals. These include cancer of the lungs, bladder, liver, breast, brain, blood (**leukemia**), multiple myeloma, and non-Hodgkin's lymphoma.

Warning signs or a test showing something may be wrong should not be ignored. See a health worker for advice and treatment right away.

People exposed to toxic chemicals over a long time have a greater risk of getting these cancers than people with little or no toxic exposures. Knowing about their risk may help them get treatment early.

Finding and treating cancer early

Finding cancer early can often save a person's life, because the person can get treatment before the cancer spreads. Some warning signs of cancer are tiredness, chronic weight loss, lumps, and pain in the body. These can be signs of other illnesses as well. One way to find out if a person has cancer is to have a test that takes a few cells from the affected part of the body. Someone trained to recognize cancer examines the cells with a microscope.

Traditional and modern cancer treatments

Cancer affects people in different ways, and there is not one treatment that works for every person. Western medicine, Chinese medicine, Indian Ayurvedic medicine, and traditional medicines around the world all have treatments and ways of promoting better health for people with cancer. Unfortunately, none of them has a cure that works every time.

The best cancer treatments promote general health and well-being and involve the person in her own treatment. When seeking treatment, go to a doctor or other healer you know and trust.

The people who understand cancer best are those who have survived it. Every cancer survivor has her or his own story about what helped and what did not.

Cancer sometimes requires treatment with very strong medicines that cause hard to tolerate side effects. Cancer is rarely cured by just one kind of treatment, whether it is drugs, herbal remedies, diet, or other therapies. The best treatment combines physical treatments, such as cancer drugs or

If you have cancer, it is helpful to seek the friendship and advice of others who have cancer or have survived it.

acupuncture, with promoting well-being by eating healthy foods. Emotional and spiritual support is also important, through support groups, counseling, prayer, or meditation.

When cancer cannot be cured

Some cancers can be cured but others cannot, especially if the cancer has spread to several parts of the body.

Often, when cancer is found late, there is no cure. Then it may be best to stay at home in the care of family. This time can be very difficult. A person with cancer should eat as well as possible, and get plenty of rest. Medicines for pain, anxiety, and sleeping problems can make a person with cancer more comfortable. Talking with someone close can help prepare for death, and plan for the family's future. Caregivers can sometimes find support and help providing care from a hospice (an organization that helps people in the last stages of life).

Breast cancer

Breast cancer has many causes, including exposure to toxic chemicals from pesticides, oil, cleaning products, and air pollution. If a woman's mother or sisters have had breast cancer, she may have a greater chance of getting it too. Breast cancer is most common in women over 50.

Breast cancer usually grows slowly, and is sometimes cured if found early. Women can watch for signs of breast cancer by examining their breasts themselves. Look for lumps or unusual discharge from the nipples. If a woman does this once a month, she will be familiar with how her breasts look and feel, and will notice any changes.

How to examine your breasts

1 Look at your breasts in a mirror. Raise your arms over your head. Look for any change in the shape of your breasts, or any swelling or changes in the skin or nipples. Then put your arms at your sides and check your breasts again.

2 Lie down. Keeping your fingers flat, press your breast and feel for any lumps.

3 Be sure to touch every part of your breast. It helps to use the same pattern every time, such as a spiral or rows of straight lines.

What to do if you find a lump
If the lump is smooth or rubbery, and moves under the skin when you push it with your fingers, do not worry about it. But if it is hard, has an uneven shape, and is painless, keep watching it, **especially if the lump is in only one breast and does not move even when you push it.** See a health worker if the lump is still there after your next monthly bleeding. This may be a sign of cancer. Also see a health worker if there is a discharge from the nipples that looks like blood or pus.

Lung (Breathing) Problems

Air pollution caused by burning fossil fuels (coal, oil, diesel, and natural gas) puts many toxic chemicals and harmful particles, like soot and smoke, into the air we breathe. Air pollution causes serious health problems. According to the World Health Organization, it kills 3 million people each year.

The two main parts of air pollution are a toxic gas called ozone, and **particulates.** Particulates are tiny bits of soot, smoke, metals, chemicals, dust, water, and rubber from tires. The smallest particles are the most harmful, because they get deepest into the lungs. Exposure to particulates can cause asthma and bronchitis attacks, and increases colds, flus, and other respiratory infections. Ozone is a strong irritant, causing a person's airways to tighten, forcing the lungs to work harder, and making existing lung problems worse. It can also cause headaches, wheezing, chest pain, nausea, and fatigue, and makes a person more vulnerable to lung infections, including tuberculosis or pneumonia.

Almost immediately, smoky or dirty air causes eyes to water, a dry throat, coughing, or wheezing. High levels of air pollution can also damage the lungs. Pollution can worsen already existing heart problems or lung disease, and cause the heart and lungs to work harder to supply oxygen to the body, causing difficulty breathing, fatigue, and chest pain.

Long-term exposure to polluted air makes:

- lungs age more quickly.
- chronic lung diseases develop, such as asthma, chronic bronchitis, emphysema, and lung cancer.
- people die earlier, most often from heart attack or stroke.

Air pollution is most dangerous for people who already have heart problems or lung diseases, pregnant women, children under 14 whose lungs are still developing, and people who work or exercise vigorously outdoors.

Prevention and Treatment

- Stop smoking tobacco.
- Avoid or reduce exposure to cooking smoke, automobile exhaust, and other chemical fumes.
- Prevent chest infections by hand washing and getting vaccinations.
- Quick-relief medicines for breathing (see asthma treatment) and cough syrup (see page 477) may be useful.

Some health problems from air pollution are not curable, such as cancers, emphysema, and asthma, although people can live with these problems for a long time. Getting away from polluted air can slow the progress of many lung diseases, but this is not possible for many people.

Chronic bronchitis

Chronic bronchitis is an inflammation (swelling) of the main airways in the lungs. Smoking or second-hand smoke (see page 355) from tobacco, air pollution, chemical fumes, and dust are the main causes of chronic bronchitis.

When a person's airways are irritated, a thick mucus forms and plugs them up, making it hard to breathe. Signs of chronic bronchitis include a cough producing yellow-green mucus, difficulty breathing, tightness in the chest, wheezing, fatigue, headaches, and swollen ankles, feet, and legs.

Asthma

Asthma is a common chronic illness for children and adults. Signs are wheezing, coughing, loss of breath, and chest tightness. These problems happen when the breathing passages in the lungs close down and the lungs fill with mucus. Industrial pollution and toxics are common causes of asthma, but asthma attacks are caused by many things.

During an asthma attack, sit forward, hands on knees, hunch your back, expand your chest, and try to relax.

Treatment

To relieve an asthma attack, inhale medicines that open the breathing passages. If quick-relief medicine is not available, try strong coffee or black tea, **ephedra (ma huang)**, or **pseudoephedrine**. Quick-relief medicines control the effects of an asthma attack — they do not prevent attacks. For treatment, see a health worker.

Prevention

Long-term treatment can help prevent asthma attacks, make them milder, or less frequent. If no long-term medicine is available, use of **Nigella sativa** (black seed, kalonji, habba sawda) can prevent asthma attacks. 2 teaspoons of black seed 1 time a day with honey or yogurt will strengthen the lungs and immune system.

To prevent asthma attacks, avoid or reduce contact with what triggers the attacks, including:

- **smoke** from cooking, heating, and tobacco.
- **outdoor air pollution** from factories and automobiles. When pollution is bad, people with asthma should stay indoors and not do hard physical work.
- **chemicals** in paints, solvents, pesticides, perfumes, and cleaning products.
- **dust mites.** Remove stuffed toys and rugs from sleeping areas (see page 357).
- **animal hair and feathers,** including from pets.
- **cockroaches** and other insect pests (see pages 366 to 367).
- **mold** (see page 358).
- **emotional and physical stress** that often comes with major life changes, overwork, and hard physical exercise.

Asbestosis

Asbestos is a mineral that was once used for fire protection in buildings and some appliances. Asbestos is made of tiny fibers that get into the air and are breathed into the lungs where they cause permanent damage. Asbestos is so dangerous it has been banned by many governments.

Exposure to asbestos leads to **asbestosis** and lung cancer. Early signs of these illnesses are coughing, shortness of breath, chest pain, weight loss, and weakness. For more information about asbestos, see page 371.

Nerve Problems

Many toxic chemicals harm our nervous systems. Harm to the nerves can cause confusion, memory loss, seizures (fits), and other problems with the brain. Nerve damage can also lead to damage to taste and smell, loss of feeling in the body, and difficulty balancing and walking. Some chemicals can cause paralysis or even death. Solvents commonly used for cleaning grease, such as acetone, benzene, turpentine, and gasoline, are toxic to the nervous system.

Prevention and treatment

The best way to prevent harm to the nervous system from toxics is to reduce their use at work and in the home. If you must use them, make sure there is good **ventilation** and use gloves and masks (see Appendix A).

Skin Problems

The most common cause of skin problems and skin disease is from chemicals in the workplace. People also get rashes, blisters, and serious chemical burns from exposure to toxics in polluted air or water from industrial or agricultural chemicals and wastes.

Prevention and treatment

Protect yourself from chemicals by reducing exposure and wearing protective equipment (see Appendix A). When exposed to chemicals, wash the skin right away with cool water and soap. Avoid warm water because it opens the pores. If your skin has been damaged or made very sensitive from chemical exposures, avoid sunlight. If you must be in the sun, keep your head and body covered as much as possible.

Some skin creams can reduce pain and soreness, but reducing contact with the poison is the only way to stop the problem.

Multiple Chemical Sensitivity (MCS)

For some people, the combined effects of many chemicals or a large exposure to even 1 chemical may cause an illness called **multiple chemical sensitivity** (MCS) or environmental illness. People with MCS have strong reactions to common toxins in paint, perfume, cars, and building materials.

Signs of MCS may include runny nose, itchy eyes, headache, scratchy throat, ear ache, scalp pain, mental confusion or sleepiness, fast heartbeat, upset stomach, nausea, abdominal cramping, diarrhea, and aching joints.

Because people show different signs of MCS, many health workers do not believe it is a real illness caused by chemicals. Instead, they think it is caused by emotional distress. MCS is also often mistaken for common allergies (see page 357), but it is different from allergies for these reasons:

- Signs appear each time the person is exposed to chemicals.
- The effects are long lasting (**chronic**) and not seasonal.
- Signs appear with less and less exposure.
- The signs go away when the triggering chemicals are removed.
- Signs appear in the presence of different and unrelated substances (such as paint and perfume, or plastics and cigarette smoke).

Prevention and treatment

The best way to prevent MCS is to stay away from chemicals that may cause it. Because each person reacts differently, treating MCS depends on the person who has it, although all improve when the toxins are removed from their environment.

Our Chemical Body Burden

Some chemicals leave the body quickly after a person is exposed. Others may remain in fat, blood, or bones for a long time. For example, **arsenic** usually stays in the body for only 3 days after a person is exposed 1 time. Other chemicals, such as the pesticide DDT (see page 150), can stay in the body for 50 years or more. The **chemical body burden** is the amount of toxic chemicals that are present in the human body at any time.

Just because we have these chemicals in our bodies does not mean that every one of us will get sick. Some people may get sick even though they have few toxic chemicals in their bodies. Others who have more chemicals may not get sick (see page 321).

Children often have a greater body burden than adults. Although they may have a shorter period of exposure because of their age, their bodies have not yet developed ways to protect themselves from toxics or to remove toxics from their bodies.

Toxic mixtures

There are so many chemicals in our environment that often we cannot know which ones we are exposed to or how the combination may affect us. This chemical mixture makes it especially difficult to trace a person's health problems to chemical exposure. In most cases, though, chemical mixtures are more harmful than each chemical by itself.

Scientists study each chemical alone to see how it can harm a person's health. But many chemical products, such as cleaners, dyes, plastics, paints, and glues, are a mixture of several chemicals. For example, paint contains solvents, pigments, and other materials. Solvents cause 1 set of health problems, and pigments cause another. Mixed together, they can cause a third set of health problems, including ones that each chemical alone might not cause. Most waste from industry, such as smoke from a smokestack or chemical waste dumped into waterways, is also a mixture of many chemicals.

How toxics move through the environment

Many toxic chemicals travel far from their sources through air, water, and food, and in products we use every day, such as plastics, cleaners, and pesticides. Some of these chemicals remain in the environment for a long time. Every person on earth carries toxic chemicals in their bodies.

Toxic chemicals collect in the fat of people and animals, and in some plants. When people or large animals (such as bears, owls, hawks, or large fish) eat smaller animals, fish, or plants, toxic chemicals in them are passed along through the **food chain** or **food web** and accumulate in the bodies of those eating them.

Toxic chemicals turn the web of life into a web of death.

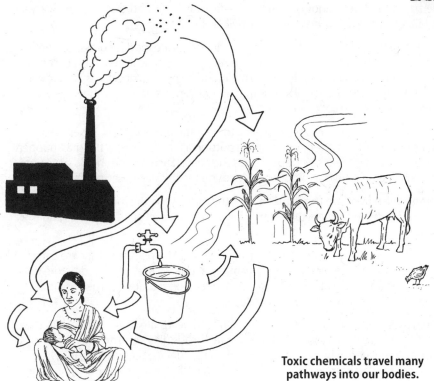

Toxic chemicals travel many pathways into our bodies.

Deadly links: Toxic chemicals pass from animals to people

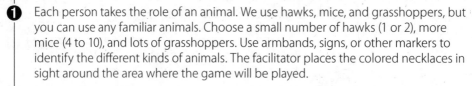

In this activity, people play the parts of different kinds of animals to show how some toxics are passed from one to another. At least 7 people are needed for this game, the more people the better!

Time: ½ hour to 1 hour

Materials: 20 or 30 necklaces made of colored beads. About half are of one color, such as yellow, and the other half have beads of two colors, such as yellow and red.

❶ Each person takes the role of an animal. We use hawks, mice, and grasshoppers, but you can use any familiar animals. Choose a small number of hawks (1 or 2), more mice (4 to 10), and lots of grasshoppers. Use armbands, signs, or other markers to identify the different kinds of animals. The facilitator places the colored necklaces in sight around the area where the game will be played.

❷ The facilitator announces that the colored necklaces are food for grasshoppers. What she doesn't say is that the red beads are toxic chemicals that have collected in the food. The grasshoppers collect their food by putting necklaces around their necks. Each grasshopper collects as much food as possible, remembering how many necklaces she collected in total.

❸ Next, release the mice into the play area to hunt the grasshoppers. Whenever a mouse catches a grasshopper, he or she puts on all the necklaces the grasshopper was wearing and the grasshopper leaves the game. Each mouse should have time to catch one or more grasshoppers and put on the necklaces he collects.

❹ Release the hawks into the game to hunt the mice, while the mice are hunting grasshoppers. Any mouse caught by a hawk turns over all of its necklaces and then sits out.

❺ Once the hawks have collected all the necklaces, all the players gather in a circle. Ask each grasshopper and mouse how many necklaces they collected before they were eaten and if any of these necklaces had red beads on them. Then ask the hawks to show the necklaces they collected.

❻ Begin a discussion, telling the group that the red beads are toxic chemicals in the food. Explain that the hawk with the most red beads dies because the most toxics have accumulated in her body. Other hawks may survive, but will lay eggs with thin shells or hatch sickly chicks. Ask the group to discuss how toxic chemicals get into their water or food. What foods do people eat that may have toxic chemicals in them? How can we keep toxic chemicals from accumulating in our bodies? How can we keep them out of the environment?

Heavy Metals

Heavy metals such as **lead, mercury, cadmium,** and **chromium,** are harmful to people, animals and plants, even in very small amounts. Heavy metals are released into the environment by many industries, such as oil drilling and refining, mining, metal **smelting,** tanneries, and **incineration.**

Heavy metals are harmful when people breathe in or swallow dust or fumes, or get them on the skin or in their eyes and absorb them into the blood. Heavy metals may also collect in plants and animals and cause harm when people eat them.

Signs of heavy metal poisoning

Heavy metal poisoning usually does not happen from one large exposure, but from exposure to small amounts over time. Early signs include shaking, irritability, difficulty concentrating, tiredness, and weakness in the hands and feet. Other signs include:

Headaches, dizziness, sleeping problems, memory loss (especially in mercury poisoning), difficulty thinking

Skin rash, irritations of eyes and nose

Bleeding gums, blisters in the mouth, toothaches, jaw pain, metal taste in the mouth

Rapid heartbeat, anxiety, and a very weak or very strong pulse

Stomach pain, bloating, diarrhea or constipation, a need to urinate often

Muscle spasms, pain and stiffness in joints and muscles, cold hands and feet

Heavy metal poisoning can also cause damage to the kidneys and the reproductive system, and other serious long term health problems.

IMPORTANT: If you suspect heavy metal poisoning, see a health worker for testing right away. If you are exposed to heavy metals day after day, medicine will not stop the poisoning. The only way to stop the poisoning is to stop being exposed. If you do have heavy metal poisoning, it is likely that others in your community will also.

The next few pages discuss problems of mercury. Other heavy metals have similar problems. See problems from lead on pages 368 to 370.

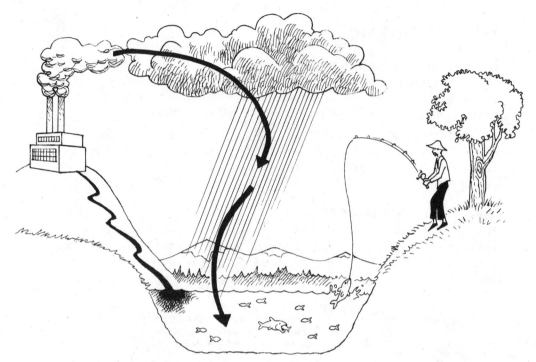

Heavy metals travel through the air, into water, fish, soil, and plants, and into our bodies.

Mercury poisoning

Mercury is a heavy metal that can cause serious health problems when it is released into the environment by mining, burning coal, or when products that contain mercury become waste. Mercury is highly toxic.

When mercury collects in rivers, lakes, and streams and combines with rotting plants, it can turn into a more toxic form called methyl mercury. Even a very small amount of mercury can poison all the fish in a pond or river. Methyl mercury in the environment is toxic for centuries.

Health problems from mercury

Breathing in or absorbing through the skin even a very small amount of mercury can cause damage to the nerves, kidneys, lungs, and brain, and birth defects. The health problems can take many years to show up.

Mild mercury poisoning causes tingling in the lips, tongue, fingers, and toes, and trembling in the hands and feet. In some cases, these signs do not appear until long after exposure.

Severe mercury poisoning causes headaches, memory loss, difficulty coordinating movement and vision, dizziness, metal taste in the mouth, muscle spasms, pain and stiffness in joints and muscles, rapid heartbeat, and a very weak or very strong pulse.

Exposure to mercury in men can lead to loss of ability to have sex, and sterility.

Exposure to mercury in women can lead to failure to have monthly bleeding and other problems in having babies.

In pregnant women, even small amounts of mercury can cause their babies to have developmental problems (see pages 322 to 324).

Mercury in fish

Methyl mercury collects in the bodies of fish, animals, and people. Fish that live in polluted water can be dangerous to eat, even though the water itself may not be harmful to bathe or swim in.

Because larger fish and animals usually eat many smaller ones, the mercury builds up in their bodies.

Small amounts of mercury can pass through the body without causing harm. If we stop eating food that contains mercury, our bodies begin to get rid of the mercury that has collected. But when we take in more mercury than our bodies can get rid of, mercury causes serious health problems.

Fish are good food, full of protein. Fish are sometimes called "brain food" because they have fats that are good for the brain. They are part of traditional diets for many people. But if they are caught in waters where mines drain or where mercury has been dumped, they may have unsafe amounts of mercury.

Fish and food safety

You cannot tell if a fish contains mercury by looking at it. Because mercury is stored in the flesh of the fish, there is no special way to clean or cook fish that will prevent mercury exposure. Some types of fish are likely to have less mercury in them, due to their feeding habits or life histories, and are safer for people to eat. If you live in a mine-drainage area,

it is more dangerous to eat:
- larger, older fish.
- bottom-feeding fish, such as catfish and carp.
- only fish as your main food.
- fish organs, especially the liver.

it is safer to eat:
- smaller, younger fish and fish that feed on insects.
- less fish. Red meat, chicken, rice with lentils or beans, eggs, milk, and cheese are other good sources of protein.
- fish mixed with foods like rice or potatoes. This will not reduce the amount of mercury in the fish, but it will reduce the amount of fish you eat at your meal.

Treatment for heavy metal poisoning

Heavy metal poisoning is very difficult to treat. The main treatment is called chelation (pronounced kee-lay-shun). Chelation uses herbs and medicines to carry toxic metal out of the body. It is most effective for poisoning caused by sudden exposure to a large dose of metals (**acute** poisoning). Most exposure to heavy metals is from daily contact over a long period, so this treatment may not be useful.

Good nutrition can protect the body

When people do not have enough vitamins, calcium, iron, or protein in their diet they may suffer more severely from heavy metal poisoning. The body will use toxic heavy metals to fill in for the missing nutrients — leading to serious illness.

Foods that help the body resist heavy metal poisoning include: Beans, whole grains, meat, nuts, eggs, red, yellow and green vegetables, dark leafy greens, coriander, cabbage, and fruits.

IMPORTANT: People who have goiter or may have chronic cyanide poisoning should avoid foods that make goiter worse, such as cabbage and cassava.

No foods will treat severe poisoning from heavy metals or other toxic chemicals. However, improving the diet helps in treating most illnesses, including illnesses caused by heavy metals. In areas where people are very poor and are exposed to heavy metals and other toxics, such as mining communities, the best approach may be a community nutrition program to ensure that everyone is well-fed, strong, and resistant to illness. (For a story about a nutrition program in a mining community, see page 475.)

POPs (Persistent Organic Pollutants)

One group of chemicals called **POPs (Persistent Organic Pollutants)** becomes more dangerous as each chemical passes from air or water to accumulate in animals, fish, and people. **Persistent** means they stay in the environment and in our bodies for a long time. **Organic** means they can enter and affect all living things. **Pollutants** means they are dangerous for the environment.

The most common POPs are **dioxins** (a chemical waste from manufacturing and incineration), **PCBs** (a chemical fluid used in electronics and many household products), and many kinds of pesticides (including DDT).

But we do not use any toxic chemicals!

Chemicals travel in wind and water, in plants and animals we eat. We have poisons in our bodies we have never even heard of.

POPs travel through air, water, and soil. They collect in the bodies of living things and accumulate as they pass along the food web (see page 335). Because of this, POPs are found everywhere in our environment, even in places far from where they were produced.

Dioxins are some of the most toxic POPs. Most dioxin is released when PVC plastic, bleached paper, coal, diesel fuel, and other things that contain the chemical **chlorine** are burned. Dioxin is also released from metal smelting, cement making, papermaking, and some pesticides. Dioxin released into air and water sooner or later gets into our food and drinking water. Dioxin causes cancer.

PVC plastic is commonly used to make pipes for water systems. PVC is also used in baby bottles, toys, food containers, and other everyday products. As PVC plastic gets old and worn down, it can release toxic chemicals, causing serious illness. When burned, PVC plastics release the harmful POPs dioxins and furans.

PCBs (Poly chlorinated biphenyls) are one kind of POP formerly used in electrical equipment, such as transformers and switches, and in products such as carbonless copy paper and dyes. Because they are known to be very toxic, PCBs are now banned internationally and replaced in some cases by other chemicals called PBDEs. But PBDEs also stay in our bodies for a long time, and also cause serious health problems such as damage to the brain and nerves.

Replacing one toxic chemical with another is no solution to the problem.

We can begin by stopping things we know are bad, like dioxins and PCBs.

Health problems from POPs

Even small exposures to POPs cause problems such as sterility and birth defects. Some POPs cause the body to become more sensitive to other chemicals as well (see page 333).

Protecting your community from POPs

POPs are a part of many products used every day. The only way to prevent harm from POPs is to stop buying them, stop using them, and stop making them.

- Avoid buying products made from PVC. PVC products often smell strongly when first used or exposed to hot sun, and are often marked with the "3" or "V" symbol on the bottom of the product. If you have to buy plastic, those with numbers 2, 4, 5, and 1 are the safest.

- Do not use plastic bags and disposable (often bleached) paper products. Instead, use cloth bags and reusable plates and cups.

- Avoid burning trash, especially plastic trash (see pages 409 and 423).

- Grow and buy foods without chemical pesticides. Support farmers who use sustainable farming methods (see Chapters 14 and 15).

- Ask your health workers if they can get and use medical products that are not made of PVC plastic.

- Support laws that ban incineration of waste.

- Join the campaign calling for the total elimination of POPs (see Resources).

Radiation

Radiation is an invisible form of energy. Some radiation, such as sunlight, is good for us. But some radiation, from heavy metals such as uranium (see page 491), causes **radiation poisoning,** cancers, skin diseases, and birth defects. Radioactive materials poison the land and water for many generations.

Most radioactive materials are produced by the military and used for making war. Radiation exposure is most common where weapons are made, tested, and used, such as military bases and war zones. Radioactive materials used by the military are sometimes recycled and show up in other metal products, causing harm to people who have no way to know they are exposed.

Radioactive metals are also used in some products such as electronics, causing harm to workers exposed to them. People who work at nuclear power plants, uranium mines, or nuclear dumping sites are also at serious risk for radiation exposure. (To learn more about radiation poisoning from mining, see pages 473 and 491.)

Radiation sickness

Radiation can cause cancer of the lungs, thyroid, and blood, as well as diseases that affect the bones, muscles, nervous system, stomach, and digestive system.

Most exposure to harmful radiation occurs in small amounts over a long time, causing health problems to develop slowly. Uranium miners, for example, may work for many years with no signs of illness. Years later, they can develop lung cancer and other illnesses related to their work with radioactive materials (see page 473).

Soldiers who handle radioactive missile shells (depleted uranium shells) and people in war zones where the shells are left among the rubble of destruction are also developing radiation sickness.

Nuclear accidents or explosions can cause death right away or within several weeks. People who survive 6 weeks after an explosion may recover for a while, but serious illness can return years later.

Radiation can pass to nursing infants through breast milk. Radiation sickness can not be passed from person to person, but the damage it causes can pass down from parents to children and grandchildren, as birth defects, cancers, and other health problems.

Signs

Early signs of radiation sickness include nausea, vomiting, diarrhea, and fatigue. These signs may be followed by:

- hair loss
- burning feeling in the body
- shortness of breath
- swelling of the mouth and throat
- worsening of tooth or gum disease
- dry cough

- pain in the heart
- rapid heartbeat
- permanent skin darkening
- bleeding spots under the skin
- pale or transparent skin, gums, and fingernails (anemia)
- death

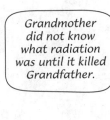

Grandmother did not know what radiation was until it killed Grandfather.

Organizing against radiation poisoning

Asian Rare Earth Company, owned partly by Mitsubishi Corporation of Japan, ran a factory for 10 years in the village of Bukit Merah, Malaysia, to produce a rare metal that was used to make the red colors in television screens.

The factory dumped radioactive waste in the village and many villagers suffered cancers and birth defects caused by the radiation. The factory had not fenced off the waste site, posted any warning signs, or taken any other measures to reduce harm to the villagers.

Community residents brought a lawsuit against the company to shut down the factory. Along with the lawsuit, they held many public protests that were widely reported on local radio and television. After 7 years, a Malaysian court ordered Asian Rare Earth to close its plant in Bukit Merah and remove all its radioactive waste and toxic chemicals.

By using public protest, media, and lawsuits, the villagers prevented further health problems by forcing the factory to shut down.

Healing Toxic Injuries

Toxic chemicals are so widespread that it may seem impossible to be free of them, and to prevent and heal the illnesses they cause. However, people all over the world are developing new treatments for toxic injuries that combine modern medicine with traditional ways of healing.

Sambhavna Clinic

Since the 1984 chemical disaster in Bhopal, India, thousands of people there live with chronic health problems. These include breathing problems and fevers, and also reproductive problems, loss of vision, cancers, and birth defects in the next generation of children. (To read more about the disaster, see Chapter 4.)

Perhaps the greatest lessons from the Bhopal disaster come from the people's campaigns for health and justice. Sambhavna Clinic was built by survivors of the disaster and other volunteers to provide health care to the whole community. In seeking ways to relieve the severe health problems following the poison gas leak, the health workers discovered new medical treatments, proving that good care and creativity are the keys to healing toxic injuries.

How the clinic runs

The Sambhavna Clinic has treated more than 12,000 people for no charge. Half of the clinic staff are survivors of the Bhopal disaster. The clinic also carries out studies that are helping the world understand the long-term effects of chemicals.

In their own words, these are the guiding principles of Sambhavna clinic:

Disaster survivors participate in monitoring community health. This is part of the struggle for memory and against forgetting.

We run our own clinic without corporate charities, large grants from foundations, or government assistance.

People can and should be active participants in their own healing.

We can build hope in a situation of despair through creative and collective action!

Clinic treatments

Health workers at Sambhavna use many kinds of treatments, including herbal medicines and yoga, breathing and movement exercises that treat body, mind and spirit. Every person that comes to the clinic has a choice of which kind or combination of treatments they want to use. In this way, the clinic encourages people to participate in their own healing, and the health workers learn that different treatments work for different people.

A mental health specialist treats problems such as panic attacks, disturbed sleep, depression, irritability, and impaired memory. Drugs may be given, though drugs with harmful effects are avoided. Herbal medicines, massage, and baths in hot water and medicinal oils are used to **detoxify** the body (cleanse by removing poisons).

Many people practice yoga to improve the health of both mind and body.

Yoga helps heal the internal organs, manage pain, and control each person's disease process. Though many survivors, especially Muslims who do not traditionally practice yoga, were skeptical at first, yoga has been found to be one of the most helpful treatments, particularly for people suffering from chronic diseases.

Finally, the clinic prepares and provides medicines using local herbs. All medicines are free of cost, and clinic workers provide information to make sure that people are well informed about what they are taking. The clinic is also built and maintained in a way that reduces toxic exposures (see page 40).

A candle against the darkness

The word *Sambhavna* means "possibility" in the Sanskrit and Hindi languages. Often, the people most affected by environmental disasters, such as in Bhopal, have little hope for recovery, justice, or for health. By using creativity, caring, and faith in the ability to heal, the health workers at Sambhavna have turned despair into hope.

17 A Healthy Home

In this chapter:

A Healthy Home

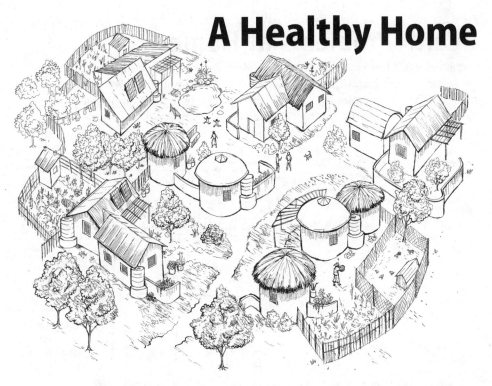

The ideal home is not just a building for shelter. A home should be a place free from harm, that supports physical, mental, and social well-being, and provides dignity and a sense of community. A healthy home protects against extreme heat and cold, rain and sun, wind, pests, disasters such as floods and earthquakes, and pollution and disease.

Unfortunately, many people's living conditions do not protect their health. Poor living conditions may even cause illness, or make health problems worse. Whether people live close together or spread apart, poor housing, **indoor air pollution,** pests, and toxic chemicals in household products can cause many illnesses.

As more people move from rural areas into cities and towns, the way people live and maintain their homes changes, often for the worse. People who spend a lot of time in the home, such as children, the elderly and disabled, and people with long-term health problems such as HIV/AIDS, suffer the most.

How to improve living conditions by making homes safer and more comfortable depends on local traditions, available materials, and climate. Unfortunately, it also depends on income and ownership. People who rent their homes often have little control over their living conditions and must depend on their landlords to make improvements. People in shantytowns, marginal communities, or other "temporary" settlements (which too often become permanent) live in homes that rarely provide security or comfort. But whether a person owns, rents, or lives in makeshift housing, working with neighbors is the most effective way to improve living conditions in the whole neighborhood.

Health Problems at Home

Our homes are not separate from the environment. They can have many of the same environmental health problems we find in our communities and workplaces. When planning a new home or improving the home you live in, you can protect your health by considering problems caused by how and where houses are built, how they are furnished, and what work is done at home.

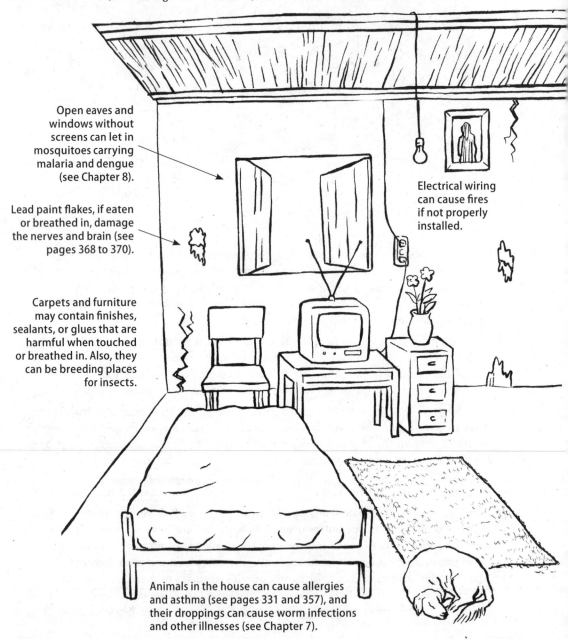

Open eaves and windows without screens can let in mosquitoes carrying malaria and dengue (see Chapter 8).

Lead paint flakes, if eaten or breathed in, damage the nerves and brain (see pages 368 to 370).

Carpets and furniture may contain finishes, sealants, or glues that are harmful when touched or breathed in. Also, they can be breeding places for insects.

Electrical wiring can cause fires if not properly installed.

Animals in the house can cause allergies and asthma (see pages 331 and 357), and their droppings can cause worm infections and other illnesses (see Chapter 7).

Air pollution from outside the home, especially in cities, industrial areas, and where large amounts of pesticides are used, causes asthma and other illnesses of the lungs, nose, throat, and eyes.

Rodents, mosquitoes, and other insects can live and breed in roof thatch and cracks in the walls and floors, spreading diseases such as Chagas (see page 367).

Cracks in foundations, floors, and walls, and unsealed roofs and windows cause heat loss and dampness. This allows mold to grow on walls, bedding, and furniture. Mold can cause breathing problems, rashes, and other illnesses (see page 358).

Cleaning products, pesticides, and other chemicals can cause skin rashes, respiratory illnesses, and other long-term health problems (see page 372).

Lead water pipes pollute drinking and cooking water, leading to birth defects and other serious health problems (see pages 368 to 370).

Germs from food or food surfaces where food is prepared cause diarrhea and food poisoning (see page 375).

Burning any fuel without ventilation releases carbon monoxide (CO) and other harmful gases into the air, leading to serious illness (see page 354).

Open fires make harmful smoke that causes illnesses of the nose, throat, eyes, and lungs, and cause burns and house fires (see page 365).

Indoor Air Pollution

When people burn wood, dung, coal, charcoal, gas, and
crop wastes indoors for cooking or heating without
good **ventilation**, smoke fills the house. This smoke
contains harmful gases (**fumes**) and tiny **particulates**
(soot) that cause breathing problems and other illnesses.
Headaches, dizziness, and fatigue are often followed by
serious illnesses such as asthma, pneumonia, bronchitis, or
lung cancer. Indoor air pollution from smoking fires also
increases the risk of getting TB (see page 356).

Women and children are the most exposed to harmful
cooking smoke. When pregnant women are exposed to
a lot of smoke every day, it can cause their children to
be born very small, grow slowly, and have difficulty
learning later on. In some cases, it can even cause
children to be born dead.

**When men cook more,
they will become better
cooks and burn less food.**

To reduce indoor air pollution, you can:

- improve ventilation (see pages 352 to 354).
- improve stoves (see pages 359 to 362, and
  Resources).
- use cleaner fuels (see page 362 to 364, and Chapter 23).
- use safer cleaning products (see page 358, and 372 to 374).
- reduce air pollution from outdoors (see Chapter 20).

Poor ventilation harms health

Ventilation is the way fresh air moves into a room or building, and how old
and polluted air moves out. If a house has poor ventilation, smoke and polluted
air stay inside. Poor ventilation also traps moisture in the house, causing
dampness and mold. The easiest way to reduce indoor air pollution is to improve
ventilation. To know if your house has poor ventilation, look for these signs:

- Smoke stays in the house, or the ceilings are black from cooking or
  heating smoke.
- Moisture collects on windows or walls.
- Clothing, bedding, or walls grow mold.
- Bad smells from toilets or sewers stay in the house.

If you cook with gas and often suffer from dizziness and confusion, this may be
a sign of poor ventilation or a gas leak.

Improved ventilation solves many problems

Ndito, a mother of 3 children, once began every morning with a terrible coughing fit. When she built a fire in the kitchen to heat water and prepare food, the house filled with smoke, causing Ndito to wheeze. Each breath was painful and labored. The smoke in Ndito's kitchen gave her asthma.

Because of her health problems, Ndito and her husband Refa agreed to join the Kenya Smoke and Health Project. Refa learned to measure the air pollution in their house, and found that the amount of smoke was very unhealthy. Refa and Ndito decided to make changes to reduce the smoke pollution.

Project workers helped Ndito build a hood over her stove with a chimney to remove smoke from the house. Also, Refa built new, larger windows to improve ventilation. With less smoke in the house, the family spends more time together. The windows also make it easier for Ndito to watch over their livestock, and they let in more light, making it easier to do beadwork.

Before these changes, Refa stayed away from the kitchen. Now he wakes up before dawn to start the fire and puts on a pot of water for tea. Ndito is relieved from waking up early and doing all the chores by herself. The new smoke hood and chimney have reduced the amount of soot, so Ndito has less to clean. Her coughing fits are less common now. Refa and Ndito had to pay for the smoke hood, but the changes they made improved Ndito's health and will protect the whole family from illness. Better health improved their livelihood, so the money they spent on the smoke hood is an investment in their future.

To improve ventilation

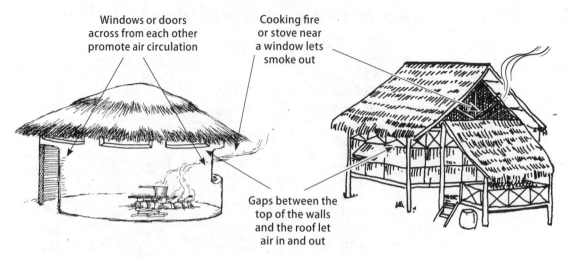

Windows or doors across from each other promote air circulation

Cooking fire or stove near a window lets smoke out

Gaps between the top of the walls and the roof let air in and out

Carbon monoxide (CO) poisoning

Stoves or appliances that burn natural gas, liquid petroleum (LP gas), oil, kerosene, coal, charcoal, or wood may produce carbon monoxide (CO), a poisonous gas with no color, taste, or smell. CO is also produced by cars.

People often close a room tightly to keep warm or use less fuel. But heating without ventilation can be dangerous. In a poorly ventilated space, CO can cause serious illness, or even death.

Signs

CO poisoning seems at first like flu, but without fever. Signs include headache, fatigue, shortness of breath, nausea, and dizziness.

Prevention

The best way to prevent CO poisoning is to make sure your home has good ventilation. Check chimneys and flues for cracks, blocks, rust, and loose connections. Never burn charcoal, gas, wood, or other fuel inside a home, vehicle, or tent with poor ventilation. Do not use gas appliances such as stove tops, ovens, or clothes dryers to heat your home. Avoid using gasoline-powered tools and engines indoors. If you must use them, make sure there is good ventilation and place the engine so exhaust fumes will go outdoors.

Cigarette smoke

Smoking tobacco can cause many health problems for the smoker and for other people exposed to the smoke. Health problems from smoking include:

- serious lung diseases, such as lung cancer, emphysema, and chronic bronchitis.

- heart disease, heart attack, stroke, and high blood pressure.

- cancer of the mouth, throat, neck and bladder.

Second-hand smoke is the mixture of smoke that comes from cigarettes, pipes, and cigars, plus the smoke breathed out by the smoker. Second-hand smoke makes smoking dangerous for everyone who lives with a smoker, especially children. It causes the same health problems as does smoking.

To stop or help someone stop smoking

People who smoke become addicted to a drug in tobacco called nicotine. Without a cigarette, they may feel sick or nervous. As every smoker knows, it is difficult to stop smoking because nicotine is a very addictive drug.

Because tobacco companies market their products aggressively, many people begin smoking at a young age and continue smoking because of the addiction to nicotine. Cigarette companies say smoking is a personal choice, not an addiction. **This is not true.** Understanding that smoking is a harmful addiction and not a personal choice is the first step toward stopping.

Telling people "DO NOT SMOKE," is rarely successful in helping smokers to stop. Some ways to help break the addiction and stop smoking include:

- Practice deep breathing every time you crave a cigarette.

- Exercise daily.

- Replace smoking with a healthy habit such as drinking a cup of tea or walking.

- Drink plenty of water to flush nicotine out of the body.

- Ask for support from friends and family.

She looks so cool when she smokes!

But smoking cigarettes makes you sick. What is so cool about that?

Tuberculosis (TB, consumption)

Tuberculosis (TB) is a disease that most often affects the lungs. It passes easily from person to person because when someone with TB coughs, the germs get into the air and live for many hours, letting other people breathe in the germs. TB spreads quickly in crowded homes and neighborhoods, in factories, work camps, prisons, refugee camps, and other places where people live or work closely and there is little ventilation.

Who gets sick from TB germs?

Many people have TB germs in their bodies, but only 1 out of 10 of them will get sick with TB. People are more likely to get sick if they are already weak from illnesses like asthma, malaria, or HIV, or if they are very young, very old, or malnourished. Smoking tobacco and breathing polluted air increase the risk of TB.

Signs

Tuberculosis is curable if it is treated early and completely. A person may have all or some of these signs when they first get sick:

- a cough that lasts longer than 3 weeks, often worse just after waking up
- a slight fever in the evening and sweating at night
- pain in the chest and upper back
- steady loss of weight and increasing weakness

Young children may have frequent fevers, steady weight loss, swellings in the neck or belly, or a lighter skin color.

Treatment

If you think you may have TB, cover your mouth or cough into your shirt when you cough around other people, and wash your hands often. Go to a clinic right away. If the health worker finds you have TB, you will need to begin taking medicines. To cure TB, people take 3 or 4 different medicines every day for 6 to 12 months. If someone in the home has TB:

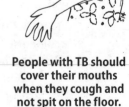

- Test the whole family for TB and begin treatment for those who are sick.
- Vaccinate all children against TB.
- The person with TB should eat and sleep apart from the children if he or she has any cough at all.

People with TB should cover their mouths when they cough and not spit on the floor.

TB is less of a problem when homes and workplaces are well-ventilated. But as long as people in the community have TB germs, it will be a threat. Reducing poverty and training people to recognize and treat TB are more likely to stop the spread of TB than any other solution. To learn more about the signs of TB and ways to prevent and treat it, see a health worker or a general health care book such as *Where There Is No Doctor*.

Allergies

Allergies are signs of the body's reaction to substances it finds difficult to tolerate. Allergies are often difficult to recognize and treat because they have the same signs as many common illnesses. Common **allergic reactions** include difficulty breathing, coughing, itchy throat, runny nose, tiredness, red or itchy eyes, and skin rashes.

Many things in the home can cause allergies, such as cleaning products, chemicals in carpeting and furniture, mold, pollen, animal dander, feathers, waste, dust and dust mites, cockroaches, rats, mice, and other pests. Exposure to toxics can lead to Multiple Chemical Sensitivity (MCS), which is similar to allergies (see page 333). Some ways to prevent allergic reactions are:

- Improve the flow of air through the house.
- Reduce contact with the pollutant causing the allergic reaction.
- Keep the house clean and free of dust.

Dust and dust mites

Dust mites are tiny, invisible bugs that are the biggest cause of indoor allergies. They irritate the eyes and nose and cause asthma attacks (see page 331). Dust mites live in warm, humid places filled with dust such as bed pillows, mattresses, carpets, stuffed toys, clothing, and furniture.

To get rid of dust and dust mites

Cleaning sleeping areas and bedding will help reduce dust, dust mites, and animal hair. Covering mattresses and pillows with tightly woven fabrics or plastic, and washing these covers in hot water regularly will help get rid of dust mites. If someone in the home is allergic to dust or dust mites, you may want to avoid having carpets, rugs, or other fabrics in the home.

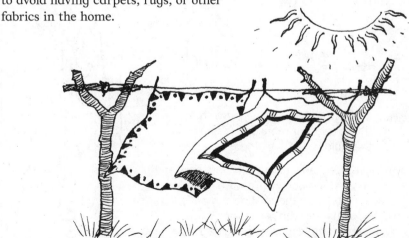

Regular cleaning and airing materials outside in the sun will help to get rid of dust and dust mites.

Mold

Mold is a kind of fungus, a simple plant that grows on soil and other plants. In the home, it grows on walls, clothing, old or spoiled foods, and in any damp place. Mold is also called 'mildew.' Most molds and mildews look like black or yellow powder, tiny threads, or white and blue fuzz.

Outdoors, molds are important to the environment. Molds help dead things decay and turn back into soil. But mold releases tiny spores that can cause health problems for people who breathe them. Molds also destroy the things they live on, so having mold inside the home is never good.

Molds cause breathing problems, headaches, skin irritation, and can trigger asthma attacks and allergic reactions. Rarely, exposure to some molds may lead to serious health problems and death, especially in infants. People with HIV are especially vulnerable to the health problems caused by molds.

To prevent and get rid of mold

Molds grow in damp places with poor ventilation. To prevent and get rid of mold, try to do 1 or more of these things:

- Fix leaks in walls, roofs, and pipes.
- Improve ventilation. When more air passes through the home, it keeps everything drier and helps prevent mold from growing.
- Wash areas where molds grow with bleach solution.

How to make a bleach solution

Mix: 1 cup of bleach, ¼ teaspoon of liquid soap, and 4 liters (1 gallon) of warm water

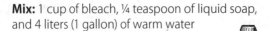

 (Adding one cup of vinegar will help this solution kill more germs along with the mold.)

Wear gloves and a face mask or cloth over your nose and mouth, and keep windows open while washing surfaces with this bleach solution. Let the solution stay on for 10 to 15 minutes, then rinse with plain water. Wipe the surfaces dry to prevent mold from growing back.

Improved Stoves

Smoky cooking stoves cause many serious health problems. Reducing smoke from stoves is an important way to improve family health.

The type of stove people use depends on what foods are cooked, what fuels and stove-making materials are available, and traditional cooking methods. To improve stoves and solve the problems of indoor air pollution, development workers and health promoters need to work together with the people who will use the stoves. Only an improved stove that pleases the cook while using less fuel and reducing smoke will be used and seen as a real improvement.

Women improve stoves for fuel and flavor

Like many women in Guatemala, Inez used to cook her family's meals on a hand-built stove that burned a lot of wood and filled the kitchen with smoke. When an organization that builds improved stoves came to her town, she went with other women to hear them speak.

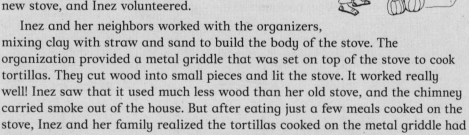

People from the organization had designed a new stove that used less wood, made less smoke, and cost very little to build. They asked who wanted to try the new stove, and Inez volunteered.

Inez and her neighbors worked with the organizers, mixing clay with straw and sand to build the body of the stove. The organization provided a metal griddle that was set on top of the stove to cook tortillas. They cut wood into small pieces and lit the stove. It worked really well! Inez saw that it used much less wood than her old stove, and the chimney carried smoke out of the house. But after eating just a few meals cooked on the stove, Inez and her family realized the tortillas cooked on the metal griddle had no flavor.

Months later, when people from the stove group returned, Inez thanked them. Then, in a small voice she said, "There is one problem with the stove. I think it makes tortillas taste bad." The organizers listened, and asked why tortillas tasted different on this stove. "The old griddle was made of clay," she said. "Maybe that's the difference."

That afternoon Inez, her neighbors, and the organizers made a griddle from local clay. They molded it, let it dry a few days, and then replaced the metal griddle with the clay one. Inez let the stove heat slowly while her daughter made tortillas. When the stove was hot enough, she laid the tortillas on the griddle. When they were ready she shared them with her family. They tasted good! Now, Inez and her family truly have an improved stove.

How a good stove works

Here are simple ways to improve stoves so they will burn less fuel, produce less smoke, and cook foods more quickly.

A hot fire burns fuel completely. A fire smokes when fuels do not burn completely. To make the fire hot, use small, dry pieces of fuel.

A grate under fuel for the fire creates a draft (moving air), helping the fire burn hotter.

Heat from the fire touches the pot. When more of the pot bottom touches the fire, heat goes into the pot and cooks food faster.

No heat is lost to the air because the pot sits right on the fire.

A chimney, hood, or vent to carry away smoke. This also moves air inside the stove, making the fire hotter and cooking food faster.

The stove is made with material that keeps heat inside the stove (insulation), so foods cook faster using less fuel.

Vent cooking and heating stoves

Good: Place the stove near a window. Having 2 openings helps air move through the room.

Better: A hood with a chimney above the stove carries most of the smoke outside. A hole in the roof or a space between the wall and the eaves will also help remove smoke.

Best: A stove with a chimney attached carries most smoke out of the house.

Improving open fires

The most basic "stove" is an open fire. It is sometimes called a 3-stone fire because in many parts of the world the fire is made with 3 stones to surround the burning fuel and to hold up the food or cooking pot.

With small changes, open fires can be made safer, create less smoke, and use less fuel. For example, burning only small pieces of wood which are dry and not "green" makes less smoke. Making a small wall of mud or stones around your fire pit can prevent accidents that lead to house fires or injuries from burns.

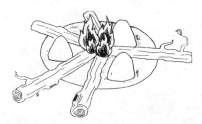

In a clean fire, just the tips of the wood burn, creating less smoke and using less fuel.

In a dirty fire, the wood burns all over, creating a lot of smoke and using a lot of fuel.

Simple clay stove

A simple clay stove with a metal grate to lift fuel off the ground takes very little material to make. It burns hot and clean, and uses less wood than an open fire. To make a simple clay stove, mix:

- 6 parts sand
- 4 parts clay
- a few handfuls of fine sawdust or chopped straw
- enough water to make the clay hold together so it can be shaped into a ring

The pot sits inside the clay ring.

A small space between the pot and the ring, about the width of your smallest finger, will heat the pot best and reduce smoke.

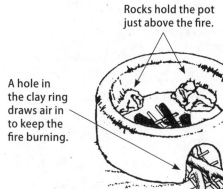

Rocks hold the pot just above the fire.

A hole in the clay ring draws air in to keep the fire burning.

Firewood rests on a grate made of scrap metal, allowing air underneath.

Haybox cookers save fuel

A haybox cooker is a way to prepare slow cooking foods (like stew, beans, and rice) and to keep food warm while saving fuel. A haybox cooker is made from hay or whatever insulating materials are available to you. It can be made from a cardboard box, a basket filled with straw or newspapers, or by simply wrapping your cooking pot in a heavy blanket or cloth.

After the food on the stove boils for a few minutes, remove the pot and place it in the haybox. The food will continue to cook for 2 or more hours. The more food in the pot, the more heat it will keep. Haybox cookers do not work well for small amounts of food.

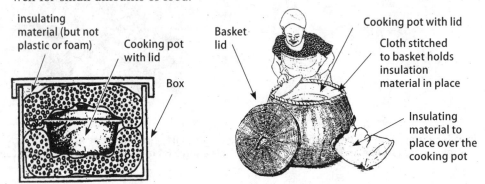

insulating material (but not plastic or foam)

Cooking pot with lid

Box

A haybox cooker made with a box.

Basket lid

Cooking pot with lid

Cloth stitched to basket holds insulation material in place

Insulating material to place over the cooking pot

A haybox cooker made with a basket.

An improved metal stove

The rocket stove is a small metal stove that can be used in temporary living situations such as refugee camps, or any place where people do not have the resources to build a full-size stove. It burns fuel cleanly with little smoke. The rocket stove can be made from inexpensive, locally available materials.
(For more detailed instructions on how to build a rocket stove, see Resources and *Where Women Have No Doctor,* page 396.)

How the rocket stove works:

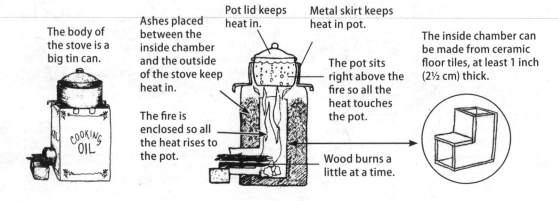

The body of the stove is a big tin can.

Ashes placed between the inside chamber and the outside of the stove keep heat in.

The fire is enclosed so all the heat rises to the pot.

Pot lid keeps heat in.

Metal skirt keeps heat in pot.

The pot sits right above the fire so all the heat touches the pot.

Wood burns a little at a time.

The inside chamber can be made from ceramic floor tiles, at least 1 inch (2½ cm) thick.

COOKING OIL

Fuels for Cooking and Heating

Wood, crop wastes, coal, dung, and charcoal are the most widely used cooking fuels. But when they burn, they can all cause pollution and breathing problems. And in many places, wood and charcoal are scarce resources.

Many people are turning to other cooking fuels such as sunlight, processed plant wastes (rice husks and other crop wastes made into pellets or briquettes), and **biogas** (a gas produced by rotting plant matter and human and animal waste).

Crop wastes (residues)

Dried crop wastes, such as rice and maize husks and coconut shells are used as fuel in many places. When these materials are used without processing, they cause smoke that can lead to health problems. Chopping the material and pressing it into blocks (fuel briquettes) can make it burn longer and cleaner.

Mixing chopped crop wastes with water, and pressing and drying them, makes a cleaner burning fuel.

Stacking wood in the house helps it dry and burn with less smoke.

Making fuel briquettes requires some machinery and an energy source, both of which can be costly. Some people do not like the taste of food cooked with briquettes. But in areas where there is a shortage of fuel, or where people want to limit the use of coal and charcoal, briquettes may be a good choice.

Firewood

Wood is one of the best sources of fuel, but it is scarce in many places. To conserve valuable forest resources and reduce smoke, use dry wood, cut into small pieces.

Biogas

Biogas, a natural gas that is mostly methane, is a valuable source of energy. By turning the organic matter in human, animal, and plant waste into energy, biogas turns waste products into a resource less harmful to the environment and community health than other fuels. (To learn more about biogas, see page 540, and Resources.)

Cooking with sunlight

You can use the sun's heat to cook in solar cookers. Solar cookers require changing your regular cooking habits, and many solar cookers cook more slowly than a fire or a stove. But by using the solar cooker when the sun shines brightly, and using the regular household stove at night or when the weather is cloudy, you can save fuel. Some cookers can pay for themselves in just a few months because they reduce expenses for charcoal, gas, or firewood. Solar cookers can also be used to disinfect water for drinking (see page 98).

Guidelines for cooking with sunlight

There are many kinds of solar cookers you can make or buy (see Resources). All of them work in basically the same way. They:

- **change sunlight to heat energy.** Dark surfaces get hot in sunlight. Food cooks best in dark, shallow, thin metal pots with tight-fitting lids to hold in heat and moisture.

- **retain heat.** A clear heat trap around the dark pot lets in sunlight and traps heat. Use a glass top, an upside-down glass bowl, or a clear, heat-resistant plastic bag marked HDPE.

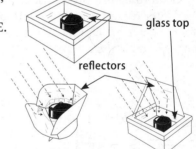
glass top

reflectors

- **capture extra sunlight.** Shiny surfaces reflect extra sunlight onto the pot to help cook food faster. Aluminum foil mounted on cardboard provides a good, low-cost shiny surface. Sheet metals and metallic paints are not reflective enough to work well.

IMPORTANT: Never look directly into the sun or at the shiny surface of a solar cooker while it is cooking. This can damage your eyes.

When building a solar cooker, do not use materials that will melt or give off fumes, such as styrofoam, polyvinyl, or some plastics.

How to use a solar cooker

Use a black pot with either a black or clear glass top. To help it cook faster, cut food into small pieces and add a small amount of water. Place a blanket or other insulation under the oven and place the oven in full sun just before and during the hottest part of the day. Be sure that the solar collector opening faces toward the sun. Turn the oven every 30 minutes or so to face directly into the sun. If the sun goes behind a cloud, surround the oven with more insulation. If the the food is hot but not cooked, finish cooking the food on a stove or fire.

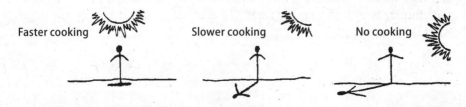
Faster cooking Slower cooking No cooking

Fire Safety

An important part of a healthy home is preventing fires.

- Keep cooking fires enclosed.
- Keep fires away from children, and keep children away from fires.
- Keep flammable and toxic materials (such as gasoline, paint, paint thinner, solvents and kerosene) out of the house and in well-sealed containers. If such materials are in the house, keep them far from any heat source.
- Make sure electrical connections are safe.
- Keep a covered water bucket, a bucket of sand or dirt, or a fire extinguisher near the stove.

IMPORTANT: DO NOT put water on a fire caused by cooking grease. This will make the fire spread! Grease fires are put out by stopping them from getting air. To put the fire out, cover it with a blanket or heavy cloth, or throw sand or dirt on the grease.

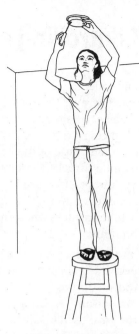

Smoke alarms warn if a fire has started, and are available at low cost in some countries.

Electricity

Even a small amount of electricity makes a big improvement in people's lives, for cooking, light, refrigeration, and so on. But unsafe electric wires can cause electric shocks and fires. To prevent harm:

- Make sure electric lines are properly installed and grounded.
- Never run electric wires under carpets.
- Avoid connecting many electric extension cords together to form one long cord. If they are not designed to be connected, they can cause fires.
- Do not install outlets or switches where they can get wet from water pipes, taps, or sinks.

Electric transmission wires

High-voltage electrical cables give off large amounts of electric radiation that can cause headaches, stress, irritation, and may lead to more serious health problems such as cancer of the blood **(leukemia).** Just as light from a candle becomes dimmer as our eyes get farther away from it, the harm from electricity grows weaker with distance. To reduce the danger:

- Build houses 50 to 70 meters away from high-voltage power lines.
- Utility companies should not build power lines or cellular telephone towers near schools or hospitals.
- Power lines should be buried when possible, rather than run above ground.

Controlling Pests

Insect pests, such as cockroaches and rodents (rats and mice), live wherever there are food crumbs, trash, and places to hide. They carry illnesses and are a common cause of allergies and asthma attacks. Unfortunately, the sprays often used to get rid of insects and rodents also cause asthma attacks and other health problems.

Many people use chemical pesticides to control insects and rodents in the home. Pesticides are poison (see Chapter 14). If they are used at all they should be used, handled, and stored with great care.

The best way to control household pests is to get rid of the conditions that attract them:

- Sweep and clean regularly to get rid of food scraps, crumbs, and materials in which rodents can nest.
- Clean and dry surfaces where food is prepared after cooking and eating.
- Store food in tightly covered containers.
- Fix leaking pipes and keep sinks dry. Cockroaches and other insects like water.
- Keep household waste in covered containers, and remove it regularly.
- Fill holes and cracks in walls, ceilings, and floors to prevent pests from entering. Fill small holes with materials such as steel wool, fine mesh screens, mortar, sheet metal, etc.

Many pests can be driven away using organic materials that are less harmful and less costly than chemical pesticides.

Pest control without chemicals

Sometimes keeping the house clean is not enough, and more active pest control is needed.

For cockroaches, make a mixture of sugar and boric acid or baking soda. Sprinkle it on surfaces where cockroaches crawl. They will eat it and die. OR, mix boric acid with water to make a thick paste. Add corn flour and make little balls. Leave them around the house, but take care that children do not eat them!

For ants, sprinkle red chili powder, dried peppermint, or crushed cinnamon where they enter.

For fly maggots, soak crushed basil leaves in water for 24 hours. Filter and spray onto maggots.

To learn how to make a simple fly trap, see page 57.

For termites, make sure wooden building materials do not come into direct contact with the soil. Do not store firewood next to the house.

To kill rodents, use traps. Poisons should be used only by people trained in their use, with great care, and with good safety equipment.

Some insect pests, such as "chinches" that cause Chagas' disease in Mexico, and Central and South America, live in cracks in the floors, walls, and roofs of houses, especially those made from mud, adobe, and thatch. Sealing wall cracks with plaster, and plastering the walls completely or even just the bottom meter of wall, will help prevent insect breeding. (To make earth plaster, see page 382.) Replacing thatch roofs with tile, metal, or cement, or lining the inside of the roof will also keep the insects out.

How to make a simple roach trap

1 Fill the bottom of a jar with beer, boiled raisins, or some other sweet substance.

2 Smear a band of petroleum jelly inside the jar below the rim to prevent roaches from crawling out.

3 To kill the captured roaches, dump them in hot, soapy water.

Toxics in the Home

Building materials, paint, furniture, cleaning products, and other things used at home may contain harmful chemicals. Asbestos and lead paint have been banned in some countries, but other toxics are still common.

Lead poisoning

Lead is a toxic metal found in common products such as paint, water pipes, some glazed ceramic pots, dishes, and floor tiles, tin cans, gasoline (petrol), and engine exhaust. A single high dose of lead can cause severe health problems. But it is more common for lead poisoning to build up slowly from repeated exposure to small amounts of lead. There may not be any obvious signs of lead poisoning, but over time it causes serious health problems.

Lead poisoning is more harmful to children than adults because it affects children's developing nerves and brains. The younger the child, the more harmful lead can be. Over time, even low levels of lead exposure can harm a child's mental development. (For more about how toxics affect children, see page 322.)

Ways people are exposed to lead

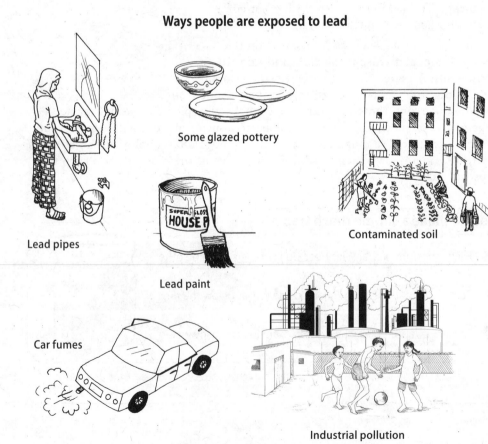

Some glazed pottery

Lead pipes

Lead paint

Contaminated soil

Car fumes

Industrial pollution

Like other toxics, lead gets into the body through eating or drinking, or being absorbed through the skin. Lead can damage the kidneys and blood, nerves, and digestive system. Very high levels of lead in the blood may cause vomiting, staggering, muscle weakness, seizures, or coma. Health problems get worse as the level of lead in the blood gets higher.

Signs

If you think someone has lead poisoning, test her blood at a health center or clinic. By the time a person has signs of lead poisoning, there is already a lot of lead in the person's blood. This is why it is important to prevent lead poisoning before it starts. Signs of lead poisoning include:

- being angry all the time.
- low appetite and low energy.
- difficulty sleeping.
- headaches.
- when young children lose skills that they had before.

- **anemia** (weak blood).
- constipation (difficulty passing stool).
- pain and cramping in the belly (this is usually the first sign of a high, toxic dose of lead poison).

Prevention

Preventing exposure to lead is the best treatment:

- Find out if local health authorities test water for lead. If your water is high in lead, find a different water source for drinking and cooking.
- Let tap water run for a minute before drinking or cooking with it.
- Do not use pottery with lead glazes for eating or cooking.
- Avoid foods from cans that may be sealed with lead.
- Throw out old painted toys if you do not know if the paint contains lead.
- Do not store liquids in lead crystal containers, as lead can leach into the liquid.
- Avoid growing food, building houses or digging wells on or in soil that may contain lead. If you find batteries, paint flakes, oil drums, and other industrial waste either on or buried in the soil, it is a sign that the soil may be contaminated.
- Wash hands before eating, especially if you have been working or if children have been playing outside.

Prevent poisoning from lead paint

When paint becomes old or is poorly applied, it breaks down and often peels or flakes off of walls, railings, and furniture. These flakes can be easily breathed in or swallowed by small children. If the paint has lead in it, this is very harmful. The best way to prevent lead poisoning from old paint is to remove it from surfaces and repaint with paint that does not contain lead.

Cleaning surfaces often with a wet cloth will help reduce exposure to dust and flakes from lead paint.

When removing old paint:

- Always wear gloves, masks, and safety glasses.

- Keep children away from work areas or from playing in areas that may be contaminated.

- To keep paint dust out of the air, wet surfaces with water as you sand and scrape.

- Clean up all paint dust carefully after each work session. Use damp mops and rags, not a broom.

- Collect paint flakes and dust in a tin can or other strong container, seal in plastic bags, and bury in a safe burial pit (see page 438).

Prevent poisoning from lead water pipes

Some signs that your water may be contaminated with lead are rust-colored water and stained dishes and laundry. Water from lead pipes should never be used to prepare infant formula, and if possible lead pipes should be replaced with pipes made of iron, copper, or plastic.

Because lead from pipes dissolves in hot water more easily than it does in cold water, it is better not to use hot water from lead pipes for cooking or drinking. Let the water run until it is as cold as possible before using it. Some water filters will filter out lead (see Resources).

IMPORTANT: Boiling water does not get rid of lead, it makes it worse!

To prevent lead poisoning from outside air pollution

To trap some dust from outside that may contain lead, put damp rags under doors and in windows. To reduce lead poisoning in the air, governments and industry must work together to reduce the use of lead in industrial products and restrict how much air pollution industries are allowed to create.

Asbestos

Asbestos is a material that was once commonly used for insulation and fire-protection in buildings, paint, and in some appliances (especially older ones) such as toasters, ovens, broilers, and refrigerators. Asbestos is made of tiny fibers that get into the air and are easily breathed into the lungs where they cut and scar the lung tissue, causing permanent damage many years after the fibers are breathed in. Because asbestos is so dangerous, many governments no longer allow it to be used in new buildings or industrial products. But it remains in many older ones.

Exposure to asbestos leads to **asbestosis** (a disease that scars and damages the lungs), and lung cancer. Early signs of these illnesses are coughing, shortness of breath, chest pain, weight loss, and weakness.

How are people exposed to asbestos?

When asbestos gets old, it begins to break down. If asbestos is used when a house is built, but is sealed off and not touched or moved afterward, it does no harm. When materials or appliances that have asbestos in them are moved or taken apart, dangerous fibers are released into the air. This causes great harm to anyone who breathes them. People who mine asbestos (see Chapter 21) also have a high risk of asbestosis.

Prevention

Asbestos can be removed from buildings and building materials, but only at great cost. Because removing asbestos can lead to exposure, it must be done by people with proper training and protective equipment.

IMPORTANT: Do not try to remove asbestos without professional help and proper protective equipment.

Treatment

Once asbestos is breathed into the lungs, it cannot be removed. It takes years for signs of asbestosis or lung cancer to appear, and these diseases cannot be reversed once they have started. Treatments can make a person have less pain, but will not cure them.

Toxics in furniture and fabrics

Some carpets, curtains, clothing, and furniture made with fabrics are made with toxic chemicals. Some of these chemicals, called **BFRs (brominated flame retardants)**, prevent fabrics from catching fire or wearing out quickly. However, they can be harmful to our health when our skin is in contact with them for long periods, when we breathe dust that carries them, or when they burn and we breathe the fumes. (To find out more about these chemicals and ways to reduce harm from them, see Chapters 16 and 20.)

Children, and also household pets, spend a lot of time on carpeting and furniture, and can develop health problems if these contain toxic chemicals.

Home cleaning products

Many cleaning products are made with toxic chemicals that make people sick. When these toxic products are breathed in, swallowed, or absorbed through the skin, they can cause health problems right away or illnesses that may appear years later, such as cancer.

The labels on most products do not say if they are toxic, or how to protect yourself. Some labels sometimes say "caution" or "keep out of the reach of children." That is a good sign you may want to change to a different product. But lack of a warning on the label does not mean you should not be careful.

Usually, if a product smells very strong and makes your eyes water, your chest hurt, or creates a bad taste in your mouth, it is

Some common home cleaning products are harmful to health.

toxic. The best way to get rid of the health risks from chemicals used in the home is to safely get rid of the chemicals (see page 410) and use safer cleaning products. Often, cleaning with soap and water is just as good, safer, and less costly than using harmful products.

Safer cleaning products

Unlike some chemical cleaners, natural cleaners work more effectively when you let them soak in before scrubbing, use tools like scrubbers and spatulas to lift grease and scum, and apply the cleaner more than once.

Soap is better than detergent because it is not made from petroleum and does not leave toxins in the water. Borax and washing soda (sodium carbonate) are safe for cleaning surfaces. White vinegar or lemon juice can be used to clean away kitchen grease and to unclog drains. These cleaners can be stored more easily because they are safe, do not go bad, and do not need to stay cold. But they still should be kept out of the reach of children.

Cleaning without toxic chemicals leaves the house smelling good, and it doesn't harm my health!

How to make safer cleaning products

▶ All-purpose cleaner

Ingredients

2 teaspoons borax, 1 teaspoon liquid soap, 1 quart of warm water, plus ¼ cup undiluted white vinegar or washing soda to clean away grease

Directions

Mix all the ingredients and store in a spray bottle or a bottle with a lid. Shake until mixed. Use for cleaning walls, stoves, cooking or food preparation areas, carpets, and upholstery.

▶ Glass cleaner

Ingredients

1 quart water plus ¼ cup white vinegar or 2 tablespoons lemon juice

Directions

Mix ingredients and store in a spray bottle.

▶ Laundry starch

Ingredients

Corn or yucca starch, 1 pint cold water

Directions

Put starch in a bottle with a small amount of water and shake until all the starch dissolves. Fill the bottle with water and shake again. Seal bottle with a sprinkle cap or lid to store. Sprinkle damp clean garment with starch, lay flat or hang to dry.

▶ Surface disinfectant

Ingredients

½ cup borax, 2 liters hot water

Directions

Dissolve borax in hot water. Wipe the surface that needs cleaning with the solution on a sponge or rag, followed by warm water. To prevent mold or mildew from forming, do not rinse off the borax solution.

Natural home cleaning protects health

When Maribel came to the United States from Nicaragua, she found a job with a cleaning company. Every night she cleaned 3 offices, washing floors and windows. Sometimes she got dizzy, nauseous, and confused after several hours of work. She went to a doctor who gave her some medicine that only made her feel worse. As long as she worked, her sick feeling did not go away.

One day her job ended. Though she was out of work, she soon began to feel better. Then she learned about another cleaning company, the Natural Home Cleaning Professionals, which used nontoxic cleaning products. The women at Natural Home Cleaning said that many cleaning products people used were harmful and made people feel ill. Suddenly Maribel knew what had made her sick!

Natural Home Cleaning is a worker-owned cooperative. The women who are the cleaners own the business, so they decide what products to clean with. The workers decided to use only healthy products like vinegar, baking soda, liquid soap, and warm water. With practice, they learned how to make these materials more effective by using cleaning tools like spatulas and scrubbing sponges. As part of their work, they also trained other women to clean using natural methods.

When Maribel started working with Natural Home Cleaning, she told her neighbors, friends, and even strangers at the market how to replace toxic cleaners with natural ones. Cleaning with natural products is sometimes harder than working with chemicals, but it is healthier. While she works, Maribel remembers how her grandmother used to clean, and she wants to hand this knowledge down to her sons and daughters. For Maribel, training people in natural home cleaning is not just part of her job. It is now an important part of her life as well.

Safe Food Preparation

Preparing food for the family is the center of home life. But food itself, and the surfaces on which it is prepared, can carry many kinds of germs. Eating food or drinks contaminated with germs can cause food poisoning, stomach pain, cramps, diarrhea, swollen belly, parasites, fever, hepatitis, typhoid, weakness and dehydration, constipation, and other problems.

Because germs are invisible, they can cause illness even in kitchens that look clean.

Reduce food-borne illness at home

Spoiled food — Throw away food that smells bad, or has mold on it, or strange textures. Do not eat food from cans that are dented or bulging because the food inside is spoiled by germs that are already inside the can.

Food handling — Wash hands before and after preparing food.

Food surfaces — Clean dishes, pots, and surfaces where food is prepared with hot water and soap before and after preparing food and eating. To remove germs from cloths used to clean kitchen surfaces, wash the cloths with soap and hang them in the sun to dry, or iron them.

Fruits and vegetables — Wash or peel all fruits and vegetables before eating.

Cooking — Heat kills germs. To make sure food is safe, make sure it is well-cooked, and eat it soon after it is prepared. Cook meats until they are no longer bloody or red in color. Cook eggs until the yolks and whites are firm. Cook fish until it flakes easily with a fork.

Meat handling and storage — Because germs from raw meat, chicken, and seafood spread easily to other foods, store meat separately or wrap it carefully so juice does not drip onto other foods. Use a separate cutting board and knife when preparing meat, and clean cooking tools well with hot water and soap before cutting other foods. It is not safe to place cooked food on a plate or surface that held raw meat.

Safe food storage — Store leftover food safely in secure containers in a cool and dry place, and dispose of trash right away. (See Chapter 12 and Chapter 15 for ways to safely store food and crops.)

Do Not Bring Work Hazards Home

People who use toxic materials in their jobs in farm labor, mining, health care, and factory work often bring toxics home on their clothes and bodies. This can harm the workers and everyone in their homes. (To avoid these risks, see Chapters 14, 20, and 21.)

Many health problems are caused by jobs done at home with toxic materials and dangerous machinery, such as assembling electronics or textiles, or taking apart batteries or computers (see page 460). Doing these kinds of work in the home is especially dangerous because companies usually do not provide people who work at home with protective equipment. Nor do they pay fair wages or other rights that all workers deserve. This dangerous work also exposes other family members, especially children, to toxic materials.

Keeping toxic work materials in a locked cupboard will help keep children safe.

When working at home with dangerous materials, take precautions.

- Know what chemicals you are using and how to handle them safely.

- Make sure there is proper ventilation (see page 352 to 354).

- Use protective equipment if you can get it (see Appendix A).

- Keep children away from work areas and materials.

- Try not to work long hours that make you tired, and make the work more dangerous.

- Talk to other people who do similar work, and organize to demand your rights to health and safety.

Building a Healthy Home

Homes designed with care contribute to communities that are safe and healthy. Putting a house in a place that takes advantage of sun and shade can help with heating, cooling, lighting, and ventilation. Choosing building materials right for your climate is also important.

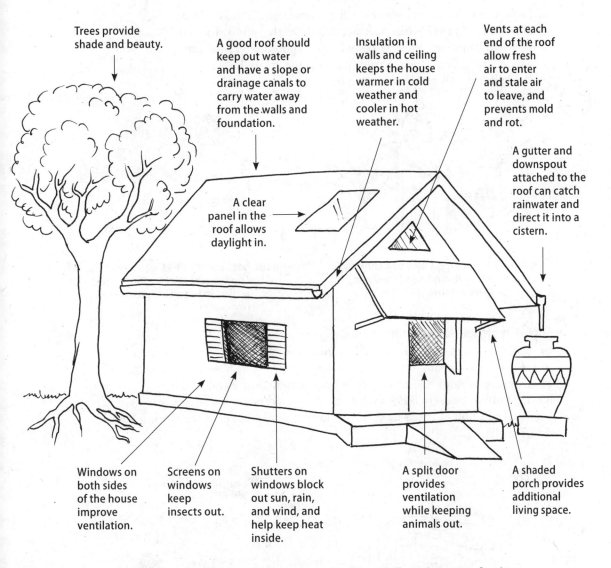

Trees provide shade and beauty.

A good roof should keep out water and have a slope or drainage canals to carry water away from the walls and foundation.

Insulation in walls and ceiling keeps the house warmer in cold weather and cooler in hot weather.

Vents at each end of the roof allow fresh air to enter and stale air to leave, and prevents mold and rot.

A gutter and downspout attached to the roof can catch rainwater and direct it into a cistern.

A clear panel in the roof allows daylight in.

Windows on both sides of the house improve ventilation.

Screens on windows keep insects out.

Shutters on windows block out sun, rain, and wind, and help keep heat inside.

A split door provides ventilation while keeping animals out.

A shaded porch provides additional living space.

A foundation and platform provide stability and protection from dampness, flooding, and pests. Platforms can be built with a ramp instead of a step, making it easier for children, the elderly, and people with disabilities to get in and out of the house.

Make best use of sunlight

When building a house or a settlement, consider where the sun will be at different times of the year in order to make best use of the sun's heat. In hot months, the sun rises high overhead at noon and provides direct heat for much of the day. In colder months, the sun is lower in the sky, gives little heat, and travels a different path through the sky.

In southern countries, houses will be more comfortable if most windows and exposed walls face north, where the sun is. In northern countries, most windows and exposed walls should face south. This general rule will help the entire house capture and retain the sun's heat.

In the cold season, the low sun shining on exposed walls and windows helps keep a house warm.

In the hot season, trees planted on the side of the house where afternoon sun shines will help keep the house cool.

Choose materials for warmth

In places that get cold, some building materials help capture and store heat in the house. Materials with more thickness store heat best. Stone, brick, and blocks made of mud and straw store heat better than wood or unfilled concrete blocks. Filling concrete blocks with earth or concrete helps them store heat better. Using any of these materials, the best wall thickness for storing heat is 4 to 5 inches.

When the sun shines on the house, heat collects in the walls and floor.

When the sun sets and the air cools, the walls and floor release heat into the room.

Protect against heat and cold

Insulation is material that protects against
heat and cold. Rather than having a single thin
wall and a roof without a ceiling, a well-insulated
house has a space between the outside and inside
walls, and a ceiling below the roof. These spaces are
filled with materials such as sawdust, wool, straw,
cork, or cardboard or paper soaked in diluted borax and
dried (to prevent termites from eating it).

**In wooden houses,
double walls with insulation
between keep heat in and cold out.**

If you cannot
build double walls,
cover inside walls with
paper, foam, cardboard, or similar
materials. This will add some insulation.

**Sealing cracks in the walls
makes a big difference in
keeping cold out and heat in.**

Thatch roofs give good insulation. So do
floors of brick and compacted earth. To keep
heat in or out of the house, seal cracks or holes
around windows and doors. Cover windows to
help keep the home cooler during the day and
to retain heat at night. Windows that open will
also allow air to flow for good ventilation.

Choosing building materials

The materials used to build a house can make the difference between an
uncomfortable shelter and a healthy, beautiful one. But when forests and
watersheds are damaged, natural building resources such as wood, thatch, and
other plant materials are lost. And when large amounts of concrete and other
"modern" materials become available, traditional materials and knowledge of
how to build with them is lost, or is no longer valued by many people. The best
building materials:

- come from the earth, and can be reused or returned to the earth
  when the life of the building is over.
- are harvested and produced locally, and fit the local climate.
- do not contain harmful chemicals or require large amounts of
  energy to produce.

Teenagers produce improved building materials

In the neighborhood of Santo Antonio on the outskirts of Brasilia, the capital of Brazil, most houses are built in a few days using clay bricks and concrete blocks that are bought outside the community. There are few skilled builders and no one has much money, so residents build their houses with the help of unskilled workers.

Because of this, materials are often poorly prepared, by adding too much water to make cement, or by leaving out reinforcing steel.

Rosa Fernandez, an architect, visited Santo Antonio and saw how the lack of skills led to poor planning and building. She set out to improve the situation. With the help of government funding, she trained a group of teenagers in Santo Antonio to make compressed earth blocks. These were made from 2 parts sand to 1 part clay, with a small amount of cement, and then were pressed in a simple hand-operated machine. After the teenagers had learned to make the blocks, Rosa taught others in the community how to build with them, and the teenagers began a business of making and selling the blocks.

Now, many new houses are built with this safer, stronger building material. The money people use to buy the blocks stays in the community and helps to build a stronger future. And with all the practice and training the teenagers received, Santo Antonio now has many skilled builders.

Traditional and modern building materials

Most traditional buildings use combinations of mud, sand, clay, stone, straw, wood, and plant materials such as bamboo, thatch, and vines for roofs and walls. These materials are strong, locally available, and cost little or nothing. But they also have some problems. Mud walls may erode in the rain, thatch roofs can become homes for insect pests, and buildings that use only these materials may not last long.

Factory-made materials such as concrete blocks and metal roofing have replaced traditional materials in many places. People often use concrete because it is easy to handle and a house can be built in stages, with additions built on as the family earns more money. For some people, building a concrete home means economic success and a modern lifestyle.

But houses built with factory-made materials may not be best for peoples' health or the environment. Often they are not well insulated for cold weather. Making concrete requires a lot of water and a lot of energy. If they are not reinforced, concrete block buildings collapse easily in earthquakes. Also, these materials are costly, and often are only available to people in large towns and cities.

When planning to build a home, consider the good and bad qualities of different materials that may be available. Just because others build their homes in a certain way does not mean it is the best way for everyone.

How to make natural earth plaster

Covering an earth, straw bale, or mud and stick house with plaster protects it from rain and prevents insects from living in the cracks in the walls. Plaster also makes a house more attractive. You will need:

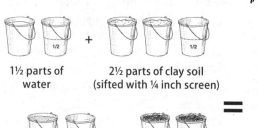

1½ parts of water

\+

2½ parts of clay soil (sifted with ¼ inch screen)

\+

1¼ parts of sand

\+

2 to 3 parts of chopped straw

=

❶ Add sand and clay soil to water. Let it sit until clay and sand absorb the water.

❷ Mix by hand until there are no lumps.

❸ Add chopped straw and mix again until there are no lumps.

If you are plastering a mud wall, wet the wall. For adobe, straw bale, or other surfaces you may need to apply a layer of clay before applying the plaster. Apply plaster to a small section of wall with your hands and then smooth it with a trowel. When it dries, test it. Does it crack easily or crumble when you press it with your thumb? Does it break away from the wall easily when you pull it, or break down easily when you sprinkle water on it? If it cracks, add more straw. If it crumbles, try adding a paste made from wheat flour and water. If it breaks down easily in water, add longer straw. Once you have plaster that does not crumble, crack, or break down easily, apply it to your walls.

To plaster a floor, add more sand to this mix. Press down the surface to make it smooth and level before you start the new floor. Then apply plaster, smooth it, and let it dry for several weeks to prevent cracking later. If possible, seal the floor with linseed oil after it dries.

Earthquake resistant building

Many lives are lost every year because people live in houses that do not withstand earthquakes. Houses of unreinforced concrete block, or unreinforced brick or earth, and houses without solid foundations, are most vulnerable to earthquakes. Houses made of traditional and flexible materials, such as mud and sticks, wood, or piled earth mixed with straw (called "cob"), or straw bales stacked and tied together and covered with plaster (see Resources) are better able to withstand damage from earthquakes.

Combining traditional materials with improved building methods, such as foundations, cross-braces, and waterproof plaster, can make houses safer, more comfortable, and affordable. To reduce the risk of earthquake damage to earthen houses:

- Build low, single story, small buildings.
- Make walls curved if possible, especially at the corners.
- If you build in a square shape, reinforce corners with wooden cross-braces. If wood is not available, you can use wire.
- Build a foundation on solid ground using lime mortar or concrete with broken brick or large stones. Anchor the foundation materials together by including sticks, bamboo, iron wire or metal rods in the mix.
- Secure the wall to the foundation using rush matting, sticks, nails, metal, or iron wire cemented into the foundation.
- Use light materials for the roof (thatch or corrugated metal).
- To make brick or block houses safer, fasten the layers of brick or blocks together. Attach crossbeams from one wall to the other, and set horizontal braces between the beams to prevent the building from moving side-to-side. Attach the roof to the crossbeams.

Light materials, like straw bales, make walls that are safer in earthquakes, and help keep inside temperatures mild.

Planning with Communities

When people plan and build their own homes and communities together, they have more control over their lives and can develop a plan that fulfills their needs, hopes, and desires. As much as possible, governments and community development agencies should involve people in planning and maintaining their own housing projects. Remember, at its best, a community is more than a group of houses. In a vibrant community, each home is connected by shared public spaces, such as gardens, water and washing facilities, markets, schools, and other places where people interact.

Building housing requires people to work together. If planners, builders, development agencies, and housing providers encourage people to work together in ways that promote education, skill-sharing, and full participation, they will not only build housing, they will build healthy communities.

Building homes and community

For many years, poor people in South Africa have lived with a housing crisis that makes their poverty and health problems worse. The government tried to solve this by building housing for poor people. But the new houses were small, dark, too close together, and built in such a way that they were either too hot or too cold. They were far from schools, health centers, and shops, and had poor access to water, poor sanitation, did not keep the bad weather out, and needed to be repaired often. They just kept poor people poor.

In response to these problems, a group called Tlholego came together to build a new kind of village. They designed homes using locally available materials like earth, bricks, and straw. Using mud bricks on stone foundations, they designed and built houses that were healthy and attractive for the lowest possible cost (a little more than US $1000 for each house).

Besides being comfortable, the houses were designed to make the best use of local conditions. They had electricity, tanks to collect rainwater, gardens that reused water from the kitchen and bath, composting toilets, water heated by the sun, and window screens to keep insects out. With windows facing the sun, shade trees all around, and solid mud brick walls, the houses were protected from extreme heat and cold. Tlholego taught people how to build the houses. This saved on construction costs, and made sure each family had a house they were proud to live in.

The houses were planned and built around common spaces, such as roads, gardens, and public buildings. This way, each family's home was a part of the larger community. Tlholego organized an education and training program for adults, and a school where children could learn reading and math, and also about farming, health, and the environment.

Tlholego is an "eco-village," a village built in harmony with the environment and the needs of its people. Rather than building cheap homes for poor people, Tlholego built a community. Through their success, Tlholego showed it was possible for people who were once forced to live in poverty to use their own resources to build homes and a community rich in dignity.

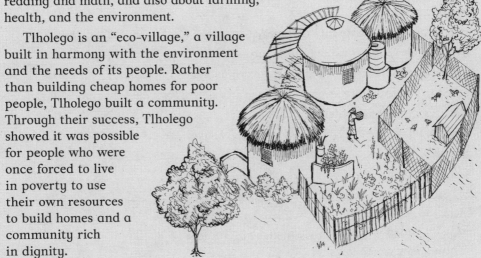

18 Solid Waste: Turning a Health Risk into a Resource

In this chapter: **page**

Solid Waste:
Turning a Health Risk into a Resource

Solid waste is called trash, garbage, rubbish, and many other names. Solid waste does not have to cause health problems. It can even become a source of income and of resources for making new products. But when solid waste is not safely collected, separated, reused, recycled, or properly disposed of, it can be ugly, smelly, and cause serious health problems.

Many of us throw things away assuming that someone else will somehow take care of our trash. Too often, it is the poorest people who are forced to live in, on, and with the waste created by the rest of society. And it is the poorest people who usually do the work of collecting, sorting, cleaning, and recycling waste into usable resources **(resource recovery).** While everyone agrees this is important and necessary work to protect our health and environment, rarely are the people who do it paid well or treated with respect.

To manage waste so it does not harm people or the environment, we need to reduce the amount of waste we create and turn what we can back into useful materials and resources. Everyone, but especially industries and governments, must take responsibility for the wastes they create and for preventing waste in the first place.

How Eseng gained better health and respect

Every day, Eseng went around the city of Bandung, Indonesia, to collect trash. Because his house was far from the neighborhoods with the best trash, he spent almost all his time walking back and forth carrying heavy bags.

Each night, Eseng sorted the trash to sell to dealers the next morning. Some dealers bought glass, others bought scrap metal, and others bought paper. But the things no dealer would buy piled up around Eseng's house. His yard became a messy, dangerous garbage dump, but there was nowhere for Eseng to get rid of the trash. Sometimes he got infections that lasted for months and made it difficult to work. Now and again he got a bad fever and chills from malaria because mosquitoes bred in the tires in his yard. And, despite his hard work, the police often bothered him when they found him sorting through trash in front of shops or in the street.

Eseng and some other waste collectors decided to organize a center to help them sell what they collected, and to provide other benefits by sharing knowledge, tools, and information. They visited a local organization that worked for the environment and workers' rights, and together they came up with the idea to develop a more complete resource recovery program.

People from the environmental organization asked the city government to support the resource recovery program, and to make the police and shop owners treat the waste collectors better. The city government agreed, and a center was set up where Eseng and the others could sort the waste they collected. Each of the waste collectors was given a cart with wheels, making it easier to collect waste and bring it to the center for sorting or take it directly to junk dealers.

The resource recovery center provided gloves and boots to protect the workers from sharp objects and contaminated trash. When the people from the environmental organization learned that Eseng had malaria, they helped him get care and medicine at a health clinic.

Eseng still works hard collecting waste, but his health has improved and his house no longer looks like a garbage dump. The police and shop owners give him and the other waste collectors the respect they deserve for helping to keep the community clean. And the city is proud of the resource recovery center and their cleaner city.

Some Waste Does Not Go Away

Waste is a problem almost everywhere because we make so much of it. And, as we see all around us, waste made from plastics, glass, and metal does not go away.

Food and other goods were once wrapped in natural or reusable materials, such as banana leaves or newspaper. Containers and other useful things were made from clay, wood, or other materials taken directly from the earth. When they were discarded, these materials did not become trash, because they quickly decayed and returned to the earth.

Now, with industry using materials such as plastics, metals, and chemicals, most manufactured products become trash when we are done using them. Everything from bottles, buckets, and bags, to cars and computers is made of materials that are strong and light, but that take a long time to decay. Packaging things in cans, bottles, and plastic bags makes them easy to transport and sell, but it also creates much more waste.

The life cycle of a plastic bag

People used to use baskets and cloth bags to carry things. Now we use plastic bags, making them one of the most commonly used plastic products. Millions of them are made and thrown away every year.

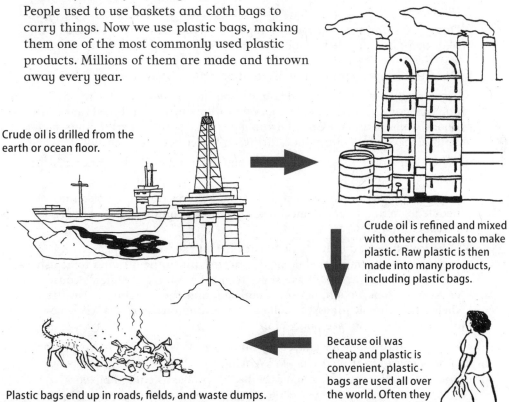

Crude oil is drilled from the earth or ocean floor.

Crude oil is refined and mixed with other chemicals to make plastic. Raw plastic is then made into many products, including plastic bags.

Because oil was cheap and plastic is convenient, plastic bags are used all over the world. Often they are used for just a few minutes before they are thrown out.

Plastic bags end up in roads, fields, and waste dumps. They clog waterways and drains, and choke animals to death. Burning them releases toxic gases. Buried, no one knows how long they take to break down completely.

Poorly Managed and Mixed Waste

When waste piles up or is scattered around our communities, it is ugly, smelly, unpleasant and bad for health. When wastes are not separated, the amount of waste and the problems it causes are bigger than they need to be. When harmful wastes, such as old batteries and health care wastes, are mixed with wastes like paper and food scraps, the mixture becomes even more difficult and dangerous to deal with.

Some waste can be reused or recycled. Some kinds of waste take a long time to decay. Other kinds never go away!

When it is not properly disposed of, waste causes health problems.

- Open piles of trash breed rats, flies, mosquitoes, cockroaches, and other insects that carry diseases such as malaria, dengue fever, hepatitis, typhus, and others.

- Dump sites and trash heaps breed germs. These can infect children who play there and people who pick through the waste for things to use or sell. Germs in trash can cause health problems such as diarrhea and cholera, scabies, tetanus, fungus, and other skin and eye infections.

- Trash clogs waterways and drainage channels causing water to back up. This can create stagnant pools that allow insects to breed and cause floods when it rains. Flooded drainage channels that carry human or animal feces also contaminate drinking water supplies and soil.

- When large piles of waste collapse they harm people who work with the waste or live nearby.

- Toxic chemicals in waste seep into water sources and soil, poisoning people for many years. Sometimes waste piles containing toxic materials explode or catch fire.

- When plastics and other toxic wastes are burned in the open or in incinerators, harmful chemicals are released into the air, and toxic ash pollutes soil and water. In the short term, these toxic chemicals cause chest infections, cough, nausea, vomiting, and eye infections. Over time, they cause **chronic** illnesses such as cancer and birth defects. (For more about incineration, see page 423.)

To treat the health problems caused by waste, see *Where There Is No Doctor* or another general health care book. Wearing gloves, face masks, and boots or closed shoes can prevent many of the health problems caused by working with solid waste. (For protection while working with waste, see page 406 and Appendix A.)

Community Clean-up and Resource Recovery

Protecting our communities from harmful waste and turning waste into a resource improves community health, the environment, and also saves money. For example, a group of waste collectors in Argentina found that if all the waste paper in the city of Buenos Aires was collected and recycled, it would save $10 million US dollars a year. If this money was used to pay all of the waste collectors in the city, each person would earn over US $150 per month.

Every person and every community can take responsibility for reducing and safely disposing of waste. But, while communities can do a lot on their own, waste is a political problem that can only be solved when government, industry, and communities work together, with improving people's health as the goal. Governments must act to reduce the burden of waste on people and the environment by requiring industry to manufacture products with as little waste as possible (see page 458). Government support of programs to encourage people to reuse, recycle, and safely dispose of waste saves money, creates jobs, and helps solve community problems (see pages 395, 401, 408, and 416).

A Community Trash Walk

A community trash walk provides an opportunity for people to look at and discuss trash problems. People can voice their concerns about trash and their hopes for a cleaner and healthier community. During and after the walk, the group can discuss what steps are necessary to clean up the community and to plan for resource recovery.

Organize a trash walk

 Invite people to participate in a trash walk

To make a trash walk most effective, involve not only people from the neighborhood, but also people who work with waste and those who have the power to change how waste is collected, transported, and managed. Include:

- workers in small industries.
- second-hand dealers and waste transporters.
- buyers who collect or purchase waste directly from households or businesses.
- waste collectors who recover materials from the streets or dumping sites.
- government officials who can support a community clean-up.

continues on next page...

Organize a trash walk (continued)

❷ Hold a meeting before the trash walk

It is helpful to have a meeting to talk about the reasons for the walk, what to look for, and what each person hopes to achieve by joining the trash walk. It is helpful to understand what motivates each of them. Some people may earn their livelihood collecting resources that others throw away. Others may want to improve the health and beauty of the community.

Thirty years ago we grew all of our food. Now we buy most of our food at the store.

Everything comes wrapped in plastic that we throw in the street.

Now there is garbage everywhere!

❸ Plan your walk

Decide where to walk and together make a list of things to look for, such as:

- trash clogging drainage ditches, other waterways, and streets.
- human feces and animal waste along streets and waterways.
- toxic wastes.
- animals eating from trash piles.

Ask older members of the community to describe how it was 20 or 30 years ago. Was there more or less or different kinds of trash? What did people do with their trash then? Think about this during the walk.

Organize a trash walk (continued)

4 Walk!

Break into teams to walk around different parts of the community. Because different groups will notice different problems, you might form teams of only men or only women, or have a youth group walk separately from adults. Or you may have all mixed teams.

Notice where trash collects and the most common ways trash is disposed of. Are there public trash bins? Do people burn trash or dump it in the open? Bring it to a landfill or incinerator? Are some things collected and reused or recycled, such as glass bottles or newspapers? What about waste from businesses?

Have someone in each team keep a list or make a drawing of the problems you find on the walk, including what kinds of waste you see.

5 Look at waste in people's homes. How much and what kinds are there?

As a part of the walk, go to some volunteers' homes to see what kinds of waste and resources are there. Take a full trash can and dump its contents on the ground. Separate the waste into 5 piles:

- food scraps and other wet, organic waste
- plastics
- paper
- metal
- other wastes

Which pile is biggest and which is smallest? What is done with each of these kinds of waste, and what could be done rather than throwing them in the trash? Take some of the waste from several households to the group discussion that follows.

Remember to put the rest back in the trash cans!

6 Come together to discuss what people saw

Later the same day (or the next day), bring all the teams back together to discuss what was learned.

Ask everyone to share what they saw during the walk. Have each person show a piece of household waste and say if she noticed the same kind of waste elsewhere in the community creating a problem or being reused or recycled. Did people see any possible or current health problems due to poor waste disposal? What were the better ideas about waste disposal that some families were using?

Organize a trash walk (continued)

 List the causes and effects of the problems

TRASH WALK

<u>Causes</u>	<u>Problems</u>	<u>Health effects</u>
• no composting	• bad smells & smoke	• coughing
• burning trash	• trash piles	• children sicker with asthma
• lots of bottles and cans		• polluted water

> *Since the new supermarket opened, everything they sell comes in plastic. This should go under the 'causes' list.*

A facilitator can write the problems people raised on a chalkboard or large paper. Ask everyone to think about the causes of the community's waste problems and write these in a column next to the problems list. Then ask how each problem affects the health of the community. Write or draw a different health effect related to each problem in another column.

8 **Plan next steps**

Ask the group to review the problems and think about possible actions they can take to resolve them. Next steps can start with ways to reduce the health effects of a problem, or try to get rid of a problem completely. Ask questions such as:

- How can each household reduce the amount of trash it produces?
- How can we promote more composting and separating wastes?
- Can a community group or business be formed to collect and reuse waste?
- Is there land to build a compost site or resource recovery center?
- Where is the nearest recycling plant?
- How can local government, community leaders, factories, and businesses each take responsibility to solve problems caused by waste?

A community trades trash for cash

The shantytowns of Curitiba, Brazil, had many open waste pits. They were breeding grounds for disease-carrying rodents. To deal with this problem, the Curitiba city council launched a program called "Don't Throw Away Your Garbage—We Buy It." The city council figured out how much it would cost to clean up the open dumps. Then, instead of hiring an outside company to do the job, they figured out what the cost would be for each bag of trash, and offered this amount to the residents.

Besides earning money for the trash they collected, every person was given a free public transit ticket for each bag they delivered to a municipal collection truck. Because these neighborhoods are located far from the city center, these tickets were highly prized. The city also donated money for each bag collected to develop community gardens and other projects. Areas that were once piled high with garbage were transformed into urban gardens or parks with trees. Community health improved.

Recent immigrants, people with disabilities, or others who needed work were given safe jobs sorting waste at a resource recovery center. Food scraps and garden waste were composted for use in city parks and local farms and gardens. Plastic and metal were sold to local industries. Plastic foam was shredded and used to fill blankets.

A few years after the program began, the city made the project even better. They began buying food directly from farmers close to the city at a fair price, and offered people a bag of fresh food in exchange for a bag of garbage. This helped the farmers sell their produce, improved the nutrition of the families in the shantytowns, and cleaned up the city.

A Community Solid Waste Program

Once a community has a shared understanding of the problems caused by waste, it can take steps to solve these problems, starting with projects that best meet the community's needs and abilities.

A complete community solid waste program would include all of these steps (find more about each step on the next few pages):

- **Reduce** the amount of waste created, especially toxic products and products that cannot be recycled.

- **Separate wastes** where they are made to make them easier and safer to handle.

- **Compost** food scraps and other organic wastes.

- **Reuse** materials whenever possible.

- **Recycle** materials and organize for government and industry to develop community recycling programs.

- **Collect, transport, and store** wastes safely. Respect and pay fair wages to the people who do this work.

- **Safely dispose** of all wastes that cannot be reused or recycled.

> Not all communities will be able to take all of these steps, especially at the beginning.

> Consider people's needs and abilities, and begin with what you can achieve together in the short term.

Reducing waste

Waste that ends up in our streets, homes, and fields begins with the industrial manufacturing of products that cannot be reused or recycled. One goal of a community waste program is to reduce waste over the long term by helping people use less of the materials that become waste in the first place. Some ways to reduce waste are:

- not buying products wrapped in a lot of packaging materials.

- choosing glass and cardboard over plastic and metal.

- using your own shopping bag or basket, and refusing plastic bags at the store.

- buying food in larger quantities to reduce the amount of packaging you bring home.

Communities can work with shop owners and local governments to prevent materials that cause disposal or health problems from entering the community in the first place. Community organizing can pressure governments to make laws that force businesses to take responsibility for the wastes they create.

Banning plastic bags

Outside the village of Emmonak in Alaska, plastic shopping bags often escaped from the town landfill and were carried by the wind. In the nearby town of Galena, they got stuck in trees or drifted into the nearby Yukon River. By Kotlik, where the river runs into the sea, plastic bags were found wrapped around dead seals and salmon.

Since the 3 villages banned plastic bags in 1998, this no longer happens. Following these villages, 30 other communities around the state of Alaska banned plastic bags, and the ban is growing. In towns and villages, people are encouraged to use paper bags or to carry cloth bags that can be used over and over, for years.

As part of the campaign against plastic waste in Alaska, the State Department of Environmental Conservation and the Yukon River Inter-tribal Watershed Council began a program to teach people how to reuse the plastic bags by making them into other things. Now people cut the bags in strips and weave them into backpacks, handbags, doormats, baskets, and other useful items. They even sell them, making money from things that once clogged the sewers and littered the roads.

Separate wastes at the source

Keeping food wastes from mixing with paper wastes or glass, and so on, makes it easier to reuse, recycle, and get rid of materials, and helps prevent the health problems caused by mixed waste (see page 390). Separating waste is the first step in better waste management, though it only solves the problem if there is a good way to deal with waste after it has been separated. Waste separation is part of a system that includes reuse, composting, regular collection, recycling, and safe disposal.

Ways to separate wastes

The biggest part of the waste produced in both urban and rural areas is **organic** or **wet waste** (food scraps and garden wastes such as dead plants and leaves). Organic waste is broken down by sunlight and water, or eaten by living things (worms, insects, and bacteria), and turned into compost (see page 400).

There is usually a lot of paper, glass, metals, and plastics in waste. A large part of this waste is discarded packaging. Household waste may also include toxic materials such as paint, batteries, plastic diapers (nappies), motor oil, and old pesticides and cleaning product containers.

Separation into 2 types of waste

Wet waste becomes compost

Wet waste

Dry waste

Dry wastes are sorted and reused, recycled, or sent to a landfill

Separation into 3 or more types of waste

RECYCLE PAPER

Wet waste becomes compost

Dry, reusable, and recyclable materials are sorted and reused, recycled, or sent to a landfill.

Toxic waste needs special handling and disposal (see page 410)

Who is responsible for separating waste?

Waste can be separated by the households and businesses that produce it, or by the people who collect it. Whatever system your community uses to separate and collect waste for reuse, recycling, or disposal, it is important for those who do the work to be respected and paid for their efforts.

Collectors may earn money by separating out and selling the more valuable items and by bringing the rest of the separated waste to a recycling center. Some collectors pay householders a small amount for separated waste, or charge a small fee for collecting waste that is not separated.

If waste is separated at home, dry material may be kept in containers indoors until they are collected. Containers for wet waste can be kept outside and made into garden compost at home, or can be collected by a neighborhood compost project (see pages 400 to 403).

Making compost: Changing organic waste to fertilizer

Because organic matter is usually the largest part of most waste, separating and composting food scraps helps reduce waste a great deal. Adding compost to the soil is a way of adding crop **nutrients** back to the earth.

The best way to make compost depends on the amount of space available. Small amounts of compost can be made in containers in each household or business. Larger composting sites can be set up in towns and cities and on farms where there is space for larger waste piles. (To use compost, see page 287.)

Good, finished compost smells good and feels soft like dark, rich forest soil.

How to compost with earthworms

Earthworms are one of nature's best composters. A small box with healthy earthworms will eat household food wastes and turn the waste into rich soil for your garden. A worm box provides a way to compost food scraps when you have no land for a compost pile.

❶ Make holes in the bottom of a wooden or plastic box to let air in, and water and soil out.

❷ Place a second box or tray under the box with holes. This will collect the rich soil the worms make.

❸ Fill the top box with shredded paper, straw, and food scraps. Get a good shovelful of worms from a gardening center or a farmer, and put them in this box.

❹ Add food scraps often and keep the box damp but not too wet. Cover the top to protect the worms from sunlight.

As the worms eat what you put in the box, they make rich soil, and the worm colony grows. Some worms may drop down into the lower box or tray. Just put them back into the top, or add them to your garden with the new soil.

A worm box can be very simple...

...or more complicated.

Community composting and recycling

Porto Novo, the capital of Benin, once had heaps of trash as tall as 4-story buildings rotting in the streets. As you can imagine, this caused many health problems. And the terrible smell made it an unpleasant place to live. Some people decided to start a composting center to change the waste into useful fertilizer.

With funding from a social service organization, they found a large site to set up a recycling and compost plant. A French organization provided the Porto Novo group with a tractor and 2 trailers. They parked the trailers near the train station and a football stadium, and encouraged people to put their trash in them. Now, every evening the tractor tows the trailers full of waste to the recycling center where young people sort the trash.

Organic waste is thrown in pits and covered with palm leaves to make compost. The compost "cooks" check the humidity, air flow, and heat regularly to make sure the waste decays quickly. After 2 months, the compost is ready for use.

Some young people from the project began to use the compost for market gardening. With funds from the United Nations Development Programme, the center bought seeds and land to grow crops. In this region of Benin, the soil has never been rich and has become poorer due to overuse. But with their compost to enrich the soil, the young gardeners are able to grow nutritious, fresh vegetables. Villagers also buy the compost to fertilize their own gardens.

The money the compost center earns from selling vegetables and compost is used to buy more equipment and hire more unemployed youth to work as waste sorters and market gardeners. In this way, the project supports itself and continues to grow.

How to make slow compost

This way of making compost requires little space and little work, and produces compost in about 6 months.

1 Dig a hole in the ground 60 cm by 60 cm wide and 1 meter deep.

2 Put a mix of dry and wet organic waste in the hole.

3 Cover every 20 cm depth of organic material with 3 cm soil and add water to keep it damp (just moist, not soaked).

4 Cover the hole to keep the rain out. After a week, the compost should start to break down. The pile of waste will heat up and shrink as it breaks down.

How to make fast compost

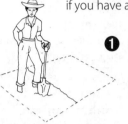

This is a way to produce a lot of compost in 1 to 4 months, if you have a large open space.

1 Choose a flat area 1½ meters wide by 4 meters long. Mark the area with stakes. Loosen the soil to a depth of 30 cm. This will help the compost pile drain, and help worms enter the pile and break down wastes. If the soil is very dry, water it.

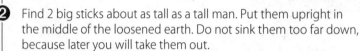

2 Find 2 big sticks about as tall as a tall man. Put them upright in the middle of the loosened earth. Do not sink them too far down, because later you will take them out.

3 Mark lines on the posts at 20 cm from the ground, then 5 cm above that, then 2 cm above that. Repeat these marks 7 or 8 times until the whole post is marked with measuring lines.

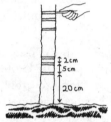

4 Make a pile of food and plant wastes (a mix of dry and wet materials is best) up to the 20 cm mark on the sticks. The pile should cover the entire area of loosened earth and be of an even height. If it is very dry add water until it is moist, but not soaked.

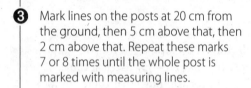

5 Put a layer of animal manure up to the next line (5 cm). Fresh manure is best because it is hot and will help the compost break down quickly. On top of the manure, add a layer of soil up to the next mark (2 cm). Continue building up layers in this order as organic material becomes available. Add a little water to each layer so the entire pile will be damp. Over time you can build the pile up to a height of 2 meters or so. Then cover the entire pile with a layer of soil, and wet it more.

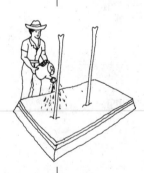

6 After 2 days, remove the sticks. This will leave wide holes for air to enter the pile and help it break down. After 3 weeks, turn and mix the pile with a shovel. Do this again every week or so. The more you turn it, the faster it will break down. The pile will heat up and shrink as it breaks down. After 1 to 4 months, the pile should turn into sweet smelling, dark, fertile soil.

To know if the compost is working

No matter which method you use, there are ways to know if your waste is becoming good compost and not just a big, stinky mess.

- To break down, compost needs both wet waste like food scraps and dry waste like straw, brown leaves, husks, or shredded paper. If the pile remains a pile of rotting food rather than heating up and turning to soil, it may need more dry, brown plant matter.

- If the pile smells bad or does not shrink, it needs more air. Turn the pile with a shovel or open holes by poking sticks into it.

- If the pile does not heat up, it could be from too much or too little water. Turn the pile with a shovel. If it is very dry, add more water. If it is very wet, add less water. Covering the pile with a black plastic sheet will also help it stay warm.

- If the compost has ants, add water.

- If it attracts flies, it needs to be covered better with soil.

A working compost pile heats up as the waste breaks down.

After a while the compost should turn into sweet smelling, rich black soil. (To learn how to use compost on plants, see page 287.)

What cannot go into the compost?

People have different ideas about what makes good compost and what does not. For example, some people keep meat scraps or paper out. Many people agree that manure from horses and cattle is good for compost, but feces from dogs and cats are not.

Large branches or very thick leaves will break down too slowly. If paper or cardboard are added, it is best if they are shredded and kept damp so they break down more easily. Meat, bones, and greasy kitchen waste attract pests and break down very slowly.

Some things are never good for compost. Plastic, metal, glass, and anything else that is not directly from the earth will not break down. Plants that poison people or other plants, like castor bean and eucalyptus, will not make good fertilizer.

Do not put these things in the compost.

Reuse what you can

One person's trash is often useful to someone else. All over the world, people save money and protect the environment by inventing methods to safely reuse discarded materials.

From **tires,** make sandals, buckets, and planters.

From **tin cans,** make lamps, planters, and candle holders.

From **waxed food containers,** make shopping bags.

From **coconut shells,** make cups, forks, and spoons.

From **banana tree leaves,** make plates and bowls.

Many new products are easily made by reusing discarded wastes.

From **scrap metal,** make stoves, lamps, and art.

Paper can be shredded and compacted for home insulation or to make briquettes for burning.

Sawdust can be used in composting, in dry toilets, or pressed into briquettes with manure and other dry organic matter and burned as fuel.

Recycling turns waste into a resource

Recycling takes products that are no longer useful and turns them into source materials to make new, useful products. Recycling some materials (such as metals and rubber) must be done in factories. Other materials, such as paper and glass, require less equipment and space and can be recycled in small workshops or people's homes.

Recycling is an important way to reduce waste. But recycling requires support from government and industry, as well as a commitment by communities and people. If there is no market for recycled products, or if they are not recycled safely, recycling is no solution at all.

Recycling just one 6-pack of aluminum cans saves enough energy to power a TV for 18 hours!

Recycling reduces waste by changing it into new products, and also saves energy used in manufacturing. For example, it takes ²/₃ less energy to recycle paper than to make new paper, or to make steel from scrap metal rather than raw ore. Making aluminum from scrap takes a tiny amount of the energy it takes to make aluminum from raw bauxite ore.

Recycling:

- reduces the amount of solid waste polluting our environment.
- reduces the amount of solid waste in need of disposal, saving space and money.
- reduces resource use by using the resources more than once.
- helps the local and national economy because fewer raw materials need to be imported.
- provides jobs.

Recycling preserves resources you and I need to live!

What materials can be recycled?

The materials that can be recycled depend on the local recycling industry.

Glass is made from sand, soda ash, and lime. When disposed of, it wears down but does not break down into its source materials again. To recycle glass, it is sorted by color, melted into a liquid, and shaped into new containers. Some glass is also recycled into materials used in roads or buildings.

Aluminum is made from a metal ore called bauxite that is mined from the earth. It does not break down to its original ore, but gets worn down like glass. Aluminum is recycled by melting and reshaping it into new cans and other things.

Tin coated steel cans, such as soup and fruit cans, are recycled by separating the tin from the steel. The steel and tin are then washed and sold to make more cans or other products.

Rubber is made from natural tree resin and petroleum. Rubber is sometimes recycled by melting or chipping it and remolding it into new things.

Paper is made from wood, cotton, and other plants with strong fibers. Paper is one of the few materials that can be recycled into itself again. Commercial paper is often recycled in industrial plants. Paper can also be recycled by hand to produce beautiful paper products for the home and for sale.

Products that contain toxic materials, such as computers, batteries, electronics, paints, solvents and pesticides, and the containers that store them, need careful handling so recycling workers are not exposed to toxic chemicals (see pages 410 to 411, and 459 to 462). Some of these products cannot be recycled at all, which is why it is better to produce fewer of them in the first place.

The problem with recycling plastics

When plastic is recycled, its quality decreases. A plastic bottle is not recycled to become another plastic bottle, but is made into something of lesser quality. Because of this, plastic can be recycled only a few times before it can no longer be used.

Recycling some plastics releases toxic gas that is harmful to workers and communities (see pages 409 to 423). And a lot of plastic intended for recycling ends up being dumped in landfills. This is why it is best to use as little plastic as possible.

Waste collection, transport, and storage

If your community does not have a reliable waste collection service, you can organize one with the help of local government and businesses. As you make plans, keep in mind what will be collected and whether it will be taken for resale to larger recycling businesses or to a community recycling program.

The less distance your waste travels the better. But many communities are not able to recycle waste locally, so other solutions must be found.

Ways to prepare waste

The way waste is prepared for collection, transport, and storage depends on how much space you have, who will do the work, who will buy the discards, and what they will be used for. To prevent bad smells and spreading germs, materials should be cleaned, dried, and flattened or stacked to take up as little space as possible and to reduce the possibility of accidents.

Computers, radios, and televisions contain many sellable and recyclable parts, but much of what they contain is toxic. These materials are best taken apart after receiving training for each product, and using protective safety gear (see Appendix A) and good ventilation. All toxic materials' containers need special handling (see pages 410 to 411).

Health and safety for waste collectors

Waste collectors are at risk for all the health problems that come with waste. To prevent harm, waste collectors need training in how to prevent health problems and where to go for treatment if problems do arise.

If waste collectors organize into cooperatives or small businesses, it may be easier to pool resources, provide training, and gain government or other community support to purchase safety equipment and make the work as safe as possible.

Eyewear

Gloves

Waste cart

Face masks

Closed shoes

Starting a community resource recovery center

A resource recovery center is a place where reusable and recyclable materials are collected for sale or reuse.
It can also be a place to start a community composting project and market garden, make new products from old materials, and exchange goods such as clothing, curtains, appliances, furniture, shoes, glass bottles, pots, utensils, building materials, and so forth.

Some of this trash is useful... but I don't know who could use it!

People working together make a community a beautiful place to live.

Resource recovery centers

Several communities in the Philippines have resource recovery centers set up by local governments and an organization called Mother Earth Foundation. These resource recovery centers have inspired community solid waste programs throughout the country, and have helped change the entire system of waste management.

Households are encouraged to separate their wastes and to clean the materials that can be reused and recycled. Some communities passed a law to reduce bad smells by preventing people from piling wastes outside.

People keep organic wastes in closed containers in the house or carry them to compost bins set up throughout the community. Every day, workers from the resource recovery center travel through the communities on 3-wheeled carts to collect organic wastes, recyclables, and wastes to be discarded. Sometimes people are paid for their recyclables. Everything is brought to the resource recovery center, which has 2 main parts:

- an ecology garden, where organic matter is composted and used to grow vegetables for sale to the community.

- an eco-shed or warehouse, where clean recyclables are stored before being sold to junk shops, recycling companies, or factories.

Some centers also provide work areas where people make new products out of old materials. Juice cartons are flattened and sewn together to make carrying bags. Glass bottles are shaped into drinking glasses.
Old newspapers are shredded and woven together to make baskets and bags that are covered with clear glue or resin to make them stiff and durable. These things are sold to provide income for the people who made them and to pay for the costs of running the resource recovery centers.

The centers have dramatically reduced the amount of trash in their communities. Rather than living with smelly piles of waste, people now earn extra income from reused and recycled materials, and produce more vegetables using composted food waste.

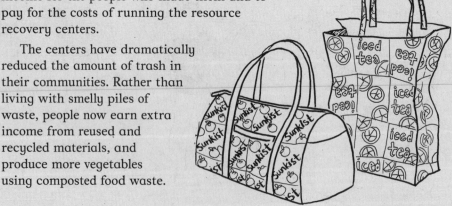

Getting Rid of Trash Safely

Whatever cannot be reused, recycled, or composted should be gotten rid of safely. Some people say burning trash is best. Others prefer to bury it, to avoid the smoke produced by burning trash. The fact is, both of these ways of disposing of trash have problems.

In places where paper and cardboard cannot be reused, recycled, or composted, they can be shredded and burned in fires for cooking and heating. But burning even small amounts of plastic or rubber releases toxic chemicals such as dioxins, furans, and PCBs that cause many health problems (see Chapter 16 and page 423).

Waste that cannot be handled in any other way can be buried in small pits or in a sanitary landfill (see page 412.) For small pit burial, simply dig a pit in an area away from water sources, put waste in the pit, and cover with soil.

When trash that contains harmful chemicals is buried, these chemicals can leak into the ground and contaminate drinking water. If there is no safe way to get rid of toxic trash (for example, by returning it to its manufacturer or treating it so it is no longer toxic), it is best to put it in a safely-lined sanitary landfill.

Toxic wastes

Toxic wastes are wastes containing chemicals that are very harmful to our health and the environment. (See Chapter 16 for how toxics harm us.)

The best way to prevent harm from toxic waste is to stop it from being produced. Governments should ban toxic products and production processes. Communities can promote the use of alternatives to toxic household products and labor unions can promote alternatives in industry. Making collection or drop off centers for toxics convenient can keep them from polluting land and community water systems.

(For safer substitutes to commonly used household toxics, see page 373. To learn more about toxics, see Chapters 14, 16, and 20.)

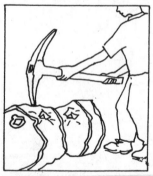

Destroy toxic materials containers so they cannot be used to store other things, especially food or water.

Safe handling and disposal of toxic wastes

Because safe disposal of toxic wastes can be complicated and costly, it is best if governments enforce guidelines for the use, storage, and disposal of toxics. This should include education and training of community members to safely handle and get rid of toxic wastes. Here are some practical guidelines for handling toxic wastes:

- Store toxic products away from food and water, and away from where children can reach them.

- Keep toxic products in their original containers, and never remove the labels. This helps prevent the containers from being reused for water or food storage.

- Keep toxic wastes separate from other household wastes.

- Do not burn toxic wastes! This spreads the chemicals through ash and smoke, and sometimes it creates even more dangerous chemicals.

- Do not put toxic materials down latrines, toilets, drains, drainage channels, in waterways, or onto the ground.

Check with local health authorities and resource recovery centers to learn the best ways to get rid of toxic wastes in your area.

Disposing of common toxics

These common household products create harmful waste if they are not handled with care and gotten rid of safely.

Paint and paint containers. Store closed paint cans in a cool place. Once all the paint is used, flatten paint containers, wrap them in newspaper, put them in plastic bags, and bury them in a sanitary landfill. Latex paint is less toxic than other paints, but needs the same disposal methods as other paint.

Solvents (degreasers, turpentine, paint removers). Store solvents in closed containers in a cool place, so they will not cause a fire. Once all the solvent is used, punch holes in the containers so they cannot be reused. Flatten the containers, wrap them in newspaper, put them in plastic bags, and put them in sanitary landfills or sealed containers.

Used motor oil. Never pour oil onto the ground or into waterways. Store it in closed containers. Used oil can sometimes be recycled by auto servicing stations. Used motor oil can also be used to coat wooden posts for building, to prevent them from rotting in the ground, and can also be burned as heating oil in some heaters.

Batteries. In some places, batteries can be recycled. But recycling batteries by hand is dangerous and should not be done without proper training and protective equipment.

Pesticides. Make holes in or destroy pesticide containers so they cannot be reused. Bury them in a sanitary landfill. To learn how to use fewer pesticides in farming or in the home, see Chapter 15 and page 367.

These common products are harmful, and make harmful waste, if not handled with care.

Waste from health care activities such as bloody bandages, dirty needles and other sharp tools, discarded medicines, and so on. To learn how to reduce, store, and best handle health care waste, see Chapter 19.

Sanitary Landfills

A sanitary landfill is a pit with a protected bottom where trash is buried in layers, compacted (pressed down to make it more solid), and covered. A sanitary landfill can reduce harm from waste that has collected, and is safer than an open dumping site. But even the best sanitary landfill will fill up and, after many years, probably start to leak. To solve our waste problems, we still need to prevent waste in the first place.

Open dumps can be turned into sanitary landfills. Or a community can build a new sanitary landfill and clean up the old site by transporting trash to the new one. A sanitary landfill protects community health when:

- it is built away from where people live.
- it is covered to prevent insects and other disease-carrying animals from breeding.
- it has a lining of hard-packed clay soil or plastic to prevent chemicals and germs from contaminating groundwater.

Because building and maintaining a sanitary landfill is a lot of work, it usually needs to be done in partnership with the community, local government, and other organizations, such as churches or businesses.

A landfill protects community health only if it is well managed. Good management includes training and support for landfill workers, and working together with resource recovery centers, toxic waste collectors, and local government.

Selecting a site

The first step in planning a landfill is choosing a site. In most places, the government requires a site assessment (a close look at the conditions of the site) before construction. This means a study of the type of soil and rocks, the kinds of plants that grow there, and the distance from water sources and homes. For health and safety, a landfill site should be at least:

- 150 meters from coastal waters.
- 250 meters from fresh water, such as streams, ponds or swamps.
- 250 meters from protected forests.
- 500 meters from homes, and from wells or other drinking water.
- 500 meters from earthquake fault lines.

The bottom of the pit must be at least 2 meters above the highest groundwater level.

Making the landfill

The size of the landfill pit depends on the amount of trash that will go into it. All pits should be narrower at the bottom than the top to prevent them from collapsing. This shape also helps compact the trash because there is more weight on top than on the bottom.

A sign posted by the landfill gate with the hours it is open helps landfill workers better control what is dumped, and when, and how.

A well-built and well-equipped landfill

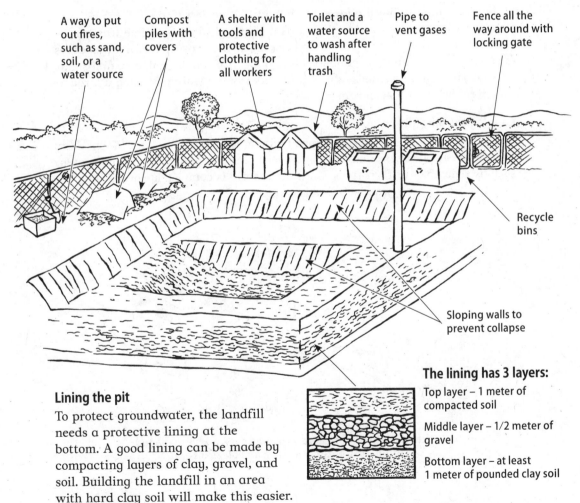

A way to put out fires, such as sand, soil, or a water source

Compost piles with covers

A shelter with tools and protective clothing for all workers

Toilet and a water source to wash after handling trash

Pipe to vent gases

Fence all the way around with locking gate

Recycle bins

Sloping walls to prevent collapse

Lining the pit

To protect groundwater, the landfill needs a protective lining at the bottom. A good lining can be made by compacting layers of clay, gravel, and soil. Building the landfill in an area with hard clay soil will make this easier.

The lining has 3 layers:

Top layer – 1 meter of compacted soil

Middle layer – 1/2 meter of gravel

Bottom layer – at least 1 meter of pounded clay soil

If there are resources to provide a better protective lining, layers of thick plastic sheeting and thick fabric will give more protection, and a system of pipes and pumps can be built to remove liquids.

Filling the landfill

The way you fill a landfill depends on the amount of trash, how much time people have to do the work, and the local climate.

In places with high rainfall and little trash, such as towns that practice zero waste (see page 416), each week or month you can dig a new hole lined with clay and gravel (in thinner layers than a larger landfill would need). Someone takes responsibility for bringing trash, filling the hole, compacting the trash, and covering it with soil. Burying trash little by little prevents water from collecting in the pits.

For a community with a large trash load, it is easiest to dig a large pit. Landfill workers add waste to the pit as it is brought in. Each time waste is added it is pressed down to make an even layer, then covered with large leaves (such as palm, banana, or palmetto) and a layer of soil, or soil, ash, and sand. This will prevent bad smells and stop insects from breeding. Making a large roof over the pit will keep rain out.

Capping the landfill

When the pit is full it should be capped with a layer of soil at least 90 cm deep. Wildflowers or grasses can be planted over it, but not plants that will be eaten, such as vegetables or fruit trees. Until the landfill is completely covered by plant life, it is best to keep grazing animals away.

After it has been completely covered over, a well-managed landfill may become a green and pleasant area.

Difficulties with sanitary landfills

A pit where trash is dumped and then covered with soil can be maintained safely with few problems. But it can develop problems if liquid waste and gas (methane) collect in the pit.

Liquid waste (leachate)

If rainwater soaks into the landfill, it creates bad-smelling liquid waste that can carry poisons from trash into the groundwater. This is why it is important to line the landfill well and not to make it near a river, stream, or lake.

The best way to prevent leachate is to keep the landfill covered with a roof, or a canvas or plastic cover, until it is capped.

Dangerous gas

In landfills containing mixed waste, bacteria can grow and create methane gas. Methane can explode or catch fire if not managed carefully, and it adds to global warming (see page 33). In many places, methane from landfills is captured and used to generate electricity. If you have no resources to do this, the best thing to do with methane is to provide vents for it to escape.

A simple vent consists of a chimney made of small rocks held in a circular or square shape by a wire mesh, or you can use 200-liter drums with the bottoms removed. The height of the vent is raised as the height of the landfill increases. The number of vents needed depends on the size of the pit and the type of trash in the landfill.

Gas vents in a landfill

A landfill that has been capped and has grass or plants growing on it may still release methane. If there are patches of dead grass, particularly if they are shaped like a circle, this is a sign that methane is escaping from the landfill. Place signs and warn people to stay at least 10 meters away from the area, because an explosion could be caused accidentally. Trained professionals should examine the landfill to decide how best to prevent an explosion.

Getting to Zero Waste

Communities around the world are finding ways to reduce their waste to almost nothing, with the goal of producing zero waste. Zero waste means reducing waste and recycling the rest back into nature or the marketplace in ways that protect health and the environment.

To reach the goal of zero waste, industries must take responsibility to produce less or none of products used only once, such as plastics. Cities and towns can develop solid waste programs that compost, recycle and reduce waste. To be successful, planning must include the people most affected by waste. (To learn more about zero waste, see Resources.)

A town struggles with solid waste and wins

Kovalam, a beautiful beach town in southern India, is a popular place for tourists. But tourism in Kovalam nearly ended because of too much trash.

During 30 years of tourism, Kovalam never had a safe way to get rid of waste. No trash bins, no recycling program, little use of compost, and thousands of visitors year after year left Kovalam buried in garbage. Plastic bags clogged the town's water pipes, mosquitoes bred in piles of trash, and the town grew ugly and unhealthy.

Local government officials decided to start a waste collection program and to install an incinerator to burn the waste. But many people argued that burning would only turn the waste into toxic smoke and ash that would fill the air. After much debate, the incinerator was not built, and the government asked the groups that opposed it to suggest an alternative.

Led by an organization called Thanal Conservation Group, the community proposed a zero waste system. People from other communities visited to share ideas about their zero waste programs. One woman, Murali, showed how she made and sold bowls, cups, spoons, bags and other useful items from discarded coconut shells, palm leaves, and scrap paper. By promoting composting and new ways of reusing discards, Zero Waste Kovalam was born.

Within a few years, Kovalam was clean and beautiful, and more prosperous than ever. It now has a new tourist attraction: the Zero Waste Center. Many local restaurants now use coconut shell cups and plates made from leaves. The women of the Zero Waste Center grow vegetables and bananas in soil enriched with compost, and the town built a plant that uses human and animal waste to make electricity (see page 540).

Kovalam has become an example for all of India and the world by showing how zero waste can restore and improve a community's health and natural beauty and protect the environment for future generations.

Waste and the Law

Most governments have policies and guidelines for managing waste. One of the goals of community action is to make sure these policies protect people's health and the environment. Another is to change the policies if they do not.

Philippines outlaws incineration and toughens waste laws

For many years, waste in the Philippines piled up in open dumps or was burned. But as pollution got worse from more and more waste, many communities began to pressure the government to ban waste burning, to establish a recycling program, and to prevent open dumping.

The campaign began in 1985 with an education program. Activists traveled across the country teaching communities about better ways to prevent wastes from being created. They showed people how to reduce waste and how to separate wastes to be composted, reused or recycled. They invited people from all walks of life, from peasants to politicians to priests, to work together to reduce waste in their communities.

At the same time, they educated communities and government officials about the toxic contamination released by burning waste. The campaigners showed how toxins from burning wastes turned up in eggs and other common foods.

Their pressure on the government paid off when incineration was banned in 1999 by a new law called the Clean Air Act. In 2000, the government began a recycling program and also passed a law to turn all open dumps into sanitary landfills. In 2001, the government passed the Ecological Waste Management Act to establish resource recovery centers in many towns and cities. The campaigners continue to work to make sure the laws benefit those most affected: the people who collect, sort, and recycle waste.

Laws like these are important in setting the standard for how waste is handled. When people take responsibility for their own wastes, and pressure lawmakers to make and enforce laws fairly, everyone benefits.

19 Health Care Waste

In this chapter: **page**

Health Care Waste

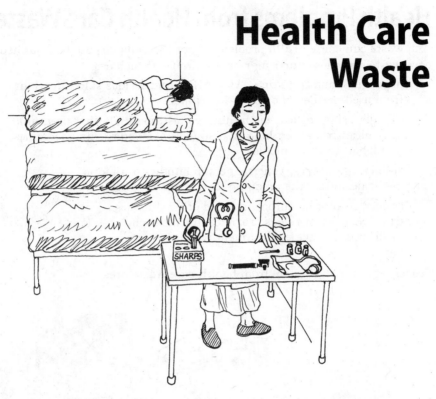

Health workers do their best to help people stay healthy. But if waste from health care is not handled safely, it can spread illness to the health workers and the surrounding community.

Health care waste includes waste from clinics, hospitals, laboratories, blood banks, dental clinics, birth centers and animal hospitals. It also includes waste from **vaccination programs** (also called immunization campaigns) and medical aid missions, and waste produced from caring for the sick at home.

Most waste from health care is ordinary waste like paper, cardboard, and food scraps. But some health care waste is contaminated with blood or body fluids that may carry harmful germs and spread disease. Used needles and other sharp tools **(sharps)** can cause injury and spread disease. Some health care waste, such as plastics, contain toxic chemicals. When waste that carries harmful germs or toxic chemicals is mixed with ordinary waste, the mixed waste becomes a threat to all who handle it. That is why separation of waste is so important.

Safe handling of health care waste uses the same basic methods used to dispose of other solid wastes (see Chapter 18). But wastes contaminated with body fluids and germs must be **disinfected** and disposed of in ways that protect the health of people and the environment.

Health Problems from Health Care Waste

Any waste can cause health problems if not carefully disposed of. But health care waste can cause particular health problems such as:

- hepatitis B and C, tetanus, HIV/AIDS, and serious skin infections from used needles and sharp instruments.

- allergies, skin rashes, eye irritations, asthma and other breathing difficulties from breathing in disinfectants, detergents, medicines, and laboratory chemicals.

- **antibiotic resistance.** When a person handles antibiotic medicines often, they may no longer work for her.

- cancer, respiratory problems, and other illnesses from wastes that release toxic chemicals such as dioxins into the environment when they are burned.

People most at risk of harm from health care waste are:

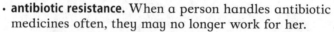

people who live near where health care waste is dumped or burned

people who remove trash from health centers and those who collect, recycle, or sell trash from dump sites and landfills

workers and patients in health centers

Sangu's story

Sangu was born in a small village in India. After years of drought and crop failure, she and her mother and baby brother moved to the city in search of a better life. They lived with her mother's family on a steep hill over a dump site. Other children showed Sangu how to pick out things to sell from the dump site. Before school every morning, she collected scraps of tin, glass bottles, plastic bags, and other things. Sangu used the money she made to buy lunch and hot tea after school.

Life was hard in the city, and Sangu's mother was soon working away from the house all day. Sangu had to take care of her baby brother and could no longer go to school. Every day she spent many hours sorting through garbage at the dump with her brother in a sling on her back.

Sometimes Sangu found bloody bandages, needles, and other hospital waste mixed in with the rest of the trash. Sangu's thin sandals did not protect her from sharp things in the trash. Broken glass and rusted metal would sometimes cut her feet and ankles. One day a syringe needle pierced her sandal and went right into her foot. Soon after, Sangu got very sick with fever, tiredness, and a swollen sore throat.

Sangu felt better after some weeks. But several months later she began to feel sick again. She was tired all the time, had fevers and sores in her mouth, lost her appetite, and grew very thin. Her mother and family worried about her, but they had no money to take her to a doctor. Finally, her mother borrowed money from a cousin and took Sangu to the health center. The doctor listened to Sangu's story, examined her, and then took some blood for a blood test.

The next day, they returned to the clinic and the doctor told Sangu's mother that Sangu had HIV. She needed medicine, but her family had no money to take her to the hospital where she could get it and the attention she needed. With great sadness, Sangu's mother took her home. Sangu rested in bed, but everyone knew she would not recover. A few months later, Sangu died.

Why did Sangu die?

Sangu died from HIV/AIDS after she was infected by stepping on a contaminated **syringe** needle.

Her illness and death were caused by an environmental problem: poor disposal of health care waste; and a social problem: poverty.

What could have prevented Sangu's death?

Because many different social problems contribute to poverty, poverty can be difficult to solve. These questions show some of the problems:

- Why was Sangu not in school?
  - Why did Sangu need to collect waste to earn money?
    - Why did Sangu not have good shoes to protect her feet?
    - Why was she not able to get health care and medicine?

Thin shoes, no money to get medicine or health care, and a desperate need to earn money, combined with the malnutrition and other problems that are a part of poverty are some of the answers to these questions. Finding solutions to social problems like these may take a long time.

Health care waste affects many people, including those too poor to go to a health center.

The environmental problem may be easier to solve in the short term. We can begin by asking these questions:

- Why was harmful health care waste mixed in with other trash that could be recycled or reused?
- Why was so much harmful waste dumped in the open, rather than disposed of safely?

Responsible management of health care waste can improve living conditions for everyone, especially those forced by poverty to live on scraps.

The Problem of Burning Waste

To destroy health care waste and the germs it carries, many clinics and hospitals burn it in an **incinerator** (an enclosed, high-heat fire). Burning health care waste seems like an easy solution because different kinds of waste can be collected and simply thrown into the incinerator. But burning waste this way creates more health problems than it solves.

Burning waste, either in an open fire or an incinerator, releases toxic chemicals into the air as smoke, and into the soil and groundwater as ashes. Wastes containing mercury, lead, and other heavy metals release these poisons into the environment when they are burned.

For every 3 bags of waste burned,

1 bag of toxic ash is produced, and other toxic chemicals go into the air, soil, and water.

Plastics used to make IV and blood bags, tubes, and some syringes produce highly toxic chemicals called **dioxins** and **furans** when they are burned. These chemicals have no color or smell and can cause cancer, make both women and men infertile (unable to make a baby), and lead to other serious health problems (see Chapter 16 and Chapter 20).

Sometimes incinerators do not burn hot enough or long enough to burn waste completely. Some incinerators are built to handle particular wastes, such as immunization wastes, but end up being used to burn medicines, pesticides, and other toxic materials.

Often, the first steps in safely handling health care waste are to separate materials that can be recycled or reused, then to disinfect waste that carries harmful germs. By using safer alternatives to incineration, the health worker's oath to "do no harm" can be applied even to the difficult task of getting rid of waste.

Preventing Harm from Health Care Waste

Whether in a small health post, a larger clinic, or in the home, medical tools and health care waste must be managed safely to prevent harm.

- **Reduce** the amount of waste by choosing medical supplies carefully.
- **Separate** wastes where they are created.
- **Disinfect** wastes that carry germs.
- **Treat** chemical wastes to make them less harmful.
- **Safely store and transport** waste.
- **Dispose** of health care wastes in the least harmful way possible.
- **Train** everyone who handles health care waste about safe methods.

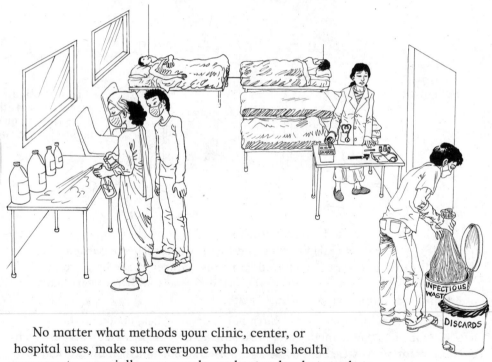

No matter what methods your clinic, center, or hospital uses, make sure everyone who handles health care waste, especially new people, understands what needs to be done and why. Often, people will bring up new ideas that can make work easier and safer for everyone. Some clinics have a team of people who are responsible for training and checking safe practices (see pages 443 to 446).

Reducing waste

Using fewer and less harmful materials will reduce the amount of harmful health care waste. When choosing materials for your clinic, think about what kind of waste will be produced, how harmful it will be, and how you will dispose of it.

To reduce the amount of harmful waste:

- Avoid using disposable items if a reusable choice is available and safe to use. (Syringes and needles should not be reused, see page 434.)

- Use non-mercury thermometers if they are available. They cost more but are more durable and less dangerous if they break.

- Do not buy more medicines than you need, and use them only when necessary.

- Use pills instead of injections.

- Use non-plastic items when possible.

- Use the least toxic products to clean and disinfect whenever possible.

- Look for IV bags, tubing, and other materials made without PVC. They are cheap and available in some places, and are always safer for patients and the community.

Separating waste

Separating waste where it is created is another important step in safe handling of health care waste.

Separating wastes greatly reduces risks to health center workers and to people who collect, sell, and recycle waste. Separation also reduces the amount of waste that must be treated or buried later and reduces the cost of waste management.

Food waste from the health center can be composted and used in gardens.

Separating waste into colored containers

Many health centers separate wastes into different colored containers at the places where waste is created. For this to be a useful method, everyone in the health center needs to understand which waste goes into which color container. Different countries use different colors for each type of waste. For example, in some countries the color red means "danger." So containers for used needles and other sharp tools, and other harmful or toxic wastes are red or marked with red paint, marker, or tape.

More than half of all waste from health centers is just like household waste: paper, cardboard, bottles, cans, and kitchen scraps. When this waste is separated out, it is much easier to manage the harmful waste.

Regular waste can be put into bags and bins and, as much as possible, recycled, turned into compost, or reused.

Harmful waste should be separated and treated carefully (see chart on page 436).

Containers should be:

- placed close to where waste is created.
- clearly marked with colors and symbols.
- strong enough so they do not leak or break.
- easy to seal and transport without risk of spills, leaks, or breaks.
- big enough to hold a full day's waste when only $3/4$ full.

It is best to use containers and bags that are the same color for the same kind of waste. If this is not possible, mark them with colored tape or paint. Always using the same colors can help workers who do not read — and even those who do — remember which containers are for regular waste and which are for harmful wastes.

Storing and transporting waste

Health care waste needs to be stored carefully until it can be safely taken to its final disposal site. Health care waste containers should be placed where waste is created and disinfected, never in hallways, bathrooms, or other places where people might spill them or fill them with mixed waste.

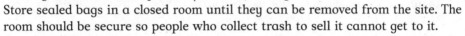

Seal waste bins and bags when they are ³/₄ full. Bins and bags ³/₄ full are less likely to spill or break, and will reduce the chances of injury to a worker picking them up. Never put used needles and other sharp instruments in bags (see page 434.) If a bag breaks or leaks, put it inside another bag. Store sealed bags in a closed room until they can be removed from the site. The room should be secure so people who collect trash to sell it cannot get to it.

Health care waste can be stored safely only for a short time. Soon it begins to smell bad and can spread infection as it decays. It is best to remove waste daily. Never store waste for more than 3 days. Your nose will tell you when you have waited too long!

Use carts or trolleys that are easy to clean to remove waste from the center. It is safest to clean carts after each use, and to use carts that have no sharp edges that could damage bags or containers during loading or unloading.

Prevent harm when handling waste:

- Wear protective clothing to reduce risks from needles or other sharp tools, germs, or splashes from blood, other liquids or chemicals (see Appendix A).
- Immediately after they are used, put used needles and other sharp tools in sharps boxes. Do not put sharp things in bags or with other waste.
- Wash hands after handling waste, and before and after working with every patient.
- Never carry uncovered (uncapped) needles.
- Do not let waste touch your skin. If protective clothing gets soaked through with contaminated wastes, take it off immediately, and wash yourself with lots of soap and water.
- Protective clothing only protects if it is clean. After each use or at the end of each shift, wash or disinfect (see page 428) gloves, aprons, glasses, and masks. This will protect the next person who uses them.

If your center does not have protective clothing, use available materials for protection. For example, use plastic garbage bags to make protective aprons, pants, masks, and hats. Some protection is better than none at all.

Disinfecting Waste

Disinfection means killing germs that cause infection. As much as possible, health care waste should be disinfected in the same place where it is created. The most common ways to disinfect are to use chemicals (such as **chlorine bleach**, **hydrogen peroxide**, or other chemicals) or heat (boiling, steaming, **pressure steaming**, **autoclave**, or **microwave**).

After waste is disinfected, it can be safely buried.

What is sterilizing and what is disinfecting?

Some health care manuals use the word **sterilizing** rather than **disinfecting.** Sterilizing and disinfecting are not the same and many people confuse them.

Sterilizing means killing all of the germs on something. It is very difficult to do this. **Disinfecting** means killing enough of the germs on something that so it will not transmit infection.

Many people use the word sterilization for proper treatment of health care equipment, and the word disinfection when talking about cleaning floors and other surfaces with 'disinfecting cleaners.' But there are different levels of disinfection.

The treatments described in this book are **'high-level disinfection'** which means killing almost all the germs on something. For this reason, we use the word disinfection for all of the methods in this book.

What wastes need to be disinfected?

Any materials in a health center that are contaminated with blood, body fluids, or feces, or that have been in close contact with a person with a contagious disease, need to be disinfected to prevent the spread of infection and disease.

Wastes that need disinfection:

- used needles and other sharp tools
- blood and other body fluids
- bandages, swabs, and other wastes that carry body fluids
- other items contaminated with blood, body fluids, or feces
- feces from people with infectious disease (such as cholera)
- bedding and bedpans from all people

Wastes that do not need disinfection:

- body parts
- wastewater from disinfection and cleaning
- chemicals from disinfection, cleaning, and laboratory tests
- food waste
- any materials not contaminated with blood or body fluids (cardboard, paper, plastics, glass, metal)

Disinfecting with Chemicals

All chemicals used to disinfect can be harmful and need to be used with great care. Some chemicals commonly used to disinfect include hydrogen peroxide (6%), chlorine bleach, ethanol (70%), and isopropyl alcohol (70% to 90%).

Chemical fumes can be harmful!

Many common cleaning and disinfecting products contain **glutaraldehyde** or **formaldehyde**. Regular exposure to glutaraldehyde and formaldehyde can cause cancer and death. These chemicals should not be used. (See pages 430 to 432 for safer ways to disinfect with chemicals, and page 440 for safe disposal of chemicals.)

Many health centers use these guidelines for safety when using chemicals:

- Use chemical disinfectants outside, or in well-ventilated rooms where there is a good exhaust fan.

- Use only the amount of chemical disinfectant needed to do the job.

- Wear gloves, safety glasses, a mask, and protective clothing to protect your skin, eyes, and breathing when using or disposing of chemicals (see Appendix A).

- Store disinfecting chemicals in their proper containers. Label the containers. Do not reuse those containers for anything else.

- Do not store or mix chemicals in water buckets, or containers or bottles that may be used for food or drinks.

- Keep chemical containers tightly closed and stored upright. Check them for breaks, leaks, and weak spots.

Wastes that do not need chemical disinfection

It is often thought that body parts need to be disinfected with chemicals. But body parts, including the **placenta** (afterbirth) and umbilical cord, are most easily disposed of by putting them in a latrine or burying them deep in the ground. In many communities, burying the afterbirth is an important ritual. If it is done safely, burial is also a good way to protect the community from germs that may grow in the afterbirth or other body parts. (See pages 436 to 440 for safe methods for disposing of waste.)

Disinfecting with safer chemicals

Some health centers use cleaning products that contain harmful chemicals, such as glutaraldehyde, to disinfect and clean (see page 440). But surfaces in health centers can be kept clean and germ-free by using less dangerous and less costly cleaning products. Hot water and soap is effective for routine cleaning of surfaces such as floors, walls, and furniture.

This stuff is great! It kills everything.

Including us!

When choosing a product, ask: Is it harmful? Is it difficult to dispose of safely?

In areas where people with infectious diseases wait or are treated, it is important to use a stronger disinfectant to prevent the spread of disease. Hydrogen peroxide solutions that contain orange oil and other natural oils are effective for disinfecting floors and surfaces. They do not cause health problems and do not have to be treated before disposal. A safe disinfecting solution can also be made with vinegar and hydrogen peroxide.

How to make a safe disinfecting solution

Mix together equal amounts of white vinegar and hydrogen peroxide. (A 3% peroxide solution is common, but 6% is better.) Mix only as much as you need for one day. Keep it in a closed container.

Pour a small amount of the mixture on a wiping cloth and scrub the surface to be disinfected with strong rubbing motion.

This mixture is best for use on tabletops, bed railings, and other surfaces.

1 Liter

Disinfecting with bleach

Many health centers use bleach to disinfect surfaces such as walls, floors, and tables. Care must be taken when disinfecting with bleach because it can cause harm to your skin and eyes if it splashes on you, and the fumes are dangerous when breathed in. Adding white vinegar to the bleach makes it an even more effective disinfectant.

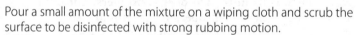

How to make a disinfecting solution of 5% bleach

If your bleach says:	Use:
5% available chlorine	Only bleach
10% available chlorine	Add 1 part bleach to 1 part water
15% available chlorine	Add 1 part bleach to 2 parts water

bleach

bleach + water

bleach + water + water

If you add 1 cup of white vinegar to a gallon of 5% bleach solution, it will disinfect better. Mix just enough solution for one day. Do not use it again the next day. It will not be strong enough to kill germs any more. To get rid of used bleach, see page 439.

Use a bleach bucket

Keep a bleach bucket wherever there is infectious waste such as used bandages, cotton swabs, gloves, and blood bags. Prepare the bleach bucket every day, or before each shift if you make a lot of waste. You may want one bleach bucket for waste to be disposed of and a different one for disinfecting tools and equipment to be reused. Cut gloves, syringes, IV bottles, tubing, and other things that are not intended to be reused into small pieces before dropping them into the bleach bucket.

The bucket should always contain enough bleach solution to completely cover the materials. The materials must stay in the bleach for at least 10 minutes. Keep a tight-fitting cover on the bleach bucket to prevent spills, and to keep the bleach solution strong enough to disinfect. Uncovered, the chlorine will evaporate away.

How to make a bleach bucket

One way to safely disinfect with bleach is to use a bleach bucket. A bleach bucket has 2 parts: a bucket or container that holds bleach solution, and a smaller inner container or basket with many small holes like a strainer or loose woven basket that holds the wastes. A bleach bucket must also have a tight-fitting cover. To prepare a bleach bucket:

Make a 5% bleach solution (see above). The main bucket should be at least ½ full of the bleach solution.

Place the smaller container, strainer, or basket inside the main bucket so the bleach solution passes through the holes. Make sure the inner container does not float on top of the solution, but that the bleach solution passes though the holes so it completely covers the waste materials.

IMPORTANT: Bleach should never be mixed with other chemicals, especially ammonia. Bleach and ammonia mixed together will produce a toxic gas that can cause death if breathed in, and enough heat to cause an explosion. Always wash carefully after handling bleach.

Laundry

In the past, many hospitals used carbolic acid to sterilize sheets. This is only necessary for the sheets of people being treated for burns. To disinfect bed linens and clothes, soak them in a bleach bucket for 10 minutes before washing with hot water and soap. Use gloves when taking them out of the bleach.

Disinfecting with Heat

Many health centers use autoclaves or microwaves (see page 433) to disinfect syringes, other medical tools, and some waste. If you have no autoclave or microwave, then boiling, steaming, or pressure steaming materials for at least 20 minutes will disinfect them. Disposable wastes should **not** be disinfected with tools that will be used again, because it is difficult to keep the reusable tools clean when you separate them after disinfection.

Wear gloves and a mask to cut plastic and cloth items such as catheters, IV bags, tubing, large bandages, and so on into small pieces.

How to make sure items are disinfected

For boiling, steaming, and pressure steaming, start to count the 20 minutes after the water is fully boiling. Do not add anything new to the pot once you begin to count. After 20 minutes, turn off the heat and let it cool.

Materials that will be reused after they are boiled or steamed must be removed using sterile gloves or tongs, placed right away inside a disinfected container, and then sealed. The boiled water can be safely poured down a drain.

Boiling

You can use boiling to disinfect metal, rubber or plastic tools, and cloth. After you wash and rinse the tools, put them in the pot, cover the tools with water, bring the water to a boil, and boil for 20 minutes.

Steaming

You can use steaming to disinfect gloves, masks, and things made of metal and plastic. The water does not need to cover everything in the pot, but you must use enough water to keep steam coming for 20 minutes. The pot should have a lid that fits tightly.

Pressure steaming

Use pressure steaming to disinfect metal, rubber, plastic, and cloth. Wash and rinse the materials to be disinfected and put them in the pressure cooker with water. Close the lid and heat it on the stove. After it boils, cook at 15 to 20 pounds of pressure for 20 minutes.

Autoclave

An autoclave is a small machine that disinfects things using steam heat and pressure. Autoclaves have been used for many years to disinfect medical instruments. They are used more and more to treat waste as well.

It is safest to use 2 separate machines — one for reusable instruments and one for waste. For health centers with very small amounts of waste to be disinfected, a pressure steamer is less expensive and works as well as an autoclave. It is possible to build gas, kerosene, or solar-powered autoclaves for areas with no electricity.

Microwave ovens

Microwave ovens heat the moisture in objects placed inside them. The heat, together with the amount of time an object is in the microwave oven, leads to disinfection. Because microwave ovens vary greatly in power, use care when disinfecting with this method. To make sure of high level disinfection:

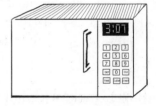

1. Put the waste in a non-metal container with enough water to cover it.
2. Put a loose-fitting cover over the top of the container to reduce the loss of water during heating.
3. Microwave waste materials for at least 20 minutes.
4. Let the container cool before opening. Dispose of any microwaved liquid waste in a leaching pit (see page 439) or you can safely pour it down the drain.

IMPORTANT: Do not put metal objects in a microwave oven. It can ruin the machine.

After Disinfection

No matter what kind of disinfection you use (chemical or heat), disinfected waste should be safely stored in bags or disposed of right after disinfection. Keep waste away from patients, and make sure that infected waste does not get mixed with disinfected waste.

Treatment and Disposal of Sharps

Many health problems from health care waste are caused by sharps. Needles, blades, lancets, and other sharp objects can cause wounds and infections, so they need to be handled with great care. Outside the health center, sharps may put the people who collect and recycle waste in danger.

To reduce sharps waste, use injections only when they are needed. (For information about when to inject and when not to, see *Where There Is No Doctor*, pages 65 to 74.)

Safe disposal of needles and syringes

After injections, needles should be removed from syringes and put into a sharps container right away. Putting caps back on needles is dangerous and best avoided. Unless you are using reusable syringes, always dispose of needles where they are used. There are many ways to remove needles from syringes. Any method should:

- use only one hand, to prevent needle sticks.
- dispose of needles in a hard container that they cannot poke through.
- be easy and comfortable for health workers to use.

How to make a keyhole box to dispose of sharps

A keyhole box is a metal box with a long slot in the top that is wide on one end and gets narrower on the other. You can buy them or have a metal worker make them. They can also be made from coffee cans or other rigid metal containers. What is important is that they let you remove needles from syringes without touching the needles.

❶ When you have finished using a disposable syringe, put the needle into the slot and slide it down to the narrowest point.

❷ Now pull up on the syringe and the needle will fall off into the box. Put the syringe in a waste container.

❸ When the sharps container is ¾ full, seal it with tape and put the box into a sharps pit or a sharps drum. (See page 439 for how to safely bury sharps waste.)

Kinds of syringes

Reusable syringes can be used again and again. Reusable syringes make less waste and can save money, but they must be washed very carefully and disinfected after every use. **Never** use a syringe without washing and disinfecting it first. HIV, hepatitis, and other diseases are spread easily if needles and syringes are not carefully disinfected between uses.

Disposable syringes are made to be thrown out with the needle attached after one use. Some disposable syringes can be taken apart, boiled or steamed, and reused several times. This is not recommended, because if the syringe or needle is not completely disinfected it can spread disease.

Auto-disabled syringes become locked or cover the needle after the syringe is used, so that it cannot be reused. However, auto-disabled syringes still have a needle inside, so they still have the danger of needle-stick accidents inside or outside of the health center. For safe disposal methods, see pages 438 to 439.

IMPORTANT: Never reuse a syringe and needle without cleaning and disinfecting first!

How to wash and disinfect a syringe and needle for reuse

Using a needle more than once can spread HIV or other diseases unless it is properly cleaned and disinfected, and so is best avoided.
But many communities do not have enough syringes and needles to afford to dispose of them after a single use. For this reason, we include information on how to wash and disinfect a syringe and needle for reuse.

1. Put on a pair of heavy gloves to protect your hands from germs.

2. Draw 5% bleach solution (see page 431) up through the needle into the syringe barrel.

3. Squirt out the bleach solution.

4. Repeat several times. Rinse everything several times with clean water.

5. Take the syringe apart and boil or steam the syringe and needle (see page 432).

Disposing of Infectious Waste

The chart on this page shows when and how to disinfect and dispose of infectious wastes in small health centers. Some health centers may not be able to use all of these methods, or may have their own, better ways to treat wastes. The important thing to prevent infection is to use a system that everyone in the health center understands and follows.

IMPORTANT: Follow all laws on how to get rid of health care waste.

➡️ **Separate by type**	**SHARPS** Needles, blades, lancets, broken glass, other sharp objects	**ITEMS CONTAMINATED WITH BLOOD OR BODY FLUIDS** Blood bags, dialysis kits, syringe barrels, gloves, masks, bandages, cotton swabs, other wastes		**BLOOD, BODY FLUIDS, FECES** Liquid blood, fluids from suction canisters, feces, and other contaminated body wastes	**BODY PARTS** Amputated limbs, tissues, skin tags
Separate using colored containers	put in sharps container	put in colored bag or container	*or* carefully cut or shred waste and put in bleach bucket	put in colored bag or container	put in colored bag or container with tight-fitting cover
Seal containers	when ¾ full, seal container with tape	when ¾ full, seal bag or container	*or* keep tight-fitting cover on bleach bucket	seal bag or cover container with tight-fitting cover	when ¾ full, seal bag or container
Disinfection or safe burial	*or* drop into a sharps pit / put container into a drum	disinfect using a heat method	*or* leave in bleach bucket for at least 10 minutes, then drain	wearing protective clothing, carefully add bleach to container and let stand for 10 minutes	put in safe burial pit, add lime, and cover with soil
Final disposal	*or* when almost full, seal the pit with concrete / when ¾ full, fill drum with concrete and bury drum in a landfill	put in safe burial pit, cover with soil. When pit is almost full, cover with soil and seal with concrete.	*or* dry and reuse or recycle glass, metals, and plastics or discard with other solid waste	put liquid waste into safe leaching pit or into sanitary sewer or septic tank	when pit is almost full, cover with soil and seal with concrete
For more information	see pages 434 to 435 on handling sharps, and page 439 on burying sharps	see pages 429 to 433 on ways to disinfect with heat and chemicals		see page 428 on handling feces and body fluids, and page 439 for burial and leaching pits	see page 428 on handling body parts, and page 439 for safe waste burial

Immunization Programs

Large numbers of people around the world are protected from diseases such as measles, tetanus, and polio by receiving special injections through **immunization** (also called **vaccination**) programs. Immunization programs are often run by international organizations like World Health Organization (WHO) and UNICEF, together with national and local governments, and with the companies that make and sell vaccines.

These programs often do not include good plans for disposing of waste. In many cases they leave waste behind to be handled by the communities receiving the immunizations. This often leads to incinerating or burning the wastes in the open, creating health problems for people and their environment.

Immunization programs can take responsibility for waste

With sufficient planning and support, an immunization program can safely get rid of its waste by:

- using the same trucks that deliver immunization supplies to carry away waste for treatment and disposal. If it is a regional program, a central waste treatment center might set up an autoclave and safe burial pits.

- helping communities set up health care waste disposal systems, which can remain long after the immunization program is gone.

- using new technologies such as immunization guns that produce less waste because they do not use needles or syringes.

Burying Health Care Waste

Burial pits are useful for disposing of sharps, body parts, and expired medicines. Try not to fill waste pits with materials that can be composted (such as food waste), reused (some glass and plastic materials), or put in a landfill after disinfection (plastics, cloth, bandages).

If there is waste collection and a landfill nearby, disinfected waste can be collected and safely buried there. If there is not, consider building small waste pits at the health center to make sure waste is safely buried. Because sharps are the most dangerous wastes, it is always best to bury needles and other sharp tools in a safe pit at the health center.

Burying waste is safest when everyone who handles the waste understands and follows the process.

Safe waste pits

For a waste pit to be safe, it should be located downhill from nearby wells, in an area where the groundwater is not near the surface, and at least 50 meters from rivers, streams, springs, and other water sources. Pit sides and bottoms should be lined with clay to prevent liquids from passing into the soil and groundwater. The pit should be well-marked and have a fence around it to keep people and animals out.

50 meters from any water

50 meters from buildings

HEALTH CLINIC

KEEP

Locking gate

50 meters downhill from a well

Use the 50 meter rule when you dig a pit to bury wastes.

How to make a waste pit with a concrete cover

This kind of pit is best used only for infectious waste and not for regular garbage.

❶ Dig a pit 1 to 2 meters wide and 2 to 5 meters deep. The bottom of the pit should be at least 1½ meters above the highest level of groundwater (water table).

❷ Line the bottom of the pit with a layer of clay at least 30 cm thick.

❸ Build up a ridge of earth around the top of the pit to prevent surface water from running in.

❹ Build a fence around the area where the pit is located to keep children safe and animals out.

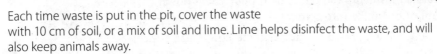

Each time waste is put in the pit, cover the waste with 10 cm of soil, or a mix of soil and lime. Lime helps disinfect the waste, and will also keep animals away.

When the waste rises to ½ meter from the surface, cover it with ½ meter of soil and seal it with a layer of concrete at least 10 to 30 centimeters thick.

How to seal sharps in containers with concrete

Place disinfected sharps and sharps containers in a hard container such as a metal drum. When the container is mostly full (¾), add a mixture of 1 part cement, 1 part lime, 4 parts sand, and ⅓ to ½ part water. Lime works as a disinfectant, and it also helps the cement flow into empty spaces to completely surround the waste. Seal the container and bury it in a trench or landfill.

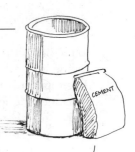

Disposing of liquid waste

Many health centers pour bleach, contaminated water, or other liquids from the health center down a drain. This is only safe if the drain does not lead to a stream or other water source. Dilute the liquid with a lot of water before dumping it. To protect water sources, it is better to put used bleach and other liquids into a safe leach pit. Chemicals such as glutaraldehyde and formaldehyde should be treated before disposal (see page 440).

To build a safe leach pit

In a place where the ground does not flood, and far from waterways and wells, dig a pit ½ meter to 1 meter deep. In the bottom of the pit, put a layer of sand a few centimeters deep. Then put a layer of gravel a few centimeters deep, and a layer of larger stones on top. Put a cover on the pit to prevent rainwater from getting in.

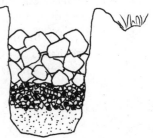

Safe Disposal of Chemical Wastes

Most health centers, small or large, end up creating chemical wastes that need to be disposed of safely. Larger centers may also have waste from x-rays, chemotherapy, and laboratories. We do not include ways to dispose of these kinds of waste in this book because they are too complicated. (For information on handling these wastes, see Resources.)

Chemicals used to clean and disinfect

Bleach can be diluted and then dumped into a leaching pit (see page 439). Hydrogen peroxide solutions can be disposed of with no special treatment. You can safely pour them down the drain of a sink or into a toilet.

Glutaraldehyde and formaldehyde can cause cancer and death. But if your center uses these chemicals for disinfecting and cleaning, there are ways to get rid of them safely. To treat glutaraldehyde or formaldehyde for disposal, add caustic soda (sodium hydroxide) solution to change the acidity (pH). Measure the pH with litmus paper or a pH meter. Bring the pH to 12 and stay at that pH for at least 8 hours. After 8 hours, bring the pH to a neutral level (pH 7) by adding hydrochloric acid (HCl). If you do not have the proper materials to make glutaraldehyde or formaldehyde safe for disposal, do not use them — they are that dangerous. After processing, it is safe to pour them into a leach pit.

Carbolic acid, used to sterilize sheets, causes breathing and skin problems. A worker should wear protective clothing including eye protection and a mask when using or disposing of carbolic acid. The wastewater should be added to a solution of sodium hydroxide, then poured into a leach pit.

When preparing liquid chemical wastes for disposal, wear protective gear (see Appendix A), and be careful not to splash.

Mercury

Mercury is the silver liquid inside a thermometer. It is also used in other medical equipment, such as the meters attached to old blood pressure cuffs, as well as in batteries and lamps.

Mercury is a very toxic heavy metal. Absorbing it through the skin or breathing in even a very small amount of mercury can damage the nerves, kidneys, lungs, brain, and cause birth defects (see page 338).

Mercury is not destroyed by burning. In fact, burning mercury turns it into even more harmful gas.

The best way to reduce harm from mercury is to use as few mercury-containing items as possible. If possible, keep equipment with mercury on metal trays, so if it breaks the mercury will not soak into wood surfaces like tables or floors. Use non-mercury thermometers if they are available in your area (see Resources).

How to clean up a mercury spill

When a thermometer or other item containing mercury breaks, the mercury scatters as small pieces. Keep people and animals away from the spill area. Turn off any heaters, fans, or air conditioners, and open windows to let air in. To clean up the spill you will need gloves, an eyedropper, 2 pieces of stiff paper or cardboard, 2 plastic bags, sticky tape, a flashlight, and a glass container with water in it.

To collect the mercury safely:

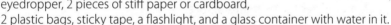

❶ **Do not touch the mercury.** Open windows or doors.

❷ Remove watches and jewelry. Mercury sticks to other metals.

❸ Shine a flashlight on the area to make the mercury easier to see, even during the daytime.

❹ Wear chemical resistant gloves if possible. If you have only latex gloves, wear at least 2 pairs.

❺ Use small pieces of stiff paper or cardboard to gather the mercury into a small pile.

❻ Use an eyedropper to suction up the mercury beads, and put the mercury in a glass container with water.

❼ Pick up any mercury that is left using sticky tape.

❽ Place sticky tape, eyedropper, gloves, and cardboard in a plastic bag.

❾ Label the bag "mercury waste" and put the bag in the glass container with the water in it.

❿ Seal and mark the container. Put it inside another plastic bag.

⓫ Dispose of it as toxic waste (see page 410).

Antibiotics and other medicines

Old medicines are another kind of chemical waste that need to be disposed of safely. Getting rid of antibiotics and other medicines safely means keeping them out of water sources and away from people who handle waste. Unfortunately, health centers, pharmacies, and drug companies often get rid of old medicines unsafely, in open dump sites, waterways, or down the drain.

When antibiotics are dumped into the environment, they can cause **antibiotic resistance** in people, animals, and even germs that come into contact with them. This means that when people take antibiotics to fight infections, the medicines will be less effective because fewer germs will be killed by them.

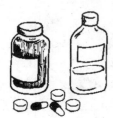

Buy and use fewer antibiotics

Do not use antibiotics for health problems they cannot cure. (For more information about how to use antibiotics, see *Where There Is No Doctor*, pages 55 to 58, and *Helping Health Workers Learn*, Chapter 19.) When your health center buys only the amount of antibiotics it needs, then fewer drugs will need to be dumped because they are old.

Return expired medicines to the manufacturer

The drug companies that make medicines have the equipment to safely dispose of expired antibiotics and other medicines, and they should do this. But if you are unable to return medicines to the company that made them, there are ways you can dispose of them safely.

How to dispose of medicines safely

❶ Wear gloves, safety glasses, and a dust mask.

❷ Grind up pills.

❸ Mix powder from the ground up pills with cement.

❹ Add water and form cement into solid balls.

❺ Bury these cement balls in a sealed waste pit.

Do a Health Care Waste Assessment

Evaluating how health care waste is created, handled, and disposed of can help everyone in a health center find ways to work more safely. An assessment can identify the problems in how waste is created and handled, and can help find solutions.

Steps in doing a health care waste assessment

1. Meet and discuss problems with all health center staff.
2. List what is in the pharmacy and supply room.
3. Make a map of the center.
4. Walk through the health center and note problems.
5. Learn about different choices for treating and disposing of waste.
6. Find out how waste is handled and disposed of, both at the health center and in the community.
7. Take action!
8. Regularly educate and train all workers.

❶ **Meet and discuss problems with all health center staff.**

Everyone at the center should help with the assessment. Doctors, nurses, waste handlers, and cleaners are likely to have different ideas about where waste is coming from and what the problems are.

Penicillin
Co-trimoxazole
Hydrogen peroxide
Sulfur
thermometers
syringes
gauze bandages
Mebendazole
bags
gloves

❷ List what is in the pharmacy and supply room.

Since most materials are ordered through the pharmacy or supply room, start your assessment by making a list of what you find in those places. As you look at each item, ask what kind of waste will be produced, and how harmful it will be.

Can disposable items be replaced with non-disposables? Can fewer or safer chemicals be used? Can the center use less plastic, fewer items that contain mercury, or make any other changes to reduce the amount of harmful waste?

❸ Make a map of the health center.

Show all rooms, doors, and windows, and note what each room is used for. Use different colors to mark places where waste is created, where waste containers are kept, and where waste is stored as it is collected and transported from its source to its final storage or disposal site.

This map can be changed as the group walks through the health center. After the assessment, make a new map to show any changes that have been made. Notice especially where containers are kept for collecting waste.

❹ Walk through the health center and note problems.

Visit all the areas where waste is produced. Look in the trash bins and note what kinds of waste are there. Do this walk-through several times over the next few weeks, and try to do it at different times of day. Then you can see the waste in different conditions and how it is handled throughout the day.

Do the walk-through with different workers. Cleaners will see things differently from doctors and nurses, and each may have important ideas about how to best handle waste.

The safest way to protect myself from used needles is to have them put in puncture-proof boxes.

The safest way to protect myself from used needles is to toss them straight into the waste pail.

The safest way to protect myself from used needles is to let the nurse give injections.

To manage waste safely, we need to think about each other as much as we think about ourselves.

❺ Learn about different choices for treating and disposing of waste.

After several walks through the health center, have a group discussion about the problems and possible solutions. Solutions do not have to be expensive or technical. Most solutions require only organization, cooperation, and commitment.

Try to make a plan that starts with the most harmful waste — sharps — and then chemicals, blood and other body fluids, and so on. The goal is to improve your entire system, not just 1 part of it.

❻ Find out how waste is handled and disposed of.

Follow waste from where it is made, to where it is stored, and where it leaves the health center. Is the waste picked up regularly? How is it collected? Do waste handlers wear gloves, shoes, or other protective clothing? Is it transported in safe containers?

Waste handlers often sell whatever they can to junk dealers. This can be safe or dangerous depending on how waste is separated and disinfected. Do waste collectors pull reusable and recyclable materials out of the waste safely? Is there a way to make a safer system for those who make a living handling or selling waste?

Is the waste taken to a dump site or an incinerator? If possible, visit the place where waste is dumped. Does it remain separated, or is it mixed with other kinds of waste? Does it lead to health risks for the community, such as sharps in an open dump site?

❼ Take action!

What happens in the health center eventually touches everyone in the community. Taking even small steps to make waste handling safer will reduce harm to people and the environment. Which improvements are possible for the health center to make now? How can the health center influence what happens to waste once it is taken away to a landfill or incinerator?

❽ Regularly educate and train all workers.

The success of any safety plan relies on continuing to educate and train everyone who handles and creates health care waste. It is easy to become careless with safety practices when nothing harmful seems to happen. Repeating a waste assessment every year can help remind people of the importance of being careful.

Community Solutions

Some systems of waste collection, treatment, storage, transportation, and disposal are more costly than many health centers can afford. But if several centers in a region share resources, together they can create a waste handling system that is safer and more complete than any could do on their own. And if they can coordinate their purchases of supplies, they can better influence suppliers to offer health care supplies that produce less dangerous waste.

If your health center does not have an autoclave and a safe waste pit, wastes can be disinfected, separated into safe containers, and transported to a center that has a safe waste pit or sanitary landfill. A regional system of sharps collection, transport, and disposal can be organized to serve many health posts in both urban and rural areas.

If there is municipal waste collection in the area, disinfected waste can be collected and sent to the landfill. And toxic wastes can be sent to the toxic waste site (if there is one). If there is no waste collection in the area, consider working toward a community solid waste system (see Chapter 18). Which methods your center uses depends on what your resources are and what works best for you.

What happens in the health center eventually touches everyone in the community.

20 Preventing and Reducing Harm from Toxics

In this chapter:

Preventing and Reducing Harm from Toxics

As we learn more about the harmful effects of toxic chemicals on our health and our environment, more and more people are organizing to prevent harm and to find healthier and more sustainable ways of producing things.

Business owners, government leaders, and some scientists try to justify the dangers of toxic pollution by saying that a certain amount of risk is acceptable as the price of development and progress (so we can have electricity, medical care, transportation, computers, and so on). But what they do not tell us is that it is possible to have these benefits in ways that are safer for people and for the environment (see page 458). Rather than accepting unnecessary risks, we can choose to promote safer production of food, manufactured goods, and energy while still preventing toxic pollution as much as possible.

Avoiding and Controlling Toxics

Preventing exposure to toxic pollution begins with the precautionary principle (see page 32), which is thinking about the harm an action or product might cause before doing it or using it. While we can make personal and community decisions to avoid harm as much as possible, we also need to demand that business owners and our governments put the long-term health of all people, both rich and poor, and the environment before corporate and personal profit.

Many things we do every day affect how much we and others are exposed to toxics. There are some everyday exposures that we cannot control through personal decisions. But there are some exposures we can limit by making choices that help keep ourselves, our families, and our communities safer and healthier. Personal choices will often lead to community action, since we soon see how impossible it is for any one person to control the harm we are facing from toxics by ourselves.

To stop harm caused by toxics, we need to:

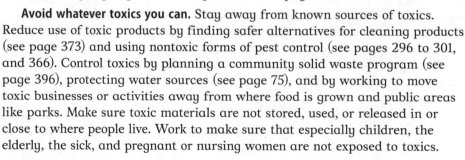

Educate ourselves. Learn and teach others what is toxic and how toxic substances cause harm. Read this book, talk with people, and learn from organizations providing information about toxics. Schools, health centers, workplaces, community centers, and our homes can all be places to educate the community about toxics and health. (For a community discussion activity on toxics, see page 468.)

Find sources of toxic exposure in our homes, water supply, neighborhoods, workplaces, schools, and region. To assess the impacts of toxic pollution on your community, do a trash walk (see page 391), do a health survey (see page 500), or set up a group to monitor pollution (see page 456).

Avoid whatever toxics you can. Stay away from known sources of toxics. Reduce use of toxic products by finding safer alternatives for cleaning products (see page 373) and using nontoxic forms of pest control (see pages 296 to 301, and 366). Control toxics by planning a community solid waste program (see page 396), protecting water sources (see page 75), and by working to move toxic businesses or activities away from where food is grown and public areas like parks. Make sure toxic materials are not stored, used, or released in or close to where people live. Work to make sure that especially children, the elderly, the sick, and pregnant or nursing women are not exposed to toxics.

We cannot choose what air we breathe, what water we drink, or what materials our employer makes us work with, and we often cannot know what we are being exposed to in the things we eat or the products we use. For this reason, we need to organize businesses and governments to reduce the use of toxics and the threat of toxic pollution. Many people working together in the shared belief that something is too harmful have the power to make change.

We can force companies to clean up

The responsibility for toxic pollution lies mostly with polluting industries like power plants, manufacturing, or oil and mineral extraction, while the burden of living with toxic pollution and cleaning it up usually falls on the people who live near the problem. Some communities have been able to shift the responsibility and show that a particular industry or company creates a problem and should clean it up and commit to safer practices. (For stories of communities that have forced companies to clean up, see pages 344, 465, 483, and 521.)

The chemicals we work with are making us sick.

The company could use fewer toxic chemicals and give us better protection.

But the company won't admit these chemicals are problems. It's up to us to make the company take our safety seriously.

Pressure governments for better safety standards

It is government's responsibility to protect people from pollution. But powerful corporations and international financial institutions pressure them to get rid of or ignore regulations about the use of toxics. It takes a lot of community pressure for governments to make and enforce laws that protect people, especially in countries struggling to attract businesses to invest there. But community-based campaigns can force changes in laws (see pages 417, 465, 466, 473 and 480) as well as use existing environmental laws (see Appendix B).

Press for changes in how products are made

Many industries have developed ways to replace toxic materials and production methods with ones that are more sustainable and less damaging to people's health and the environment. See page 458 for more about clean production methods and ways to influence businesses to adopt them.

Change consumption patterns

In the end, there is too much consuming by the wealthy. Less consumption and waste, using enough but not too much, is a big part of the solution.

Hidden Costs and Who Pays Them

Many industries that produce and use toxic materials tell people their materials and products are safe and necessary. But this is not true. Many chemicals and products that people once thought were safe and necessary, such as PVC plastic, leaded gasoline, or pesticides, are now known to cause great harm. And many toxic chemicals have safer alternatives, if industry would only seek them out and use them.

Industrial development has many "hidden costs" in the form of damage to the environment and health problems for people. These hidden costs are usually "paid for" by the people who must live with the harm from toxics, not by the industries that cause this harm. Allowing these costs to be disconnected from the businesses engaged in toxic-spreading activity is one way business protects and increases their profits. These profits are often very large, certainly big enough to support safer practices and protection of people's health.

The people who suffer the worst effects of industrial pollution are usually the workers in polluting industries. Also affected are those who live nearby and cannot move to less polluted places. Many health problems from toxics cannot be cured (see Chapter 16). So, even when someone can afford costly treatments, and most of us cannot, the harm to our health is often permanent. The real solution is to ban the use of very toxic materials and tightly regulate the use of toxics that are necessary and do not have safer replacements.

Industries must pay the cost for safer alternatives and better safeguards for workers, communities, and consumers everywhere.

The cycle of production and toxic waste

Even though industries are responsible for making and using toxic chemicals and toxic wastes, each of us, no matter whether we live in a small village or a large city, is affected by the global cycle of production and waste. Whether it is the plastic bags that are used by people worldwide (see page 389), or the many toxic substances and production methods that go into making a single computer, car, or cell phone, we are each connected to a worldwide cycle of toxic production and toxic waste.

Producing electronics — and toxic waste

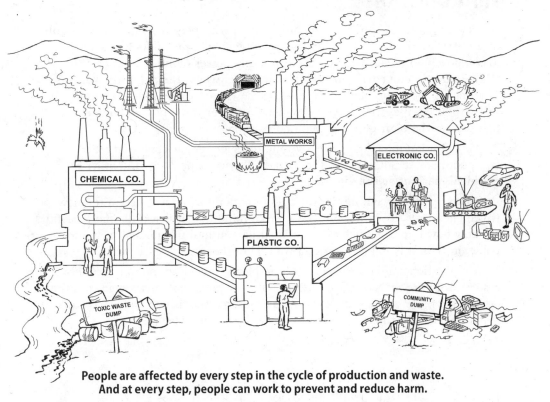

**People are affected by every step in the cycle of production and waste.
And at every step, people can work to prevent and reduce harm.**

Some common sources of industrial pollution

Oil refineries and electric power plants pollute air, water and soil with toxic chemicals and heavy metals. For more about refineries, see page 513.

Smelters release heavy metals like mercury and lead (see pages 338 and 357), and toxins like dioxin (see page 341).

Factories of all kinds may cause pollution, but can improve their safety by using clean production methods (see page 458).

Industrial waste dumps leak chemicals into soil and groundwater, causing serious problems for many years.

Incinerators release toxic chemicals into the air, water and soil (see page 423).

Small-scale industries such as tanneries, electroplating, garment, and battery manufacturers can cause pollution and serious health problems for both workers and people nearby (see pages 459 to 464).

Military bases and war zones cause devastating pollution, from radiation to dioxin, and leave harmful waste that may last for many generations.

Air Pollution

Air is polluted when it becomes contaminated with poisonous gases and small dust particles. Most air pollution is caused by burning **fossil fuels** (oil, coal, diesel, gasoline) to run engines, factories, and power plants (see page 526). Wind and rain can carry air pollution far from where the pollution was made. This causes health problems for people everywhere. Air pollution is usually worse in cities, industrial areas, low-lying areas or those circled by mountains, and places where air gets trapped and does not move well.

Air pollution may contain heavy metals such as mercury and lead (see pages 337 to 340, and 368 to 370), POPs (see page 340), and other toxic chemicals such as sulfur dioxide.

If you are doing community air pollution monitoring, it is useful to know which chemicals are in the air. But keep in mind that it is usually more useful to know how to protect yourself and your community from harm from air pollution than it is to know exactly what is in the air.

Air pollution causes serious health problems, including many cancers and respiratory illnesses (see pages 327 to 331). Air pollution causes acid rain that damages forests, water sources, and buldings, as well as our lungs. Also, air pollution is one of the main causes of global warming (see page 33).

Air pollution monitoring

Air pollution monitoring is a method used by a community during a campaign against a polluting business or industry. The monitoring allows many people to participate in the campaign as well as building a base of evidence that can be used to pressure the companies or industries to stop polluting.

Monitoring or checking for air pollution begins with your senses and your common sense. To know what effect air pollution is having in your community, ask people to keep a record of what they smell, see, hear, taste, or feel. The more people that do this, the better chance the community will have to identify and stop the pollution.

The bucket brigade method

Some communities monitor the air using a simple, low-cost method called the "bucket brigade." A 5 gallon plastic bucket with a valve and a special bag are used to take air samples. By opening the valve when there is a toxic release, or any time the air seems especially polluted, a small amount of air is sucked into the bag. The bag is then removed from the bucket and sent to a laboratory to find out what chemicals it contains. (See Resources.)

Having the air sample tested in a laboratory is the most costly part of the bucket brigade. Most countries do not have laboratories that can — or will — test the air sample properly, so it may need to be sent to Europe or the United States. Some communities raise money for a bucket brigade by collecting door-to-door, or by holding dances, parties, or house meetings.

Many communities use the bucket brigade along with other community organizing activities such as interviews and surveys. They also report toxic releases to the media and government, and try to force refineries and other polluting industries to use safer equipment and reduce emissions.

GroundWork's bucket brigade

Durban, South Africa, is a city surrounded by oil refineries and pipelines, a large chemical storage area, chemical plants, textile and paper factories, and toxic landfills. Every day, people in Durban are exposed to high levels of air pollution, water pollution, and all of the health problems that come with constant exposure to toxic chemicals. Industrial accidents, leaking storage tanks, and broken pipelines are common, causing fires and destruction of nearby wetlands and groundwater resources.

In 1999, a group called GroundWork formed to help people in Durban monitor air pollution. Using the bucket brigade method, the community began testing the air for toxics whenever there was a gas flare, an explosion, or a toxic release. Then they sent the bags full of air pollution to a laboratory in the United States for testing.

The lab tests found high levels of toxics, including sulfur dioxide, nitrogen oxide, and benzene. Test results from air samples collected near a school showed that children were exposed to levels of pollution as high as if they had stood all day, every day, on a busy highway.

The activists showed the test results to the government and the polluting industries, and also announced them on the radio, newspapers, and around the community. The state-run oil company said the tests were not accurate and took their own air samples. But when their samples were tested, they found even higher levels of poisons!

The bucket brigade method helped build a nationwide movement against pollution in South Africa. Under pressure from the growing environmental justice movement, the government passed the Air Quality Act in 2004. The city of Durban also set up its own air monitoring system. Since then, there has been a noticeable decrease in air pollution.

The bucket brigade helped community members feel stronger, braver, and more able to challenge polluting industries. With this increased confidence, they forced the government to listen to them.

There is still a serious pollution problem in South Africa. As chemical plants, refineries, and pipelines get older, the danger of accidents increases. But by combining strong community organization with a tool for collecting samples of toxic pollution, the people of Durban have made themselves safer. And they have shown the rest of their country and the world that people can make industry and government take responsibility for their pollution.

When there is a toxic release

Chemical plants, oil refineries, and other factories can have accidents that release large amounts of toxic chemicals very suddenly. Refineries also release toxic gases as part of 'regular maintenance.' A toxic release may look like a cloud of smoke or a large fire, or it simply may be a sudden strong smell. This can be frightening. It can also be deadly.

In the short term, there are steps people can take during and after every toxic release and chemical spill to reduce harm (see Appendix A). In the long term, it takes community organizing to pressure industries and governments to enforce better safety regulations.

During a toxic release:

- Depending on the situation and how quickly you can respond, sometimes it is safest to just stay indoors. In other situations, it is safer to leave the area as quickly as possible. Training and a good community emergency plan will help you know when to stay and when to leave.

- Make some kind of record. Mark the time of day the release happened, and how long it lasted. Also note any strange smells, sights, sounds, physical reactions (feelings in your body), and reactions of other people and animals nearby. This information may be useful later for taking community action.

- Take photos and video if it is safe to do so. These can be used later in court or campaigns.

After a toxic release:

- If people have been exposed to chemicals, help them go to a clinic or hospital right away.

- Contact local government and media to report what happened.

- Call a meeting to let everyone in the community know about what happened, and to organize a response.

- Encourage community members to share their experiences and feelings. This will help people to recover from the event and build solidarity in the community.

TUESDAY	WEDNESDAY	THURSDAY
14	2:25pm 15 White smoke from factory. Smell of rotten eggs.	16
21	22	23

Making notes directly onto a calendar is a good way to keep a record of toxic releases.

Clean Production

Technologies and methods exist to produce and sell products without causing pollution or toxic waste. **Clean production** protects people's health and the health of the environment.

How a paper factory uses clean production

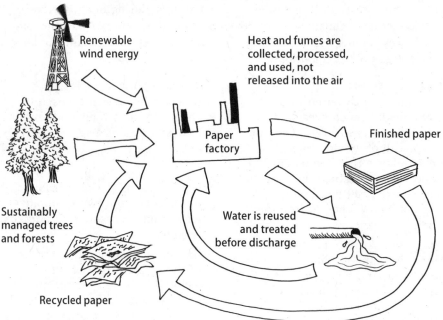

A paper factory uses trees, water, electricity, and chemicals such as chlorine. A clean production paper factory reduces pollution by using:

- mostly recycled paper, and trees from sustainably managed forests.
- a renewable source of energy (such as solar or wind energy) rather than electricity from fossil fuels such as oil or coal.
- no chlorine or other toxic chemicals.
- as little water as possible. Water is reused several times and then treated to make it safe to put back in the environment.

Most industries can use a clean production process. Heat from factories can be used to generate electricity, and waste products from one process can often be used as materials in another. Clean production can reduce waste to almost nothing. And because clean production reuses materials and energy, it also saves money.

But because companies usually do not pay to clean up or prevent the pollution and harm they cause, they usually must be forced by popular pressure or government regulation to change to clean production methods.

Promoting cleaner businesses

When business owners and workers understand how chemicals and industrial waste can harm them and everyone in the community, they are often willing to make changes in production materials and methods to reduce harm. Sometimes, however, it is necessary to pressure them in both positive and negative ways to achieve changes that will benefit community health. There are various ways to influence business to choose cleaner production methods.

Government can: ban or regulate the use of toxic chemicals and dangerous production processes; refuse to purchase products that are produced in harmful ways; provide funds to businesses to change to cleaner production methods; charge less taxes to businesses that use clean production, and collect more taxes from businesses that use harmful methods.

People can: educate themselves, business owners, and workers about the dangers of toxics and the benefits of cleaner production methods; boycott (refuse to buy) products made by a company or sold by a business that is polluting; let others know about nontoxic alternatives that can be substituted for toxic products; use the media to both denounce toxic corporate practices and celebrate the successes of nontoxic, sustainable businesses.

Workers can: learn about, follow, and enforce rules about safe handling of toxics, and write protections against toxics for workers and the community into their union contracts.

Cleaner small businesses

Sometimes, small business owners do not fully understand the harm toxics can cause. When they and their workers use, store, and dispose of toxic chemicals in unsafe ways, they are usually just trying to save money, time, and labor. After all, many businesspeople live in the same communities they are polluting, and are friends and neighbors of the people affected. Or they may know about cleaner production methods but feel they cannot afford the cost of making changes. But over time, the high costs of health care for injured workers and environmental clean-up for damage in the community will often end up costing more time and money, rather than saving it.

When small businesses change to cleaner production practices, they help make the entire community, and their future as a business, more sustainable.

Dyeing

Many dyes are made with heavy metals and other toxic chemicals. The waste from making dyes is often poured into waterways, filling them with pollutants that are dangerous and difficult to clean up.

How to reduce pollution

Small businesses in the dye industry can reduce harmful waste by following these guidelines:

- Avoid the most toxic dyes, such as azo dyes, and look for safer alternatives. Azo dyes, known to cause birth defects, are commonly used in printing, textiles, paper manufacturing, pharmaceuticals, and food industries.
- Control the amount of toxics used.
- Reuse byproducts from dyeing as materials to make other products.
- Reuse cleaning water to make the next batch of dye.
- Use high-pressure hoses for cleaning to reduce the amount of wastewater.
- Label and store toxic materials in secure areas away from waterways.

Tanneries

Leather tanneries use large amounts of water, salts, and toxic chemicals, such as different forms of chromium. At the end of the tanning process, these chemicals are often dumped as waste into rivers and other waterways. As a result, communities around tanneries often have highly contaminated drinking water.

In the short term, these toxics can cause bronchitis, asthma, and other breathing problems. In the long term, repeated exposures can cause birth defects and cancers.

How to reduce pollution

Some tanneries use nontoxic or less toxic production methods. Traditional methods of tanning use animal parts for safer and cleaner tanning. For tanneries that use chromium, there are ways to recover and recycle chromium so that less is used, and less ends up as waste. This reduces costs as well as toxic pollution. The water used in tanning baths can be recycled, and the wastewater can be treated to make it safer before dumping.

Cleaner production in tanneries

The city of León, México is famous for its high quality leather shoes. The tanneries in León are small businesses, important to the economic survival of the community. Unfortunately, the tanning operations used to dump chemical waste directly into local waterways, causing serious illness.

Over many years, León passed laws to regulate the pollution, but the tanneries almost never obeyed them. Many tannery owners thought reducing pollution was too costly and would hurt their businesses.

However, when thousands of birds died from pollution in a wetland near León, the local trade organization representing the tanneries began to look for ways to reduce pollution without hurting business. This was when they learned about clean production.

Over the next several years, the trade organization helped the tanneries reduce pollution, and many of the tanneries changed their practices. They did not do this only because they wanted to protect local drinking water or migrating birds. They also did it because they saw that clean production could save them money and produce higher quality leather.

Tanneries in Africa and Asia worked with the United Nations Industrial Development Organization (UNIDO) to find different ways to recover and reuse the chemicals used in tanning. UNIDO's Cleaner Production Project showed that more than half of the pollution from tanneries could be reduced through careful and efficient use of natural resources – using smaller amounts and using them with greater care.

The tanneries of León learned from the UNIDO project and began to practice cleaner production methods. First, they used a new process in which more of the chromium in the tanning bath came in contact with the hide, and less ended up as waste. Next, an enzyme (a natural product that causes chemical changes) replaced the harmful chemicals used to soften hides. Some tanneries that produced lower quality leather began using vegetable tanning rather than chromium tanning, eliminating a very toxic and costly part of the process.

Tanneries that could find no alternative for chromium began reusing it, rather than dumping it after the first use. The same was done with the large amounts of chemical-filled water. Some tanneries built wastewater treatment systems to clean the water and recycle it for reuse, protecting and preserving water resources.

Now the leather workers of León know about clean production. When you ask them why they use these new methods, they may tell you it is to protect local waterways. But they will also tell you they now produce higher quality leather for a lower cost than before.

A taste of clean production

The beautiful views from the hills of San Francisco, USA, attract tourists from around the world. So does the variety of foods served by its many small restaurants. But with so many restaurants, waste oil from cooking became a problem, clogging sewers and costing the city money. The city requires that all restaurants use a "grease trap" to prevent oil from entering the sewers, but emptying and cleaning grease traps is expensive. Many small businesses owned by recent immigrants can not afford it.

San Francisco's Public Utilities Commission, in charge of the city's sewers, decided that instead of charging large fines to restaurants for not disposing of their oil properly, they would offer a solution. They would collect the waste oil and use it to run city buses!

When the diesel engine was invented, it burned light fuels such as vegetable oil. But because petroleum was cheap and plentiful, and the companies that produced it were powerful, most diesel engines began to use petroleum. Now, with the serious pollution and global warming caused by petroleum, people are returning to vegetable oil as a cleaner and less costly fuel.

Vegetable oil can be used after making a few changes to a diesel engine, or the oil can be turned into "biodiesel," which can be used with no changes. Burning biodiesel dramatically reduces the air pollution that causes asthma and cancer, and it does not cause global warming. Compared to other fuels, such as natural gas, it is also less expensive.

Making biofuels by recycling waste oil is different than growing a new crop just for fuel. It keeps a waste product out of the sewers and puts it to use.

To make clean production work, the San Francisco Public Utilities Commission hired native speakers of many languages to visit restaurants and collect waste oil. The restaurant owners no longer pay to get rid of their oil, and the city benefits by having fewer clogged sewers and cheaper fuel for its buses.

Now, instead of smelling like traffic, the streets of San Francisco smell like fried food. Which brings more tourists than ever to local restaurants.

Unsafe Disposal of Toxic Wastes

Companies that do not use clean production methods often produce a lot of toxic wastes. For some industries, like the chemical industry and the mining and oil industries, toxic waste may be their biggest product!

Because toxic wastes can be extremely costly and difficult to dispose of safely, dangerous dumping of wastes is common. And not surprisingly, the dumping usually adds yet another source of illness to the burden of health problems faced by people in poor communities.

More and more businesses are being organized to keep toxic products out of the waste by recycling some or all of their parts. But even environmentally friendly activities such as recycling must be done carefully to prevent toxic materials from harming workers and the environment.

Making sure industries dispose of wastes responsibly is only one part of the solution. To truly end the problem of toxic waste, we must change the way industry works. The only safe way to dispose of toxic waste is to stop creating it in the first place.

The African Stockpiles Project

Corporations and development agencies have promoted pesticides to farmers for decades as part of a solution to hunger. But many scientists and farmers now recognize that pesticides create more problems than they solve. Who will dispose of these deadly chemicals? How can it be done safely?

In countries across Africa, more than 50,000 tons of unused and unwanted pesticides and other toxic wastes are stored in leaking containers. To clean up these toxics and to prevent the dumping of more poisons, a group of government agencies and international organizations formed the African Stockpiles Programme (ASP).

The groups in the ASP have different ideas about how to clean up the waste. Some say the easiest and cheapest way is to burn it. The World Bank and several governments are building incinerators to do this. Other groups in the ASP say burning these wastes would release more poisons into the air and water, and suggest safer disposal methods. As of now, there are no truly safe ways to destroy these chemicals. Developing safer methods will be costlier than burning and will take time.

As the ASP works to solve this problem, toxic wastes blow in the wind and leak into groundwater. These poisons and the sicknesses they cause are part of the deadly legacy of the chemical companies and development agencies that made them and promoted their use.

Battery recycling

Lead acid batteries from cars are commonly recycled for the metals they contain. In most places, this is not an organized industrial process, but is done in homes and backyards. Battery recycling creates serious lead pollution, damaging health and the environment. Short-term exposure to high levels of lead can cause vomiting, diarrhea, convulsions (seizures, "fits"), coma, or even death (see pages 368 to 370).

In some places, small household batteries are taken apart and the black powder inside is used to make dyes, inks, and cosmetics. This powder is very poisonous. It is made of cadmium, lead, zinc, mercury, and other toxic heavy metals. The powder should be handled with gloves and face masks, disposed of safely, and never reused.

Reducing harm

The best way to reduce exposure to toxins in batteries is for battery producers to collect used batteries and make sure they are recycled under safe conditions. Some countries have laws regulating safe battery recycling.

Electronics recycling

Producing electronic equipment, such as computers, televisions, cell phones, and radios, requires a large amount of resources. Electronic equipment also contains many toxics such as lead, cadmium, barium, mercury, flame retardants (see page 372), PCBs, and PVC plastic (see page 341).

Electronics often end up in landfills where the toxics they contain leach into groundwater. Or they are taken apart and the materials they contain are recycled, often by hand, using dangerous solvents. This causes serious health problems for the people doing the recycling, and moves the toxic materials into other products that will cause more health problems later.

The safest solution is to require companies that produce electronics to take responsibility for safe recycling and to redesign their products to use less harmful materials and to last longer. And the people who buy and use electronic products can reduce harmful waste by having them fixed when they break rather than throwing them out.

Wearing masks, gloves, and other protective equipment will help protect people who recycle computer parts.

Toxic trade

Toxic trade is the export from one country to another of toxic wastes and harmful materials. Because rich countries often try to dump their waste far away, and because governments of poor countries are often powerless to stop them, toxic trade most often means rich countries and rich communities dumping their waste on poorer countries and poorer communities.

Despite international agreements to protect health and the environment, toxic trade is part of global business. Even though they are harmful, products such as tobacco, pesticides, GE foods, asbestos, leaded gas, broken electronics, and others are commonly sent from rich countries to poorer ones.

Some toxic trade is banned by international law (see page 467). But as many health and human rights activists know, laws only protect people when people organize to enforce them.

Take your toxic waste and go home

The Khian Sea was a ship loaded with 14,000 tons of toxic incinerator ash from the city of Philadelphia in the United States, to be dumped anywhere outside the United States. But wherever it went, people rejected it.

First the ship went to the Bahamas, then the Dominican Republic, but these countries did not accept the waste. It sailed on to Honduras, Bermuda, Guinea-Bissau, and the Netherlands Antilles. But no country wanted the toxic ash.

Desperate to unload, the ship's crew lied about their cargo. Sometimes they said the ash was construction material or roadfill. But environmental activists kept one step ahead of the ship, letting the countries know what was really in the ash. No one would take it until it got to Haiti. There, the US-backed government allowed the ash, now called "fertilizer," into the country. 4000 tons of the ash were dumped onto the beach in the town of Gonaives, Haiti.

Before long, public outcry forced Haitian officials to admit they were not getting fertilizer. They ordered the waste returned to the ship. But the Khian Sea had already slipped away in the night.

For 2 years, the Khian Sea went from country to country trying to dispose of the remaining 10,000 tons of ash. The crew was even ordered to paint over the ship's name. Still, no country was fooled into taking the toxic cargo. A crew member later testified in court that much of the waste was dumped into the Indian Ocean. In the end, 2000 tons of the ash was put in a landfill back in Philadelphia, thanks to years of effort by activists.

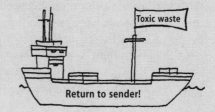

Urban construction can unearth toxic waste

Unfortunately, ignoring toxic waste doesn't make it go away. When new development projects are begun in cities, usually people are excited about the new markets, housing, recreation, and jobs that will be created. But especially when these projects are built where a factory or military base had been, people must be careful to make sure that the very ground itself has not become a toxic waste dump. And if it has, the toxic wastes must be disposed of safely.

A home run for health

When the city of San Diego, USA, began to build a new stadium, fans of the San Diego Padres baseball team were excited. The new stadium would be better for watching games, and building it would bring jobs to the community. But an environmental impact assessment (EIA) showed the project would also have bad affects on the environment and people's health.

The proposed site was contaminated with toxic chemicals. The plan called for the toxic soil to be dug up and burned right in the middle of the city. Members of a local group, the Environmental Health Coalition (EHC), knew this would cause serious health problems. So they organized the community to demand an alternative.

EHC and community members asked city officials to reject the plan, but the city denied their request. The community then organized more than 100 residents to protest at the building site. When the local media reported it, the San Diego Padres looked like they did not care about their fans. Soon the owners of the team agreed to find another way to get rid of the toxic soil.

The EHC also showed how the new stadium would cause an increase in traffic, air pollution, and asthma among neighborhood children. After many meetings, the Environmental Health Coalition helped develop new, healthier building plans.

Even when public meetings are scheduled and environmental impact assessments are produced, this does not mean that a project will be free from harm. In the case of the San Diego stadium, the developers wanted to go ahead with the project even though they knew about the harm from burning toxic soil and the problems with the stadium plans. It took an organized and dedicated group to study the reports, attend the meetings, and protest in the streets to get the government to reduce harm.

Many people in San Diego pay attention to every game the Padres play. Now they can support their team and know it has not made them sick.

International agreements on toxic waste disposal

For years, rich countries of North America and Europe used Africa, Asia, Latin America, and Eastern Europe as toxic dumping grounds without any legal pressure to stop. Finally, community action in the poorer countries, together with pressure from environmentalists around the world, won international agreements outlawing toxic trade.

The first agreement was the Basel Convention on the Control of Transboundary Movements of Hazardous Wastes and their Disposal (1992). This was won mostly because of the activists who followed the Khian Sea, the ship that traveled around the world trying to dump its cargo of toxic ash. Countries that sign the Basel Convention agree to treat, reuse, and dispose of toxic wastes as close as possible to where they are made, rather than shipping them to other countries.

In 2001, 92 nations signed the Stockholm Convention on Persistent Organic Pollutants (POPs, see page 340). It bans production and use of the 12 most harmful POPs (called "the Dirty Dozen") and makes trading them illegal, unless the use of a certain chemical will prevent more harm than it causes (such as targeted use of DDT to control malaria, see page 150).

A third agreement passed in 2004, the Rotterdam Convention on Prior Informed Consent, requires a country to notify and get permission from another country when it wants to export harmful chemicals.

When people know about and use these agreements, they can be an important tool to make our world healthier and more just. But there are many ways for countries and corporations to get around the law. For more information on ways to use these and other national and international laws in your struggles for environmental health, see Appendix B.

Snakes and ladders game

Snakes and ladders is a popular board game used in health education. This version can be played to show the ways that toxics harm us, and how to prevent and reduce harm. You can make your own game board by copying the game board below onto large paper, cardboard, or wood.

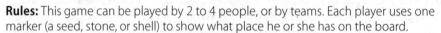

Materials: Dice, and seeds, stones, or shells as game markers, and a game board

Rules: This game can be played by 2 to 4 people, or by teams. Each player uses one marker (a seed, stone, or shell) to show what place he or she has on the board.

The first player throws the dice and moves his or her marker according to the number shown, beginning from square 1, marked START.

If a player rolls a 6, the player move 6 spaces and then rolls the dice for a second turn. Otherwise, the dice moves to the next player.

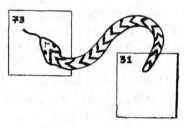

If a marker lands on the head of a snake, the player reads the message on the square out loud, then moves the marker to the snake tail, and reads the message on that square. The player's next turn starts from there.

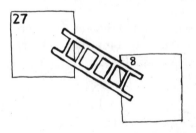

If a marker lands at the bottom of a ladder, the player reads the message on the square out loud, then moves the marker to the top of the ladder, and reads the message on that square. The player's next turn starts from there.

The first player to reach the last square wins. A player must throw the exact number needed to land on the final square.

This game works best when you adapt the messages on the "snake squares" so they refer to health problems and toxics in your community. Also adapt the messages on the "ladders squares" to possible actions to reduce exposure and other solutions relevant to your community.

Encourage the players to discuss the problems (snakes) and solutions (ladders) they land on during the game. When the game is over, ask if there are other problems with toxics that were not mentioned, and what actions people can take to protect their health.

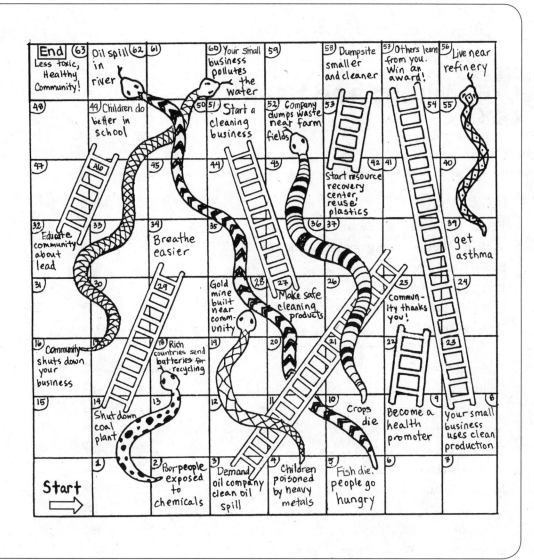

End (63) Less toxic, Healthy Community!	Oil spill (62) in river	61	Your small (60) business pollutes the water	59	Dumpsite (58) smaller and cleaner	Others learn (57) from you. Win an award!	Live near (56) refinery	
48	Children do (49) better in school	50	Start a (51) cleaning business	Company (52) dumps waste near farm fields	53	42	41	40
47	46	45	44	43	Start resource recovery center, reuse plastics		54	55
Educate (32) community about lead	33	Breathe (34) easier	35	36	37		get (39) asthma	
31	30	29	Gold (28) mine built near community	27	Make safe (26) cleaning products	Community thanks you! (25)	24	
Community (16) shuts down your business	14	Rich (18) countries send batteries for recycling	19	20	21	22	Become a (9) health promoter	Your small (8) business uses clean production
15	Shut down (14) coal plant	13	12	11	Crops (10) die			
Start →	1	Poor people (2) exposed to chemicals	Demand (3) oil company clean oil spill	Children (4) poisoned by heavy metals	Fish die, (5) people go hungry	6	7	

For more information on creating and using board games, see Chapter 11 of Hesperian's **Helping Health Workers Learn.**

21 Mining and Health

Mining and Health

People mine the earth for metals such as gold, silver, and copper; for gems such as diamonds and rubies; and for minerals such as uranium, asbestos, coal, sand, and salt. All mining is dangerous, and it is difficult for miners to earn a livelihood while also protecting their health and the environment. But there are ways to make mining safer and to pressure the mining industry to do less harm.

Mining is done in very large open-pit surface mines or deep underground mines operated by large corporations, as well as in small-scale mines run by local people. Large-scale mining causes greater damage because it requires clearing large amounts of land, digging huge pits and tunnels, and moving massive amounts of earth. But small-scale mining can also hurt people and the environment.

Mining conditions are very different depending on the location, type, and size of the mining operation. By understanding mining's threats to health and long-term well-being, and by taking precautions to reduce harm in all mines, miners and other people in mining communities can better protect their health and improve their lives.

Health Problems from Mining

Mining causes serious accidents such as fires, explosions, or collapsed mine tunnels that affect miners and people living in communities near mines. Even in places where mining happened long ago, people can still be exposed to health threats from mining waste and chemicals that remain in the soil and water. Mining damages health in many ways:

- **Dust, chemical spills, harmful fumes, heavy metals and radiation** can poison workers and cause life-long health problems.

- **Heavy lifting** and working with the body in awkward positions can lead to injuries to the arms, legs, and back.

- **Use of jackhammers or other vibrating machinery** can cause damage to nerves and blood circulation, and lead to loss of feeling, very dangerous infections such as gangrene, and even death.

- **Loud, constant noise** from machines can cause hearing problems, including deafness.

- **Long hours working** underground with little light can harm vision.

- **Working in very hot conditions** without drinking enough water can cause heat stress. Signs of heat stress include: dizziness, weakness, rapid heartbeat, extreme thirst, and fainting.

When working in the heat, drink as much clean water as possible, and rest in the shade often.

- **Water pollution and overuse of water** resources leads to many health problems (see Chapters 5 and 6).

- **Land and soil are destroyed,** leading to food scarcity and hunger.

- **Air pollution** from power plants and smelting factories built near mines causes serious illness (see Chapter 16).

Mining and sickness among the Dineh

The Dineh tribe and other Native people from the deserts of the western United States tell of 2 kinds of yellow powder the Creator put in the ground. One kind is the yellow pollen of maize. For the Dineh, maize is a sacred food, and its pollen is used in religious rituals. The other yellow powder is known as "yellow cake," or uranium. The Dineh believe that uranium was supposed to stay under the ground and never be dug up or used.

In the 1940s, when the US government discovered how uranium could be used to make nuclear weapons and nuclear energy, mining companies began to dig for uranium on Dineh land. Young Dineh men, who had formerly earned their living raising sheep, eagerly took jobs in the new mines. Uranium mining quickly became one of the most important ways Dineh people earned money. But over the years, uranium mining made many Dineh people very ill.

The government and the mining companies knew the dangers of uranium mining, but the miners and their families had to find out about the dangers on their own. Dineh miners died young from the harmful effects of radiation. Many women had miscarriages or had children with birth defects and other health problems. Men who worked in the mines developed lung cancer and breathing problems. Some lost the ability to walk. Even cattle and sheep near the mines grew sick and died before they could give milk or wool.

These problems continued for over 50 years. In 2005, the Dineh finally banned uranium mining on their land. But Dineh land still has hundreds of abandoned uranium mines and piles of toxic waste. The US government is paying some families of people who died from uranium poisoning, but not very much. And there is great pressure from the nuclear industry for the Dineh to open more mines.

Dineh land also has some of the largest deposits of coal in the United States. With the loss of jobs from closing the uranium mines, coal mining has become one of the only sources of well-paying jobs for Dineh men. But coal mining is also dangerous to health as well as the environment, both when it is dug out of the ground and when it is burned to make electricity in power plants.

Like many people, the Dineh are being asked to choose between poor health and poverty. Many things must change for the Dineh to have better choices, especially an end to the racism that denies Native people the right to control their own communities, resources, and futures. And the whole world, but especially the United States, must use less harmful ways of producing energy than coal and uranium.

Social Problems

Mining affects people's health directly, when people work in dangerous conditions and are exposed to toxic chemicals. It also affects people's health through the social problems it brings. Mining towns and camps develop quickly, with little planning or care. This usually causes many problems. Men come looking for work in the mines, women who need income become sex workers, and this combination can lead to the rapid passing of HIV/AIDS and other sexually transmitted infections. The sudden wealth and sudden poverty that mining brings is often accompanied by increased violence against women and children, abuse of workers by mine owners, and fights for control over resources. Many people are forced to leave the community by the violence or because it becomes impossible for them to continue living as they did before the mine opened.

Mining provides a livelihood for millions of people, often in areas where there are few other sources of income. But riches in the ground do not always result in wealth for miners. The nature of the mining industry is to exploit every last piece of earth and every available worker, sacrificing the health, human rights, and environment of mining communities.

Women bear an enormous share of the costs to people and the environment from large mining projects.

Joining or forming a workers organization has proven to be the most effective strategy for miners to earn a decent living, and to defend their human and environmental rights. Miners' unions have forced companies and governments to make and follow rules that protect miners' health and safety. However, unions often place more importance on miners' short-term needs for jobs and income than on preventing long-term health problems caused by mining and mineral use (for example, pollution from burning coal for energy).

The union protects my health, my job, and my benefits. When the company is so big and powerful, workers have to get organized.

When a mining operation is too dangerous, unhealthy, or polluting, it should be shut down. But mine workers should not be abandoned to unemployment and poverty. Plans for their well-being and livelihood should be included in plans for and costs of shutting down the mine.

Protecting Children

Children often work in mining to help their families. Working long hours under difficult conditions is dangerous for them, creates serious problems for their growing bodies and soft bones, and leaves them no time to go to school. Child labor is illegal under international law (see Appendix B.)

If mining companies provided good wages and benefits for adult workers, children could go to school instead of to work.

School and nutrition for child miners

When men and women go to work in the stone quarries in India, their children often go to work with them. This is the way it has always been. Without education and organizing for change, this is the way it will always be.

In Pune, India, the children who work in the stone quarry are malnourished and covered from head to toe in rock dust. Some social workers started a volunteer group called Santulan to work with these children. "Children have basic rights to education, good health, and childhood," they said. To promote these rights they started schools in the quarries.

First, Santulan trained new teachers. Some women quarry workers were taught songs and other teaching methods, and given pencils, paper, chalkboards, and books. Some quarry owners offered spaces for Santulan to hold classes. In other quarries, the workers themselves organized classrooms.

Once the children started going to school, the teachers realized they would not learn without food to eat during the day. Santulan began to provide rice, lentils, and boiled eggs. This gave the parents another reason to let their children go to school. Not only did the children learn, but they came home with full bellies.

A few years after the quarry schools opened, over 3000 children were participating in classes. Many are the first in their families to read and write. The children sing songs, learn history, and, above all, learn they have the right to education and the right to childhood.

Illnesses from Dust

Lung damage caused by rock and mineral dust is a major health problem. Whether you are mining underground or above ground, you may develop lung damage if:

- dust covers your clothes, body, and equipment as you work.
- you cough a lot and have trouble breathing.

Once dust has damaged the lungs, there is no way to reverse the damage. Dust is a threat both to mineworkers and to communities near mines.

The most dangerous kinds of dust are coal dust, which causes **black lung disease,** and silica dust, which causes **silicosis.** Dust that contains asbestos (page 371) or heavy metals (page 337) is also dangerous.

Signs of lung damage

Dust from mining can make it difficult to breathe. Large amounts of dust can make the lungs fill with fluid and swell up. Signs of lung damage from dust include:

- shortness of breath, coughing, wheezing
- coughing up green or yellow sputum (mucus that comes up from the lungs)
- sore throat

- bluish skin at ears or lips
- fever
- chest pain
- loss of appetite
- tiredness

Black lung disease and silicosis, as well as asbestosis (see page 371), are serious conditions with no cure. It is best to prevent exposure to harmful dust. Because these diseases worsen very quickly, by the time you have signs all you can do is keep the disease from getting worse. If you have any of the signs above, or have been exposed to these kinds of dust, see a health worker right away.

Because smoking greatly increases the risk of lung damage from dust, it is particularly important that miners do not smoke tobacco.

Black lung disease and silicosis

Black lung is caused when coal dust blocks the lungs, causing severe and permanent breathing problems. Underground coal miners, and children and women who work separating rocks from coal, are most affected by black lung.

Silicosis is caused by exposure to silica dust. Silica is a common mineral released from sand and rocks during mining, exposing many miners to harm.

Treatment

Black lung and silicosis cannot be cured. But you can reduce the suffering they cause.

- Drink plenty of water to help loosen mucus from the lungs.

- Keep breathing passages open. Fill a bowl with steaming hot water and strong-smelling herbs such as eucalyptus, oregano, mint, or thyme. Put your head over the bowl, cover yourself with a towel or cloth, and breathe the vapors. Do this for 15 minutes at a time, several times a day.

- Medicines called **bronchodilators** can help open the breathing passages. The kinds that are inhaled work fastest.

- Hospitals may give oxygen to help a person breathe more easily.

- Home-made cough syrup can reduce painful coughing. Mix:

| 1 part honey | 1 part lemon juice | Take a teaspoonful every 2 or 3 hours |

- Some people believe dairy foods like milk, cheese, and butter make mucus thicker and more difficult to cough up. If eating these foods makes you feel worse, avoid them as long as you can get good nutrition from other foods.

IMPORTANT: **It is not true** that drinking alcohol clears the lungs of dust. Drinking alcohol only makes health problems worse.

Related health problems

People with black lung disease or silicosis have a higher risk of developing other health problems such as:

- tuberculosis (TB) (see pages 356 and 481)
- chronic bronchitis (see page 331)

- heart disease
- lung cancer
- pneumonia
- asthma (see page 331)

- rheumatoid arthritis
- lupus
- rheumatic fever
- sclerosis

See a general health book like *Where There Is No Doctor* for more information.

Preventing harm from dust

By limiting the amount of dust you breathe in, lung damage can be prevented.

Mine operators should provide equipment to reduce dust in mines

- Pump fresh air into underground mines. Mines should have many openings to the surface. Air pumps and fans can bring fresh air in and push dust and dirty air out.

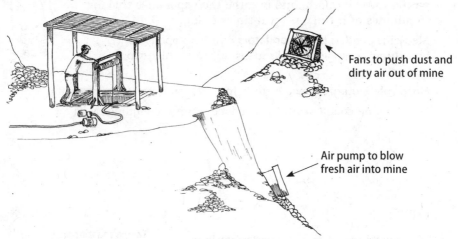

Fans to push dust and dirty air out of mine

Air pump to blow fresh air into mine

- Provide water sprinklers to damp down dust. Store water in a tank above, and pump it or let it run down into shafts and tunnels through pipes with small holes or shower heads. "Sour water" not fit for drinking works fine. Howver, miners need plenty of fresh water to drink.
- Provide cutting and grinding equipment that sprays water to trap dust.

Mine operators should provide materials to protect miners from breathing dust

- Provide supplies such as crushed limestone and blankets to cover blasting areas.
- Provide proper masks and make sure they are cleaned and maintained (see Appendix A).

Workers need a place to change out of dusty clothes and bathe before leaving the mine site, and a clean area to store clothes. Mine operators also have a responsibility to find ways to keep dust from mining operations out of the surrounding communities.

IMPORTANT: Dust can kill. Miners have a right to demand that all possible methods are used to reduce dust, including protective equipment provided by the company. Dust masks prevent lung damage only if they fit tightly and are cleaned often. If you use a paper mask, change it often. If you use a plastic or cloth mask, or a bandana, wash it often.

Regular use and cleaning of dust masks can prevent lung damage.

Miners can reduce the amount of dust they breathe in

- **Wet surfaces before cutting or drilling** to prevent dust from rising.

- **Spread crushed limestone** to prevent silica or coal dust from rising into the air.

- **Cover blasting and grinding areas with a wet blanket or tarp** to trap dust. After blasting or grinding, spray the area with water.

- **Let dust settle** after blasting and before entering an area.

- **Wear protective clothes and equipment.** The best mask for miners is a rubber respirator that fits tightly and has filters for the materials you work with. Miners should receive training in how to choose, use, and maintain masks. If no dust mask is available, wear a cloth around your mouth and nose, and wash it daily. Glasses or goggles will protect your eyes. (For more information on protective equipment, see Appendix A.)

- **Wash hands and face before eating, drinking, or smoking, and during and after work.**

- **Wash gear often.** Do not shake out dusty bags — this throws more dust into the air. Wash the bag instead. If you must shake the bag, make sure the wind carries dust away from you. Cloth bags trap a lot of dust — use plastic bags if you can.

Prevent mine dust from entering your home

- Wash after work and before entering the house.

- Leave dusty work clothes at the mine, or change out of them before entering your home.

- Clean floors with a damp mop to remove dust. Sweeping will put dust in the air.

- If it is dusty outside, keep doors and windows closed. If your house does not have doors and windows that close, hang curtains or large banana leaves in doors and windows.

Treatment for miners with silicosis

Lal Kuan is a village in India dedicated to mining and stone crushing. Everything in Lal Kuan is covered by a thick layer of dust. The dust is so bad it is difficult to see. For many people, the dust has also made it difficult to breathe.

Budh Ram came to Lal Kuan 20 years ago to operate stone-crushing machines. After 10 years of work, he began to have difficulty breathing. He was treated for TB by a government clinic. The TB drugs helped him for a year, but after that he began to get sick again. Budh Ram was not alone in his illness. Despite getting treated many times for TB, many workers and villagers died with terrible pain in their chests, unable to breathe.

When S.A. Azad, coordinator of an organization called People's Rights and Social Research Centre, came to Lal Kuan, his goal was to teach the villagers to read and write. But when he saw they were dying in great numbers, he took on a different task: to help the villagers get treatment and compensation for their illness.

Azad realized that workers were being treated for TB, but they were dying of silicosis. Most workers, like Budh Ram, did not even know what silicosis was. And mine operators did not want to know about silicosis, because under Indian law they were responsible for illnesses caused in the workplace. For mine operators, it was best if no one knew the workers were dying of silicosis.

Azad contacted other organizations to build support for the people affected by silicosis, and to demand compensation and health care. After several years of organizing, the Chief Minister of Delhi agreed to hold a meeting to hear of the misery in Lal Kuan. The meeting resulted in a great victory when the Chief Minister agreed to meet the demands of Azad and the people of Lal Kuan.

Now, after many years of suffering, the people of Lal Kuan have a community center for the treatment of work-related diseases. A mobile medical van visits the area 4 days a week giving free medical care. The government has promised to do a health survey in Lal Kuan and to give a pension to all victims of silicosis, as well as training and support to help them find other ways to earn money and support their families.

This victory has given the miners and villagers a new sense of empowerment. The air in Lal Kuan is still full of dust. But it is also full of possibility for a better future.

Tuberculosis (TB)

Because miners often live in crowded conditions, work long hours without enough food, and have little access to health care or medicines, they have a high risk of getting TB. Signs of TB include a bad cough that will not go away, fever, coughing up blood, feeling weak, weight loss, and night sweats. Without proper treatment, a person can spread TB to others and can die.

TB can be fatal to anyone, but is especially dangerous for people weak from hunger or other illnesses like HIV/AIDS. Lung damage from dust increases the risk of TB even more.

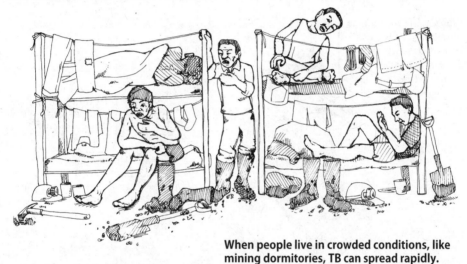

When people live in crowded conditions, like mining dormitories, TB can spread rapidly.

Good **ventilation** will reduce the chance of TB spreading through a mine, miners' dormitories, or homes. The best way to prevent TB among miners, or any workers, is to create the conditions for good health through:

- better pay
- shorter work hours
- safer work conditions
- safe, clean living conditions
- clean water
- healthy food
- good health care

To prevent the spread of TB, it is important to make sure everyone with TB gets proper treatment and medicine. Many governments provide free TB treatment; to get medications, see a health worker. (For more information on TB, see page 356 or a general health book such as *Where There Is No Doctor.*)

Contaminated Water

Mining uses large amounts of water and leaves large amounts of waste, contaminating water sources and the people who depend on them. While all mining operations tend to pollute water, big companies usually cause the biggest problems. Surface water and groundwater in mining areas may remain contaminated for many years. Water loss can leave the land barren and unusable for farming or raising animals. The long-term damage of water contamination will last much longer than the short-term economic gain from mining.

Preventing and reducing water pollution

Leaking waste ponds are one of the main causes of water pollution from mining. To prevent pollution, waste ponds should be:

- built away from water sources or watershed drainage areas.
- lined to prevent leaks into groundwater.
- built according to the best international standards.
- monitored to prevent leaks and spills.
- emptied of wastes and safely closed when mining operations end.

Cleaning water once it has been polluted by mining is difficult, costly, and not always successful.

Community action saves a river

In the northern Philippines, the Abra River runs from high in the mountains through lowland farms and into the China Sea. For many generations, communities along the Abra River made their living from farming, fishing, handicrafts, and small-scale mining of gold and copper. In recent years, large corporations have begun mining the area's gold, causing great harm to the river, the wildlife, and the people who live there.

Mining companies cleared forests to dig the mines, causing the river and the streams that feed it to fill with silt and dry up. Many kinds of birds, animals, and plants have disappeared. The river has been poisoned by chemicals spilled from waste ponds and from acid mine drainage. People living along the Abra River suffer from headaches, dizziness, coughing, chest pain, nose and eye irritation, skin rashes and diarrhea, as well as long-term problems like hunger from crop loss year after year.

In response to these problems, local people formed a group called Save the Abra River Movement (STARM). STARM protects land and water rights in many ways. STARM educates communities and government officials about the dangers of mining. It organizes petitions and rallies to make local demands known. It monitors water quality through a partnership with local universities, which contribute equipment and scientists, and local people's organizations that act as witnesses, guides, and water collectors.

Armed only with cell phones and cameras, community-based water monitoring teams alert each other about unusual events. For example, when a lot of fish started dying downstream, community leaders upstream investigated and found that an unusual chemical smell was coming from the mine drainage. University scientists were alerted and quickly sent water containers so they could sample river water for toxics.

Dangerous mining continues along the Abra River. But the Save the Abra River Movement is forcing mining companies to stop the most harmful practices, and the communities are asserting their rights to a safe and healthy environment.

Acid mine drainage

Acid mine drainage happens when water and air mixes with the sulfur deep in the ground (sulfide) to create acids that dissolve heavy metals and other toxic mine wastes. This toxic mixture eats away at rocks and goes into the soil, groundwater, rivers, and lakes. At first, there may be few signs of danger, but slowly the poisons in the water sicken people, plants, fish, and animals. Acid mine drainage destroys life downstream from a mine for hundreds or even thousands of years.

Any mine can create acid mine drainage. Because it is nearly impossible to stop, **companies should prove before opening a mine that there will be no acid mine drainage.** Prevention, clean-up, or containment of acid mine drainage is so costly that a campaign against it may prevent a company from opening a mine in the first place.

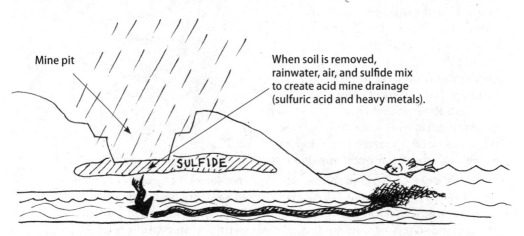

Mine pit

When soil is removed, rainwater, air, and sulfide mix to create acid mine drainage (sulfuric acid and heavy metals).

SULFIDE

Acid mine drainage poisons water downstream and is nearly impossible to clean up.

Take action against acid mine drainage

- Identify abandoned mines and have them tested by trusted scientists. Do not let the mining company do the tests and simply tell you the results. They lie.
- Demand the mining company provide an Environmental Impact Assessment report that includes acid mine drainage (see page 560).
- Learn how mines can be monitored, and involve the community in making sure they are safe (see Resources).
- Insist that the only safe way to deal with acid mine drainage is to prevent it in the first place.

Chemicals Used in Mining

Chemicals used in mining and processing minerals contaminate the land, water, and air, causing health problems for workers and people living near mines. Toxic chemicals used in mining include:

- cyanide, sulfuric acid, and solvents for separating minerals from ore
- nitric acid
- ammonium nitrate and fuel oil ("ANFO") used in blasting tunnels
- heavy metals such as mercury, uranium, and lead
- gasoline, diesel fuel, and exhaust fumes from vehicles and equipment
- acetylene for welding and soldering

Cyanide

Cyanide is used to separate gold from ore. In its pure form, cyanide has no color and smells like bitter almonds. It may lose this smell when it combines with other chemicals. It can be used in powder, liquid, or gas forms.

Cyanide is deadly when swallowed. An amount the size of a grain of rice is enough to kill a person. Exposure to low doses over a long time may cause a swelling in the throat **(goiter)**, which can also be caused by malnutrition.

Cyanide is often spilled into waterways during gold mining, and when ponds filled with mine wastes burst and spill. Mining companies say that cyanide in water quickly becomes harmless. But this is true only when there is lots of sunlight and oxygen. Even then it leaves behind other harmful chemicals. If cyanide is spilled underground, or if the weather is cloudy or rainy, it can remain harmful for a long time, killing fish and plants along rivers and making water unsafe for drinking and bathing.

Sulfuric acid

Sulfuric acid is a toxic chemical used in copper mining. It is also a byproduct of many kinds of mining, mixing with water and heavy metals to form acid mine drainage. Sulfuric acid smells like rotten eggs. Contact with sulfuric acid can cause burns, blindness, and death.

Treatment

Chemicals used at mine sites can spill on the skin and clothes, splash in the eyes, or be breathed in as fumes. If someone is hurt, get medical help as soon as possible. (To learn how to treat chemical spills and chemicals burns while waiting for help, see Appendix A.)

Prevention

The best way to prevent harm from toxic chemicals, including heavy metals, is to not use them. But there are also ways to prevent and reduce harm if toxics are still being used.

- Use protective equipment whenever possible (see Appendix A).
- Wash your hands many times a day. Do not touch your face, smoke, or touch other people while working with or near toxics unless you wash your hands first.
- Demand that mine operators reduce dust and water pollution.
- Never eat where chemicals are being used, mixed, or stored.
- Store chemicals safely.

Storing chemicals

Many chemicals can cause fires, explosions, or release of toxic gases. Safe storage of chemicals can help prevent accidents and reduce harm at mine sites. Store chemicals:

- away from explosives, electrical sources, all sources of water, and motor vehicles.
- away from where people eat.
- in containers that are clearly labeled. If you move chemicals from one container to another, label the new container. **Never** put chemicals in containers used for food or drinks — someone may accidentally eat or drink the chemical. After a chemical container is empty, it should never be used for food or drinks, even if you wash it out.
- in strong, locked cabinets designed and labeled for chemical storage.

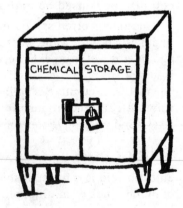

Heavy Metals

Heavy metals such as arsenic, mercury, cadmium, uranium, and lead are harmful to people even in very small amounts (see page 337). Because many metals are found together at mine sites, it is often hard to know which metal may be causing health problems.

If you know what metals are likely to be found in your area and the health effects of these metals, this will help you know if you have heavy metal poisoning. Some miners demand testing from the mine operator to know what heavy metals they are exposed to, and training about ways to reduce harm.

Mercury is mined on its own and is also used to separate gold from ore.

Lead is often found with copper, silver and zinc.

Copper is found with silver and zinc.

Arsenic is often found with gold, copper, and zinc.

Cadmium is found with silver and zinc.

IMPORTANT: If you are exposed to heavy metals day after day, medicine will not stop the poisoning. The only way to stop the poisoning is to stop being exposed. If you have heavy metal poisoning, it is likely that others in your community do as well.

Mercury poisoning

When artisinal miners process silver or gold ore, they often mix the ore with mercury to make a soft substance called amalgam. When burned off to collect the gold, the mercury turns to a gas that can be breathed in by anyone nearby. Mercury can also become a gas if it is spilled or left in an open container. Breathing in mercury fumes is very dangerous. Mercury is also dangerous if it is absorbed through the skin or eaten when it passes from someone's hands to food (see page 338).

Some signs of mercury poisoning are easy to confuse with malaria. If you live in a gold mining community and malaria medicine does not seem to work, talk to a health worker about the possibility of mercury poisoning.

Mercury poisons the environment by settling into the water and soil, where it can remain for many years. Lakes and rivers in California, USA, are still poisoned by mercury from gold mining over 100 years ago. (To learn more about mercury poisoning in water and fish, see page 339.)

Prevent mercury poisoning

Artisinal silver and gold miners can prevent mercury poisoning by using a **mercury retort.** A mercury retort captures mercury gas before it gets into the air. This prevents miners and others from breathing the poison, and allows miners to save money by reusing mercury rather than losing it to the air.

Always separate gold from mercury in the open air or in a well-ventilated area. This will reduce the amount of mercury fumes that collect on, and in, the bodies of people nearby. Wear thick gloves when handling mercury.

Some gold miners simply put a banana leaf over the gold heating pan to capture mercury. When heated, the mercury turns to gas, and turns back to liquid on the leaf. Covering the heating pan with a leaf is much better than leaving it uncovered. But this still allows the mercury to poison the worker and the environment, and the mercury is not recovered. A better solution is to use a closed retort.

There are many kinds of mercury retorts. All of them require strong, directed heat. A blowtorch or a fire with an air blower will help to recover all the gold as quickly as possible.

How to make a bowl-style retort

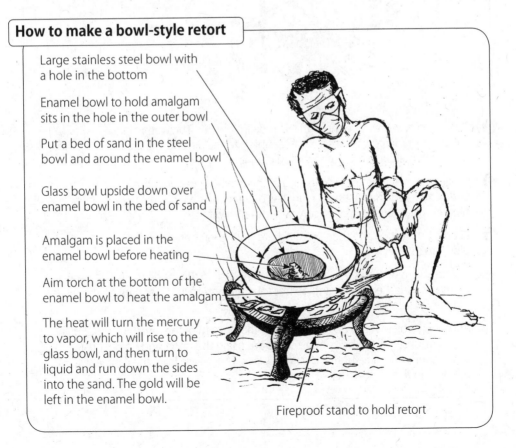

Large stainless steel bowl with a hole in the bottom

Enamel bowl to hold amalgam sits in the hole in the outer bowl

Put a bed of sand in the steel bowl and around the enamel bowl

Glass bowl upside down over enamel bowl in the bed of sand

Amalgam is placed in the enamel bowl before heating

Aim torch at the bottom of the enamel bowl to heat the amalgam

The heat will turn the mercury to vapor, which will rise to the glass bowl, and then turn to liquid and run down the sides into the sand. The gold will be left in the enamel bowl.

Fireproof stand to hold retort

How to make a galvanized pipe retort

This retort is made from standard pipes and plumbing connections. Wear gloves, glasses, and a mask when using it.

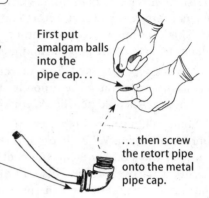

First put amalgam balls into the pipe cap...

...then screw the retort pipe onto the metal pipe cap.

❶ Form gold amalgam into little balls. Always wear gloves (or plastic bags) on your hands while doing this. Put the little balls into the pipe cap.

❷ Screw the retort together tightly so that no mercury escapes.

❸ Put the body of the retort into a bed of hot coals, with the bent pipe in a glass or bowl of cool water. This retort works best if it is heated evenly.

glass or bowl of cool water

❹ The mercury will escape through the pipe into water. The water will prevent mercury fumes from releasing into the air, and will cool down the mercury so it becomes liquid again.

❺ When no more mercury is collecting in the water, all the gold has been extracted and all the mercury has been recovered. Tap the pipe to make sure all the mercury falls into the water.

❻ Let the retort cool, and then open it. Pure gold is left behind in the pipe cap.

One problem with this retort is mercury may stick to the inside the first several times it is used. Be patient, and do not touch the mercury. Over time, all the mercury will come out.

Another problem is the gold may stick in the bottom of the retort. To avoid this problem, unscrew the bottom piece before using the retort and hold it upside down over a lit candle until it is coated black. The grease from the candle will prevent gold from sticking.

Uranium radiation

Uranium is a metal that releases harmful **radiation** (see page 342). Radiation causes cancer, skin diseases, and other serious health problems. People are exposed to uranium through mining it, processing it, or living near uranium mines or waste dumps.

Uranium is used to make 2 things: nuclear weapons and nuclear energy. Both are costly, dangerous, and not needed. No country can trust its leaders or military with nuclear weapons built to kill huge numbers of people. What we need is peace.

Nuclear energy is also dangerous, and accidents in nuclear power plants can kill thousands of people. The waste from nuclear energy remains very harmful for thousands of years and cannot be disposed of safely. Electricity can be made in safer ways (see Chapter 23).

Safety at Mine Sites

Mining companies are responsible for making mines operate safely. Governments, miners, and their unions are responsible for making sure the companies do that. Unfortunately, many governments do not enforce health, safety, and environmental regulations. (For information about how laws protect the human and environmental rights of miners, see Appendix B.)

Workers and communities need the right to protect themselves from harm, information, and equipment and training to reduce exposure to harmful materials. Miners and communities often form safety committees to make sure conditions are as safe as possible. Safety committees can also prepare for emergencies with plans to transport hurt workers and evacuate anyone in danger.

Mine operators should provide protective equipment for all workers and maintain it in good condition. Mine operators should also make sure every mine operation has first aid supplies, and that all workers have access to them (see Appendix A). Most importantly, all workers should be trained about the dangers of chemicals.

To make sure mining does as little harm as possible to the environment, water and air near mine sites should be monitored for signs of pollution. People who may be exposed to toxic chemicals, excessive dust, or other dangers should be tested by health workers on an ongoing basis, and be given treatment at the first signs of health problems.

Organizing to improve miners' lives

Miners around the world have improved their lives, safety, and health by forming labor unions and cooperatives, and by pressuring mining companies to obey laws and the government to enforce them. They have also organized campaigns to enforce international treaties to regulate mine health and safety. Miners and others have also used strikes, demonstrations, and blockades to stop mining operations when they are unfair, unsafe, or destructive to the environment.

Miners know that by working together, we can move mountains!

Women miners organize a cooperative

In Bolivia, women collect scraps of gold, silver, and tin from waste piles dumped near the mines. Many women are forced to do this difficult work after their husbands die in mining accidents or from silicosis. The women work long hours, often in contaminated water, and with no protection. They earn very little money. In the past, they were not even recognized as workers by the government. They were like invisible people.

One day, a mining company began blasting a road through the waste dump where a group of women were working. The women climbed to the top of a hill to protest the destruction of their only source of income. They were not able to stop the blasting, but they continued to fight for their rights.

They formed a cooperative to demand more money from the companies who bought their scraps. The companies refused to pay more. But the government recognized their struggle and passed a law that made the companies pay the women when they missed work because of illness. This was a small step, but it was the first time the women's work was recognized by the government. This small victory inspired the women and other mine workers to continue building cooperatives and unions, and organizing for justice.

Holding corporations accountable

Many mining operations are run by multinational corporations whose headquarters are in countries far from the mine site. This makes it difficult to pressure them for change. But people around the world have organized and forced corporations to change their practices.

Asbestos miners finally win in court

When Audrey was a child, she worked at a mine in South Africa for the Cape Mining Company of Britain. Her job was to step up and down on piles of asbestos powder so that it could be packed into bags for shipping. A supervisor watched her and the other children to make sure they never stopped working. If she stopped, he would whip her. Audrey became very sick from breathing in asbestos, and so did many other workers.

Thirty years later, Audrey joined thousands of other South Africans to sue the British company for causing her health problems. The company spent 3 years arguing that the South African courts should hear the case. Audrey and the people she worked with believed a South African court would not give them a fair trial against a big company that brought a lot of money into the country. Audrey and others traveled to other countries to tell people about their struggle and win support. Finally the courts agreed to hear the case in Britain, the home base of the asbestos company.

After almost 5 years of legal battle, the company gave up. They paid the miners tens of millions of dollars for the harm they caused. Today, most countries ban asbestos mining and many countries ban the use of asbestos altogether. Finally in 2008, South Africa went from being one of the world's largest producers of asbestos to prohibiting the use or manufacture of asbestos or any asbestos product.

When a Mine Closes

Before a mining operation begins, the company must study what the environmental and social effects of the mine will be. This study, called an **Environmental Impact Assessment** or **EIA** (see Appendix B) should plan for ways to reduce harm and to clean up the site when the mine is closed. It should also make sure that people and communities harmed by mining activities are paid for any damage they suffer.

When a mine is closed, the mining operator, with oversight from the government mining authority, is responsible for restoring the site to make it safe for future use. Mining companies and mine operators should:

- remove toxic materials, machinery, and mining structures.

- fill holes, close off tunnels, fence dangerous areas, and clearly mark these areas with signs.

- stabilize cliff faces, pit walls, and waste dumps to reduce erosion and prevent collapse.

- restore soil and cover the area with healthy soil and plants.

- restore damaged waterways.

In some countries, mining companies are required to put up money (called a bond) before they begin work. A bond is effective only if it is large enough to prevent the company from causing too much harm. If the amount of the bond is less than the costs of restoring land and paying for damages from mining, the company may not fulfill its responsibilities. To make sure that companies fulfill their responsibilities, some communities negotiate for the highest possible bond. It may also help to demand one large bond for an entire project, rather than smaller bonds for each separate part of the project.

Restoring damaged land

If land is damaged by erosion and loss of topsoil, it can be restored over time (see Chapter 11). But land that is badly damaged by mine waste and chemicals may be very difficult to restore, if it can be restored at all.

After mining and before restoration

Restoring and replanting damaged land should be the responsibility of mine owners and operators. But mining communities, with or without support from government, usually must pressure the mining companies to make sure they fulfill this responsibility.

To restore and replant mined lands, toxic waste must be prevented from washing or blowing away, and acid mine drainage must be prevented. It takes a lot of work over many years to bring land back to a healthy state.

If land cannot be mined safely and responsibly, it should not be mined at all.

New plants growing 5 years after replanting

Full plant cover 20 years after replanting

Responsible Mining

The World Bank and other international agencies now promote what they call "sustainable mining." But large-scale mining is always destructive and the amount of minerals that can be safely mined is limited. Mining is a "boom and bust" industry, meaning there may be great wealth when a new mineral deposit is discovered, but this is followed by great poverty when the minerals are gone. As yet, there has been no such thing as "sustainable mining."

While mining probably cannot be done in a way that is truly sustainable, it can be done in ways that are less destructive and more beneficial to workers and communities.

Develop environmental and social plans

All mine operations should include a plan to protect the environment and support community needs. Mining companies want to take out as much wealth as possible with as little cost, so community pressure will be necessary to force mining operations to develop these kinds of plans. For any plan to be effective, people from nearby communities must be involved in all decision-making. A responsible plan will include:

- an environmental impact assessment (EIA) carried out with the participation of the communities that will be affected (see Apendix B).
- social services such as health clinics and schools, and providing safe drinking water, sanitation, and other necessary services.
- long-term, comprehensive health care for miners, their families, and affected communities.
- a plan for closing mines, restoring land, and providing safe, sustainable work for those who worked in the mines.

22 Oil, Illness, and Human Rights

In this chapter:

Oil, Illness, and Human Rights

Petroleum, or oil, is part of many products used every day, such as gasoline, propane, kerosene, heating oil, and asphalt, as well as many plastics, paints, pesticides, solvents, and cosmetics. Even some clothes and medicines are made from oil. But oil is toxic and has harmful effects on our health and the environment, starting with the methods used to find it, transport it, and refine it, as well as the ways in which it is then used.

People in oil-rich areas hope that oil will bring wealth. But in most cases, the wealth goes to the oil companies while the people in the communities are left with poverty, pollution, sickness, and the violence that seems to spill over wherever oil is found. Because the world economy depends on oil, the oil industry has the power to influence governments and international policies. This often leaves poor people in oil-rich communities struggling to protect themselves and their land, and people in wealthy or developing communities struggling with air pollution.

Oil, coal, and natural gas are **fossil fuels.** They are made from the remains of plants and animals that died millions of years ago, and there is only a limited amount of them. In the past 100 years, oil has become the main energy source for most of the world. Now, much of the world's oil resources have been used up. Burning so much oil and other fossil fuels has led to global warming (see page 33), one of the biggest environmental problems facing the world today. More and more, people around the world are calling for an end to the oil economy and for the development of cleaner and more sustainable forms of energy (see Chapter 23).

Oil and Community Health

In places where oil is discovered, the economy develops rapidly, but it is an economy of misery. Poorly built oil camps are carved out of the landscape and bring with them many social problems, such as forced displacement, alcoholism, sexually transmitted infections and HIV/AIDs (see also page 474). Oil companies and governments regularly wash their hands of the communities most damaged by oil development. These communities are often left on their own to try to determine how much and what kinds of harm oil has caused, and to search for ways to restore their community's health.

Natural gas also causes health problems

Burning natural gas produces less carbon dioxide (a cause of global warming) and other pollutants than burning oil. But drilling for natural gas is similar to oil drilling, and it brings many of the same social problems. Almost everything that is true about oil in this chapter is true of natural gas as well.

Communities affected by oil organize a health study

In 1992, a group of health promoters in the Amazon jungle in Ecuador studied the way oil drilling was affecting local communities. They knew oil companies were destroying their land, but there was little understanding about how the oil affected people's health. So the health promoters began to collect information in their towns and villages.

> We live in an area that is rich in oil. But no one here is rich.

The health study took a lot of work and a lot of time. When they began, the health promoters did not know what they would learn. They tell their story in their own words throughout this chapter.

For thousands of years this region has been home to indigenous people. In our part of the Amazon jungle live many different peoples: Shuar-Achuar, Runa, Quichua, Huaorani, Siona-Secoya and Cofan. Each of these cultures has its own language and art, and its own vision of reality.
Before modern times, all of these tribes lived in harmony with nature. Then this harmony was broken. If we want to understand what is happening to us, we have to look at our history.

> In 1492 people from Europe arrived here...

This was the beginning of breaking the balance between our ancestors and nature. First, the Spanish searched our lands for gold and silver. Our ancestors were forced to work as slaves digging gold and silver out of the earth. Then the English came. Instead of gold, they wanted rubber. They made slaves of us to take rubber from our lands. After this, the oil companies came. They did the same thing.

We know the oil companies are destroying our health. This is why our health promoters decided to study the pollution and how it affects us. We want to work together for a better economic, political, and cultural situation.

The health promoters learned that people in oil-polluted communities have more sickness than in unpolluted communities. Women in these communities suffer from many miscarriages. Children suffer from malnutrition, and often die at an early age. Many people have skin diseases that do not go away. (To learn more about the health problems caused by oil, see pages 506 to 507.)

This is just some of what they learned. After their study, they produced a book called *Cultures Bathed in Oil* so other people could learn from the work they had done.

First we formed a team, adding people who had technical and medical knowledge to people from our community organizations.

Our team was made up of 6 people: 3 health promoters (2 who worked in communities and 1 who worked in a health laboratory), and 3 health technicians (a doctor, a biochemist, and a medical technician).

Here are the steps we followed to do our study, so you can do the same thing:

1. We gathered information.
We collected information about the type of oil exploitation in our area, the chemicals used, and the health effects of these chemicals. We learned that the chemicals were known to cause miscarriages, birth defects, cancer, and other illnesses. We also learned that people get these illnesses by drinking water polluted with these chemicals.

2. We chose which communities we would study.
We chose 7 communities that had water polluted because of oil development and extraction. Choosing polluted sites was easy, because nearly every community in our area is polluted by oil wells, waste ponds, or pumping stations. We also chose 3 communities that had no oil activity, but that were similar in all other ways to the first 7 communities.

3. We collected medical histories from people in these communities.
We collected information from 4 years past to see what illnesses were most common from one year to the next. We learned that many, many people suffered from accidents and illness.
Until we collected this information, we did not know so many of us were sick!

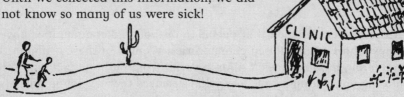

4. We contacted scientists to help us... but they would not help.
We went to a local center of health studies and asked for a class in popular research methods. They were interested at first, but in the end they would not help us. Then we asked for help from the medical school nearby, and they would not help us either. The students there recommended that we study the chemicals in our drinking water. Since this was expensive, they suggested we try to raise money in other countries.

Nobody wanted to help us do the study. So we decided to do the study ourselves.

5. We organized a meeting of people from all the communities in our area.
We explained why we wanted to do this study and asked if the
communities were prepared to help. At the end of the meeting, everyone
voted to do it. We organized a committee including health promoters,
people from different communities, and people with knowledge of how
chemicals affect people and the environment, to carry out the study and
analyze the results.

The Problems of Oil

6. We made a work plan.
We planned to take 5 months to do the study. We would go to a different
community every 15 days and stay for 3 or 4 days in each place. We would
survey the community and collect samples of blood, urine, and feces for
testing. When we had the test results from a lab in the city, we would
return to the community to share the results. This was very important to
allow us to make decisions together. We also planned to have a meeting
every 2 months, where the coordinating committee and community
representatives could talk about how the study was going.

7. **We searched for funding for our work and the laboratory costs.**
   We formed a commission to find the money. After a lot of searching, we got money for the study from a group of doctors in Spain.

8. **We made maps of the communities.**
   People from each of the communities made maps showing oil wells, polluted water, and locations of villages and farms. At the same time we made a list of all the people who live in each community (a census). The list included each person's name, age, and whether they were a man or a woman.

9. **We began visiting the communities and doing the study.**
   Instead of sending samples to the city, we set up a lab in the community school where we tested people's blood, urine, and feces. (You need lab equipment and some training to do these tests, so we won't explain them here.) In the mornings we went from house to house collecting the samples. Afterwards, another group went to each house doing surveys to gather information and the health promoters did a medical check-up of each person.

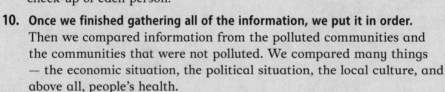

10. **Once we finished gathering all of the information, we put it in order.**
    Then we compared information from the polluted communities and the communities that were not polluted. We compared many things — the economic situation, the political situation, the local culture, and above all, people's health.

11. **The last step was to write it all down and discuss it together.**
    This helped all of the communities involved to decide how to take action to improve our health.

On the last day in each town or village, we had another meeting with the community about what we would do next and what more we hoped to learn.

The health study led to community action

The work of the health promoters showed people that many of their health problems were caused by oil pollution. Toxic chemicals from oil were found in the water and soil, and in people's blood, urine, and feces. Knowing this helped them begin to work toward a solution. They knew that as long as the contamination continued, it would be difficult to have safe water, healthy food, or clean air.

A group formed, calling itself the Committee of Affected People, to petition the government for help. And the organization of health promoters continued supporting people's health and showing how their health problems were caused by oil.

Another organization, the Front for the Defense of the Amazon, began a lawsuit to sue the oil company for the damage it had caused. (To learn about this lawsuit, see page 522.) Huge areas of the rain forest had

Health promoters and other people in the community realized their study was only the beginning of their struggle for health and justice.

been destroyed, and environmental laws about how damage had to be repaired were ignored. The foreign-owned oil company just took its profits and left.

The community study and lawsuit inspired other organizations to get involved in the struggle to save the rainforest and its people. Universities and medical schools in Ecuador, England, and the United States did more studies to support the lawsuit against the oil company, and to show that oil caused terrible health problems. These studies also helped the authors of this book learn about the health effects of oil.

But the key work was done by the health promoters. By teaching themselves how to study the health effects of oil, they worked locally on an issue of global importance. By showing how their neighbors' health was being devastated by the destruction of the rain forest by multinational oil corporations, they brought local issues to the international arena. They were an inspiration to us as we wrote this book.

Oil Causes Serious Health Problems

As with other toxic chemicals, health problems from oil may be difficult to prove because they take a long time to affect people. But most people who live and work near oil drilling sites and refineries are familiar with the pollution of air and water from oil. Drilling for oil, refining it, and burning oil as fuel all lead to many serious health problems, such as the ones listed below and those discussed in more detail on the pages that follow:

- **blurred vision** and other eye problems

- **headaches,** hallucinations, euphoria (sudden feelings of happiness), tiredness, slurred speech, brain damage, coma

- **convulsions** and unusual deaths

- **nose sores** and nose bleeds

- **ear infections**

- **asthma, bronchitis, pneumonia** and other respiratory diseases

- **lung and throat** infections and cancers

- **increased risk of TB** (tuberculosis)

- **heart attacks**

- **digestive problems,** including vomiting, ulcers, and stomach cancer

- **damage to liver,** kidneys, and bone marrow

- **menstrual problems,** miscarriages, stillbirths, and birth defects

- **skin** rashes, fungus, and cancers

In some places, people sniff petrol (gasoline) fumes for drug-like effects. This is very dangerous. For some people, breathing in gasoline deeply, even once, can cause sudden death.

Long-term health effects

Oil causes reproductive health problems

Breathing fumes or swallowing food or liquids contaminated by oil and gas causes reproductive health problems such as irregular bleeding cycles, miscarriages, stillbirths, and birth defects. These problems may have early warning signs such as abdominal pain or irregular bleeding (see Chapter 16 for more information).

Oil causes cancer

Regular contact with oil and gas causes cancer. Children living near oil refineries are much more likely to get cancer of the blood (**leukemia**) than those who live farther away. People living in areas where oil is drilled are much more likely to develop cancers of the stomach, bladder, and lungs than people living in other places. Workers in oil refineries have a high risk of cancer of the lip, stomach, liver, pancreas, connective tissue, prostate, eye, brain, and blood. (For more information about cancer, see Chapter 16.)

In the area of Ecuador where oil is drilled, 1 out of every 3 people has some form of cancer.

When Texaco began drilling for oil in Ecuador, cancer was not known in the region. Forty years later, in 2 of the most heavily exploited oil regions of the Amazon, the community health workers did a survey of 80 communities. They found that 1 of every 3 people has some form of cancer.

Every Part of Oil Production is Harmful

Understanding the damage caused to both health and the environment during each stage of oil production can help you respond.

Exploration

When companies first start looking for oil, forests are cut down and homes are destroyed. Roads are built, and streams and rivers are blocked up. The search for for oil often involves a series of explosions set off to help oil companies know what is underground. This is called **seismic testing.** Seismic testing damages homes, wildlife, and the land.

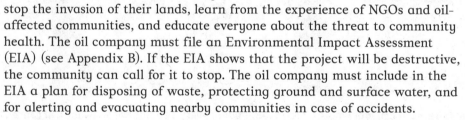

Before companies start the search for oil, community groups can visit government officials to try to stop the invasion of their lands, learn from the experience of NGOs and oil-affected communities, and educate everyone about the threat to community health. The oil company must file an Environmental Impact Assessment (EIA) (see Appendix B). If the EIA shows that the project will be destructive, the community can call for it to stop. The oil company must include in the EIA a plan for disposing of waste, protecting ground and surface water, and for alerting and evacuating nearby communities in case of accidents.

Oil drilling

Oil wells are drilled to bring oil out of the ground. Oil drilling can cause fires, explosions, and other accidents that endanger workers and the community. When oil spills it pollutes groundwater and waterways, harms plants and animals, and damages resources for hunting, fishing, and farming.

Communities can use cameras, video, radio announcements, written reports, and even children's drawings to document the harm from drilling. This documentation can be used as evidence when a community makes a demand to stop oil drilling and environmental destruction, to enforce the standards of the Environmental Impact Assessment, or to take legal action against the oil company.

Separation

Oil comes out of the ground mixed with gas, heavy metals, and toxic water. The oil must be separated from these other materials.

The dumping of the toxic water is often the largest cause of pollution. Laws about drilling in wealthy countries require the toxic water to be put back into the ground rather than dumped on the surface. This practice should be followed everywhere.

The other wastes are separated and dumped into **containment ponds.** Oil companies often do nothing more than dig a hole and dump in crude oil, drilling wastes, toxic water, and other wastes. These ponds often leak into the groundwater or overflow, contaminating groundwater and land.

Containment ponds should be lined with concrete. The ponds must be monitored for leaks and spills, and cleaned up before the oil operation ends.

Gas flares

The gases found with oil are often separated by burning them off. Gas flares (see pages 511 to 512) expose workers, communities, and wildlife to pollution that causes cancer, skin diseases, asthma, bronchitis, and other health problems. The flares pollute the clouds, causing a "black rain" that poisons water sources.

Transport and storage

Oil is often spilled during transport through pipelines, trucks, and ships. Oil can also leak from storage tanks. These spills may cause damage that lasts for years to soil, groundwater, animals, and people. Oil companies should warn communities when a spill happens, contain the spill, and clean it up right away. (To reduce harm from oil spills and to learn about oil spill clean-up, see pages 514 to 519.)

Environmental Impact Assessments for oil operations should include plans for pipeline building and use. You can build regional support by organizing communities along the pipeline to oppose unsafe oil company practices.

Refining

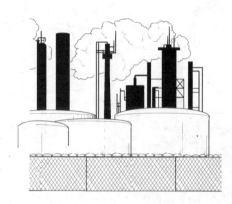

Refineries are factories where oil is made into products such as gasoline, diesel and heating fuels, asphalt, lubricating oils, and plastics. Refineries release toxic waste into water, soil, and air. Pollution from refineries leads to asthma, bronchitis, cancer, reproductive problems, and abnormal development of the brain and nervous system in children. This pollution also adds to global warming. (For more information about how communities can prevent and reduce harm from refineries, see pages 455 to 458, and page 513.)

Burning oil as fuel

Burning oil and gas in factories and in automobiles creates different kinds of air pollution. One gas created is carbon dioxide, which traps heat in the air. This is one of the major causes of global warming, causing disasters like floods, storms, droughts, and rising seawater. It also affects crops, animals, and insects, allowing diseases like malaria to spread to new areas. At the gasoline station and in crowded cities, people are exposed to toxic fumes that can cause cancer and many other illnesses.

Gas Flares

When oil is found together with natural gas, oil companies may burn the gas to separate it from the oil. Burning gas makes giant flares that light up the sky and make a loud, terrible noise. Gas flaring is dangerous, wasteful, and very polluting.

Oil companies can sell the gas rather than burn it off. But this is more costly and difficult because gas must be stored under pressure, increasing the risk of fires and explosions. So companies flare off the gas simply because it is less costly, even though it increases the harm to people and the environment.

Health and safety around gas flares

All gas flares pollute the air and can cause health problems. But some flares are worse than others.

Gas may be flared occasionally as a safety measure to prevent explosions (called **safety flares**), or every day as part of oil operations (called **routine flares**). Each kind of flaring requires a different response.

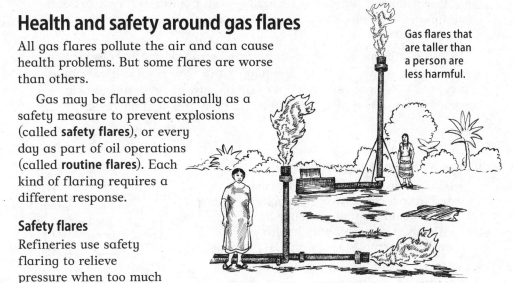

Gas flares that are taller than a person are less harmful.

Gas flares that are the height of a person, or flares that are horizontal to the ground, are very dangerous.

Safety flares

Refineries use safety flaring to relieve pressure when too much gas is in the pipes. Even though it does not happen all the time, it is still very harmful! **If there is safety flaring in your community,** demand advance notice from the company about when flares will occur. The company should always warn nearby communities 24 hours before flaring will happen.

When there is a flare, everyone should stay as far away as possible. Stay inside with doors and windows closed. (For what to do in an emergency, see page 457.)

Routine flares

In some places, gas is flared every day, simply because it is cheaper for the company. It is very difficult for people who live near routine gas flaring to take precautions all the time. The only way to be safe from routine flaring is to stop it.

Flaring can be stopped!

The worst routine gas flaring in the world occurred for many years in the Niger Delta of Nigeria. Gas flaring by international oil companies in Nigeria has cost many lives. And the poisons released by Nigerian gas flares have contributed more to climate change and global warming than all other sources in sub-Saharan Africa combined.

Comrade Che Ibegwura, a man from Rivers State, Nigeria, said: "For years, we have lived with continuous flaring of gas. Our farmlands have been polluted. We labor hard to plant, but little comes out. Our roofs are corroded. Our air is polluted. Our children are sick. Even the rainwater we drink is contaminated with black soot from the gas flares. We cannot continue with this suffering."

In 2005, after many years of protest and struggle, routine gas flaring was outlawed in the Niger Delta. A judge ruled that all the oil companies in Nigeria must stop gas flaring right away because of the health problems it causes, and because it violates the human right to a healthy environment.

If there is routine flaring near you:

- Discuss the dangers of gas flaring and form a committee to complain to the company and government officials. Also speak with health workers, journalists, and NGOs.

- Keep a record of your campaign. Encourage people to mark the days and times of flares and the problems they caused.

- Organize meetings to share these records with other communities, journalists, and government officials. Keep records of your talks with them. Writing down or filming what the officials say will also show that you are serious. Most importantly, do not give up!

The company refuses to talk to us about the flaring. Who can we try to talk to next?

These actions may not stop flaring right away. But the common goal of stopping the flaring can unite the community and build strength to protect everyone's health in the long term.

Oil Refineries

Oil refineries are factories where oil is made into gasoline and other fuels, and into materials such as asphalt and plastic. Oil refineries are a major source of air pollution for people who live near them and work at them. Chemicals in and around refineries cause cancer, reproductive harm, breathing problems such as asthma and emphysema, and birth defects, as well as other health problems such as headaches, nausea, dizziness, and stress. Refineries are also a major source of the gases that cause global warming.

Making refineries safer

Refineries do not have to cause such terrible health problems. Pollution could be prevented if oil companies would do all they could to prevent accidents and contain toxic gases and liquids at all stages of the refining process. If you and your community are working to make a refinery safer, your campaign might focus on some of these ideas:

Air pollution monitoring can identify problems and stop emergencies before they happen. The companies should monitor the air and respond to problems immediately. If they will not monitor pollution, communities can (see pages 455 to 457).

Gas flares can be replaced with safer methods, such as recovering the gases for reuse (see page 511).

Tanks used to store crude oil, gasoline, and other substances sometimes release toxic fumes when they are filled, emptied, or cleaned. These fumes can be contained with better equipment and procedures. Tanks and valves must be inspected and repaired regularly to prevent leaks into the air and the groundwater.

Tankers and barges filled with oil and gasoline release fumes into the air and leak liquids into water. Safety systems should be used at all times to prevent spills and toxic fumes. Tankers should have double- or triple-lined hulls to prevent spills.

Wastewater containing toxic chemicals often spills or leaks into groundwater. By building and maintaining wastewater systems, these problems can be avoided.

Dirty crude oil makes more waste and pollutes air and water, especially if a refinery was built to process cleaner, lighter forms of oil. Refining cleaner oil results in less pollution.

Oil Spills

Wherever there is oil, there are oil spills. Ships and trucks have accidents, and pipelines leak. It is the oil companies' responsibility to prevent spills and to clean them up when they happen.

There is a saying: "Oil and water do not mix." But when oil spills in water, toxic chemicals from the oil do mix with the water and stay there for a long time. The thicker part of the oil spreads over the surface and prevents air from getting into the water. Fish, animals, and plants that live in the water are not able to breathe. When oil spills in water, the chemicals left behind may make the water unsafe to drink, even after the oil we can see is removed.

When oil spills on land, it destroys the soil by choking out the air and killing the living things that make soil healthy. Something similar happens when oil gets on our skin or the skin of animals. The oil covers the skin and blocks air from getting in. Toxins from the oil also enter the body through the skin, causing illness.

Do oil and water mix?

This activity can help people understand the effects of an oil spill in water.

Time: 1 ½ hours

Materials: Clear glass jar, water, vegetable oil

❶ Fill a jar with water. Add 2 spoonfuls of vegetable oil. Shake the jar to mix the oil and water. Leave the jar alone for an hour.

❷ Return to the jar. You will see that most of the oil has settled on top. Vegetable oil is harmless, but imagine the jar is a river with an oil spill. Begin a group discussion about the effects this might have. Imagine fish trying to survive in this river with a layer of oil, blocking air and sunlight. Imagine what happens to birds trying to hunt for fish in the river.

❸ Use a spoon to try to skim oil off the surface. After you have skimmed off as much oil as you can, see if some bubbles of oil remain in the water. This is oil that sinks into the water. Consider the old saying, "Oil and water do not mix." Discuss with the group what happens when oil and water do mix.

Water pollution from oil

It is very harmful to drink water that has oil in it. The water that comes out of the ground when oil is drilled is also very toxic.

Filters that clean oil and toxic chemicals out of water are very costly. Boiling water, using solar disinfection, and adding chlorine to water (see pages 92 to 99) kill germs but **cannot** get rid of oil pollution.

Adding chlorine actually makes oil pollution worse because it combines with some of the chemicals called "phenols" to form an even more toxic chemical called "chlorophenol."

If an oil spill has been cleaned up, even if you do not see oil in the water, the water is still probably not safe. Many of the toxins in oil settle into the water and stay for a long time. The only way to be sure water is safe is to have it tested.

How to keep safe after an oil spill

- Avoid contact with the oil. Keep children and animals away from the spill. If possible, put a fence around the area and post a warning sign.

- Use a source of water upstream from the spill. Even if you have to walk a long way, it is worth it to prevent health problems. Where oil has spilled, rainwater may be the only safe water to drink.

- Avoid eating animals that live in water such as crabs, shrimp, and snails near the spill and areas downstream. They soak up toxins like sponges.

- Avoid bathing in affected water. If somebody falls in the water, they should wash right away with strong soap and clean water.

- Notify neighbors, government officials, the press, and NGOs that are concerned about health and the environment.

- Teach people about the dangers of oil at schools and community gatherings.

Let's go get water at your uncle's farm instead.

Cleaning up oil spills

Cleaning up spills is the responsibility of the oil company. Companies claim they can clean up any spill. But the truth is, even with the best equipment, oil spills and oil spill clean-ups are very dangerous and difficult. In most cases, people affected by spills have no protective equipment.

Whenever there are spills, on water or on land, the chemicals in the oil poison people, animals, plants, land, and water.

The oil company should start clean-up as soon as spills happen. Because toxins from oil settle into water and soil, removing the black sludge from the surface does not always remove the source of harm (see page 514).

Oil spill clean-up makes workers sick

When an oil tanker named Exxon Valdez ran aground off the coast of Alaska in 1989, it spilled millions of gallons of oil into the water. The spill killed countless animals and birds, and destroyed the local fishing industry. The oil caused damage that continues to this day.

The Exxon company hired 10,000 workers to clean up the oil and rescue the animals. Using the best equipment, they worked 12 to 16 hours a day for many months cleaning the spill and trying to prevent the oil from spreading. They wore protective clothing to keep the oil off their skin and masks to keep them from breathing toxic fumes.

At the end of each day, the workers removed their raincoats, boots, and gloves. The suits and the workers themselves were cleaned with chemical solvents. The next day they put the suits back on and went back to work. But despite the protective gear, many workers complained of coughing, headaches, dizziness, and runny noses. "At night, in the bunks, everyone was coughing. It was like a TB ward," said one worker. Ten years later, many of the workers have developed memory loss, lung damage, and cancer. Hundreds of them have died.

Exxon was sued to pay for the damage. But all these years later, they have paid nothing at all.

What to do in case of an oil spill

When oil spills or leaks from a storage tank, it should be contained and absorbed. Once it is absorbed, the oil and any material used to absorb it must be removed and disposed of safely, for example, in a pit lined with concrete, so they will not pollute the groundwater.

Oil spills on water can also be contained and absorbed, but this is difficult without special equipment. Anyone who enters the water to clean up spilled oil can get very sick. Trying to remove oil from water by collecting it in buckets is dangerous and does not work well. With proper equipment and training, this is how oil spills in water are cleaned up:

Some materials that absorb oil are straw, sawdust, ground corncobs, feathers, clay, wool, and sand.

Oil is kept in place with a boom, a kind of floating fence held by anchors, or tied to boats or to things on shore. The boom prevents most of the oil from floating away.

A machine called a skimmer takes oil off the surface of the water and sucks it through a hose into a waste storage tank.

Oil that remains in the water is absorbed with materials like sawdust, peat moss, feathers, or clay.

After as much of the oil as possible is skimmed from the surface, soaked up, and removed, what is left is set on fire and burned away. Burning the oil makes toxic smoke, but may be better than leaving oil in the water.

If you clean up an oil spill, protect yourself!

Whether you and your community have to clean an oil spill on your own or are paid by an oil company to clean an oil spill, you should know:

- Oil is always toxic. Touching or breathing it can lead to serious health problems (see page 506).

- Solvents used to clean oil are also toxic and can lead to serious health problems (see page 516).

- High-pressure hoses commonly used to spray oil off of rocks cause oil to **vaporize** (become a gas) and make the oil easy to breathe in. This can lead to problems of the throat and lungs.

- The company responsible for the spill and for cleaning it up should provide you with protective clothing, including a body suit, gloves, boots, respirator, safety glasses, and a head covering (see Appendix A).

- Working long hours in oil-contaminated water or being exposed to solvents can cause serious health problems. It is best to work fewer hours and to rest away from toxic fumes between work shifts.

Make a safety plan for emergencies

If you live where there is oil drilling or refineries, work with your community to make a safety plan to protect everyone's health in case of emergencies such as flares or spills. (To learn what a safety plan includes, see page 545.)

Map your community

Part of a safety plan is to know where problems may break out and where the resources are to prevent and recover from an emergency. Mapping the community can help.

Together with others from the community, draw a map of where you live. Include oil wells, drilling sites, pipelines, waste pits, refineries, and other sources of pollution. Also, include places where you get water, grow or collect food, and keep animals, as well as community resources.

Talk about where there have been spills, accidents, or pollution in the past. What was the impact? Mark the map where you have seen the effects of oil spills. Then make a list of your available resources and a plan for how to use them in case of an emergency.

Meet and make your plan

WHAT WE NEED

- An upstream water source or a community water tank.

- Change stored water every 6 to 12 months.

- Trucks or other vehicles to get people safely away.

- Choose 1 or more people to alert nearby communities, officials, and the media in an emergency.

- A school, church, or other meeting places.

- Telephone or radio to call for help, and alert officials and media.

- Telephone numbers for hospitals, clinics, and health workers.

RESPONSIBLE

- Joseph

- Sala, Naisha, Njuma

- Ahmed's taxi, Kwame's truck

How many of us have mobile phones we can use in an emergency?

How to hold the company responsible

The oil company should have filed an Environmental Impact Assessment (EIA) before drilling for oil. The EIA states what the company is legally responsible for in case of a spill. Discuss how your community can use the EIA to hold the company accountable in an emergency. For example, can you demand they shut down the pipeline that caused the spill until they clean it up? Can the company supply the community with drinking water, or pay for health services and damage to property? (To learn about EIAs, see Appendix B.)

Restoring land damaged by oil

Oil spills cause severe long-term harm to land. If the oil is cleaned up and land is left to recover for many years, it may be possible to restore land to make it fertile again. But it will take a long, long time. (For more information on restoring land, see Chapter 11 and page 496.)

A new way to clean spilled oil?

After a diesel fuel spill in the USA, different companies were asked to see what they could do to clean it up. The soil where the oil spilled was mounded up in piles, and each company was given one pile to work with.

One of the companies was a small business devoted to growing and selling edible mushrooms. The man who ran the business had seen mushrooms growing after forest fires and other natural disasters. He believed mushrooms had the power to restore damaged land. His team went to work filling their oil-soaked pile with the root fibers of oyster mushrooms. Then they covered the pile and waited.

When they uncovered the pile 6 weeks later, what they saw was amazing. The soil was covered with huge mushrooms, some as big as 30 cm across. They took the mushrooms and soil to a laboratory and tested them. The mushrooms had no trace of oil or any of the toxic chemicals that oil contains. The mushrooms had completely cleaned the soil!

The exciting part of the story is what happened next. After the mushrooms matured, flies came in and laid eggs in them. Maggots appeared, birds flew in, and other small animals began to eat the mushrooms and the maggots. The birds and animals carried in seeds, and plants started growing. The polluted pile of dirt was transformed into a rich garden of life.

This method worked in the experiment, but no one knows yet if it will work as well in all conditions and all places. More work needs to be done to find out if mushrooms or other "natural remedies" can clean up oil spills.

Environmental Justice

One of the only ways for people to protect their health in oil-rich areas is to make sure that whoever controls oil resources works in a way that protects people from the health risks and provides them with the benefits. Because oil is so valuable, they have a lot of wealth to work with.

Women protest oil exploitation

The Niger River Delta in Nigeria was once a fertile land with plenty of fish, wildlife, and healthy farms. When oil companies first came to this region, they promised economic benefits to all the people. But after more than 30 years of oil development, the companies have not kept their word. As one Nigerian woman explained, "We are angry. Since 1970 when the company came here, they have denied us every living thing. We have nothing to show except the pollution of our rivers and creeks, destruction of our forests and mangroves, and the terrible noise of the gas flaring. We have no hope, while they are making millions with our gifts from God. They do not care or hear our cries."

(story continues on next page)

Nigerian women began a campaign of peaceful protest involving people from every tribe in the region. The women demanded that Chevron-Texaco, one of the main oil companies working in the region, provide jobs, resources for education, water, electricity, and community development. And they demanded compensation for all of the damage the oil company had done.

Chevron-Texaco called for the government to respond with an iron fist. Police and the military fired tear gas and attacked the women, beating and torturing them. Many were injured and some were killed. But the women responded with determination and creativity. Some picketed the oil company headquarters, others occupied the main export terminal, and hundreds more took over 4 flow stations in the Niger River to stop the companies from shipping the oil. Chevron-Texaco lost over $100,000 each day the women occupied the terminal and flow stations!

The oil company officials finally gave in. Chevron-Texaco agreed to create jobs and to set up a microcredit program to help women start their own businesses. They also promised to provide schools, hospitals, and water and electricity for the villages.

The brutal actions of the oil companies and their government allies in Nigeria show they will stop at nothing to increase their profits. The women in Nigeria have inspired people around the world to demand a share of the benefits, not the suffering, from oil development. Otherwise, they will stop oil development altogether.

Oil and the Law

Many countries make laws to protect people, water, and wildlife from pollution, and to gain safe working conditions. Regional and international laws and agreements also exist to hold oil companies accountable for spills. But laws are effective only if people work together to make sure they are enforced. (For more about international laws, see Appendix B.)

The case against Texaco

When Texaco came to drill for oil in Ecuador, the Cofan people there had no idea the US oil company would destroy their lives. For over 20 years the company dumped millions of liters of oil and toxic waste water into the environment.

Rivers that had supported the Cofan for generations became useless as sources of food. People spent many hours each day searching for drinkable water and hunting for animals. Many people fled the area due to the destruction. The Cofan leaders say that Texaco destroyed their traditional way of life and caused illness for thousands of people. The Cofan population shrank from 15,000 people to only about 500.

The victims of Texaco's contamination formed the Front for the Defense of the Amazon. They organized medical care for those suffering from serious illnesses. They helped to organize studies of the health effects of Texaco's oil operations. They talked to environmental activists from the capital city of Quito and to lawyers in the United States. Together they came up with a plan. The leaders and activists traveled by foot, canoe, and plane to New York City to file a billion dollar lawsuit against Texaco.

Texaco tried to have the case dismissed. The company claimed the case should be tried in an Ecuadoran court because the pollution happened in that country. The activists worried that it would be hard to get justice in Ecuador. They explained to the judge that the decisions to pollute the Amazon had been made in the United States. The judge agreed to listen to them. This was the first time an international case had been accepted in an American court! The Cofan leaders were overjoyed.

For 10 years Texaco fought to dismiss the case. A new judge decided that the case should be tried in Ecuador, but if a just outcome was not given, the case could be retried in New York. The lawsuit is still not over. The people continue to suffer health problems as oil is pumped out of the rainforest. Their persistence in seeking justice from the Texaco Corporation has taught many people about the damage done by oil, and has forced Texaco and other oil companies to use safer methods of drilling for oil.

23 Clean Energy

In this chapter: **page**

Clean Energy

It takes energy to light a home, to cook a meal, to lift and carry water, and to do all of the things we do every day. Sometimes this energy is human energy, such as the strength to walk, chop wood, or lift a bucket. Often this energy comes in the form of electricity to power lights, water pumps, fans, and other machines.

Electricity makes our lives and our work easier. It allows us to have light to work and study by, refrigeration to keep food and medicines cool so they do not spoil, washing machines, drills, and so on to make work easier, and radio and television to keep us informed and entertained. All these things can make our lives healthier and more comfortable.

Unfortunately, access to electricity is a far-off dream for many people. Most of the electricity used in the world is in cities and the wealthy countries of the North. Of the world's 6 billion people, 2 billion have no electricity.

We also use energy for transportation, usually from **fossil fuels** such as gasoline (petrol) or diesel to power automobiles, buses, trucks, railroads, and airplanes. As with electricity, the wealthy countries of the North use more than their fair share of transportation fuel.

To prevent pollution and to reduce global warming (see page 33), the world must burn less less oil, coal, and natural gas. Especially people in rich countries, who use too much, must use less. For everyone to have enough electricity and transportation without increasing global warming, we must change to non-polluting power sources (**clean energy,** also called renewable energy). These include wind power, solar power, water power, and biogas.

How Electricity Is Produced

Most electricity today is made by burning fossil fuels (oil, coal, and natural gas). Some energy also comes from nuclear power, and from large dams (see page 170). To understand why we need clean energy to replace fossil fuels, nuclear power, and energy from large dams, it helps to understand how electricity is made and how it causes harm if it comes from sources that are not clean or renewable.

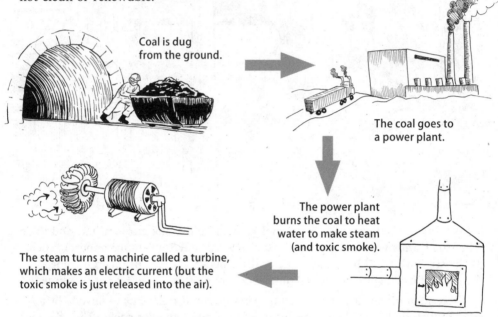

Coal is dug from the ground.

The coal goes to a power plant.

The power plant burns the coal to heat water to make steam (and toxic smoke).

The steam turns a machine called a turbine, which makes an electric current (but the toxic smoke is just released into the air).

Whether from coal, oil, or natural gas and nuclear power, making electricity is all done the same way. First the power source makes heat, which is used to make steam, which turns large turbines to make electricity. Large hydroelectric dams use falling water, rather than steam heat, to turn a turbine to make electricity. But all of these kinds of energy lead to toxic pollution, destruction of communities and watersheds, and many serious health problems. None are healthy or sustainable, especially when they are used on a very large scale.

Fossil fuels are growing scarce and becoming more expensive to find. Fossil fuels are **nonrenewable**, meaning that once they are used up, systems based on them will literally run out of fuel. At the same time, the danger of global warming (see page 33) and pollution from burning fossil fuels has grown to become a serious environmental health problem for every single person and place in the world.

Health problems from nonrenewable energy

Burning fossil fuels in large power plants is the way most electricity is made. Digging up and burning fossil fuels pollutes air, soil, and water, leading to respiratory and skin problems. It also produces toxic chemicals that cause cancer and birth defects (see Chapter 16, and page 506). Our use of fossil fuels leads to global warming, and to wars for control of oil resources.

Big hydroelectric energy (using water from large dams to make electricity) leads to people being forced to leave their homes, go hungry, and lose valuable land, and causes an increase in diseases such as malaria and schistosomiasis (see Chapter 9). Small dams have many fewer problems.

Nuclear energy is very

dangerous because of the toxic materials it uses (see page 491), the threat of accidents, and the harmful waste it leaves behind, causing health problems for many generations. Nuclear energy is not clean energy.

High voltage wires (the cables that carry electricity from where it is made to where it is used) can cause health problems such as cancer of the blood **(leukemia)** and other cancers. It is best not to build homes very close to high voltage wires, especially directly beneath them.

High voltage wires are just as dangerous when used with clean energy as with fossil fuels. Making energy locally, which is an important part of clean energy, reduces the need for high-voltage wires.

Benefits and Costs of Clean Energy

Clean energy is energy that can be made with few negative social, cultural, health, and environmental effects. Clean energy is also called **renewable** or sustainable energy, because it is produced from sources that do not run out, such as:

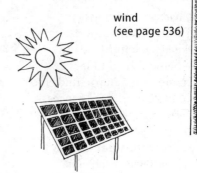

wind
(see page 536)

falling water from small dams
(page 534)

sunlight (page 537)

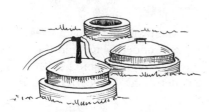

biogas and other biomass
(page 540)

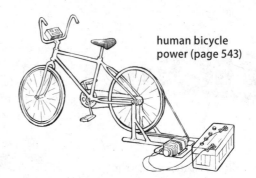

human bicycle
power (page 543)

By using clean energy, we reduce harm to both human health and the environment caused by finding and using fossil fuels and other forms of polluting, nonrenewable energy. Clean energy can provide power in rural villages, in big cities, and in factories without causing harm.

Each way of making clean electricity has advantages and disadvantages. And each depends on local conditions such as how much wind, sunshine, or falling water there is in each place. Electricity, even clean electricity, may be too costly for many people to afford. But as more and more people use clean energy, and as the ways to make clean energy are improved, it will likely become easier and less costly to make and use.

Paying for clean energy

Home energy systems that run on solar, wind, or water power cost money to install. But once they are in place they cost little to run and maintain. The income generated by labor-saving electric machines such as grain grinders and water pumps, and the ability to work after nightfall, can often pay for the initial costs.

People in many countries are developing ways to make it possible for everyone to have access to clean energy. Forming village cooperatives to pay for energy collectively is one solution. Another solution is microcredit programs (see page 539). Microcredit programs allow families to pay small amounts over time, rather than a large amount all at once. By paying into a "revolving credit fund," money is made available to help more people install home energy over time.

There are no longer any technical reasons why people in poor countries or rural areas should not have electricity. The reasons they do not have electricity have to do with a scarcity of social justice.

Storing energy

Any form of energy, in order to be useful when and where it is needed, must be stored. For gas or oil-powered transportation, this means storing fuel in the tank of a car or bus so it can be burned along the journey. For electricity, it means using batteries.

Even if energy is made using clean sources such as wind, water, or sunshine, it must be captured in batteries. Batteries can often be among the most costly parts of a clean energy system. They also contain toxic materials and must be replaced after several years. So far, there is no good replacement for batteries as a way to store electrical energy.

Energy Distribution

Large power plants run by private industry and
governments generate electricity and distribute it
through high-voltage wires to different areas.
Then the electricity passes through transformers (machines
that change the electricity from high voltage to a lower
voltage that can be used in homes and businesses). Low
voltage wires bring the electricity into houses or factories
to run lights and machines.

Transformer

   The problem with the way most electricity is produced
today is not only that it is dirty, but that it
is produced on a very large scale and sent
over long distances. This is very expensive.
Because this distribution system is so
expensive, smaller communities may wait
years for the national electric system to
arrive, if it ever arrives at all.
So most electricity goes to the
biggest users: industry
and cities.

**It is very costly to transport
electricity through high-voltage
wires over long distances.**

Clean energy from wind, sun, and water can be made in smaller quantities
at a lower cost, so clean energy is easier to use close to where it is produced.
Communities that use clean energy can have control over their own energy
resources. When electricity is made locally from sunlight, water, or biogas, it
reduces dependence on fossil fuels, and on expensive, high-voltage distribution
systems. It also avoids having faraway government agencies or large
corporations setting prices and controlling where the energy can go.

Clean energy works best if a mix of different sources is used. If one source becomes unavailable, such as sunshine on cloudy days, or falling water in the dry season, the other sources are still able to make power.

Fossil fuel energy distributes electricity, dependence, and pollution. Clean energy distributes electricity, independence, self-reliance, and sustainability.

Solar-powered rural clinics

In a remote part of Burma near the border of Thailand, people of the Karen ethnic community live in constant struggle with the Burmese military. Due to this oppression, no governmental or non-governmental organization (NGO) is able to provide health care in this area. But Karen groups on the Thailand side of the border have built a network of medics supporting over 28 clinics that care for almost 100,000 people in the region. The medics treat land mine victims and other people wounded in the conflict, as well as other health problems.

Two NGOs, Green Empowerment and a local group called Border Green Energy Team, brought solar panels and batteries to the border and trained Karen villagers, refugees, and medics to assemble and use them. The medics carried the equipment through the jungle. Now all 28 clinics in the war zone have electricity to run lights, laptop computers, and life-saving medical equipment, and villagers know how to repair and maintain their own solar energy systems.

Making the Best Use of Electricity

Aside from using clean energy, an important way to reduce pollution from electricity is to use it more carefully. If we waste less electricity, our power plants will not have to produce so much — or produce so much pollution. There are many ways governments can promote better energy use, including regulating industry to use cleaner production methods (see page 458), and improving existing power plants and power lines.

Compact fluorescent light bulbs last much longer than regular (incandescent) light bulbs, saving electricity and money.

Reduce waste, reduce demand

Reducing the demand for more electricity by people and industries that use too much is the best way to reduce the use of fossil fuels. Governments can reduce the demand for energy by encouraging factories, businesses, and people who live in cities to use energy more efficiently. When less energy is used, it reduces both the cost of making energy and the harm to peoples' health and the environment.

Governments can charge more or ask for higher taxes from industries that use the most electricity. Governments can also encourage electricity use at different times of the day, so that it is not in demand all at one time.

The corporations that make electricity are like other businesses. The more they make and sell, the more they profit. Because our health and environment is harmed by too much production of electricity from fossil fuels, the energy corporations must be forced to conserve, not expand.

Improve existing power plants and power lines

Power lines carry electricity from power plants to wherever the electricity is used. The way electricity moves through a power line can be compared to how water moves through a pipe. Just as a leaky pipe wastes water, a poorly maintained power line wastes electricity. Poor quality power lines waste a lot of electricity.

Repairing power lines saves a lot of electricity.

Existing power plants can also be improved to produce more, cleaner, and safer electricity. Improving power plants costs less and causes less harm to people and the environment than building new ones.

Transportation

Along with electricity, the biggest use of energy worldwide is as fuel for transportation in trains, airplanes, trucks, buses, and automobiles. Just as with electricity, people in wealthy countries use more fuel for transportation than people in poor countries. Pollution from burning fuel for transportation is a major cause of illnesses such as asthma, bronchitis, and cancers, and also causes global warming.

In order to burn less fuel and have more fairness in transportation, people in wealthy countries, especially the United States, must use more public transportation (trains and buses) and fewer private automobiles. Cities and transportation systems must encourage bicycles instead of cars.

The problem with plant-based fuels

When the automobile engine was invented, it was made to run on fuels made from plants, such as vegetable oil or alcohol. But soon after, when petroleum became cheap to produce, gasoline and diesel fuel (both made from petroleum) became the main fuels used to power automobile engines, as well as motorcycles, trucks, and airplanes. The petroleum industry worked very hard to prevent plant-based fuels from being used.

Now that oil has again become expensive, many countries are turning to plant-based fuels to replace petroleum. Fuel made from palm, soybeans, canola, maize or other plant oils is called "biofuel" or "agrofuel." This seems like a good solution because plants are renewable. But there are many reasons why agro-fuels will cause more problems than they solve.

- Producing oil from plants that could be used for food leads to competition between growing fuel for cars and growing food for people. With so many people suffering from lack of food, we cannot afford to turn food into fuel.

- One reason to reduce dependence on fossil fuels is to decrease global warming. But to produce the amounts of crops needed to make biofuel requires the use of petroleum fertilizer, farm machinery, and transportation of the fuel crop from where it is grown to where it is processed and distributed, and finally to where it is used. In the end, producing biofuels uses more energy than it produces, and causes more global warming than petroleum!

- When forested land is cleared to grow biofuel crops, the trees that absorb global warming gases are destroyed. For example, biofuel made from palm oil causes 10 times as much global warming as diesel oil.

Small Dams

Small dams can be used to generate electricity from running or falling water (called small hydropower, and micro-hydropower when it is very small). Where there is enough water from rivers or streams, micro-hydropower is the least costly way to provide electricity to rural communities. These projects can be set up and managed by villagers. In China, India, and Nepal, thousands of small hydropower projects supply power to villages and towns.

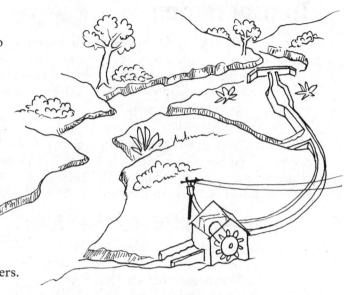

Water is taken from the river, run downhill to a turbine, and then flows back into the river.

In small hydropower projects, water is channeled from a river or stream and runs downhill through a pipe. The falling water in the pipe turns a turbine, and then returns to the river or stream. Small dams do not displace people or change the flow of the river the way large dams do. Micro-hydropower projects use dams only a few meters tall to direct water toward the turbine.

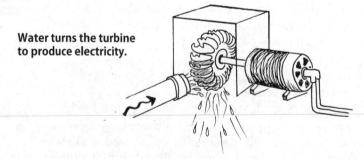

Water turns the turbine to produce electricity.

(To learn more about micro-hydro power and to contact organizations that install micro-hydro power systems, see Resources.)

Micro-hydropower unites communities

As the country of Nicaragua recovered from many years of war, people throughout the country devoted themselves to rebuilding farms, water systems, schools, and health clinics. But the country was left in deep poverty, and the government was unable to provide electricity to many rural communities.

The village of La Pita had no electricity, and the nearest power lines were 70 kilometers away. People in La Pita had fought on opposing sides in the war, and this made it difficult to carry out community projects. But after they worked together to build a school and a clinic, they decided to bring electricity to the village as well.

The villagers asked a local group called the Association of Rural Development Workers-Benjamin Linder to help them electrify La Pita. Because the village lies close to a river that runs year-round, La Pita was a good site for a micro-hydropower project. The development workers helped the villagers organize the project and get support from a small international agency called Green Empowerment, which provided funds and technical skills.

Community members worked together for many hours to build the small dam and turbine that now sends electricity to 400 villagers. The electricity is used in people's homes, the community school, 2 carpentry shops, and local farms. When the electric plant was installed and running, the community formed an association to run and maintain the system, making sure everyone in La Pita benefits. Despite differences people had in the past, electricity and the responsibility for generating it is now shared by everyone. The small village of La Pita, far from the national power lines, has its own power.

Wind Power

Energy from the wind has been used
for hundreds of years to pump water
and grind grain. In recent years, wind
is being used to generate electricity in
Europe and North America, India, China,
South Africa, and Brazil. Large and small
windmills generate electricity as the force
of the wind turns the blades.

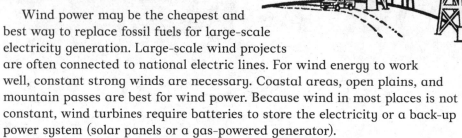

Wind power may be the cheapest and
best way to replace fossil fuels for large-scale
electricity generation. Large-scale wind projects
are often connected to national electric lines. For wind energy to work
well, constant strong winds are necessary. Coastal areas, open plains, and
mountain passes are best for wind power. Because wind in most places is not
constant, wind turbines require batteries to store the electricity or a back-up
power system (solar panels or a gas-powered generator).

Small-scale wind energy

Wind turbines are used to charge batteries for homes in some parts of the
world. But because wind energy relies on constant wind, requires careful
measurements to set up and maintain the turbines, and wind turbines may
be costly, this may not be the best choice for home or village electricity.
Wind may seem better at first glance than solar, because a wind turbine
may cost less than solar panels, but in the long term it needs more repairs
and maintenance.

(To learn more about wind power and to contact organizations that install
wind power systems, see Resources.)

Solar Power

When you feel the sun heating your body or the air in your house, this is solar energy. There are many ways to make efficient use of the sun's energy to heat water (see page 538), to make water safe (see page 98), and to cook food or heat a house (see page 378). The sun's energy can also be used to make electricity.

Solar panels on the roof of a house collect energy from the sun.

Solar energy requires the use of **solar panels** or solar cells to capture the sunlight and change it into electricity. Because the sun is not always shining, the electricity made must be stored in batteries before being used to run lights, motors, and other machines.

A solar energy system can be costly to install because it requires solar panels, batteries, and other parts. But sunlight is free (and endlessly renewable). Once a solar system is in place, it costs little to run and maintain. The biggest costs of maintaining a solar system are replacing the batteries every 3 to 5 years and replacing solar panels if they break.

The parts of a solar electric system

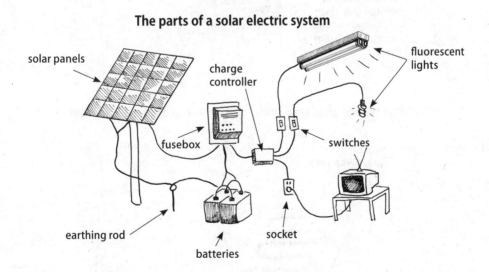

solar panels

charge controller

fluorescent lights

fusebox

switches

earthing rod

socket

batteries

(To learn more about solar energy and to contact organizations that install solar electric systems, see Resources.)

Solar hot water

In areas with a lot of sunlight, one of the most direct uses for solar energy is to heat water for drinking or bathing. Solar hot water does not require solar panels or costly equipment. All that is needed is a water storage tank, and pipe painted black to absorb the sun's rays.

In mild climates, solar collectors are needed to heat water. They are more costly than simple solar water heaters, but less costly than the solar panels needed for electricity, and less costly than heating water with nonrenewable resources.

A simple water heater

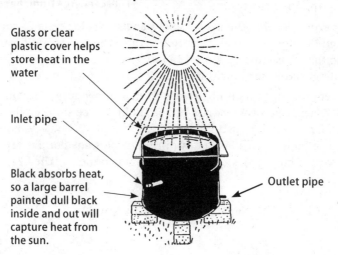

Glass or clear plastic cover helps store heat in the water

Inlet pipe

Black absorbs heat, so a large barrel painted dull black inside and out will capture heat from the sun.

Outlet pipe

Solar water heater placed in the sun on a roof or at ground level

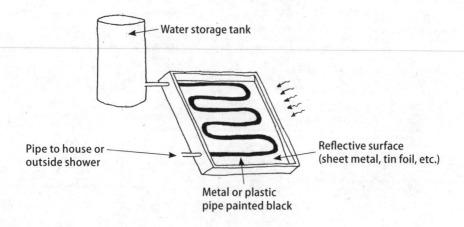

Water storage tank

Pipe to house or outside shower

Reflective surface (sheet metal, tin foil, etc.)

Metal or plastic pipe painted black

Microcredit helps fund solar power

Most homes in rural Sri Lanka are not connected to the national electric power system. But as in many tropical countries, the island of Sri Lanka has a lot of sunshine. In 1991, an organization called SELF (Solar Electric Light Fund) came to Sri Lanka to help people use their sunshine to make electricity.

Because they could not give away solar power systems for free, SELF came up with a way to help people pay for their own systems. Together with a Sri Lankan non-profit organization, they formed a "solar cooperative." The cooperative set up a microcredit fund. Cooperative members paid a small down payment to have a solar system set up, and made small payments to the fund every month for up to 8 years. As the fund grew, more families were able to use it to pay for their own solar systems. After 5 years, the first 48 families had repaid enough into the microcredit fund to allow 25 more families to buy solar systems.

Building on this success, SELF began working with Sarvodaya, the largest NGO in Sri Lanka, with over 3 million members. SELF and Sarvodaya developed a "Solar Seed" program, which introduced solar electricity to over 100 villages. The program installed demonstration solar systems in community centers, schools, and Buddhist temples. SELF then organized a microcredit fund to help Sarvodaya members buy home solar systems. The program started with 300 households. A few years later, it was so successful that Sarvodaya began planning for a "million-home" solar program.

Thousands of homes in rural Sri Lanka now have solar electricity. Using the microcredit system, thousands more will soon have solar electricity. If they continue working this way, Sri Lanka may one day be the world's first nation to run entirely on sunlight.

Biomass Energy

In many countries, **biomass** (waste material from plants and animals) is a common household energy resource. The energy in biomass materials can be released by burning it or by allowing it to rot and produce **biogas** (a natural gas).

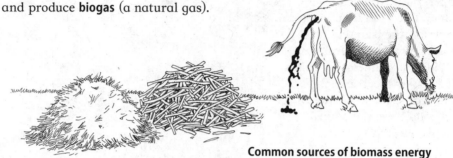

Common sources of biomass energy

Biomass from plants is renewable, but when it is burned as fuel it contributes to global warming and health problems. When you make a fire with wood or cow dung, you are using biomass energy on a small scale.

On a larger scale, crop wastes (residues) can be used to generate electricity. In Cuba, for example, a large amount of electricity is generated by burning sugarcane stalks after they have been harvested and milled for sugar. Rice husks, wood waste, and other kinds of biomass can also be used in this way. While it may be renewable, pollution from burning crop wastes is bad for the health of the community and the environment.

Biogas

Biogas is produced when organic matter rots. When biogas is captured in a closed container, it can produce a small flame for cooking, or electricity for heating, lighting, pumping water, and operating motors and farm equipment. By converting the organic matter in human, animal, and plant waste into energy, biogas turns waste products into a resource that is good for the environment and for community health. Biogas can be made from many kinds of organic matter:

- animal manure and urine
- human feces and urine
- food waste such as meat, blood, bones, and vegetable scraps
- plant matter such as crop residues, straw, leaves, bark, branches, and grass cuttings

Biogas is invisible and does not smell. When it is burned, it produces a clean blue flame. Using biogas for cooking instead of solid fuels like wood reduces illnesses from indoor cooking smoke (see Chapter 17), and reduces the pressure to cut down trees for fuel. The material left behind after producing biogas can be used as a high quality fertilizer. Burning biogas does not lead to climate change and global warming.

Make a small biogas plant

The design of the biogas plant depends on the quantity and kind of wastes you have, the climate, and the construction materials available. Different kinds of animal and plant waste create different amounts of gas, so it is difficult to say how many animals are needed to produce biogas.

Manure from cows, pigs, chickens and even human waste can be used to produce biogas. Cows produce the most, by far, and are the best source of biogas fuel. To have enough fuel to cook every day (5 hours per day on a 2-burner stove), 4 or 5 cows are needed.

Before building a biogas plant, you must be sure you have enough waste material available to generate the amount of energy for your needs.

A basic design for a biogas plant

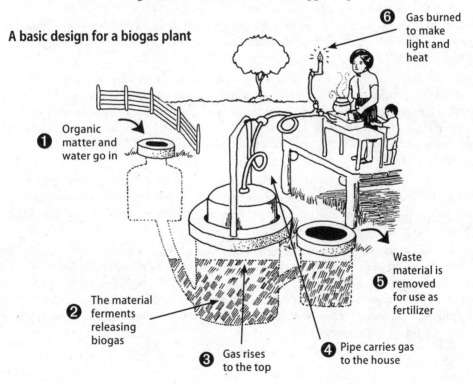

❶ Organic matter and water go in

❷ The material ferments releasing biogas

❸ Gas rises to the top

❹ Pipe carries gas to the house

❺ Waste material is removed for use as fertilizer

❻ Gas burned to make light and heat

(To learn more about biogas and to contact organizations that build biogas systems, see Resources.)

Biogas powers rural life

In Nepal, most people live in remote villages scattered across high mountains, foothills, and deep valleys. The combination of poverty and rugged terrain make it nearly impossible for the government to provide electricity throughout the country.

Because it is an agricultural nation, most households in Nepal have cattle. In the early 1990s the government of Nepal discovered that they could use cattle dung mixed with water to make biogas, providing energy for people in rural areas to have heat, light, and cooking fuel for very little money. With support from the governments of Germany and Holland, they established the Biogas Support Program (BSP).

The goal of this program is to provide a biogas system to as many homes in Nepal as possible. BSP designed a biogas system that was low-cost, efficient, and easy to use and maintain. BSP workers did outreach and education to teach rural people about the uses and benefits of biogas. They also started a microcredit program to help families pay the costs of the biogas systems.

In the first 2 years, 6000 biogas systems were installed. The program was so effective that over the next 10 years, 100,000 more systems were installed. By the year 2010, the government hopes to have installed 200,000 biogas systems.

Families all over rural Nepal now use biogas for cooking, heating, and light. By using biogas, each house saves 4 tons of firewood and 32 liters of kerosene per year. Each biogas plant also produces 5 tons of fertilizer per year, which farmers use to improve their crop yield. Thanks to biogas, many families in Nepal are now healthier, warmer, and less dependent on fuels that pollute and damage the environment.

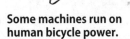

Bicycle Power

The bicycle may be one of the greatest machines ever invented. Bicycles provide an easy way to get around using only human energy, and have countless benefits for people's health and the environment. But more than this, human power can be harnessed by bicycles and used as energy for running many different kinds of machines.

Some machines run on human bicycle power.

Adding a battery, bicycles can power lights, televisions and other machines.

Maya Pedal bicycle power

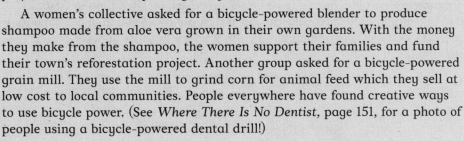

In 1997, a group came together in Chimaltenango, Guatemala, to promote sustainable development. Called Maya Pedal, this NGO promotes health, environmental protection, and a sustainable rural economy through bicycle power.

They began by collecting used bicycle parts to build bicycle-powered machines to meet the needs of rural people. Maya Pedal sold bicycle-powered machines to anyone who wanted to buy one, but groups that wanted to start sustainable development projects were offered especially low prices.

A women's collective asked for a bicycle-powered blender to produce shampoo made from aloe vera grown in their own gardens. With the money they make from the shampoo, the women support their families and fund their town's reforestation project. Another group asked for a bicycle-powered grain mill. They use the mill to grind corn for animal feed which they sell at low cost to local communities. People everywhere have found creative ways to use bicycle power. (See *Where There Is No Dentist*, page 151, for a photo of people using a bicycle-powered dental drill!)

Appendix A:
Safety and Emergencies

When working with or being exposed to dangerous substances in the workplace, the community, or the home, it is important to be as safe as possible and to be prepared for accidents. This section has information on the following topics:

- make a safety plan for emergencies
- a first aid kit
- protective clothing and equipment
- protective masks
- chemical spills

- treating harm caused by chemicals
- treating burns
- shock
- rescue breathing
  (mouth-to-mouth breathing)

The material provided here will help you prepare for emergencies, but it is not a complete first aid manual. To be better prepared, seek training in first aid and in treating chemical accidents, get a first aid manual and understand its contents, and ask your community health workers to assist in developing a safety plan.

Make a Safety Plan for Emergencies

Just as important as having protective equipment and a first aid kit is knowing what to do in case of an emergency or an accident. Every community and every workplace should make a safety plan in case of a toxic release, fire, flood, storm, or other emergency.

Post the address and phone number of the nearest medical clinic or hospital in central locations. Make sure everyone knows where first aid kits and other emergency supplies are located, and how to use them. A safety plan can also include:

- a plan for transporting injured and ill people to a clinic or hospital, and a vehicle that can be used in an emergency.

- a central meeting place such as a community center, school, or church.

- an emergency supply of clean drinking water.

- a telephone or radio to call for help and to alert officials and media.

- a list of elderly people, people with disabilities, or others in the community who may need help in case of an evacuation.

Different kinds of emergencies require different responses. Understanding the most likely threats to your community and learning to be prepared for them is an important part of any safety plan.

A First Aid Kit

Every workplace, health post, and community center should have a first aid kit to provide treatment in emergencies. Make a first aid kit in a container with a tightly fitting cover so water, dust, or chemicals cannot leak into the kit. Make sure everyone in the community or workplace, including new workers, knows where the kit is kept and how to use it.

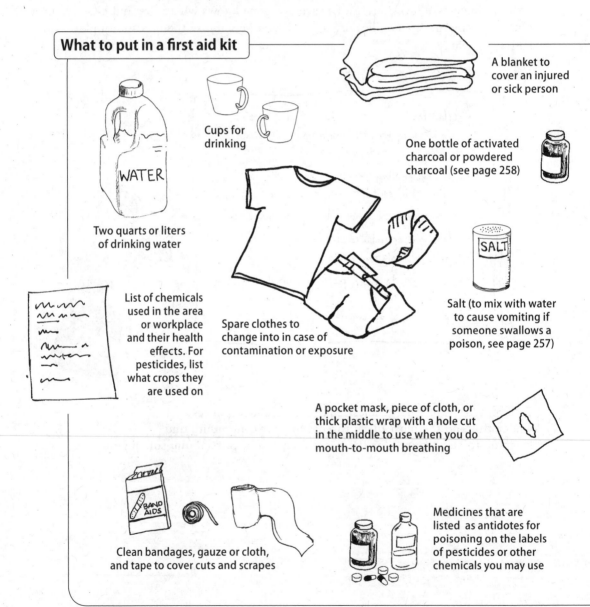

What to put in a first aid kit

A blanket to cover an injured or sick person

Cups for drinking

One bottle of activated charcoal or powdered charcoal (see page 258)

WATER

Two quarts or liters of drinking water

Salt (to mix with water to cause vomiting if someone swallows a poison, see page 257)

List of chemicals used in the area or workplace and their health effects. For pesticides, list what crops they are used on

Spare clothes to change into in case of contamination or exposure

A pocket mask, piece of cloth, or thick plastic wrap with a hole cut in the middle to use when you do mouth-to-mouth breathing

BAND AIDS

Clean bandages, gauze or cloth, and tape to cover cuts and scrapes

Medicines that are listed as antidotes for poisoning on the labels of pesticides or other chemicals you may use

Different communities and workplaces will require different kinds of first aid supplies. Consider the kinds of emergencies that may happen in your area and plan your first aid kit with this in mind. If you work with pesticides or other chemicals, read the labels on their containers to find out which medicines are recommended for poisonings.

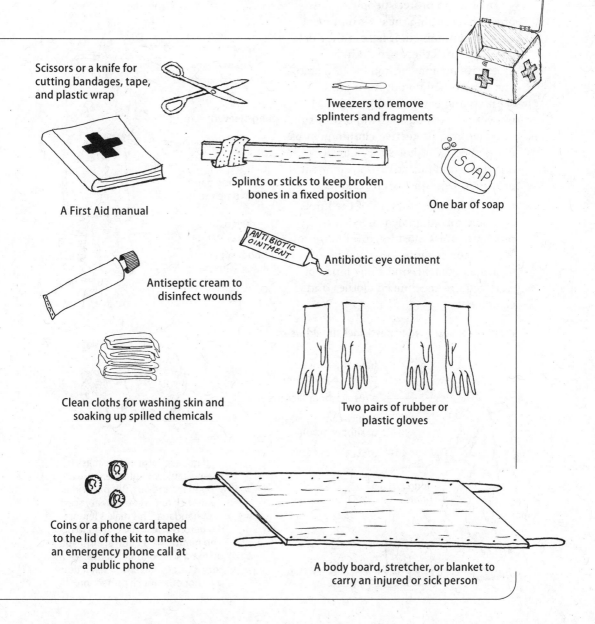

Scissors or a knife for cutting bandages, tape, and plastic wrap

Tweezers to remove splinters and fragments

A First Aid manual

Splints or sticks to keep broken bones in a fixed position

One bar of soap

Antiseptic cream to disinfect wounds

Antibiotic eye ointment

Clean cloths for washing skin and soaking up spilled chemicals

Two pairs of rubber or plastic gloves

Coins or a phone card taped to the lid of the kit to make an emergency phone call at a public phone

A body board, stretcher, or blanket to carry an injured or sick person

Protective Clothing and Equipment

Every person should wear protective clothing, also called personal protective equipment, when working with or being exposed to harmful materials. It is the responsibility of employers to provide protective equipment for workers. Workers should demand that employers respect their rights to health and safety by providing protective equipment and maintaining it in good condition.

In order to protect people, protective clothing must fit and must be well-maintained. It is said that in poor countries there are 3 kinds of protective equipment: too big, too small, and torn. If you do not have protective clothing and equipment, you can protect yourself by wearing a rain suit, or by making protective clothing out of plastic bags. Cut holes for your head and arms and put other bags on your arms and legs, and hands and feet.

This picture shows all of the kinds of protection equipment needed to protect against most harmful materials. Not all jobs or materials demand all of this equipment, and some kinds of work require specialized clothes and equipment.

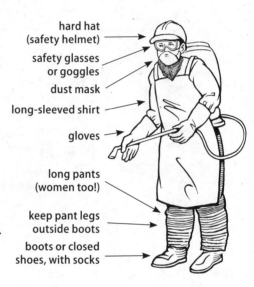

hard hat (safety helmet)

safety glasses or goggles

dust mask

long-sleeved shirt

gloves

long pants (women too!)

keep pant legs outside boots

boots or closed shoes, with socks

Farmworkers exposed to pesticides should wear:

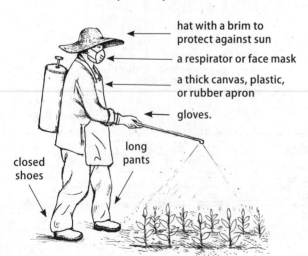

hat with a brim to protect against sun

a respirator or face mask

a thick canvas, plastic, or rubber apron

gloves.

closed shoes

long pants

If no respirator or face mask is available, people often use a bandana or scarf. But pesticides will stick to a wet or sweaty scarf or bandana. This makes it more dangerous to use these than to have no mouth protection at all. If you do use a scarf or bandana, rinse and dry it often, and know that it does not offer much protection.

Oil and mine workers are better protected when they wear:

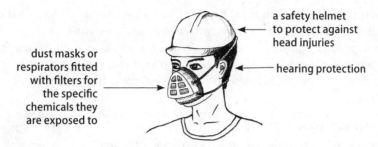

dust masks or
respirators fitted
with filters for
the specific
chemicals they
are exposed to

a safety helmet
to protect against
head injuries

hearing protection

People collecting waste, and health workers at hospitals, health clinics, and other health care settings should wear:

safety glasses to protect
against splashes

a face mask to protect
against germs

durable gloves

INFECTIOUS
WASTE

closed shoes

Protective clothing and equipment works only if it is clean. After each use, or at the end of each shift, wash gloves, masks, glasses, and other clothing and equipment to prevent the next person who uses them from being contaminated.

Protective masks

The best ways to prevent harm from breathing in toxic chemicals and dust are to have good ventilation when working with them, and to wear a protective mask made to protect against the chemicals you are working with. If you feel ill from a chemical while wearing a mask, it is a sign the mask is not working properly, or that you are being exposed to that or some other toxic chemical in some other way.

Loose cloth or paper mask

This mask will help keep out some dust. It will **not** stop you from breathing in chemical fumes. Fumes pass through paper and cloth and leak in around the edges of a loose-fitting mask.

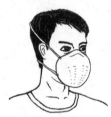

Tight fitting paper mask

This mask will protect from dust. The mask should touch your face all the way around. It will **not** stop you from breathing in chemical fumes. These masks clog up or wear out quickly and must be replaced when they no longer touch the face all around.

Plastic dust mask

This mask will protect from dust better than a loose cloth or tight paper mask. The mask should touch your face all the way around. It will **not** stop you from breathing in chemical fumes.

Rubber respirator

This rubber mask with filters MAY keep you from breathing in chemical fumes. It must fit your face tightly so no air leaks in between your skin and the mask. You will probably need a different filter for each chemical and must change the filter often. You will need special training to fit, use, and clean this mask. This mask is hot and uncomfortable to wear. When working with chemicals, take breaks often in an open, well-ventilated area where you can safely remove the mask.

How to make a cloth and activated charcoal mask

This homemade mask was designed by Dr. Maramba of the Philippines. It will give some protection from chemicals and dust.

1 Cut one cup from a padded cloth bra.

2 Remove padding from the bra cup.

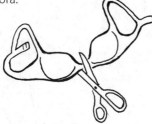

3 Cut some filter paper to make a pouch for a new pad that will fit inside the bra. Fill the filter paper pad with 100 grams of activated charcoal, making sure a layer of charcoal fills the entire filter evenly rather than settling to the bottom. Seal the paper so it will not spill, and place it inside the bra where the bra pad was.

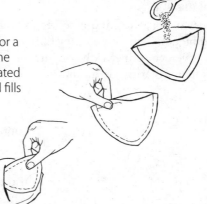

4 Fit the bra cup with elastic straps to hold it tightly to your face.

The filter should be aired out between uses. If used while spraying the most toxic chemicals, this mask is good only for 2 uses of 4 hours each. The charcoal must be replaced within 1 week, depending on the type of chemical exposure and how long it is worn.

Chemical Spills

Before you clean up a chemical spill, protect yourself, people nearby, and water sources. If there are people who are more prepared than you to clean up a spill (people who have been trained to do this work), call them for help. **Always wear protective clothing to clean up chemicals!**

Small chemical spills

If a small amount of chemicals is spilled, it is important to control, contain, and clean the spill before anyone is hurt, and before the chemicals get into waterways or soak into the ground.

Control the spill

The most important thing is to keep the spill from getting bigger. Shut down any leaking equipment, turn a fallen container right side up, or put the leaking container inside an unbroken container.

Contain the spill

Absorb the chemicals by putting soil, sand, sawdust, clay or other material on the spill. If the material may blow around, cover it with a cloth or plastic sheet.

Clean up the spill

Scoop materials into barrels or thick plastic containers. Do not use water because it will spread the chemicals and make the problem worse. Dispose of the material safely (see pages 410 to 411).

Large chemical spills

In oil drilling areas, work sites, and industrial areas where large amounts of chemicals are used or transported, it is important to be prepared for a large chemical spill.

- Make an emergency plan with workers, employers, and people living nearby. Hold regular meetings to make sure everyone is familiar with the plan.

- Post names and telephone numbers of people to contact in case of a spill. Include employers, clinics and hospitals, safety officials, government authorities, health workers and people trained to clean spills.

- Keep instructions, materials, and protective equipment for cleaning spills at the site.

- Plan and mark an escape route from the area.

- Have a supply of safe water to use in case oil or other chemicals contaminate the community water supply.

Treating Harm Caused by Chemicals

Chemicals can spill on the skin and clothes, splash in the eyes, or be swallowed or breathed in as fumes. If someone is hurt, get medical help as soon as possible.

Breathing in chemicals

- Get the person away from the area where she breathed in the poison, especially if it is an enclosed area. If the spill happened indoors, open windows and doors.

- Get the person into fresh air.

- Loosen the person's clothing.

- Sit or lay the person with head and shoulders raised.

- If the person is unconscious, lay her on her side and make sure there is nothing blocking her breathing.

- If the person is not breathing, do mouth-to-mouth breathing (see page 557).

- If there are signs of a health problem such as headaches, nose or throat irritation, dizziness, drowsiness or tightness of the chest, seek medical help immediately. Take the chemical label or name with you.

Swallowing chemicals:

- If the person is unconscious, lay her on her side and make sure she is breathing.
- If the person is not breathing, quickly do mouth-to-mouth breathing (see page 557). Mouth-to-mouth breathing can also expose you to the chemical, so cover your mouth with a pocket mask, or a piece of cloth or thick plastic wrap with a hole cut in the middle, before you start mouth-to-mouth breathing.
- If the person can drink, give her lots of clean water.
- Find the chemical package and read the label right away. The label will tell you if you should make the person vomit up the poison or not (see page 257).

When chemicals spill on the body or clothing

- If it is safe, first move the injured person away from the chemical spill.
- Remove any clothing, shoes, or jewelry the chemical spilled on. Be careful when removing pullover shirts or sweaters to prevent getting chemicals in the eyes. It may be best to cut the clothes off.
- Wash the affected area with cool water for at least 15 minutes.
- If chemicals got into the eyes, rinse with clean water for 15 minutes. Pull the eyelid away and move the eyeball in a circle so the entire eye is washed.
- If the person stops breathing, use mouth-to-mouth breathing.
- Use a rag to soak up chemicals, being careful not to spread the chemicals around.
- If the body is burned by chemicals, treat them like ordinary burns (see page 555).

Treating Burns

For any burn:

- Stop the burning by putting the burned part in cool water at once. Continue to cool the burn for at least 20 minutes.

- Relieve pain with aspirin or other pain medicine.

- Prevent shock (see page 556).

For minor burns, no other treatment is needed.

For chemical burns, radiation burns, electrical burns, and burns that cause blisters (2nd degree burns):

- **DO NOT** remove anything stuck to the burn.

- **DO NOT** apply lotions, fats, or butter.

- **DO NOT** break blisters.

- **DO NOT** remove loose skin.

- **DO NOT** put anything on a chemical burn.

- **DO** immediately wash away any chemicals from the burn with clean water.

- **DO** cover the burned area with wet **sterile dressings** (such as a clean gauze bandage) if possible.

- **DO** wash gently with cool, clean water and a mild soap if blisters are broken. Only leave the burn uncovered if you are in a very clean area, where there are no insects, dust, or chemical fumes.

- **DO** get rid of clothing that may be contaminated by chemicals, or wash the clothing separately from other clothes.

- **DO** use honey to cover a minor burn. Honey can prevent and control infection and speed healing. Gently wash off the old honey and put on new honey at least twice a day.

Then take the person to a health worker or hospital as soon as possible.

Take the person to a hospital if you think they have burned their airway. Signs include:

- burns around the mouth or nose, or burns inside the mouth.

- mental confusion, unconsciousness, or coughing a lot from inhaling smoke.

Also, take a person to the hospital who has serious burns on the face, eyes, hands, feet, or genitals.

Any person who is been badly burned can easily go into shock (see the next page) because of combined pain, fear, and the loss of body fluids from the oozing burn. Comfort and reassure the person, ease pain, treat shock, and give plenty of liquids.

Shock

Shock is a life-threatening condition that can result from a large burn, losing a lot of blood, severe illness, dehydration, severe allergic reaction, acute toxic exposure, or other emergency situation.

Signs of shock

- Mental confusion, weakness, dizziness, or loss of consciousness
- Weak, rapid pulse
- Cold sweat: pale, cold, damp skin
- Blood pressure drops dangerously low

To prevent or treat shock

At first sign of shock, or if there is risk of shock:

- Have the person lie down with his feet a little higher than his head, like this: ⟶
- Stop any bleeding and treat any wounds.
- If the person feels cold, cover him with a blanket.
- If the person is able to drink, give sips of water. If he is dehydrated, give a lot of liquid, and rehydration drink (see page 53).
- If the person is in pain, give aspirin or other pain medicine, but not one with a sedative, such as codeine.
- Stay calm and reassure the person.

If the person is unconscious:

- Lay him on his side with his head low, tilted back and to the side (see above). If he seems to be choking, pull his tongue forward with your finger.
- If he has vomited, clear his mouth right away.
- Do not give anything by mouth until he becomes conscious.
- **Seek medical help.**

Rescue Breathing (Mouth-to-Mouth Breathing)

A person can die within 4 minutes if she does not breathe. If a person stops breathing for any reason, begin mouth-to-mouth breathing right away! If the person swallowed chemicals, mouth-to-mouth breathing can also expose you to the chemical, so before you start mouth-to-mouth breathing, cover your mouth with a pocket mask, or a piece of cloth or thick plastic wrap with a hole cut in the middle.

Step 1: Quickly use a finger to remove anything stuck in the mouth or throat. Pull the tongue forward. If there is mucus in the throat, quickly try to clear it out.

Step 2: Quickly but gently lay the person face up. Gently tilt his head back and pull his jaw forward.

Step 3: Pinch his nostrils closed with your fingers, open his mouth, cover his mouth with yours, and blow strongly into his lungs so that his chest rises. Pause to let air come back out and blow again. Repeat about every 5 seconds. With babies and small children, cover both the nose and mouth with your mouth, and breathe very gently about once every 3 seconds.

Continue rescue breathing until the person can breathe by himself, or until there is no doubt he is dead. Sometimes you must keep trying for an hour or more.

Note: Unless there is an open sore or bleeding in the mouth, it is not possible to give or get HIV from mouth-to-mouth breathing.

Appendix B:
Using Laws to Fight for Environmental Rights

Human rights, and somtimes environmental rights (the right to a safe, healthy environment) are protected by the laws of many countries. This book includes many stories about how people have worked together to make new laws to protect their communities, or have demanded protection under laws that already exist.

This section of the book includes information on how to use an **Environmental Impact Assessment** or a lawsuit to fight for your environmental rights. It also contains information about where to seek international help if your local and national courts and government do not protect you.

Communities struggling to protect their environment and health often face opposition and violence from corporations or governments that want to take their natural resources or pursue development projects, regardless of the harm they will cause. These projects may displace people from their lands, create terrible pollution, endanger public safety, or produce toxics that cause serious health problems. These are all violations of human rights and environmental rights.

Large corporations sometimes have so much money and power they are able to prevent governments from recognizing or enforcing laws that should protect you. When local and national laws are not effective, there are some international laws that may offer protections to you and your community.

The idea that people have environmental rights is a relatively new area of law, so the definitions of what those rights are and how they apply are still being determined. This makes every legal battle for environmental rights very important.

Environmental Impact Assessments (EIAs)

Because industry and development projects have caused so much environmental destruction, many governments, industries, and development agencies are now required by law to use a decision-making and planning tool called an environmental impact assessment, or EIA.

An EIA describes how a project, such as building roads, mines, airports, or other industrial development will affect the people, animals, land, water, and air quality in an area. It may also look at social problems such as displacement of people and loss of cultural resources, such as traditional livelihoods, places of historic or spiritual importance, etc. An EIA must also suggest less harmful ways for the work to be done if a project is to go ahead.

An EIA may be done by a corporation alone, or it may be done by a corporation together with communities and government officials. (For stories about how 2 communities used an EIA, see pages 466 and 561.)

How EIAs work

EIAs involve 2 basic activities:

1. A study of the project's impacts and a written report describing these impacts. This is usually the responsibility of the company managing the project and may or may not involve community participation.

2. Public meetings to allow affected communities to evaluate the project before it begins.

An EIA works best when it is guided by the precautionary principle (see page 32). If an EIA shows harm may result from a project, the plan should be stopped or changed. But often EIAs are used to make a project appear harmless even though the project will cause serious harm to people and the environment, now or in the future.

Many companies write the EIA report before inviting community participation, rather than writing it with community participation. Sometimes companies do not publicize meetings about the EIA or they make the meetings difficult for people to attend. When an unfair EIA process is rushed through by a company or government agency, it often leads to a situation where the project begins while the community campaigns to stop it. Nevertheless, EIAs can be an important tool for communities and governments to evaluate and improve proposed development projects.

How communities can influence an EIA

Getting lots of information from different sources (not just from the company) and taking the time you need to understand all the potential impacts, are important parts of exercising your right to participate in an EIA. Usually, many decisions are already made by the time the people who are most affected have any say.

Participating in an EIA process can help educate and organize your community to better protect its health and resources in the long term. Even if it is not always possible to stop a harmful project, educating and organizing around an EIA can help protect your community.

Demand to participate

Communities can demand a voice in an EIA. Sometimes a court, government, or development agency will allow community representatives to take part in the EIA process. People from the community may participate, or can ask an ally, such as an NGO or a lawyer, to represent them. If community representatives take part in the EIA process, they can then report back at community meetings about what the company is planning and doing. Participation can also help build an understanding about the community's rights and responsibilities, and the ways they may prevent harm from a project or prevent the project altogether.

Get the entire EIA report

Communities have a right to see the entire EIA document, not just a summary or a partial version. EIA reports often include sections called "Security Risks," "Social Risks," "Health Risks," and "Clean-up Costs." These sections may describe problems the company would rather not share, especially at public meetings.

The problems described in an EIA, as well as the problems ignored by the EIA, can be shared with media, government officials, and the public to help build broader resistance to harmful projects. You can also share them with national or international bodies, such as the United Nations, which may result in pressure being placed on corporations or governments to respond to community concerns.

Communities resist mining

The small farming community of Junín lies in a beautiful area of cloud forest on the slopes of the Andes Mountains in Ecuador. People here are poor but they have earned a living from the earth for hundreds of years. Recently, the people of Junín faced the biggest challenge in their history: a company planned to build one of South America's largest open-pit copper mines in their region.

When a Japanese mining company came to explore the area, people in Junín knew that mining could bring pollution. But the mining company promised to build roads, health clinics, and schools, so the people of Junín let them explore for minerals anyway. Before long, the company found a large deposit of copper, and the people of Junín soon found their water supply polluted with mine waste. People were soon suffering from skin rashes and other health problems.

The community asked the mining company to stop polluting. The company didn't stop, so the people of Junín took action. When the miners were away on holiday, hundreds of villagers entered the mining camp, removed tools, furniture, and other items of value, and left them with the authorities. Then they burned down the camp. The company got the message and pulled out, but later sold the mine to a company from Canada.

The Canadian company worked to divide the community. They offered people from Junín large amounts of money to sell their land. Some people did sell, but others refused. The company knew this would cause conflicts. The company also sent a doctor to provide health care, but only to people who signed a paper saying they were in favor of the mine. After making this injustice known outside Ecuador, international supporters sent a health worker to attend anyone who was ill.

We continued organizing. Some villagers started a newspaper to spread the news and build support for our struggle.

Because the law in Ecuador requires an EIA before any development project can begin, the people in Junín made the EIA part of their plan to protect their land. The villagers knew that if an EIA was not done properly, the government would not allow the mine to be built. They also knew an honest EIA would show how copper mining would force people to move away, cause air pollution, erosion and silting of waterways, and contaminate the water with raw sewage, heavy metals, and other toxic waste.

(story continues on next page)

(continued from previous page)

The people of Junín had learned to use the law to their advantage. After the company claimed it had done the EIA, the government rejected it as incomplete.

People in Junín also used direct actions, such as refusing to let the company enter the area by blocking roads. Community leaders declared the entire municipality a non-mining zone. By using a variety of tactics, the people of Junín have prevented this open-pit copper mine from destroying their homes, their rich forests, and their water sources.

Community-based EIAs

A community-based EIA can help people in a village, town, or region come to a common understanding of the ways they use, protect, and depend on resources such as air, food, water, animals, forest products, plant medicines, sacred places, and so on. This can create a process for resolving conflicts and misunderstandings within communities about the use of resources. This can help build the unity needed to challenge corporations or governments. It can also help mobilize people to oppose industries which take advantage of divisions among people to exploit their water, timber, land, or other resources.

A community-based EIA can be as simple as discussing what resources the community uses and coming to agreements about how to best protect them from exploitation. A more complicated community-based EIA can include making detailed maps, conducting surveys, and building alliances with neighboring communities and supportive organizations.

A community-based EIA is different from an EIA carried out by corporations or governments. It may not meet the legal requirements of an "official" EIA, because it puts more importance on what communities think and the health of people and their culture than on exploiting resources. A community-based EIA recognizes that the difficult to understand structure and "scientific" language required in EIAs is not only confusing to most people, but purposely designed to exclude them. A community-based EIA is a way of saying "Another way to assess environmental impact is possible."

Many of the activities throughout this book, such as mapping (page 15), sociodramas (page 18), health surveys (see page 500), watershed protection activities (page 164), trash walks (page 391), or other activities developed by your community can contribute to a community-based EIA.

Lawsuits

One way that environmental rights and justice can be won is by going to court to sue companies that violate national or international laws. A successful lawsuit against a polluting industry or company not only protects the people immediately affected, it also protects people in other places and future generations.

To protect our rights we must use the law.

But to make the law work, we must struggle for our rights!

Will a lawsuit help your community?

Lawsuits have been used successfully in many struggles for environmental justice. But lawsuits are very expensive and they often take many years.

Even when a country has laws to protect health and the environment, it can be difficult to win a lawsuit in court. If the laws are not often used, judges and lawyers may not be aware of them. And in many countries, especially where corporations are very powerful, corruption among judges and politicians makes it difficult for poor communities to claim their rights. Unfortunately, there are many more unsuccessful lawsuits than successful lawsuits.

Before beginning a lawsuit against a corporation, industry, or government, these are some things to consider.

Think about your goals

It is important to know exactly what you want a lawsuit to achieve. Then decide if a lawsuit is the best way to reach that goal. Do you want a company to:

- clean up an oil spill or other toxic pollution?
- pay people for damages to their health, land, or resources?
- shut down and leave the region or country?

A legal battle can mobilize and educate the community. But actions such as boycotts, sit-ins, strikes, or public information campaigns may lead to negotiations or political settlements more quickly and easily than a long legal battle. Consider if these kinds of actions will be easier and more effective for your community to undertake than a lawsuit. Also consider if using both legal action and direct action will help your community to win.

Will a lawsuit be useful even if it does not succeed in court?

Of course you want to win your lawsuit. But if you are unsure whether your lawsuit can win, consider whether it will help or harm your cause if it does not win. Sometimes an unsuccessful lawsuit can bring public attention to a community's problems. If a lawsuit involving environmental damage and human rights abuse is unsuccessful in your country's courts, you may be able to take the complaint to an international body such as the Inter-American Human Rights Commission or the United Nations (see page 567). This still may not resolve the problem, but it can bring more attention to your issues; however, it also takes more time and resources.

Sometimes an unsuccessful lawsuit can make things worse. A bad result can lead judges and lawyers to think that future lawsuits should not win either. Negative publicity can cause people to think a community is unjustly demanding money or other rewards. And like any failed organizing effort, unsuccessful lawsuits can demoralize and divide a community.

Who will take the lawsuit to court?

The victim of harm, whether it is a person, a person's family, or an entire community, must be willing to take on the work and the risks of a lawsuit. Usually an organization cannot bring a lawsuit against a company on behalf of someone who was harmed but who is not willing to join the lawsuit.

Is there proof of harm?

For a lawsuit to succeed, you must be able to prove:

- The victims suffered physical or economic harm.
- The corporation caused or is responsible for the harm.

If there is not enough evidence to prove this, the lawsuit may do more harm than good. Even when it is clear a company has violated the law, without proof that they caused harm you may not be allowed to bring a case to court, and if you do, you may not win.

Is the proof available?

Only proof that can be brought to court is useful in court. People who bring a lawsuit because they have suffered harm must be willing and able to speak in court, and they must have witnesses who are willing to speak as well. They must be able to show through pictures, studies, medical records, or some other evidence that harm was done to them by the corporation being sued. Harm can be very hard to prove. For example, a company may hire a doctor to say that it was not the chemicals it used that caused cancer among its workers, but instead it was workers bad habits such as smoking tobacco, eating an unhealthy diet, or just bad luck. It can be very hard to legally prove "cause and effect" even if it seems obvious based on common sense.

Who or what caused the harm?

Lawsuits can be brought against people, corporations, and in many countries against the government for causing environmental damage.

Is the lawsuit against a multinational corporation?

Multinational corporations often have offices in many countries. To successfully sue a multinational corporation it is necessary to work both in the country where the damage was done and in the corporation's home country. This can be costly and difficult, but it can be done (see the stories on pages 494 and 522).

Multinational companies often have branches in the countries where they work, called subsidiaries. It may be easier to sue the subsidiary of a company than to sue the foreign owner. For example, when the American oil company Chevron polluted the Niger Delta in Nigeria, rather than suing the American company, local activists sued Chevron's Nigerian subsidiary.

At the same time, international activists launched a campaign to educate people around the world about Chevron's human rights abuses, to pressure the company to change its practices.

Other things to consider

- Was the harm or abuse committed recently? A lawsuit must be filed within a certain number of years after the harm was done (usually no more than 10 years). This makes it difficult to win a case about illnesses that may take many years to develop, like cancers, even though these can be the most severe illnesses.

- Are the people bringing the lawsuit, their witnesses, and their lawyers willing to risk their safety? Many corporations and governments will stop at nothing to retain their power, including physical violence and murder. Those who challenge this power may put their lives at risk.

- Is there money to pay for the lawsuit? Court fees, lawyers' fees, international travel, phone calls, gathering proof, and other costs add up quickly.

- Are you able to work many years on a lawsuit? A lawsuit can take from 3 to 10 years or more. Sometimes the victims have already died by the time their cases are resolved.

Using International Law

Many laws and conventions agreed on by countries who are members of the United Nations (nearly every country in the world) protect environmental rights for all people. Human rights belong to every person and community and cannot be taken away. These rights are recognized internationally, but in order for these rights to be effective, people must be aware of them and must exercise them. Without action to make sure they are enforced at a national level, international laws and conventions are not effective.

International agreements

Many international agreements protect human rights and the environment. Unfortunately, a person or group cannot usually file a complaint when these agreements are violated. Only a State Party (a country that has signed the agreement) can complain, and they rarely do. And these agreements can only be enforced against governments, not against multinational corporations. In many countries, international laws can be used in the courts of that country. Learning what international agreements say may also help you understand the attitudes of the international community toward particular issues, and help build campaigns to protect human rights.

If people are aware of their rights and the agreements that many countries have made to respect them, they will be better able to exercise their rights and hold governments accountable.

Here is a list of some of the international agreements that protect human rights and the environment, along with websites where you can find the agreements and information about how they are used. (See page 467 for a description of some of the agreements on toxics.)

The United Nations Charter
www.un.org/aboutun/charter/

The Universal Declaration of Human Rights
www.un.org/Overview/rights.html

The Convention on the Rights of the Child
www.unhchr.ch/html/menu3/b/k2crc.htm
www.unicef.org/crc/

The United Nations Framework Convention on Climate Change
unfccc.int/2860.php

The Convention on Biological Diversity
www.biodiv.org/default.shtml
www.iisd.ca/biodiv/cbdintro.html

The Declaration on the Right to Development
www.unhchr.ch/html/menu3/b/74.htm

The International Covenant on Economic, Social and Cultural Rights
www.unhchr.ch/html/menu3/b/a_cescr.htm

The United Nations Declaration on Social Progress and Development
www.unhchr.ch/html/menu3/b/m_progre.htm

The United Nations Vancouver Declaration on Human Settlements
www.un-documents.net/van-dec.htm

The Stockholm Convention on the Elimination of POPS
www.pops.int
www.ipen.org

The Basel Convention on the Control of Transboundary Movements of Hazardous Wastes and Their Disposal
www.basel.int/text/con-e.htm
www.ban.org

The Bamako Convention on the Ban of the Import into Africa and the Control of Transboundary Movement of Hazardous Wastes within Africa
www.londonconvention.org/Bamako.htm
www.ban.org/Library/bamako_treaty.htm

The Rotterdam Convention on the Prior Informed Consent (PIC) Procedure for Certain Hazardous Chemicals and Pesticides in International Trade
www.pic.int/

The Convention on the Prevention of Marine Pollution by Dumping of Wastes and Other Matter
www.imo.org/Conventions/contents.asp?topic_id=258&doc_id=681
www.londonconvention.org

The Dublin Statement on Water and Sustainable Development
www.wmo.ch/web/homs/documents/english/icwedece.html

The Millennium Declaration of Johannesburg
www.johannesburgsummit.org/html/documents/summit_docs/political_declaration_final.pdf

International forums and special procedures

To bring attention to their struggles for human rights, people in many countries have sought justice in international legal forums such as the Organization of American States Inter-American Court, the World Court, and the United Nations Commission on Human Rights. International attention in these forums can pressure countries to negotiate settlements or end corporate activities that cause environmental damage and violate human rights.

It may be necessary to show that going to the courts of the country where the human rights violation took place has not led to a solution, or to explain why national laws and the national court system are not fair or will probably not be successful for other reasons.

The United Nations has also established "special procedures" to address human rights abuses. These special procedures can be used by groups and individuals without the consent of their government, and do not depend on any covenants or conventions.

A person or community can use the special procedures by contacting human rights experts called "Special Rapporteurs." They investigate human rights abuses that happen within their area of work (called their "mandate"), such as the right to food, the right to health, the dumping of toxic wastes, and so on. These Special Rapporteurs can be contacted with a simple letter, along with any news reports, documents, or other written information about the problem. The Rapporteurs report these problems to the United Nations Human Rights Council, and sometimes to the United Nations General Assembly.

The names of the Rapporteurs, their mandates, and their contact information can be found on the UN Human Rights website (www.ohchr.org), under "Human Rights by Issue."

Vocabulary

Here is a list of words that may be new or difficult to understand, or that are especially important to promoting environmental health. Knowing what these words mean can help you use this book better.

Most of the words used here are explained in the chapters. The first time they are used in a chapter, the words are printed in heavier black letters.

These words are listed in the order of the alphabet:

A B C D E F G H I J K L M N O P Q R S T U V W X Y Z

A

A-frame level a tool for finding a level area across a slope, made of wood in the shape of the letter A.

Absorb to pull into. Plants absorb water from the ground.

Acetaminophen a pain-relieving medicine. *Also called* paracetamol.

Acetone a toxic solvent.

Activated charcoal a powder made from charcoal used to absorb poison and reduce the harm it causes.

Active ingredient in a pesticide, the substance that kills pests.

Acute when something happens suddenly, and is strong, serious, or dangerous. An acute illness gets bad quickly but may not last long. *Compare with* chronic.

Agroforestry growing crops and trees together so they produce many benefits, such as food, firewood, and soil conservation.

Air pollution the release of poisonous gases and small dust particles into the air. Burning fossil fuels causes a lot of air pollution.

Algae very small plants with no roots, stems, or leaves, that grow in water and in wet places.

Allergy, allergic reaction a problem, such as itching, sneezing, hives or rash, and sometimes difficult breathing or shock, that affects some people when specific things are breathed in, eaten, injected, or touched. The things that cause allergies are called allergens.

Anemia a disease in which the blood gets weak and thin from the lack of red blood cells. It is caused by a lack of iron in the diet, destruction by toxics of the body's ability to make blood or red blood cells, or loss or destruction of blood faster than the body can replace it.

Antibiotic a medicine used to fight infections caused by bacteria.

Antibiotic resistance when bacteria are no longer killed by an antibiotic. Antibiotic resistance can be caused by taking antibiotics unneccessarily, or dumping them into the environment.

Artemisinin a medicine used to treat malaria.

Asbestos a toxic material that does not burn and has been used to make fire-resistant building materials and protective clothing. Asbestos is mined and milled into tiny threads that can get into the lungs and cause a serious illness called asbestosis.

Asthma a disease of the lungs that causes difficulty breathing, often with a hissing or wheezing sound. Asthma attacks are caused by specific allergens and air pollution.

Autoclave a machine that disinfects using steam heat and pressure. Commonly used in hospitals and clinics.

B

Bacteria living things too small to see. Some bacteria cause infectious diseases, and are often called germs. Other bacteria help break down organic matter and keep soil healthy.

Benzene a dangerous solvent.

Bilharzia a disease caused by worms that live in water snails. *Also called* blood flukes and schistosomiasis.

Biodiversity the great number of different kinds of plants, animals, and insects that live on Earth.

Biogas mostly methane gas produced by rotting organic matter. Biogas burns cleanly and can be used for fuel.

Biomass waste material from plants and animals, commonly used as a fuel.

Birth defect a physical or mental problem a child is born with, such as a cleft lip or mental slowness. Birth defects are sometimes caused by toxic chemicals. *Also called* genetic defects.

Black seed a seed from India and the Middle East used in treating asthma attacks. *Also called* Nigella sativa.

Bleach a chemical used to purify water, and to disinfect surfaces and equipment.

Blood fluke infection caused by a tiny worm that lives in water snails. *Also called* schistosomiasis and bilharzia.

Brominated flame retardant (BFR) a toxic chemical used in many consumer products such as electronics, furniture, and textiles to reduce the danger of them catching on fire.

Bronchitis a lung disease that causes cough, fever, and pain in the chest.

Bronchodilator a kind of medicine used to open airways, and relieve chest pain and breathing problems.

C

Cadmium a toxic heavy metal used in electronics and other production processes.

Cancer a disease which causes cells to grow in an uncontrolled way that damages the body. Cancer can affect many parts of the body. Many cancers are related to toxic chemicals and industrial pollution.

Carbon dioxide a gas that people and animals breathe out, and that is produced when fossil fuels are burned. Carbon dioxide from burning fossil fuels is the leading cause of global warming. *Also called* CO2.

Carbon monoxide a poisonous, colorless, odorless gas produced by cars, cigarettes, burning natural gas, and other sources. *Also called* CO.

Catchment, catchment area an area of land that catches rainwater and sends it downhill into streams and rivers, or underground to be stored as groundwater. Catchment is another word for watershed, and also the highest part of a watershed.

Cell the smallest part of any living thing. All people, animals, and plants are made of cells.

Certification program lets people who buy products know that they were grown in environmentally or socially healthy ways. Crops can be certified as organic, forest products can be certified as sustainably harvested, and so on. Certification may bring higher prices to the seller.

Chemical body burden the amount of toxic chemicals present in the human body at any time.

Chlorine a strong chemical, commonly called bleach, used to kill germs and disinfect water. Chlorine is also used to bleach paper and to make PVC plastic. When products containing chlorine are burned, they release toxic gases such as dioxins and furans.

Chloroquine a medicine used to treat malaria.

Cholera a disease caused by drinking water or eating food contaminated by bacteria. Often spread by dirty water, cholera causes severe vomiting and diarrhea.

Chromium a toxic heavy metal used in leather tanning and other industries.

Chronic something that lasts for a long time or that happens often. A chronic illness lasts for many years and is difficult to treat or cure. *Compare with* acute.

Clindamycin an antibiotic used to treat malaria and other infections.

Cistern a large tank for collecting and storing water.

Clean production methods of manufacturing that greatly reduce or eliminate toxic wastes. Clean production promotes the use of renewable energy and materials.

Clear cut logging when most of the trees in an area are cut down.

Climate the weather that a place has over a period of time.

Climate change the way many places now have different weather than they used to have. Climate change is related to global warming, and is caused by burning fossil fuels.

Community all the people who live in a certain area and interact with one another. A community may be a neighborhood or an entire village, or it can be a group of people, such as farmers, mothers, or people who attend the same church, who share common interests, common needs, and common problems.

Community seed stewardship when communities maintain a diverse collection of seeds for the future and keep careful records of them.

Compact, compaction when soil is pressed down and becomes hard due to loss of organic matter, excess irrigation, or people or animals walking or driving on it. Compacted soil cannot hold much air or water, and leads to erosion.

Companion planting planting different crops together to promote healthy crops by reducing pest problems and making the best use of soil nutrients.

Compost natural plant food made from decomposed food scraps, crop and plant wastes, manure, and other organic matter.

Conservation saving natural resources from being wasted or destroyed.

Constructed wetland a pit or basin filled with wetland plants which filter and clean waste water. *Also called* a reedbed.

Consumer a person who buys or uses things.

Consumption buying and using products and resources.

Containment pond a pond built to hold waste from mining or oil drilling.

Contour, contour line the places on a hillside or slope which are level across the slope.

Contour barrier a barrier, such as a wall or ditch, built on a contour line to slow, spread, and sink water into the ground and prevent erosion.

Crop residue stalks, leaves, roots and other plant matter left after crops are harvested. Often used in compost or as a biomass fuel.

Crop rotation changing where crops are grown each year to improve soil fertility.

Cutting a piece of a plant or tree branch that can be used to grow a new plant or tree.

Cyanide a very toxic chemical used in gold mining.

D

DDT a pesticide used to kill malaria mosquitoes. DDT is a Persistent Organic Pollutant (POP). Overuse of DDT has caused it to be less effective in fighting malaria.

Decay to slowly break down and rot. *See also* decompose.

Decompose when living things are broken down by heat, insects, and bacteria. When plant matter decomposes, it turns to compost or rich soil.

Deforestation when forests are cut down and cleared.

Degradation making something less useful, less valuable, or less beautiful. When land or forests are abused but not destroyed they are degraded.

Dehydration when the body loses more water than it takes in. Dehydration is one sign of diarrhea diseases, often related to poor sanitation. Dehydration can be very dangerous, especially for children.

Delirious when a person is not in her or his right mind. Usually caused by a fever or other illness.

Dengue fever a serious illness spread by mosquitoes.

Detoxify to cleanse and remove poisons.

Diabetes a disease caused when the body cannot process sugars. *Also called* sugar disease.

Diarrhea frequent, runny stools. Diarrhea diseases are often caused by unsafe water and poor sanitation.

Dilute to make weaker by mixing with water.

Dioxins a group of very harmful chemicals released by burning plastic. Dioxins are Persistent Organic Pollutants (POPs).

Disinfect, disinfection cleaning something (water, wounds, tools, equipment, and so on) in a way that gets rid of most germs so it will not spread infection.

Disposable an item meant to be used once and then thrown away.

Diversity having many different kinds of people, animals, plants or other things in one place. *See also* biodiversity.

Drainage the way water is carried away from a place or seeps into the groundwater.

Drug resistance when certain medicines no longer work to cure an illness.

E

Ecological, Ecology the relationship among living things and their environment. Something is ecological if it is good for the environment or if it acts like a natural system.

Ecotourism a project to earn money by bringing tourists to see the natural beauty of a place without harming the environment.

Emphysema a serious lung disease caused by smoking cigarettes, mining, and air pollution.

Endometriosis a serious illness that causes the womb's lining to grow outside of the womb.

Environmental Impact Assessment (EIA) a study that shows what changes are expected to happen if a project such as a mine, a dam, or a road is built.

Enzyme a substance produced in living things that causes chemical changes to occur, such as digesting food.

Epidemic a disease that spreads quickly from one person to another, making many people sick.

Epilepsy a disease in which a person has convulsions ("fits," seizures) and loss of consciousness.

Ephedra a medicinal plant used to relieve asthma attacks. *Also called* Ma Huang in China.

Ephedrine a medicine used to help breathing.

Equator an imaginary line that divides the northern half of the planet Earth from the southern half.

Erosion when soil and rock are worn away and carried away by wind and water.

Estrogen a hormone in women's bodies that controls reproduction, along with progesterone.

Evaporation when water dries up into the air.

Excess having too much of something, such as pollution or waste.

Exotic plant or tree a plant or tree not native to the local area.

Exploit to use for profit without care for long-term health.

Exposure when a person comes in contact with something. People are exposed to pesticides and other chemicals by breathing, swallowing, and touching.

Extraction taking oil, minerals, or other resources out of the earth.

F

Fair trade buying and selling things for a price that is fair to both the seller and the buyer.

Fair trade certification lets people who buy things know that fair labor practices were used to produce them. It can result in higher and more stable prices for the producers. *See also* certification.

Farmer field school teaching programs that help farmers learn to solve problems themselves and to share those solutions with other farmers.

Ferment when food or other organic matter rots and becomes sour. This happens because bacteria enter and change the nature of the substance.

Fertile, fertility how well soil grows plants or how well animals and people reproduce.

Fertilizer material used to make the soil richer so more crops can be produced.

Food chain the way living things are connected to each other by how one thing eats another thing (or its products). *Also called* the food web.

Food safety when food is nutritious, and free of poisons and other harmful substances.

Food security when everyone has enough safe, nutritious, and appropriate food all year to lead an active and healthy life. Food security means food is produced and distributed in ways that promote a healthy environment, community self-reliance, and the sharing of food among people and communities.

Food sovereignty the right of a community, region, or nation to determine its own local food systems, including local farming, markets, fair distribution, affordable food prices, and food safety.

Food web *See* food chain.

Forest a large area of land covered with trees and other plants growing close together. A forest includes not just trees and plants, but also animals, insects, birds, and people who live in and rely on the forest.

Formaldehyde a toxic chemical used for disinfecting and cleaning, and in industrial products. Formaldehyde is dangerous and should be handled carefully, if used at all.

Fossil fuel a fuel made from the remains of plants and animals that died millions of years ago. Fossil fuels include oil, coal, and natural gas. Fossil fuels are nonrenewable resources, and when they are burned, they release carbon dioxide, leading to global warming.

Fumes odorless gases or smoke, sometimes invisible, released from chemicals or when a fire burns. Fumes are usually harmful to breathe.

G

Gasoline a fossil fuel used in cars, trucks, motorbikes, and generators. *Also called* petrol.

Genes the parts of every living thing that determines their traits or characteristics. Genes make our eyes brown or blue, give us straight or curly hair, determine the size and shape of our hands and feet, and so on.

Generate to make electricity.

Genetic damage, Genetic defect harm to genes that results in a difference that creates a problem for that person, plant, or animal. Some toxics can cause genetic damage, and some genetic defects can be passed to offspring.

Genetic engineering when scientists change the genes of plants or animals, sometimes by adding genes from a different plant or animal, to change the traits or characteristics of the resulting plant or animal.

Germ a tiny living thing that can spread disease. Different germs cause different diseases, and spread in different ways. For example, dysentery germs are spread through feces, and tuberculosis germs spread through the air.

Giardia a parasite that causes yellow, bad-smelling diarrhea, cramps in the gut, and burps that smell like rotten eggs.

Global warming the rising of temperatures throughout the world, leading to more floods, storms, rising seawater and the spread of diseases to new areas.

Glutaraldehyde a toxic chemical used for sterilizing and cleaning. Glutaraldehyde is very dangerous and should be handled carefully, if used at all.

Goiter a swelling of the lower front of the neck caused by a lack of iodine in the diet, or by chronic cyanide poisoning.

Greywater water that has been used for washing or cooking. It can be reused in gardens and other places.

Groundwater water that flows underground. Groundwater is the source of drinking water in wells and springs. The groundwater level changes depending on rainfall and how water and land are used. *Also called* water table or aquifer.

Guinea worm a long, thin worm that looks like a white thread. It lives under the skin and makes a painful sore on the ankle, leg, or elsewhere on the body.

H

Hantavirus an infectious disease spread when people breathe in the infected urine or feces of rodents.

Heavy metals metals that may be harmful when people are exposed to even very small amounts. Some heavy metals are lead, mercury, cadmium, and chromium.

High voltage wire wire that carries electricity from where it is generated to where it is used.

HIV/AIDS a disease affecting millions of people worldwide. It eventually causes the body to lose the ability to fight illness. There is currently no cure, but the disease can be controlled by medicines, and by improved diet and living conditions.

Hormones natural chemicals the body makes to control weight, body temperature, hunger, bone strength, moods and sexual feelings, and the ability to reproduce.

Hormone disruptor a toxic chemical that gets into our bodies and confuses our hormones by sending false signals.

Hybrid a plant or animal with parents from 2 different breeds or species that have been bred to have particular traits.

Hydrogen peroxide a chemical used to clean and disinfect.

Hygiene what people do to stay clean and prevent the spread of germs. Hygiene includes washing hands and bathing, storing and preparing food, and keeping the home clean.

I

Ibuprofen a medicine used to reduce pain, inflammation, and fever.

Immunization an injection of medicine that can prevent certain diseases. Immunizations are common for measles, tetanus, and polio. *Also called* vaccination.

Immunization programs mass efforts to immunize people, usually run by international health organizations like the World Health Organization (WHO) and UNICEF, national and local governments, and companies that make and sell vaccines. *Also called* vaccination programs.

Incineration burning things in a closed furnace in order to destroy them.

Incinerator a kind of oven or furnace used to burn waste.

Incline the steepness of a hill.

Indoor air pollution air pollution inside a home or building from tobacco smoke, fires, chemical products, or other sources.

Industrial pollution all of the forms of pollution caused by chemicals and waste products of industry.

Inert ingredient in a pesticide, the part that is not the active ingredient. Inert ingredients include things that make pesticides stick to plants and insects or prevent them from being washed off in the rain. These ingredients are often very poisonous.

Infection a sickness caused by bacteria, viruses, or other organisms. Infections may affect a part of the body or all of it.

Infectious disease a disease that can be spread easily from one person to another.

Infrastructure things that are built, such as homes, roads, and water systems.

Injection when medicine or other liquid is put into the body using a syringe and needle.

Integrated pest management (IPM) a way to control crop pests and diseases without chemicals. *Also called* natural pest management.

Inputs anything that a farmer uses to help crops grow, such as seeds, pesticides, and fertilizers.

Insulation material used to stop heat, cold, sound, or electricity from getting into or out of a place.

J

Jaundice yellow color of the skin and eyes. Jaundice is a sign of liver problems or hepatitis.

Junk food food or drink that may taste good but is not healthy because it contains few if any nutrients, but a lot of fat, salt, sugar, oil, or chemicals.

K

L

Leachate liquid waste that seeps from a landfill or waste dump.

Leach field a sewage treatment system that directs waste into underground pipes with holes in them that slowly let sewage soak into the ground.

Leukemia cancer of the blood and bone marrow.

Lymph system the body's system for preventing and healing infections.

Lymphoma a general term for cancers that develop in the body's lymph system.

M

Ma huang *See* ephedra.

Malaria a serious illness that causes fever, chills, aches, and can be fatal. Malaria is spread by mosquitoes.

Malnutrition when the body does not have enough of the foods it needs to stay healthy.

Manganese a toxic heavy metal used in welding and soldering.

Mercury a toxic, liquid, heavy metal that is used in gold mining, and in thermometers and other medical supplies. Mercury is poisonous to the touch. It is even more poisonous when it turns to gas and is breathed in, or gets in water and combines with other elements.

Microwave an oven that uses waves of energy to heat and disinfect things.

Mildew a fungus that looks like powder, dust, or tiny threads. Mildew grows in damp places.

Mold a fungus that grows on old food, plants, and things that are warm and wet.

Monoculture planting only one kind of crop on an area of land. *Also called* monocropping.

Mulch material spread on top of soil to protect it from sun, rain, and wind, and to prevent weeds from growing. Green manures are often used as mulch.

Multinational corporation a powerful business that works in many countries at once. Because they are so large, they have the power to influence governments and make or change global trading rules. *Also called* transnational corporations.

Multiple chemical sensitivity (MCS) an illness that causes people to have extreme allergic reactions to common toxins in paint, perfume, cars, building materials, and so on. *Also called* environmental illness.

N

Naphtha a toxic solvent.

Natural fertilizer fertilizer made from organic matter such as animal manure, crop residue, or compost.

Natural gas a gas formed underground or undersea that is stored and used as fuel.

Natural pesticide pesticides made from natural substances like plants (garlic, peppers, marigold, and so on), milk, or vegetable oil.

Natural succession the stages in which plants develop on or recover from destruction of an area of land.

Nickel a metal used in batteries, electroplating, and smelting. Exposure to nickel may cause health problems.

Nitrogen a naturally occurring chemical that is important to healthy soil.

Nitrogen-fixing plants or trees trees or plants that put nitrogen into the soil, making it richer for growing things.

Node a bump on a tree branch where the leaves grow.

Nonrenewable resource a resource that is gone forever once it is used, such as oil. *Compare with* renewable resource.

Non-timber forest product any of the many things from a forest besides wood which can be sustainably harvested and sold.

Nursery a place where plants or trees are grown and cared for until they are strong enough to plant directly into the ground.

Nutrient anything that feeds plants, animals, or people. People need nutrients in food to grow strong and healthy, and plants need nutrients in soil to grow strong and bear fruit. When farmers add compost and fertilizer to the soil, they are adding nutrients.

Nutrition eating enough and the right kinds of food to help a person grow, be healthy, and fight off disease.

O

Obesity excess weight that creates serious health problems.

Oil a fossil fuel, is a smooth, dark liquid formed underground. Oil is used to make petrol (gasoline), diesel, kerosene, plastics, and many other industrial products. *Also called* petroleum.

Oil refinery a factory where oil is made into products such as gasoline and other fuels, asphalt, and plastic. Oil refineries are a major source of air pollution.

Organic farming farming that does not use chemical fertilizers or pesticides. Before pesticides were invented, all farming was organic farming. The word organic also refers to the crops grown without chemicals.

Organic certification farmers or producers using organic or sustainable farming methods can get certified to receive higher and more stable prices for their products. *See also* certification.

Organic matter anything that is or was alive, that can rot and decompose, such as plants, animals, insects, and bacteria. Organic matter makes the soil rich.

Organic waste food scraps, crop waste, manure, and other remains of living things that break down and go back to the soil.

P

Paracetamol *See* acetaminophen.

Paralysis inability to move.

Parasites tiny worms or animals that can live in or on a person or animal, and may cause disease.

Passive solar design a way to design buildings using the location and climate for natural heating, cooling, and lighting.

PCBs Polychlorinated biphenyls are toxic chemicals used in paints, plastics and electronic equipment. PCBs are long-lasting in the environment, and difficult to get rid of safely. PCBs are Persistent Organic Pollutants.

Pesticide a poisonous chemical used to kill insects, weeds, rodents, or plant diseases.

Petrol *See* gasoline.

Petroleum *See* oil.

Pioneer species very hardy plants that are the first to grow back on damaged lands.

Placenta a spongy organ in a pregnant woman's womb through which all blood and nutrients pass to the developing baby. Unfortunately, many toxics can also pass through the placenta and harm the baby even before it is born.

Plaintiff a person who undertakes a lawsuit because he or she has suffered some sort of harm.

Plant breeding when farmers select seeds to grow plants that are bigger, resist pests, taste better, or have other desirable traits. Used by farmers throughout the ages, plant breeding has resulted in the many delicious and nutritious varieties of crops we have today.

Plastic a material made from petroleum and other chemicals. Plastic is convenient, but making it, using it, and disposing of it can expose people to toxics.

Plumb line a weight hanging on a string that is used with an A-frame to measure whether a surface is level.

Pollinate when pollen is spread from one flower to another to make a seed or fruit grow.

Pollinator an insect or animal that carries pollen from one flower to another, helping to fertilize plants. The wind also helps spread pollen.

Pollution harmful wastes that are released into air, water, or the ground.

Pneumonia an illness that causes fever, coughing, and weakness.

POPs Persistent Organic Pollutants are a group of toxic chemicals that are very long-lasting in the environment. Dioxins and PCBs are POPs.

Precautionary principle the idea that "If there is reason to believe that something may cause harm, even if we do not know for certain, then it is better to avoid it than to risk doing harm."

Predator an animal that hunts and eats other animals.

Progesterone a hormone in women's bodies that controls reproduction, along with estrogen.

Price support a price set by the government that helps farmers by setting a higher market price for some foods they produce.

Pseudoephedrine a bronchodilator medicine used to open the breathing passages.

PVC polyvinyl chloride is a kind of plastic that contains chlorine. When produced, and also when burned, PVC releases very dangerous chemicals called dioxins and furans.

Q

Quinine a medicine used to treat malaria.

R

Radiation an invisible form of energy. Some radiation, such as sunlight, is natural. Some radiation, such as that from nuclear explosions and uranium, causes serious illness.

Radiation poisoning illnesses caused by exposure to radiation. Radiation poisoning can cause cancer, skin diseases, and other serious health problems.

Recycle to make something that is no longer useful or wanted into another material that can be used again.

Refinery *See* oil refinery.

Rehydration drink a drink made of sugar, salt, and water, or from grain and water, that helps replace liquid and restore health when a person is dehydrated.

Renewable resource a resource that can be used without fear of it being used up, because it will grow again, like a tree, or is part of nature, like the wind or the sun. *Compare with* nonrenewable resource.

Reproductive health health issues that affect the parts and processes of men's and women's bodies that allow them to make a baby.

Resistance the ability of something to defend itself against something that would normally harm or kill it. Bacteria can become resistant to the effects of certain antibiotics, and mosquitoes can become resistant to pesticides.

Resource recovery turning unused or unwanted materials into resources. Resource recovery includes reusing, recycling, and composting wastes.

Residue what is left over or left behind. Pesticide residue is the dry powder or oily film that stays on crops after pesticide spray dries. Crop residues include the leaves, stalks, seed coverings, and so on that remain after the crop is harvested or processed.

Respirator a protective mask that covers the nose and mouth to prevent people from breathing in poisons.

Respiratory illness an illness that interferes with breathing. Some respiratory illnesses are asthma, emphysema, and pneumonia.

Restoration bringing something that has been damaged back to good condition.

Reservoir a human-made area of water, usually collected behind a dam.

Routine gas flare when natural gas is separated from petroleum by burning, 24 hours a day.

Runoff water that moves over the surface of the land rather than soaking into the ground.

S

Safe water water not contaminated with worms, germs, or toxic chemicals. Safe water is good for drinking, bathing, and washing clothes.

Safety gas flare when excess natural gas is separated from petroleum by burning to prevent explosions in oil pipelines.

Sanitary landfill a pit for wastes that cannot be reused or recycled. It is safer than an open dump.

Sanitation building and maintaining toilets to manage human waste in a safe and healthy way, and washing hands to prevent the spread of germs.

Scarcity not having enough of something, such as water or food.

Schistosomiasis a disease caused by worms that live in water snails. *Also called* blood flukes and bilharzia.

Septic tank a tank buried underground for collecting and treating sewage.

Sewage water used to carry away human waste in closed pipes or open ditches.

Sewage system a system of pipes or ditches that carries sewage to septic tanks, waste ponds, sewage treatment plants, or elsewhere.

Sewage treatment ways of filtering and cleaning sewage water so it can be reused or safely returned to the environment.

Sewer the pipes or ditches that make up a sewage system.

Sharps needles, blades, lancets, and other sharp medical tools or instruments. (Broken glass can also be considered a sharp.)

Silica, silica dust a substance found in many kinds of mining and used in many industries. Breathing silica dust can cause health problems.

Silicosis a serious lung disease caused by breathing in silica dust.

Silt tiny bits of rock and earth carried by water that eventually become an important part of healthy soil.

Smelting heating metals in order to work with them. Smelting often creates toxic pollution.

Soakaway pit a pit filled with sand and gravel to let water absorb slowly into the ground.

Sociodrama a short theater piece used to show a social problem and suggest solutions.

Solar energy energy from the sun used to generate heat or electricity.

Solar oven an oven that uses the sun's heat to cook.

Solar panel a flat panel used to capture the sun's rays and produce electricity.

Solid waste anything that is used and disposed of. *Also called* trash, garbage, litter, rubbish.

Solvent a substance, usually liquid, that can dissolve another substance. Water is a safe solvent. Gasoline, acetone, benzene, and xylene are toxic solvents.

Stagnant water water that does not move and often smells bad. Mosquitoes breed in stagnant water.

Sterile when people, plants, or animals cannot reproduce. Or, when something is free of germs.

Sterility inability to have children.

Sterilize to kill all the germs on something.

Surface water water that collects or runs on the surface of the earth, such as rivers, lakes, streams, and reservoirs.

Subsidy money given to increase or decrease prices for goods or services such as crops, oil, healthcare, etc.

Sustainable able to continue in an ongoing way without running out or causing excess harm, now or in the future.

Sustainability the ability to meet the daily needs of people now without neglecting the needs of future generations.

Syringe an instrument used with a needle to inject medicine.

T

Temperate climate a place where there are 4 seasons: spring, summer, autumn, and winter, normal in countries further north or south of the equator. *Compare with* tropical climate.

Toluene a toxic solvent.

Toxic anything that is harmful, usually because it is poisonous and can cause illness or death.

Toxoplasmosis a disease caused by germs on food.

Trade when people, organizations, or countries exchange goods and services. Unfair trade between countries is a major cause of poverty.

Traits determined by genes, the things that are different and specific about every living thing, such as eye or hair color. *Also called* characteristics.

Tree plantations very large farms where only 1 kind of tree is grown, such as rubber, palm oil, teak, or pine.

Tropical climate a place that is hot and has a wet season and a dry season, normal in countries near the equator. *Compare with* temperate climate.

Tuberculosis (TB) a serious, infectious lung disease.

Tumors growths in the body, often caused by cancer.

Turbine a wheel turned by wind, steam, or falling water to generate electricity.

Turpentine a toxic solvent.

Typhoid an infection of the gut that is spread from feces to mouth in contaminated food and water.

U

V

Vaccination *see* immunization.

Vaccination programs *see* immunization programs.

Vaporize to turn from a liquid to a gas.

Value-added product a product that is no longer a raw good, but has been processed for sale.

Ventilation the movement of air through a house or building.

W

Wastewater water that is dirty or polluted from use in homes, farms, or factories.

Water security regular access to sufficient, safe water.

Water table *see* groundwater.

Water treatment the different ways to make water safe for drinking.

Watershed an area of land that gathers water from rain, snow, and the water that seeps up from the ground into one big river, lake, or wetland. *Also called* catchment area.

Watershed management using and protecting the land and water resources within a watershed in a way that is healthy and sustainable.

Wetland a low area of land covered for much of the year with shallow water and plants. Swamps, mangrove forests, and flood plains are wetlands.

Wind energy electricity produced by harnessing the power of wind.

Windlass the part of a well that is turned to make it easier to raise the bucket of water.

World Health Organization (WHO) the part of the United Nations responsible for international health.

World Trade Organization (WTO) a powerful organization in which governments make agreements about trade among countries and multinational corporations.

X

Xylene a toxic solvent.

Y

Yellow fever a serious illness in Africa and some parts of South America, spread by mosquitoes.

Z

Zero waste minimizing the amount of waste produced and recycling all waste materials to protect health and the environment.

Resources

Here is a selection of organizations, printed materials, and internet resources that can provide useful information about environmental health. We have listed organizations and materials that cover as many of the topics in this book as possible, and that work in many parts of the world.

Resources are listed according to the topics in the book. Within each topic, there are organizations, printed materials, and internet resources.

Organizations work directly on environmental health issues, and can offer training, materials, and other kinds of support.

Printed materials such as books may be helpful to individuals and community groups working to improve environmental health. Often, printed materials include suggestions of other resources.

Internet resources contain information about many areas of environmental health. They also have links to other resources.

Within each heading, resources are listed in the order of the alphabet:

A B C D E F G H I J K L M N O P Q R S T U V W X Y Z

Training for environmental health and justice

Organizations

International Institute for Environment and Development (IIED)
An international policy research institute that works with many groups, from smallholder farmers and big city slum-dwellers to national governments, regional NGOs, and global institutions to promote sustainable and equitable global development.

3 Endsleigh Street, London WC1H 0DD
Tel: +44 (0) 20-7388-2117;
Fax: +44 (0) 20-7388-2826
E-mail: info@iied.org
Website: www.iied.org

Printed materials

From the Roots Up: Strengthening Organizational Capacity through Guided Self-Assessment
By Peter Gubbels and Catherine Koss

A guide to help grassroots organizations and community groups recognize their potential, identify critical issues, and decide for themselves what actions to take to build their capacity.

World Neighbors
4127 NW 122nd Street, Oklahoma City, Oklahoma 73120-8869, USA
Tel: +1-405-752-9700
Fax: +1-405-752-9393
E-mail: actionlearning@wn.org

Helping Health Workers Learn
By David Werner and Bill Bower

A collection of teaching methods, aids, and ideas for community health promoters and educators who may have limited formal education.

Hesperian Foundation
1919 Addison Street, Ste 304, Berkeley California, 94704, USA
Tel: (510) 845-1447
Fax: (510) 845-0539

Options for Educators
By Lyra Srinivasan
A book for educators about participatory education methods.

PACT/CDS
777 UN Plaza, New York, NY, 10017, USA
Tel: +1-212-697-6222
Fax: +1-212-692-9748

Participatory Learning and Action
A leading informal journal on participatory learning and action approaches and methods for community workers, activists and researchers. All the material is copyright free and users are encouraged to photocopy articles for sharing and training.

Research Information Ltd, Grenville Court, Britwell Road, Burnham, Bucks, SL1 8DF, UK, UK.
Tel: +44 (0) 1628-600499;
Fax: +44 (0) 1628-600488;
E-mail: info@researchinformation.co.uk
Website: www.researchinformation.co.uk

Tools for Community Participation
A book of educational methods.

By Lyra Srinivasan
PACT/CDS
777 UN Plaza, New York, NY, 10017, USA
Tel: +1-212-697-6222
Fax: +1-212-692-9748

Training for Transformation
By Anne Hope and Sally Timmel

A 3-part guide to help in the development of self-reliant communities, with group methods, organizational development, and social analysis.

Practical Action Publishing
Shumacher Centre
Bourton on Dunsmore, Rugby, Warwichshire
CV23 9QZ, UK
Website: www.practicalactionpublishing.org

Health problems from water, sanitation, and mosquitoes

Organizations

Aquamore, Zimbabwe
Technical support and information on ecological sanitation and community water management.

P.O. Box MP 1162, Mount Pleasant, Harare, Zimbabwe
Tel: 301115
E-mail: aquamor@mweb.co.zw
Website: aquamor.tripod.com/index.html

Biocontrol Network
Distributes BT (Bacillus thuringensis) for ecological mosquito control.

5116 Williamsburg Rd.
Brentwood, TN, 37027 USA
Outside USA: +1-615-370-4301
From USA: (1-800) 441-BUGS (2847)
Website:
www.biconet.com/biocontrol/bti.html

ICIPE African Insect Science for Food and Health
Training and resources for BT malaria control and other ecological methods. Program areas of food security, health, sustainable livelihoods and resource use.

P.O. Box 30772-00100
Nairobi, Kenya
Tel: +254 (20) 8632000;
Fax: +254 (20) 8632001
E-mail: icipe@icipe.org
Website: www.icipe.org

Potters for Peace

Information and technical support for making low cost ceramic water filters.

Ron Rivera, Coordinator of Ceramic Water Filter and Int'l. Projects, P.O. Box 3868, Managua, Nicaragua
Tel: +011-505-277-3807
E-mail: pottersforpeace@yahoo.com
Website: www.pottersforpeace.org

Practica Foundation

Information about rope pumps and other low-cost water and sanitation technologies.

Maerten Trompstreet 31, 2628 RC Delft, Netherlands
Tel: +31-15-2575359
E-mail: info@practicafoundation.nl
Website: practicafoundation.nl

Sarar Transformación SC

Technical support, information and publications about ecological sanitation, community water management, and participatory education.

AP. #8 Tepoztlán, Morelos, 62520, México
Tel/Fax: +52-739-395-03-64
E-mail: sarar@laneta.apc.org
Website: www.sarar-t.org

SODIS-Solar Disinfection

Provides technical support and information about solar disinfection.

Ueberlandstrasse 133CH-8600, Duebendorf, Switzerland
Tel: +41-44-823-50-19;
Fax +41-44-823-53-99
E-mail: wegelin@eawag.ch, regula.meierhofer@eawag.ch
Website: www.sodis.ch

WELL — Resource Centre Network for Water, Sanitation and Environmental Health

Provides information and support with water, sanitation and environmental health.

c/o Water, Engineering and Development Centre (WEDC), Loughborough University, Leicestershire, LE11 3TU, UK
Tel: +44-1509-228304;
Fax: +44-1509-223970
E-mail: well@lboro.ac.uk
Website: www.lboro.ac.uk/well

Printed materials

Create an Oasis with Greywater

By Art Ludwig

Describes how to choose, build, and use many types of greywater reuse systems for rural, urban, or village settings.

Oasis Design
5 San Marcos Trout Club
Santa Barbara, CA 93105-9726
Website: oasisdesign.net/greywater

Guidelines for Treatment of Malaria

WHO Press, 20 avenue Appia, 1211 Geneva 27, Switzerland
Tel : +41-22-791-4806 ;
Fax: +41-22-791-4857
Email: bookorders@who.int
Website: www.who.int/malaria/docs/treatmentguidelines.html

Waterlines

An international journal of appropriate technologies for water supply and sanitation.

Intermediate Technology Publications
Schumacher Centre for Technology and Development
Bourton-on Dunsmore
Warwickshire CV23 9QZ
Tel: +44 (0) 1926-634501;
Fax +44 (0) 1926-634502
E-mail: journals.edt@itpubs.org.uk
Website: www.ingentaconnect/itpub/wtl.

Internet

Emergency Sanitation for Refuges

www.lboro.ac.uk/well/resources/technical-briefs/38-emergency-sanitation-for-refugees.pdf

Kanchan Arsenic Filter

web.mit.edu/watsan/wb_filter_monitoring_plan.htm
(look for the link to the Kanchan arsenic filter)

World Health Organization (WHO)
Dengue Fever: www.who.int/topics/dengue/en
Malaria: www.who.int/topics/malaria/en
Yellow Fever: www.who.int/csr/disease/
yellowfev/en
Water, sanitation and health: www.who.int/
water_sanitation_health/en

Natural resource management and land restoration

Organizations

Center for International Forestry Research (CIFOR)

An international research institution committed to conserving forests and improving the livelihoods of people in the tropics.

P.O. BOX 6596, JKPWB, Jakarta 10065 Indonesia
Tel: +62-251-622-622;
Fax: +62-251-622-100
E-mail: cifor@cgiar.org
Website: www.cifor.cgiar.org/

International Institute for Environment and Development (IIED)

An international policy research institute that works with many groups, from smallholder farmers and big city slum-dwellers to national governments, regional NGOs, and global institutions to promote sustainable and equitable global development.

3 Endsleigh Street, London WC1H 0DD
Tel: +44 (0) 20-7388-2117;
Fax: +44 (0) 20-7388-2826
E-mail: info@iied.org
Website: www.iied.org/

International Rivers

A non-governmental organization that protects rivers and defends the rights of communities that depend on them, in collaboration with local communities, social movements, and other partners.

International Rivers, 1847 Berkeley Way, Berkeley, CA 94703, USA
Tel: +1-510-848-1155;
Fax: +1-510-848-1008
E-mail: info@internationalrivers.org
Website: internationalrivers.org

Regional Community Forestry Training Center for Asia and the Pacific (RECOFTC)

An international not-for-profit organization that works closely with partners to support community forestry and community-based natural resource management.

P.O. Box 1111, Kasetsart University, Bangkok 10903, Thailand
Tel: +66-2-940-5700;
Fax: +66-2-561-4880, 562-0960
E-mail: info@recoftc.org
Website: www.recoftc.org

World Rainforest Movement

International network of groups defending the world's rainforests.

Movimiento Mundial por los Bosques Tropicales, Maldonado 1858, 11200 Montevideo, Uruguay
Tel: +598-2-413-2989; Fax: +598-2-410-0985
Website: www.wrm.org.uy

Printed materials

Dams, Rivers and Rights: An Action Guide for Communities Affected by Dams
By International Rivers

Offers lessons and ideas for action from the international anti-dam movement and outlines successful struggles against destructive dams.

International Rivers, 1847 Berkeley Way, Berkeley, CA 94703, USA
Tel: +1-510-848-1155; Fax: +1-510-848-1008
E-mail: info@internationalrivers.org
Website: internationalrivers.org

Food and farming

Organizations

Campesino a Campesino
A method and a movement that supports the sharing of knowledge between smallholder farmers, based in Central America.

Website: www.laneta.apc.org/mexsursur

CLUSA International Program
Helps farmers and village associations start or improve existing cooperatives and community-based development projects by providing training and financial assistance.

1401 New York Avenue, NW, Suite 1100, Washington, DC 20005, USA
Tel: +1-202-638-6222; Fax: +1-202-638-1374
E-mail: clusa@ncba.coop
Website: www.ncba.coop/clusa.cfm

Developing Countries Farm Radio Network
Makes radio programs on issues facing small farmers using information from farmers world wide.

416 Moore Avenue, Suite 101, Toronto, Ontario
M4G 1C9, CANADA
Tel: +1-416- 971-6333; Fax: +1-416-971-5299
E-mail: info@farmradio.org
Website: www.farmradio.org

ETC Group
Promotes cultural and ecological diversity and human rights through research, public education, and advocacy, with a focus on sustainable agriculture.

ETC Headquarters,
431 Gilmour St, 2nd Floor, Ottawa, Ontario,
Canada K2P 0R5
Tel: +1-613-241-2267; Fax: +1-613-241-2506
E-mail: etc@etcgroup.org
Website: www.etcgroup.org/en

Fair Trade Labeling Organizations International (FLO)
Sets standards and provides information for local producers to become fair trade certified.

Bonner Talweg 177, 53129 Bonn, Germany
Tel: +49-228-949230; Fax: +49-228-2421713
E-mail FLO: info@fairtrade.net
E-mail FLO-Cert: info@flo-cert.net
Website: www.fairtrade.net

Farm-Africa
Works with farmers in Eastern and Southern Africa to manage resources more effectively, develop sustainable livelihoods, and reduce poverty and dependence on international aid. Has materials on forestry as well as food and farming.

Farm-Africa Ethiopia
PO Box 5746, Addis Ababa, Ethiopia
Tel: +251-11-467-0057;
Fax: +251-11-416-9696
E-mail: farm.ethiopia@ethionet.et

Farm-Africa Headquarters
Clifford's Inn, Fetter Lane, London, EC4a, IBZ, UK
Tel: +44 (0) 20-7430-0440;
Fax: +44 (0) 20-7430-0460
E-mail: farmafrica@farmafrica.org.uk
Website: www.farmafrica.org.uk

International Federation of Organic Agriculture (IFOAM)
Helps small farmers if they should be certified and how they should go about doing so.

Charles-de-Gaulle Str. 5, 53113 Bonn, Germany
Tel: +49 (0) 228-926-50-10;
Fax: +49 (0) 228-926-50-99
E-mail: headoffice@ifoam.org
Website: www.ifoam.org
For Organic Certification Information:
Website: www.appta.org/preseng.
htm#CERTIFICATION

Navdanya
Supports farmers conserving traditional crops and plants and provides education about the hazards of genetic engineering.

A-60, Hauz Khas, New Delhi-110016, India
Tel: +91-11-2653-5422, 2696-8077;
Fax: +91-11-2685-6795, 2656-2093
E-mail: vshiva@vsnl.com
Website: www.navdanya.org

Pesticide Action Network (PAN)
A network of NGOs, institutions, and individuals in more than 60 countries promoting healthy alternatives to pesticides. PAN provides lists of banned pesticides for different countries and information on the uses and health effects of particular pesticides (see Internet resources).

PAN International contact information for all regional centers:
Website: www.pan-international.org/panint/?q=node/33

Centre Regional Pour L'Afrique (PAN Africa)
BP 15938 Dakar-Fann, Dakar, Senegal
Tel: +221-254-914; Fax: +221-254-914
E-mail: panafric@telecomplus.sn

Asia and the Pacific (PANAP)
PO Box 1170, 10850 Penang, Malaysia.
Tel: +604-657-0271/656-0381;
Fax: +604-675-7445;
E-mail: panap@panap.po.my

Europe
Eurolink Business Centre, 49 Effra Road,
London SW2 1BZ UK
Tel: +44-207-274-8895;
Fax: +44-207-274-9084
E-mail: admin@pan-uk.org

Latin America (RAPAL)
c/o Red de Acción en Alternativas al uso de Agroquímicos (RAAA) Mariscal Miller No 2622, Lince, Lima,
Peru
Tel: +51-1-421-0826;
Fax: +51-1-440-4359;
E-mail: rapalpe@mail.cosapidata.com.pe

North America (PANNA)
49 Powell Street, #500, San Francisco, CA 94102, USA
Tel: +1-415-981-1771;
Fax: +1-415-981-1991
E-mail: panna@panna.org

Via Campesina
An international movement of peasant farmer organizations, agricultural workers, rural women, and indigenous communities from Asia, America, and Europe.

Jl. Mampang Prapatan XIV No. 5, Jakarta Selatan, DKI Jakarta, Indonesia, 12790
Tel: +62-21-7991890; Fax: +62-21-7993426
Website: http://www.viacampesina.org

Printed materials

Agrodok Series
A series of low-priced, practical manuals on small-scale and sustainable agriculture in the tropics. Agrodok publications are available in English, French, Portuguese and Spanish.

Agromisa Foundation
P.O. Box 41, 6700 AA Wageningen
The Netherlands
Tel: +31-317-412217; /Fax +31-317-419178
E-mail: agromisa@agromisa.org
Website: www.agromisalustrum.org/agromisa/

How to Grow More Vegetables
By John Jeavons
A guide to sustainable agriculture.

Ecology Action
5798 Ridgewood Road, Willits, CA 95490, USA
Tel: +1-707-459-0150; Fax: +1-707-459-5409
Website: www.growbiointensive.org/_

Practical Guides to Dryland Farming
A series of booklets for farmers, extension agents, and development workers to improve farming in arid and semi-arid regions.

World Neighbors
4127 NW 122nd Street, Oklahoma City, OK 73120, USA
Tel: +1-405-752-9700 / Inside USA:
1-800-242-6387; Fax: +1-405-752-9393
Website: www.wn.org

Two Ears of Corn
By Roland Bunch

A people-centered account of how communities can improve agricultural production by encouraging appropriate technology and small-scale experimentation that result in two ears of corn where only one grew before.

World Neighbors
4127 NW 122nd Street, Oklahoma City, OK 73120, USA
Tel: +1-405-752-9700 / Inside USA: 1-800-242-6387; Fax +1-405-752-9393
Website: www.wn.org

Internet

PAN Pesticide database
www.pesticideinfo.org

Healthy homes

Organizations

APROVECHO Research Center
Information and training about low fuel cook stoves as well as organic gardening, sustainable forestry, and appropriate technology. Produces booklets describing how to build several simple stoves.

80574 Hazelton Road, Cottage Grove, OR 97424, USA
Tel: +1-541-942-8198; Fax: +1-541-942-0302
E-mail: apro@efn.org
Website: www.aprovecho.net/

Builders Without Borders
An international network of builders who promote the use of straw, earth, and other local, affordable materials in construction.

Website: builderswithoutborders.org

Solar Cookers International, USA
Assists communities in building and using solar cookers.

1919 21st Street #101, Sacramento, CA 95814, USA
Tel: +1-916-455-4499; Fax: +1-916-455-4498
E-mail: info@solarcookers.org

East Africa
P.O. Box 51190-00200, Nairobi, Kenya
Tel/fax: +254-20-43-47144
E-mail: sci@iconnect.co.ke

Printed materials

The Barefoot Architect: A Handbook for Green Building
By Johan van Lengen

A highly illustrated guide to planning and designing buildings using a variety of natural materials. Includes material on home heating and cooling, water and sanitation and other related information.

Shelter Publications
PO Box 279, Bolinas, California, 94924, USA
Tel: +1-415-868-0280 / 1-800-307-0131
E-mail: shelter@shelterpub.com
Website: www.shelterpub.com

Boiling Point

A technical journal for people working with stoves and household energy. It deals with technical, social, financial and environmental issues and aims to improve the quality of life for poor communities in the developing world.

PO Box 900
Bromley, BR1 9FF, U.K.
Tel: +44 (0) 20-7193-3699
E-mail: boilingpoint@hedon.info
Website:
www.hedon.info/goto.php/BoilingPoint

Toxics and waste

Organizations

Clean Production Action
Promotes clean production and the use of products that are safe for people and the environment.

PO Box 369 Succ. St-Jacques, Montreal, Qc H3C 2T1, Canada
Tel: +1-514-933-4596
E-mail: bev@cleanproduction.org
Website: www.cleanproduction.org

GAIA (Global Alliance for Incinerator Alternatives, or Global Anti-incinerator Alliance)
International alliance of organizations and individuals working to end waste incineration and to promote sustainable waste management practices.

GAIA Secretariat, Unit 320 Eagle Court Condominium, 26 Matalino Street, Barangay Central, Quezon City, Philippines
Tel: +632-929-0376; Fax: +632-436-4733
E-mail: gaia@no-burn.org
Website: www.no-burn.org

Global Community Monitor
Supports communities fighting pollution through community monitoring and campaign support.

739 Cortland Avenue, San Francisco, CA 94110, USA
Tel: +1-415-643-1870
E-mail: jenanne@gcmonitor.org, dennylarson@gcmonitor.org
Website: www.gcmonitor.org

HealthCare Without Harm (HCWH)
An international coalition of hospitals and health care systems, medical professionals, community groups, labor unions, environmental health organizations and religious groups, working to make the health care industry ecologically sustainable.

Latin America
Veronica Odriozola 3 de Febrero 3062, 1429 Capital Federal, Argentina
Tel/Fax: +54-11-4701-8872
E-mail: info@saludsindanio.org

Southeast Asia
Merci Ferrer, Unit 330 Eagle Court Condominium 26 Matalino Street, Brgy. Central Diliman, Quezon City 1100 Philippines
Tel: +63-2-928-7572; Fax: +63-2-9262649
E-mail: merci@hcwh.org

For all other countries and global issues, contact:
HCWH International Coordination
1958 University Avenue
Berkeley, CA 94704, USA
Tel: +1-510-848-5343, ext.101

Toxics Link
Promotes environmental justice by collecting and sharing information about community solutions to the problem of toxic waste in India and the rest of the world.

H-2, Jungpura Extension, New Delhi - 1100014
Tel: +91-11-2432-8006, 2432-0711
E-mail: info@toxicslink.org
Website: www.toxicslink.org

Internet Resources

Collaborative on Health and Environment (CHE) Toxics database
http://database.healthandenvironment.org/index.cfm

http://database.healthandenvironment.org/links.cfm

Mining, oil, and energy

Organizations

Biogas Support Programme
Resources and support to learn how to construct a biogas plant.

P.O. Box 1966, Kathmandu, Nepal
Tel: +977-552-1742, 553-4035
E-mail: snvbsp@wlink.com.np
Website: journeytoforever.org/biofuel_library/methane_nepal.html

ENERGIA
An international network concerned with energy, sustainable development, and gender. ENERGIA's goal is to contribute to the empowerment of rural and urban poor women through a specific focus on energy issues.

ENERGIA Secretariat P.O. Box 64 3830 AB LEUSDEN, The Netherlands
Tel: +31.(0) 33-432-6044;Fax: +31 (0) 33-494-0791
E-mail: energia@etcnl.nl
Website: www.energia.org

Green Empowerment

Promotes and helps to fund international community-based renewable energy and water systems and related watershed restoration projects.

140 Southwest Yamhill Street, Portland, OR 97204, USA
Tel: +1-503-284-5774;
Fax +1-503-460-0450
E-mail: info@greenempowerment.org
Website: www.greenempowerment.org

Mines and Communities

Provides direct support and advocacy for mining-affected communities.

Roger Moody MAC, c/o 41 Thornhill Square, London N1 1BE United Kingdom
Tel: +44-20-7700-6189;
Fax: +44-20-7700-6189
E-mail: info@minesandcommunities.org
Website: www.minesandcommunities.org

Mines, Minerals, and People

An alliance of individuals, institutions, and communities affected by mining in India.

SAMATA, Plot No. 169, Ravi Colony, Tirumalagiri, Secunderabad - 500015, A.P, India
Telefax: +91-40-2799-2488
E-mail: samataindia@gmail.com
Website: www.mmpindia.org

MiningWatch Canada

Campaigns to improve mining practices and support mining-affected communities.

City Centre Building Suite 508, 250 City Centre Avenue, Ottawa, Ontario K1R 6K7 Canada
Tel: +1-613-569-3439; Fax: +1-613-569-5138
E-mail: info@miningwatch.ca
Website: www.miningwatch.ca

Oilwatch International

A network that opposes the activities of oil companies in tropical countries.

Casilla 17-15-246C, Quito, Ecuador
Tel: +593-2-254-7516
E-mail: tegantai@oilwatch.org
Website: www.oilwatch.org

Southeast Asia

Jl. Mampang Prapatan, 2 No 30 RT 004/07, Jakarta Selatan, DKI Jakarta, Indonesia 12790
Tel: +62-21-794-1559

Africa

Environmental Rights Action
214 Uselu Lagos Road, Benin City, Edo State, Nigeria
Tel: +234-52-600-165
E-mail: eraction@eraction.org

Mesoamercia

San Jose, Costa Rica
Tel: +506-283-6046, +506-225-0676

Solar Electric Light Fund (SELF)

Promotes, develops, and helps to fund solar rural electrification and energy self-sufficiency in developing countries.

1612 K Street, NW Suite 402, Washington, DC 20006, USA
Tel: +1-202-234-7265
E-mail: info@self.org
Website: www.self.org

Printed materials

Electricity in Households and Micro-Enterprises

By Joy Clancy and Lucy Redeby

Practical Action Publishing
Tel: +44 (0) 1926-634501;
Fax: +44 (0) 1926-634502
E-mail: publishinginfo@practicalaction.org.uk
Website: www.developmentbookshop.com

Micro-hydro Power: A Guide for Development Workers

By P. Fraenkel et al
Practical Action Publishing
Tel: +44 (0) 1926-634501;
Fax: +44 (0) 1926-634502
E-mail: publishinginfo@practicalaction.org.uk
Website: www.developmentbookshop.com

Environmental law

Basel Action Network
An international network that uses international law to halt toxic trade and promote clean production.

122 S. Jackson, Suite 320, Seattle, WA 98104, USA
Tel: +1-206-652-5555;
Fax: +1-206-652-5750
E-mail: inform@ban.org
Website: www.ban.org

Earthrights International
Public education, organizing, advocacy and legal action on behalf of communities whose environmental rights are under threat. Their website provides resources for education and legal action.

1612 K Street, NW, #401, Washington, DC 20006 USA
Tel: +1-202-466-5188; Fax: +1-202-466-5189
Website: www.earthrights.org/

Earthjustice
A non-profit public interest law firm dedicated to protecting natural resources, and wildlife, and defending the right of all people to a healthy environment.

Website: www.earthjustice.org

International Indian Treaty Council
Works for the rights and recognition of indigenous peoples worldwide, and represents indigenous nations at the United Nations.

2390 Mission St., Suite 301,San Francisco, California, 94110, USA
Tel: +1-415-641-4482; Fax: +1-415-641-1298
E-mail: iitc@treatycouncil.org,
alberto@treatycouncil.org
Website: www.treatycouncil.org/

International POPs Elimination Network (IPEN)
A global network of NGOs working for the elimination of persistent organic pollutants (POPs).

International Secretariat, Bjorn Beeler, 1962 University Ave. Suite 4, Berkeley, CA 94704 USA
Tel: +1-510-704-1962; Fax: +1-510-883-9493
E-mail: BjornBeeler@ipen.org
Website: www.ipen.org

General

Organizations

Centers for Disease Control
A US Government agency that provides a wide range of environmental health education programs and resources.

1600 Clifton Rd, Atlanta, GA 30333, USA
Tel: +1-404-639-3311, +1-404-639-3534, Inside USA: 1-800-311-3435
Website: www.cdc.gov

International Development Research Center (IDRC)
Magazines, other publications, and films about health, agriculture, and development. Materials in English, Spanish, French, and Arabic (some for no cost). Write for a catalogue.

PO Box 8500 Ottowa, Ontario, K1G 3H9, Canada
Website: www.idrc.ca

Friends of the Earth International
An international network of grassroots environmental groups, with offices in many countries.

FOE Secretariat PO Box 19199, 1000 GD Amsterdam, The Netherlands
Tel: +31-20-622-1369; fax: +31-20-639-2181

People's Health Movement
An international network of people and organizations committed to health for all.

Website: www.phmovement.org

Practical Action (formerly ITDG)
Helps communities to choose and use technology to improve their lives, and publishes many books on appropriate technology and community development.

E-mail: practicalaction@practicalaction.org.uk,
enquiries@practicalaction.org.uk
Website: www.practicalaction.org

Winrock International
Promotes economic opportunity, sustainable natural resources, and protection of the environment.

2101 Riverfront Drive, Little Rock, Arkansas 72202 USA
Tel: +1-501-280-3000;
Fax: +1-501-280-3090
Email: information@winrock.org
Website: www.winrock.org

India
1 Navjeevan Vihar, New Delhi 110 017 India
Tel: +91-11-2669-3868;
Fax: +91-11-2669-3881
E-mail: winrockindia@winrockindia.org
Website: www.winrockindia.org

Philippines
Jollibee Plaza Building, Unit #2401, Emerald Avenue, Pasig City 1600, Philippines
Tel: +632-632-1233; Fax: +632-631-2809
E-mail: winphil@nwave.net

Europe
European Cooperative for Rural Development (EUCORD), c/o CS, Chaussee de la Hulpe 189,
1170 Brussels, Belgium
Tel: +32 (0) 2-675-6797;
Fax: +32 (0) 2-675-5870
E-mail: info@eucord.org
Website: www.eucord.org

Printed materials

Environment Words:
A dictionary in plain English
By Glenda Kupczyk-Romanczuk (Ed.)

An easy to use dictionary of words used to talk about the environment.

Environment Words Dictionary Project, P.O. Box 201, Chiang Mai University Post Office, Chiang Mai 50202, Thailand.
E-mail: env_dict@yahoo.com

Index

The Index lists topics covered in the book in the order of the alphabet.

A B C D E F G H I J K L M N O P Q R S T U V W X Y Z

NOTES

NOTES

NOTES

NOTES

NOTES

Other books from Hesperian

Where There Is No Doctor, by David Werner with Carol Thuman and Jane Maxwell. Perhaps the world's most widely used health care manual, it provides vital, easily understood information on how to diagnose, treat, and prevent common diseases. Emphasizes prevention, including cleanliness, diet, vaccinations, and the role people must take in their own health care. 512 pages.

HIV, Health, and Your Community, by Reuben Granich and Jonathan Mermin. Essential for community health workers and others confronting the growing HIV/AIDS epidemic. Emphasizes prevention and also covers virus biology, epidemiology, and ideas for designing HIV prevention and treatment programs. Contains an appendix of common health problems and treatments for people with HIV/AIDS, along with other practical tools for health workers. Now updated to include antiretroviral treatments and new advances in therapy. 245 pages.

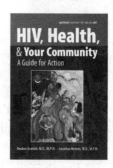

Where Women Have No Doctor, by A. August Burns, Ronnie Lovich, Jane Maxwell, and Katharine Shapiro, combines self-help medical information with an understanding of the ways poverty, discrimination, and cultural beliefs limit women's health and access to care. Clearly written and with over 1000 drawings, this book is an essential resource for any woman who wants to improve her health, and for health workers who want more information about the problems that affect only women, or that affect women differently from men. 584 pages.

A Book for Midwives, by Susan Klein, Suellen Miller, and Fiona Thomson. Revised in 2004, ideal for midwives, community health workers and those concerned with women and babies' health in pregnancy, birth and beyond. Covers helping pregnant women stay healthy, care during and after birth, handling obstetric complications, breastfeeding, and includes expanded information for women's reproductive health care. 544 pages.

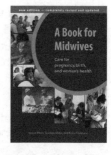

A Health Handbook for Women with Disabilities, by Jane Maxwell, Julia Watts Belser, and Darlena David. The social stigma of disability and inadequate care are often greater barriers to health than disabilities themselves. This groundbreaking handbook, full of useful advice and suggestions from women with disabilities worldwide, will help women with disabilities improve their general health, self-esteem, and abilities to care for themselves and participate in their communities. 406 pages.

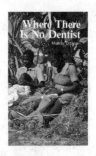

Where There Is No Dentist, by Murray Dickson, promotes care for the teeth and gums, and prevention through hygiene, nutrition, and education. Includes information on using dental equipment, placing fillings, taking out teeth, and new material on HIV/AIDS and oral health. 237 pages.

Helping Health Workers Learn, by David Werner and Bill Bower. Indispensable for teaching about health, this heavily illustrated book promotes effective community involvement through participatory education. Includes activities for mothers and children; tips for using theater, flannel-boards, and other techniques; and ideas for producing low-cost teaching aids. 640 pages

Disabled Village Children, by David Werner, covers most common disabilities of children. It gives suggestions for rehabilitation and explains how to make a variety of low-cost aids. Emphasis is placed on how to help disabled children find a role and be accepted in the community. 672 pages.

Helping Children Who Are Deaf, by Sandy Neimann, Devorah Greenstein, and Darlena David, helps parents and other caregivers build the communication skills of young children who do not hear well. Covers signed and spoken methods, assessing hearing loss, exploring causes of deafness, and more. 250 pages.

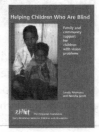

Helping Children Who Are Blind, by Sandy Niemann and Namita Jacob, aids parents and other caregivers in helping blind children develop all their capabilities. Topics include: assessing what a child can see, preventing blindness, moving around safely, teaching common activities, and more. 192 pages.

To order books in English or Spanish,
or to learn more about our work, contact us at:

Hesperian Foundation
PO Box 11577
Berkeley, California, 94712-2577
USA

tel: (510) 845-4507
fax: (510) 845-0539
email: bookorders@hesperian.org
www.hesperian.org

Learning Resources
Centre